For Alma Mater

For Gert Brieger,

with great respect + in mutual enthusiasm for institutional histories (despite my amateur status) — and in honor of your visit to the University of Illinois for the Physician-Scholar Symposium

Paula Treichler
November 1989

For
Alma Mater:
Theory and Practice
in
Feminist Scholarship

Edited by
Paula A. Treichler
Cheris Kramarae
Beth Stafford

University of Illinois Press
Urbana and Chicago

This book is printed on acid-free paper.

Library of Congress Cataloging in Publication Data

Main entry under title:

For alma mater.
   1. Sex discrimination in education—Addresses, essays,
lectures. 2. Feminism—Addresses, essays, lectures.
3. Women's studies—Addresses, essays, lectures.
4. Women—Medical care—Addresses, essays, lectures.
I. Treichler, Paula A. II. Kramarae, Cheris.
III. Stafford, Beth.
LC212.8.F67 1985   305.4'07'1173   84-16346
ISBN 0-252-01178-3

The Alma Mater, with Learning and Labor clasping hands behind her, embodies the motto of the University of Illinois and its land-grant ideal; dedicated in 1929, the statuary group was designed by the sculptor Lorado Taft. Archives photograph.

Dedication: For Alma Mater

This collection of essays, written for the most part by feminists at academic institutions, is dedicated to Alma Mater. Though it is dedicated with special affection to the Alma Mater statue at the University of Illinois at Urbana-Champaign, our home institution, in a simpler and more general sense our dedication is to the Alma Mater in spirit at every institution: a "fostering mother" who supports women and sustains us in our work. We acknowledge the ironies of a dedication to a spirit which for many of us may not always seem to exist. Indeed, a number of the contributors to this collection document the ways in which their institutions or disciplines have failed to nurture them. Nevertheless, a sisterhood of women scholars has emerged; women's studies programs continue to exist and occasionally to flourish; feminist scholarship is healthy and demonstrates great staying power in terms of force and intellectual achievement. Clearly, then, the university offers an environment in some ways suited to the needs and aspirations of the feminist scholar; in other ways, it is as clearly alien. For us, the Alma Mater embodies this duality. In many respects her history has been dominated by men, her name often inscribed upon a male landscape. This dedication seeks to reclaim her and invites her to be one of us.

Contents

Acknowledgments

A number of people have read and commented on portions of this book, and we are appreciative of their contributions, among them, Marianne A. Ferber, Jo Ann Fley, Benita Katzenellenbogen, Carol Thomas Neely, Cary Nelson, and Barbara Yates. Special thanks goes to Berenice Carroll, whose clarity of thought and purpose have helped us in this project, as in others.

While we were working on this book, Daniel K. Bloomfield, dean of the College of Medicine at Urbana-Champaign, generously and consistently supported our efforts. Hugh C. Atkinson, university librarian, has demonstrated a continuing commitment to women's studies and to this project. For their expert assistance at many stages of this effort, we thank Laura Battle, Arletta Lynn, Gerry Swift, and the rest of the staff of the Medical School's word processing center; Marilou Alender, Pat Donze, Roena Hensler, and Denice Wells, also at the College of Medicine; and Jytte Millan and the other research typists at the university library.

One reward of working on this volume we did not originally anticipate was our growing knowledge of former women students, faculty, and administrators, whose history contributes to our understanding of current and future feminist work. Our explorations in the University of Illinois archives have enriched us and given us great respect for our predecessors. We would like to acknowledge a special debt to Mary Loise Filbey, whose history of the deans of women at the University of Illinois exists in manuscript form in the archives and is cited in Paula Treichler's opening essay; we urge her to complete her account and publish it. We also appreciate the knowledge and resourcefulness of archivists Maynard Brichford and William Maher.

We thank the individual contributors for their patience and coop-

xi

eration. The comments of our anonymous readers were immensely helpful. Our editor, Ann Prisland Thorpe, made many excellent suggestions. Finally, we thank Carole Appel and Richard Wentworth of the University of Illinois Press for their continued encouragement and support of scholarship by and about women.

Introduction

We explore in this book theoretical and methodological issues in feminist research. The contributors, representing a wide range of fields, address the language of feminist scholarship, its disciplinary and interdisciplinary practices, its boundaries, and its resources. The title emphasizes the relationship between the practice of scholarship and its institutional context; within the academic institution as a working environment, feminist scholars encounter both nurturing and alienating forces. The Alma Mater, potentially a nurturing and sustaining maternal figure, has historically been appropriated for other purposes that are sometimes inhospitable to women and to their projects.

This book appears at a time when feminist scholars are calling for theoretical analysis and are developing courses in feminist theory. We are scrutinizing the boundaries of the institutions within which we live, and seeking models and maps to understand the intricate relationships between the rules and attitudes of university disciplines and departments and the freedom to practice feminist scholarship. We are trying to define what this scholarship is to embody. What makes scholarship *feminist*? Where does its difference lie? We are seeking to understand the boundaries between professional practices and personal experience. Does the distinction hold? If it does, how do the two areas animate, or contradict, each other? We are seeking to define the ways in which vision and rigor may go hand in hand. We are exploring whether feminist scholarship is to be individual or collective, integrational or separatist, central or marginal.

Like most academics, feminist scholars tend to be linked, at least originally, to an established discipline, yet we are almost inescapably drawn into interdisciplinary thinking and must encounter the language, the content, and the methodology of scholarship in new fields. After an initial period in which the pleasures of this interdisciplinary adventure were commonly celebrated, more recent inquiries have sought to understand more fully and intensely the genuine implications of such movement across boundaries, or even whether the language of such spatial metaphors is appropriate. Perhaps we should not be speaking of landscapes and maps but of power, of trade, and of access to the sea.

For Alma Mater reflects a diversity of theoretical approaches to the practice of feminist scholarship; though many disciplines are represented and explored, the book is organized to reflect our concern with feminist scholarship as a mode of inquiry about the world. This rather portentous formulation embraces highly practical realities about institutional life as well as more abstract ideas. Likewise, it suggests that to understand the scholarly enterprise we must understand the scholarly institution. This is a deliberately eclectic volume whose strength, we believe, lies in its theoretical and interdisciplinary focus and in its exploration of the "non-academic" dimensions of scholarship. We hope that the diversity of the fields included and the depth in selected fields— notably language, critical theory, history, educational policy, and medical sciences—will provide insight into the range of questions and decisions that necessarily confront the individual feminist scholar.

The original impetus for this book was a week-long conference on feminist scholarship held at the University of Illinois which brought more than thirty scholars from across the United States and abroad to the Urbana-Champaign campus. Here, they interacted formally with more than sixty local faculty members, students, and community feminists in presentations and panel discussions, and with hundreds more in other settings. Out of this has come *For Alma Mater*. Although the essays in the collection are substantially or entirely different from those presented at the conference, like any collection it is shaped in part by its origins; in working with these papers, we decided we did not wish to eliminate the diversity of voices or impose an "academic" tone as the authors rewrote or restructured their essays for this volume. We hope our readers will also take pleasure in this diversity. A number of the essays emphasize themes which have acquired particular theoretical importance in recent years: the centrality of language to scholarly inquiry, the interaction between public and private domains, racism and homophobia in academia, the importance of lived experience, and the question of visibility and invisibility. We see the book as a useful inquiry into the nature of feminist scholarship and hope it will be used to illuminate and define our shared enterprise.

There are a variety of ways to read this book. The opening essay explores the conception of the Alma Mater figure, draws upon archival material from the University of Illinois and elsewhere to trace the historical and political dimensions of the university as an environment both sustaining and alienating to women, and provides a context for the essays that follow. Our organization reflects what we see as the central issues in the theory and practice of feminist scholarship. The first group of essays (Section 2) explores language and other issues related to feminist criticism. The essays in Section 3 address the question of boundaries—between racism and sexism, between the university and the society at large, between scholarship and policy, and between disciplines. Section 4 looks at the links between theory and the ways in which feminist scholarship works itself out methodologically within a given discipline. The three essays in Section 5 focus on the female body and illustrate three different ways in which scientific investigation and feminism can intersect. In Section 6, the authors speak in more personal voices, describing relationships between feminism in their professional and personal lives: how are the two mutually informing, they ask; how are they sometimes contradictory. The final section outlines and evaluates resources for the practice of feminist scholarship.

Several themes run throughout the volume. The brief introduction to each section notes the central issues addressed and their particular disciplinary or interdisciplinary context. The book is not organized around disciplines, though given disciplines do tend to address some issues more than others. Apart from the interest individual essays may have as reports of scholarly findings, the book as a whole is broadly representative of the enterprise that is feminist scholarship. We would like it to be seen in the light of the past and the future, as part of an evolutionary as well as a revolutionary process. The Alma Mater photographs, representing various universities, remind us of our continuity with the past and our connections across institutional boundaries. The fundamental nature of the questions that many of these essays ask should point the way toward the future.

Paula A. Treichler
Cheris Kramarae
Beth Stafford

1

Section 1. On Women and the Academy

Paula Treichler's introductory essay explores and reflects upon the complexities of the institutional context in which feminist scholarship takes place. Just as feminist criticism enters a text and uses it as the particular occasion for analysis and meditation, the opening essay uses the University of Illinois as a starting point for theoretical reflection. Though in some respects unique and particular, this university embodies the trends and traditions of American higher education. Founded as a midwestern land-grant institution in the mid-nineteenth century, the University of Illinois has evolved into one of the superior research universities in the United States. Its history accurately reflects, then, both the democratic and the research commitments of higher education. It is a good place to look at the support and reception feminist scholarship receives.

Though recent feminist scholarship draws its spirit from the feminist movement of the last fifteen years, it also has longstanding traditions grounded in women's intellectual history and in the history of women in higher education. To explore these roots of feminist scholarship, we visited the University of Illinois archives and began to explore the history of women at this institution. What we found here could be found elsewhere, including not only evidence of women's scholarship and of their contributions to intellectual history and to teaching, but also including the dark side of the Alma Mater—the recurrent episodes of exploitation, humiliation, and trivialization that our predecessors experienced. Our sense of continuity became accordingly complex and ambivalent.

We felt considerable interest in the projects of these women as found in the archives. The 1914 wartime issue of the *Illio* yearbook, for example, was edited and produced entirely by women. Extraordinary photographs of simple objects—bread, brooms, white cloth—exist in the early files (circa 1910) of the Department of Home Economics. In the papers of an early twentieth-century faculty member, we found quotations torn from "The Suffragist's Calendar" and kept. We also found the correspondence between women faculty and their department heads on matters of salary and benefits, and the memoranda from deans of women to the president seeking sustenance for the population of women students in their charge. We felt dismay at the sense of familiarity about it all. The requests for funds could be written today with only a change in the size of the figures. Yesterday's battle for admission could be today's request for campus child care or retirement equity. The salary discrepancies in the graph comparing salaries of male and female faculty members fifty years ago would be similar to the discrepancies in many departments today. The opening essay explores this history in greater depth.

Alma Mater's Sorority: Women and the University of Illinois, 1890–1925

Paula A. Treichler

Feminist scholarship is rooted both in theory and in practice, enabling us to bring to the analysis of diverse phenomena feminist insights and perspectives and at the same time inevitably raising questions about the socially constituted nature of scholarship, itself a complex of attitudes and practices that shape the relationship between the scholar and her work. Self-conscious attention by feminists to scholarly practices has, of course, yielded vital methodological contributions to scholarship, yet it also suggests the inseparability of scholarly inquiry from the conditions in which that inquiry takes place. More than a happenstance of the academic landscape, our own material conditions as scholars signal the institution's hospitability to our presence and its structural incentives for our work.

This analysis starts with a contradiction: historically, many women have found the academy compatible with their values, temperaments, and professional aspirations, yet few have been adequately recognized or rewarded for their achievements; with few exceptions, the academy has proved a thorny and inhospitable environment, making its concessions to women grudgingly, in the face of political, economic, and legal pressure. Even today, in the wake of more than a decade of legislation

For their contributions to this essay, my thanks to Maynard Brichford, Berenice A. Carroll, Marianne A. Ferber, Mary Loise Filbey, Jo Ann Fley, Karl Grisso, Laura J. Huelster, Cheris Kramarae, Carol Thomas Neely, Cary Nelson, Linda Nicholson, Beth Stafford, Patricia Spain Ward, Joanne Wheeler, and Elisabeth Wittman.

and litigation on behalf of sexual equity, women lag behind men on virtually all statistical measures; in addition, they report that they continue to experience frustration and alienation in the academic environment. The identification of sexism, institutionalized discrimination against women, has given us considerable explanatory power in accounting for and predicting stratification by sex; a closer examination of the academic environment itself reveals that sexism, in turn, is dependent upon ongoing constructions of the categories "woman," "women," and "femininity." Because this process of construction transcends particular incidents, cases, and historical eras, it is important to examine its operation in some detail.

I will, therefore, examine a particular piece of the academic environment: the University of Illinois from 1890 to about 1925, a period in which the institution established itself as an important research university and in which the women's population, growing in size and heterogeneity, moved from an era of expanded opportunity to a period of increased institutional hierarchy and control. Quite apart from their intrinsic historical appeal, archival materials from this formative period are interesting because they document and illuminate the ongoing negotiation of a relationship between women and the academy whose legacies persist today. That this relationship remains problematic is all the more reason to examine its history. The fate of a particular request to the university administration on behalf of women, for example, may initially appear to be localized in time and place. Repeated negotiations over such requests, with their remarkable structural similarities over time, suggest a pervasive institutional reluctance to commit resources to women; accordingly, a variety of discursive and other practices can be identified which camouflage this often subterranean reluctance behind formal institutional discourse. Moreover, what we see at one university, uniquely constituted, we also see elsewhere; particular incidents therefore encourage reflection about more general patterns and practices.

I talk first about the symbol of the Alma Mater, using this figure as an emblem for some of the contradictions and tensions that mark women's relationship to the academy. I next describe women's entrance into the University of Illinois, particularly exploring some of the early communications between women and the university administration. The following section notes the complicated and heterogeneous make-up of the women's population at Illinois; between 1890 and 1925, the democratic land grant ideal was frequently compromised by institutional regulation. The communication between the university president and a particular dean of women during an era of strong centralized control suggests, however, that women's experiences are multiply determined, with locally generated events both enacting and complicating wider social and historical developments. After briefly reviewing the land grant union of science with household labor and the use of scholarship to define and reinforce "woman's place," I conclude that certain fundamental questions about coeducation and women's education remain problematic. Legacies of the past, embedded in the institutional structures and practices of the present, need to be identified and challenged. Feminist scholarship, representing an opportunity for the investigation of the academy itself, is thus a key element, together with women's studies and feminist activism, in the process of reclaiming Alma Mater and making the academy a fruitful place for women to live and work.

The Alma Mater

The question of co-education has never greatly stirred the University of Illinois. It has been practically settled from the very beginning. Even in the early history of the institution, women were never legally admitted, but some entered, nevertheless, imbued with the feeling that an education is part of the common human birthright; and the University, acquiescing in that spirit, has never swerved from the position then taken.

University of Illinois pamphlet, circa 1905

The very college students who most loudly hymned their "Alma Mater" most resolutely kept their sisters from the campus. Man has always liked to have some woman, especially one about eight feet high and of earnest aspect, to represent his ideas or inventions. At the same time, of course, he anxiously thwarted her attempts to utilize the inventions or pursue the theories.

Miriam Beard, circa 1920[1]

When we stood at boyhood's gate,
Shapeless in the hands of fate,
Thou dids't mold us, Dear Old State,
Into men!
Into men![2]

An academic institution is commonly called Alma Mater ("fostering mother") by its former students, who thus endow it with a female spirit. An institution's Alma Mater may be physically embodied in a song, painting, statue, or in memorabilia. Indeed, the Alma Mater is a formidable symbol at many colleges and universities, with a history that reflects institutional aspirations and self-presentation over time. Columbia University's Alma Mater sits in stately fashion on the steps leading to Low Library, a centerpiece for commencement and other rituals and a favorite graphic for the student newspaper. The dramatic Alma Mater of the City College of New York takes the form of an enormous mural, painted by Edwin H. Blashfield in 1908 and mounted in what is now the Great Hall. Alma Mater, at the center of the mural, surrounded by other female figures who represent the great universities of the world, confers a degree on a single male graduate; holding the torch of learning in one hand as he accepts his degree with another, he is flanked by other male students and representatives of several athletic teams. The female figures are in classical robes, reminiscent of the muses (to whom the Alma Mater is akin), the males in modern dress.

At the University of Illinois at Urbana-Champaign, the Alma Mater statue is part of a statuary group created by the sculptor Lorado Taft, a distinguished Illinois alumnus of the Class of 1879. The Alma Mater's outstretched arms offer a welcome to higher education. The two figures standing behind her, one in classical robes representing the arts and the other in a leather apron representing the sciences (Fig. 1), together embody the University's motto "Learning and Labor" and its land-grant mission. As one speaker put it at the statue's dedication ceremony in 1929, the land-grant universities replaced the classical view of the academy as "medicine and mathematics" with the new idea that education "goes down to the farms." The union of learning and labor implied not only mutual respect between liberal and practical learning but the very "right to have learning."[3]

What the Alma Mater signifies is complex. With the relative democratization of the university in the late nineteenth century came the need to attract to it the population of Illinois. The Alma Mater, symbol of the intellectual life, was also a symbol of this continuing "marketing campaign." Although the statue's open arms symbolize the egalitarian vision of a land-grant university, the 1929 dedication ceremony also celebrated the coming of "culture" to the prairie in the form of a major piece of sculpture by a recognized artist; the Alma Mater could thus be interpreted as a visible sign that the university's "cow college" origins had given rise to a first-class research university, a worthy competitor to

the academically elite institutions of the East. In keeping with this transformation, the Alma Mater first faced south, opening her arms toward
the agricultural school and the farms, the direction in which the campus
was expected to develop. As things happened, it grew to the north
instead, and the Alma Mater, moved to a new site, now offers her
welcome to engineering and computer sciences. Although the Alma
Mater irresistibly draws successive generations of parents, children, and
yearbook editors to photograph her, her official use is carefully over-
seen by her institutional custodians. A 1937 photo in the archives
shows a male and female student gazing up at the Alma Mater. They are
a rather sophisticated pair, especially the woman, with a fur boa draped
around her neck. A note clipped to the photo reads: "This is probably
the best, but the coed figure is objectionable. Man is all right. Both can
be sprayed out." It was very likely the fur boa that was "objectionable"—too fashionable and citified to represent young women at a
land-grant institution.[4]

These contradictory visions are rooted in tensions between theory
and practice, inclusion and exclusion, teaching and research, provin-
cialism and sophistication, populism and meritocracy. These tensions
have marked the university's development and have had both concrete
and symbolic consequences for women. The Illinois landscape is, however, only one site among many on which the ongoing negotiation of
relations between women and the institution of higher education is
constituted.

Women's history accompanies, even anticipates, this negotiation.
A 1980 Illinois catalog shows a woman student's kite tangled in the
Alma Mater's fingers; playfully childlike, the student smiles and climbs
the statue to retrieve her kite, as though deliberately to enact the role
predicted in the motto engraved on the statue's base:

ALMA MATER
To Thy Happy Children
of the Future
Those of the Past
Send Greetings

For women at colleges and universities today, struggling to define
and address our complex encounter with the academy, the Alma Mater's ironic optimism speaks to us out of the history of a complex
sorority. Indeed, the Romans gave the title *alma mater*, "nurturing

mother," to several goddesses, including Ceres and Cybele. (Ceres, the goddess of agriculture, and Cybele, the goddess of nature, no doubt join the Alma Mater at the University of Illinois.) It was in England that the term came to mean schools and universities, regarded as "fostering mothers" by their alumni and, much later, alumnae. *Alumnus* and *alumna* actually come from the same linguistic source as *alma* (Latin *alere,* 'to nourish') and mean "foster son" and "foster daughter."

"In signe and token of grete plente," reads a 1495 citation from the *Oxford English Dictionary,* "a grete female ymage was made, and callyd *Alma mater.*" Yet it is chiefly men, like the male figures in the CCNY mural, who have historically benefited from the bounteousness of this nurturing female spirit, a fact that emerged clearly in the 1970 congressional hearings which documented the existence of sex discrimination in many institutions of higher education and paved the way for more than a decade of legislation and litigation seeking greater sexual equality.[5] The academy, with few exceptions, was white and male; male faculty and male students were the adults, the creators and inheritors of institutional tradition. Women were largely excluded from the real life of the institution and deprived of its benefits. At Illinois, even with its relatively egalitarian foundations, the archival history of the Alma Mater marks this exclusion. Women in these photographs most often appear as the Alma Mater's accompaniment, childlike, passive, or silent; men, in contrast, are shown in active roles. In a representative World War II photo, a soldier, a sailor, a marine, and a WAC stand at the base of the Alma Mater behind a "coed" with bobby sox and a male civilian student with a slide rule. The men are gazing into the camera or into the distance; the women are gazing at the men. The picture suggests that the men are making direct contributions to the war effort; the women, implicitly, are onlookers, supporters, or mirrors (Fig. 2). Many photos show men in active physical relation to the statue: they are sitting on her, climbing her, photographing her, dressing her, or taking her from one place to another (Fig. 3). A recent photograph shows Paul Lewis, one of the American marines held hostage in Iran in 1980, walking past the Alma Mater, books in hand, school and normalcy his reward for patriotism. In much of the official record, the university enacts a largely male history upon a landscape peopled by males.

Women, in this history, rarely have had the opportunity to define themselves; when female self-definitions have emerged, a variety of institutional practices have obscured or revised their meaning, political force, or preservation over them. For example, Domestic Science, developed by Louisa Allen in the 1870s, was abolished and became an "extinct dep't" until its existence and history were reconstructed by a determined alumna in 1891.[6] One historian of the university describes women undergraduates in the early decades of the twentieth century as confined to the "ghetto" of the Woman's Building, thereby obscuring their presence in many academic curricula and campus activities.[7] In the naming of buildings, few women have been honored. When the Woman's Building lost its original function and was made into academic classrooms and offices for the English Department, it could well have been named in memory of Louisa Allen or Violet DeLille Jayne, significant advocates for women's interests in the university's formative years; instead, it became the English Building.[8] Women students at Illinois at the turn of the century helped create and develop a unique system of self-government which came to be known as the Women's Group System or the "Illinois Plan"; this strong tradition of decentralized women's governance, which emphasized democratic communication and small-group decision-making, is essentially unknown today.

The Alma Mater, potentially a strong, nurturing figure for an academic sorority, is herself an appropriated figure who seems to participate in this history as a male collaborator. Indeed, according to one chronicle of the American college in the early twentieth century, "it was a bad world for women. . . . *Alma mater* was a jealous deity that tolerated no feminism except her own male variety."[9] Or as a feminist academic caustically commented in the context of her tenure battle in the late 1970s, "the Alma Mater is a woman of ill repute."[10] Nevertheless, women's experience at the University of Illinois and elsewhere suggests that the Alma Mater should be reclaimed as a figure of nourishment for women in the academy, a reclamation which offers a more powerful vision of sorority and continuing possibilities for the future. Such a reclamation begins with the past.

Those of the Past Send Greetings

"Those girls back in the seventies didn't go to college because it was socially the thing to do—they went in spite of the fact that it was not the thing to do . . . and they had all the fine passion of pioneers for their undertaking."

Olive Deane Hormel, 1926[11]

And so another great door of opportunity was opened for human betterment, another chance was given for men and women, hand in hand, to work at the world's problems. That, to me, has always been one of the very great benefits that the Land-grant College has given to our daily life—the fact that the men and women have worked to-gether at the world's problems.

Isabel Bevier, 1920[12]

That last year at the university was an idyllic year; fall, winter and spring, glowing with health and youth, we enjoyed them all, the burning heat of the prairies, the dry cold of the winter snows, the smell of the upturned blue-black earth in spring.

Dorothy Day, 1952[13]

Women were admitted to the University of Illinois only two years after it opened in 1868 as the Illinois Industrial University; Regent John Milton Gregory cast the deciding vote for coeducation in 1870, even as he did so expressing his reservations about this "innovation of doubtful wisdom."[14] In many ways, the land-grant movement was hospitable to the notion that women should be educated, and in Illinois the strong agricultural lobby actively worked for their admission. Although there was less argument about women's admission to land-grant institutions than to the Ivy League colleges and universities of the East Coast, even the land-grant schools were "more tolerant than supportive" of women's higher education: many accounts document a history of dis-crimination and a pervasive perception among male faculty, students, and administrators that women's nature was marked by countless physical and mental frailties, impossible deficiencies, and, finally, a troubling "otherness."[15]

The ambivalence of Gregory's affirmation accurately fore-shadowed the institution's response to women in the years that fol-lowed. In 1898, for example, the struggle began to get a new carpet for the Woman's Parlor. As Violet DeLille Jayne (Fig. 4), the first dean of women at Urbana, repeatedly pointed out to university president An-drew Draper, a new carpet would cost no more than $100 or so, and would go a long way toward humanizing the one place on campus the women students could call their own (like the male students, most women students lived in private rooming-houses or in the homes of local citizens). The carpet on the floor clashed with the wallpaper, wrote Dean Jayne, producing "an almost excruciatingly inharmonious effect."[16] President Draper replied that such expenditures were out of the question. Furthermore, "I remember something being said about the carpet in the women's parlor a year ago, but I have come to the conclusion that the carpet is better than the paper on the walls, and am fearful that if you have a new carpet you will think it necessary to have new paper."[17] Besides, the university had no money. Dean Jayne persisted. The parlor was used daily by 100 to 200 women, she wrote; the floor and woodwork were badly in need of paint, the old desks and chairs needed repair, and the couches had given out. Besides dust in the creases of the couches, she added, she had also "found indications of living creatures that make them even more repellent."[18] Unfortunately, the president told her, the university had no money. For seven years, Jayne's requests for furnishings were either ignored or denied; on the eve of her resignation from the university to be married, the president cordially invited her to sit on his veranda and discuss women's furnishings. The university, of course, still had no money.

Somewhere in the middle of this problematic seven-year dialogue, President Draper requested $250 from the Board of Trustees to have squirrels caught and released on the campus grounds. This Squirrel Park project was dear to his heart. "The influence upon University life," he wrote, "and upon the feelings of the students, would be considerable and students would carry the influence to all parts of the state."[19] President Draper's Squirrel Park (which was approved by the trustees) illustrates a rhetorical strategy that will be familiar to most women who have ever submitted a request to a higher administrator: the president elevates and idealizes his own goals while trivializing those of women; in addition, he forces Dean Jayne into the role of supplicant, perennially asking, documenting, and persuading. Her humility and tact, like Draper's evasions, were virtually infinite: "You said perhaps if I presented the matter to you when you are not quite so tired out," she wrote, "you might see it differently. May I then bring the matter to your attention again?"[20]

The Squirrel Park episode, while at some level inescapably comic, nevertheless reveals real institutional priorities: the land-grant university was far more unambivalently hospitable to animals than to women. It also offers a rhetorical model for dialogue between women and universities from which many higher educational administrators have never shown an inclination to depart.

A different relationship, and for women readers today somewhat
more satisfying, existed between President Draper and Lucy Flower, a
wealthy and influential member of the Board of Trustees (Fig. 5). Where
Violet Jayne and successive deans of women tended, of necessity, to be
tactful and deferential in their dealings with their superiors, Lucy
Flower, with age, wealth, and influence behind her, tended to enact
rather than defend her views on women's education.[21] It was Flower
who maneuvered the reluctant President Draper into doing many things
on behalf of women that he would perhaps have preferred to have left
undone: hire women faculty, create a Woman's Department, build a
Woman's Building, hire a dean of women, establish a Department of
Household Science, and admit women students to the medical school.
The medical school decision nicely illustrates her tactics. When the
College of Physicians and Surgeons in Chicago affiliated with the university in 1897, it became subject to general university admissions
policies and thus open to women. Despite this, and despite considerable
lobbying by prospective women students, alumnae, and Flower herself,
President Draper argued that admitting women, while inevitable in
time, would have a disastrous effect on the young program by causing
scores of male faculty and students to abandon it. Mrs. Flower simply
set this aside as an empty, if ancient, rhetorical ploy and at the Board of
Trustees' meeting of June 29, 1897, successfully moved that women be
admitted to the Department of Physicians and Surgeons the following
year.[22] (Coincidentally, but perhaps in keeping with the Squirrel Park
motif, Flower's five-line motion in the Board of Trustees minutes is
followed by a lengthy and eloquent recommendation for the purchase
by the university of Morgan horses.)

With Lucy Flower, too, of course, the president attempted to
trivialize women's interests, for example in the business of establishing
a Department of Household Science. Despite pressure from women
alumnae as well as from Lucy Flower, the President delayed any decision on the matter and complained to Mrs. Flower in 1898 that
"women engaged in [Domestic Science] are assumed to be very scientific
when they are not. Our faculty people discredit them because they
assume what they cannot carry out. Again, there is no such call for the
work as some think." Further, continued Draper characteristically, "I
am very much more interested in the practical than the theoretical side
of this domestic science movement."[23] Specifically, he wanted "modern,

hygienic principles" to be used to achieve his own (not always explicit) goal: the creation and maintenance of a high-quality, convenient faculty lunch room.

So on several counts, women's science was deemed non-theoretical; the lunch room arrangement would, in addition, have placed women in a traditional domestic role, ministering to male needs. Mrs. Flower, adept at compromise, proposed in response that a suitable woman should be appointed head of the lunch room; if she proved satisfactory, she would become head of Household Science the follow-ing year. Draper responded shortly thereafter that, unfortunately, plans for the lunch room would have to be given up, for the university had "to economize in every direction."[24] At Mrs. Flower's urging, however, the Board of Trustees approved the hiring of Isabel Bevier (Fig. 6) as Head of Household Science the following spring. This story suggests a number of lessons for women today. First, this was a period in the university's history in which women's special needs were emerging and women were learning to request resources to meet those needs. Male faculty and administrators, with relatively little experience interacting with women in an academic setting, tended on the one hand to wish to acknowledge that women constituted a special population and on the other hand to resist being obliged to commit resources on their behalf. One strategy for steering between these two courses involved emphasiz-ing women's traditional feminity to argue that their professional aspira-tions were not comparable to men's and thus that comparable resources were not needed. A corollary strategy was to argue that the academic setting canceled out sexual differences and that, therefore, women had no special needs in the way of personnel or space.

Important during this period, then, were powerful allies and orga-nized advocates of women's interests. Influential people like Lucy Flower on the Board of Trustees were in positions to mandate rather than request the allocation of resources. Isabel Bevier in Household Science and Katherine Sharp in Library Science argued for the scientific basis of advanced work for women; this position was at odds with traditional views of women (Bevier engaged in a protracted battle with the farm auxiliary because she would not offer practical homemaking instruction in the absence of theoretical training) but solidified al-legiance with those who felt homemaking skills *per se* ("bread-baking") had no place in a university curriculum. Interestingly, the fact that women provided certain concrete services linked to traditional female interests and skills—for example, organizing campus social life—also argued for the continued flow of resources to them as women.

Through an ongoing process, then, women were defined as a special population and institutional commitments to them were made. Though this process reflected certain views of women's place, women were nevertheless acknowledged as a constituency with special needs, talents, and aspirations; as a result, certain positive administrative, educational, and professional consequences and opportunities followed (Lucy Flower's insistence on a Woman's Department, for example, headed by a dean of women, meant that Violet Jayne served on the university's exclusive Council of Administration). The existence of separate structures for women within a larger coeducational institution was no doubt important in developing and strengthening women's opportunities.[25] In short, the interplay between women and institutions over the question of how women are to be defined, categorized, and treated is only in part a philosophical question of women's right to higher education. It is also directly linked to the institutional commitment of resources. Thus the argument over the carpet for the Woman's Parlour only seemed to be over the carpet; in fact, it was over the commitment of institutional resources to women. Strategies to protect resources take a variety of forms in individual instances. Their embodiment as communication bears special watching. Draper's paternalistic rhetoric forced Violet Jayne to follow a conventionally feminine division of linguistic labor: taking the initiative, using tact, making supplication. In turn, her "femininity" was used as a basis for refusing her. His responses, like a father's to a child, were both capricious and personal, avoiding any appearance of institutional commitment. Above all, a concrete and timeless rule for women emerges from this story: when a university claims it has no money, look around, because someone, somewhere, is building a squirrel park.

Sisterhood and Sorority: Whose Alma Mater?

> She believed in rouge and her powder-box; in the wisdom of Prexy and the Grand Council of her sorority; in the State University's football team and in the integrity of all deans but the Dean of Women.
>
> Lois Seyster Montross, 1923[26]

Despite the influx of flappers, there are more college girls seriously studying for serious vocations than there ever were before.

Olive Deane Hormel, 1926[27]

Is the time ripe for a house for colored girls? Colored girls are diminishing in number here, going to other universities where housing conditions are better.

Interracial committee, University of Illinois, 1923–24[28]

By the turn of the century, women in the United States had been relatively successful in gaining access to higher education. Because access to education was not government-controlled, women's success was instead dependent on public opinion and economic conditions, both of which facilitated their educational goals. Despite variations in size, quality, and curricula, many single-sex and coeducational institutions were established, providing education to women in all parts of the country. In 1900, women received 17 percent of all advanced degrees; they were earning 23 percent by 1910, 34 percent by 1920, 40 percent by 1930, and 41 percent by 1940. The greatest period of increase was the 1920s, growth that has not been equaled since.[29]

During the formative period 1890–1925, there were a number of notable women faculty at the University of Illinois: Isabel Bevier in household science, Louise Freer in women's athletics, Louise Dunbar in history, Katherine Lucinda Sharp in library science, Virginia Bartow in chemistry, Allene Gregory Allen in English, and Queen Lois Shepherd in philosophy. Two novels about the University of Illinois, published by women graduates in the 1920s, indicate that these women faculty made a strong impression on their students. In Olive Deane Hormel's *Co-Ed*, the "always modish" Miss Simmons [Katherine Sharp] of the Library School expresses her views on library education: "We are not a vocational department but a professional school, admitting only college graduates and requiring two full years in intensive training for a diploma. . . . I am happy to say that most parents have come to appreciate the fact that their daughters have as much right as their sons to a professional education after college" (Fig. 7). Miss Bovard of "Home Ec" describes her Practice Cottage as a laboratory designed "to instill ideas and real possession of skill into the making of a better home life, and to transform the housewife by virtue thereof from harrassed drudge to intelligent director in the domestic demesne."[30]

Despite similarities among women faculty in terms of commitment to women's education, these women faculty differed in their philosophy of education, commitment to feminism and suffrage, attitudes toward teaching and research, personal commitments, relationship to the university, views on academic freedom, political beliefs, friendships with other women, and day-to-day behavior and dress. It was still somewhat unclear how women on coeducational campuses were to behave, outside the "henneries" of the East. Although to male faculty and administrators, the very fact of femaleness sometimes seemed to supplant other characteristics, the lives of individual women demonstrated a complex of relations, not all of which were primarily significant on the female/male axis.

This complexity is apparent in Queen Lois Shepherd, who is probably the model for Doctor Cynara Georges in *Town and Gown:* "She was a woman about thirty with red-brown eyes and a mop of mahogany colored hair. Her voice was quiet and rather deep—she watched understandingly while you recited, seemed to encourage you with 'm-*hm*,' 'm-*hm!*'—then she pounced on your conclusions with feline swiftness and tore them into shreds."[31] Here, a characteristic female mode of interaction in the form of sympathetic listening is contradicted by the "feline swiftness" of the intellectual attack. Despite the stereotypical female metaphor, the behavior described challenges female stereotypes, a challenge that continues outside the classroom. Like Shepherd herself, Doctor Georges belongs to a small group of campus radicals who meet each week to drink, smoke, and talk. A male undergraduate member of the group, alone with her, finds the conjunction of "intellect" with "woman" not to be tolerated: "If only they were in Bagdad—or Canton! It was impossible here—he was haunted by remembered quiz papers on which her red ink glistened—'Can you prove this statement?', 'You have mistaken Hume's meaning.' Damn the University anyway! It had created this barrier. . . . Spring articulate outside—and he inside, inarticulate! She was a woman. And he was a man."[32] This sketch encapsulates a woman graduate's ironic perception of a male undergraduate undone by a woman professor's intellect. For him, the coeducational situation is inescapably heterosexual as well. Shepherd is also portrayed in *Co-Ed,* whose female protagonist responds to her intellectual performance with admiration rather than the male undergraduate's resentment:

Miss Herder's "quiz section" was a weekly clearing house for points of controversy. Lucia did not often join in these discussions, for she felt an inhibiting awe in the presence of the quick, keen mind which seemed to pounce upon a fallacy—be it ever so obscure—almost before it was uttered. Miss Herder never interrupted, but Lucia came to know by a little fugitive gleam in those red-brown eyes just when a student put forth an argument which must later collapse before her superior skill, and she always enjoyed immensely the parry and thrust of the mental sword-play that followed. . . .[33]

A rather bizarre episode in the real life history of the University of Illinois allows us to see yet another side of Shepherd. In the course of a World War I Liberty Bond drive in 1917, several faculty members, Shepherd among them, returned pledge cards which, in a growing climate of patriotic fervor, were interpreted as expressing disloyalty to the United States government. A regional investigator for the FBI came to campus to interrogate the faculty members in question. Shepherd, a committed pacifist and passionate believer in academic freedom,

proved a difficult person to interrogate. After a few introductory questions about her place of employment, residence, and salary, Kerrick [the FBI investigator] asked whether she had purchased Liberty Bonds and learned that she had not. When he asked what she had done to help the war effort, Miss Shepherd refused to answer. Kerrick asked whether she was a socialist, and she asked him for his definition of socialism. He asked whether she was an atheist; again she asked for a definition of the term. . . . Turning to another line of questioning, Kerrick asked about the political opinions of her colleagues and was promptly told that he should ask them himself. At this point Kerrick lost control of his temper and began to yell at Miss Shepherd: "You are a rank, rotten, vicious, socialist and anarchist, and I knew you were before I came. . . ."

Throughout the interrogation, Miss Shepherd had been more amused than angered at Kerrick's conduct of the interrogation. She had difficulty suppressing her laughter at the ridiculousness of the occasion. Kerrick interpreted her amusement . . . as "sneering, scoffing," and "defiance" of the United States Government.[34]

These women faculty members seem to have been aware of each other and to have participated in a variety of women's activities on the campus. Of the women faculty members and administrators, most were unmarried and remained so as long as they were employed by the university. Many formed deep friendships with each other.[35] Many were interested in women's education and worked to make the coeducational institution a hospitable environment for women's development (Fig. 8). At this earlier stage, "compulsive heterosexuality" does not seem to have had the force it came to have over the next several decades. This does not mean that the institution was woman-centered, however, for many factors in its evolution as a research university worked against the formation of a unified women's community: disciplinary divisions, increasing specialization, and domination of the university administration and academic committees by men. Moreover, a number of issues engaged the faculty as faculty, dividing them from the university administration on the one hand and from the non-academic community on the other. The academic freedom issue, for example, which did not divide along male/female lines, repeatedly came up and created mistrust and bitterness that colored campus relations for years. The question of race, it may be noted, did not arise during this period, for the university did not hire a Black faculty member for several more decades.

Despite their differences and multiple identities, the women faculty were treated less well as a population than were comparable male faculty, with their promotions and salary increases occurring at a significantly slower pace. Louise Dunbar, for example, who received her undergraduate degree from Mount Holyoke in 1916 and her Ph.D. from the University of Illinois in 1920, joined the history faculty in 1920. When she retired in 1962, she had been promoted only to the rank of assistant professor. One male colleague, hired within five years of her, had become a full professor by 1950; when he retired in 1952, making $7,000, Dunbar was making just over $5,000. A second male colleague, also her contemporary, became a full professor in 1935; by 1952, he was making $9,000, and by his retirement in 1962, $15,000 (when Dunbar had not yet reached $9,000).[36] Despite such treatment, many women faculty members remained at Illinois for their entire careers. In Dunbar's papers, along with her teaching and research notes, are memorabilia of the suffrage movement; perhaps these sustained her in an environment that may often have seemed unrewarding.

The women students also represented an increasingly diverse population during this era. Violet DeLille Jayne, the first dean of women, inherited in 1897 a small number of women students who seemed to display little cohesion or cameraderie among themselves, knew little of the world outside the rural midwestern environment in which they grew up, and depended on the male students for leadership. Charged with responsibility for the women students' social and educational development, Jayne followed several strategies in seeking to build a women's community. One of these contributed significantly to the direction life would take among women students over the subsequent decades. In 1899 she encouraged a student named Emma Rhoads to speak at a general women's assembly about the possibility that the women students would take responsibility for governing themselves; this would include having chaperones at parties, leaving parties before midnight, and going to dances on Friday and Saturday nights only. The women students decided that they wished to try this system and the following fall formed the Watcheka League "with the stated aim of facilitating united action on the part of women students of the University" (the name was changed to the Women's League in 1900).[37] The Women's League became famous for organizing a number of annual social events, including an end-of-the-year party and the May Day Fete; although these responsibilities reproduced the traditional sexual division of labor in which women were responsible for social life and culture, the system of self-government, for a time abandoned after Dean Jayne left the University, was a genuine contribution by women to the organization of academic life. Its usefulness was particularly clear as the population of women students grew larger, more fragmented, and increasingly dominated by the sororities. Under the Women's Group System, or the "Illinois Plan" as the self-government system came to be known, non-sorority women, or "independents," formed "scatter groups" which were in turn represented, as the sororities were, on the Woman's League Council. By thus creating a kind of structural equivalent to the sororities, the plan aimed at bringing "the benefits of the organized to the unorganized" and involving diverse female constituencies in responsibility and decision-making.[38]

For many years, there had been efforts to have a Woman's Building built; requested from the state legislature of 1902 was $150,000 for an Agriculture Building (a curriculum in which only twenty-two students were then enrolled, yet a politically powerful lobby), $135,000 for a Chemistry Building, and $80,000 for a Woman's Building. Thanks to the efforts of Mrs. Henry M. Dunlap, wife of the state senator from the university's district, the appropriation came through in 1902 and the Woman's Building (Fig. 9) became a reality in 1905.[39] The name—with *woman* in the singular—was intended to give every individual woman a sense of proprietorship and belonging. Here women could go to retreat from the coeducational atmosphere; men's access to the building was greatly restricted, despite their requests for wider use. For some years, the Household Science Department was housed in the Woman's Building, as was the women's gymnasium (Fig. 10). Campuswide social events were held there periodically, transforming the building into such a festive sight that graduates remembered it for years.

By the 1920s, the university had succeeded in attracting to the university a large and increasingly diverse population of students; an entering student was likely to feel overwhelmed, as this fictional freshman does in Montross and Montross' *Town and Gown:* "The passing and repassing of students was dizzying. Fur-coated co-eds with rouged cheeks, men wearing bone-rimmed glasses; an instructor or two hurrying by with green bags in hand; Chinese students in groups; two colored girls, hesitant and self-effacing; couples who sauntered, gayly glancing about for acquaintances; the girl he had heard called 'Dot' accompanied by two men; and freshmen like himself, bewildered, self-conscious, frowning over the brown-covered announcement of courses."[40]

Stimulated by the growth in numbers, a great many social (as opposed to scholarly) sororities developed for women students. These "girl fraternities," as they were originally known, proliferated in part because the university repeatedly resisted spending money on dormitories; as a result, while official university publications emphasized the virtues of self-reliance, Illinois became the "Greek capital" of the United States, with chapters of most national sororities and fraternities represented. Despite the serious and even progressive social and educational goals of many sororities, they initially flourished at Illinois primarily as the growing female population strained the abilities of the local community to absorb it in private housing.

Black women, barred from national sororities of white women, were not so easily accommodated. Despite the ongoing presence of Black students at the university (Fig. 11), the climate was hostile and restrictive. They were discriminated against in housing, in the local theaters, in restaurants and stores, and sometimes even in classrooms and laboratories. They were not permitted to live in the available university housing. Male students could obtain housing and meals in the two Black fraternities, but the female students had to find private housing with local Black citizens. Even after a chapter of the Black sorority Alpha Kappa Alpha was established at Illinois in 1914, there were problems finding a suitable location for the house (a citizen's delegation protested one site to the Urbana City Council in 1923–24); a second Black sorority, Delta Sigma Theta, did not get started until 1932. Neither was represented during this period on the Pan-Hellenic Council nor included in the *Illio* yearbook.[41]

By the 1920s the female student body was much more heterogeneous than it had been at the turn of the century; as the opening quotations suggest, it included at least three distinct groups: white sorority women including "flappers"; more socially conservative women who often belonged to the Women's League; and a much smaller group of non-white (including Black and foreign) women whose concerns in the face of widespread racial discrimination often involved such fundamental issues as where they were to eat and sleep. There was a small group of campus radicals that included pacifists and socialists; Dorothy Day, who later edited the progressive newspaper the *Catholic Worker,* attended the University of Illinois from 1914 to 1916 on a scholarship; "while I was free to go to college," she wrote, "I was mindful of girls who worked in stores and factories through their youth and afterward married men who were slaves in those same factories."[42]

At least some of these women students felt excluded from the coeducational arena. Until Violet Jayne organized a special women's issue of the *Illini* in 1898, in twenty-six years women students had never contributed to the school paper. Some years later, Bernice Powell (a 1914 graduate) complained that university women believed their place in campus life was secondary: to them fall the "inevitable secretaryships, all work and no glory."[43] In Olive Deane Hormel's *Co-Ed,* a male student wins an important campus office by pledging to get women students appointed to important campus committees.

As coeducation developed, with its "terrible dangers,"[44] a female figure arose who in principle at least could be said to embody the nurturing spirit of the Alma Mater. In the position that came to be known generically as dean of women, the contradictions and tensions of women's experience in the academy were especially apparent. The dean of women was usually a woman faculty member appointed by the

institution to "oversee" the arrangements, social activities, health, and
conduct of the women students. For perhaps fifty years it was an office
in which intelligent, well-qualified, well-educated women could exercise
administrative skills and professional leadership and exert a unifying
influence on behalf of women. Many outstanding women educators
made their mark as deans of women: Marion Talbot and Alice Freeman
Palmer at the University of Chicago, Mary Bidwell Breed at Indiana
University and the University of Missouri, Lois Kimball Mathews
Rosenberry at the University of Wisconsin, Gertrude S. Martin at Cornell University, Lucy Diggs Slowe at Howard University, and Evelyn
Wight Allan at Stanford. Like Louisa Allen and Violet Jayne at the
University of Illinois, many of these deans had strong views about
women's education, the institution's role, and their own responsibilities. Their commitment to the social, physical, and intellectual
development of women was often incomprehensible to their male colleagues, as was the position itself.

In consequence, the title of the dean of women position, its functions, and the match between the two were disputed over the years.
Katharine Merrill's title at the University of Illinois from 1892–1897
was "Preceptress"; Louisa B. Allen, before her, had been "Lady Principal." Violet Jayne was the first real "Dean of Women" at Illinois; given
her excellent credentials, the title itself and the leadership it implied may
have influenced her acceptance of the position, for which she was somewhat overqualified.[45] The question of the title was central to the dispute.
"Is not the title Dean of Women then a misnomer?" asked Gertrude S.
Martin in 1911 in frustration at performing duties for which she was
overqualified, and recommended either that the title be changed (to
"proctor, or advisor, or housemother or what not") or that the position
be defined so its holder could truly function as a dean on behalf of
women: "She must know the whole field of opportunity open to the
educated woman and the demands which life can make upon her; and
she must be able to adapt a man-made curriculum to the special needs
of the woman student."[46]

It was inevitable that some deans of women, with their interests in
women and frequently strong views on women's education, were feminists. Locking the barn door after the horses had bolted by rewriting the
job description, the university tried to guard itself against this danger as
best it could. When Katharine Merrill, a feminist, left the University of
Illinois and President Draper listed the qualifications of her successor,

he specified that the new Dean of Women "must not be possessed of the idea that the world has been doing women great wrongs through the preceding centuries," adding, "we want one who has seen the world and can get along with others and not be in hot water all the time."[47] The Board of Trustees' minutes of 1897 stipulated that the dean of women should be able to represent the Woman's Department on public occasions "without engaging in extreme and doubtful projects or entering into controversies about which people are widely divided."[48] At the same time, the new job description tended to emphasize responsibilities that were concrete and understandable, like discipline or hygiene. Of all the duties carried out by the deans of women, the university administration understood discipline best and tended to emphasize conduct rather than student development.[49] Some deans at Illinois, like Eunice Dean Daniels, accepted this role and functioned efficiently as something equivalent to a housemother, attending primarily to conduct and hygiene. Ruby Mason, some years later, took the disciplinary nature of her role so seriously that she alienated much of her student constituency, a situation discussed in greater detail below. Maria Leonard, the dean of women with the longest tenure at Illinois, sought to maintain "control through friendship . . . rather than control through regulations," yet emphasized control nevertheless.[50] Miriam Sheldon, in 1947, agreed to take the position of dean of women only after it was redefined to include greater responsibility and scope for genuine leadership.[51]

As the number of women students at colleges and universities grew, and as the pioneer spirit of the nineteenth century gave way to the more spirited ways of the twentieth, deans of women were increasingly encouraged not to develop the potential of women students but to control them. Even fulfilling this role was not a foolproof way for a woman dean to keep out of "hot water." Martha Kyle's views on the new student dances and on sorority social life coincided perfectly with those of the conservative University of Illinois administration; this was fine, but she differed from the administration in believing that women's residence halls were a good idea. This, involving as it did the commitment of substantial resources, was not fine. To Dean Kyle's position that women students should not be left so much to themselves, President James retorted: "I am surprised that a strong-willed suffragette like yourself should take a gloomy view of the necessity for female supervision"; he dismissed her shortly thereafter.[52]

Two novels about the University of Illinois mentioned above suggest pretty clearly how the lines were drawn during this period. *Town and Gown,* published in 1923, is a collection of related stories by Lois Seyster Montross and Lynn Montross (Class of 1919).[53] Called "unwholesome" by some reviewers and disliked intensely by the straightlaced university president David Kinley, *Town and Gown* largely identifies the university experience with fraternity and sorority life. The non-Greek, or "barb," is excluded, despised, or invisible; though the self-absorption and cynicism of the fashionable "flapper" population are caustically satirized, the naivete and moralism of other campus figures—in whose eyes the sorority flappers are the campus "bad girls"—are even more unappealing.[54] More to President Kinley's taste was the 1926 *Co-Ed* by Olive Deane Hormel (Class of 1916).[55] Though its protagonist is also a sorority woman, she becomes disenchanted with Greek life and thereafter is able to perceive that the university's real significance lies in its intellectual resources and land-grant philosophy. Showing sympathy for the dean of women and Women's League events, she is thus in contrast very much a "good girl."

Despite their differences, the two books make clear that students had a life of their own quite distinct from their academic existence. (This is also apparent in Dorothy Day's account of her student years at Illinois from 1914 to 1916: "Really I led a very shiftless life, doing for the first time exactly what I wanted to do, attending only those classes I wished to attend, coming and going at whatever hour of the night I pleased. My freedom intoxicated me."[56]) At the same time, in the eyes of the administration the Greek system was gradually becoming a monster out of control. The evils of twentieth-century civilization reached college campuses through the sororities and fraternities, which were thus the enemies of morality, decency, and the land-grant ideal. This description is from *Town and Gown:*

> On one side Dean Agnes Watson. On the other side several thousand young virgins with knee-conscious skirts and rouged ear tips and rolled-down stockings and bobbed hair and plucked eyebrows and baby stares and affected lisps and a terrible frankness. And several thousand men students who roared about in high-power, low-slung automobiles apparently in an endless pursuit of the several thousand young virgins.
>
> The odds were all against the dean of women. . . .[57]

1. The Alma Mater statue of the University of Illinois, dedicated at Urbana in 1929, offers a democratic welcome to higher education. The sculptor Lorado Taft was an Illinois graduate (Class of 1879). University of Illinois Photographic Services.

2. Students are photographed with the Alma Mater during World War II. The male students gaze at the camera or into the distance; the women students gaze at the men. Through such constructed images, the university comes to be seen as a largely male environment in which women are onlookers. Archives photograph.

3. Photographs in the archival record show men in direct physical relation to the Alma Mater. Here, she is moved from her original site to a more visible campus location. Not until the 1980s do such photos begin to appear with women in them. Archives photograph, 1962.

4. Violet DeLille Jayne, dean of women from 1897 to 1904, inherited a population of women students with little cohesion or camaraderie. Under her guidance, the women students devised a system of self-government which came to be known as the Illinois Plan. Archives photograph, circa 1900.

5. Lucy Flower was the first woman member of the University of Illinois Board of Trustees (and thus became the first elected female official in the state); rich and influential, she persuaded the reluctant university president to take many important steps on behalf of women. Archives photograph.

6. Isabel Bevier was a pioneer in the field of home economics; she was particularly alive to the opportunities that the land-grant philosophy opened to women. Believing strongly that household science must be founded on scientific theory and method, she repeatedly resisted pressures to offer merely practical instruction in such areas as bread-baking; she stated scornfully that "neither a cooking school nor a milliner's shop was being opened in the University." In this photo, Bevier (back row, right) sits in front of the Woman's Building with the faculty of the Department of Household Science. Archives photograph, circa 1908.

7. Women graduates in library science, 1914. Developed at Illinois by Katherine Sharp, library science was a fruitful advanced field for women. As this photograph shows, this included Black women. Archives photograph.

8. Women playing hockey, 1912. Women's athletics developed at universities to combat nineteenth-century misogynist arguments that women would be physically incapable of advanced study; feminist educators sought to create conditions for the woman student that would ensure "a sound mind in a strong body." At many institutions, including Illinois, women's athletics was institutionalized before men's athletics. Archives photograph.

9. The Woman's Building, completed in 1905, was named in the singular so that each individual woman would feel a sense of proprietorship and belonging. The building was the hub of women's intellectual and social activities for many decades, a history that its current name (the English Building) obscures. *Illio Yearbook,* 1919.

10. Display of brooms, Department of Household Science, circa 1915. Arguing that the land-grant institution was designed for women as well as men, University of Illinois graduate Katherine Kennard wrote in 1891 that "science is the hand maid of home culture no less than the hand maid of agriculture." Domestic science sought to bring scientific principles into the "private sphere." Archives photograph.

11. By the turn of the century, Black women were enrolled in many curricula at the University of Illinois, including medicine. Isabella Garrett, a Black woman, graduated from the University of Illinois College of Physicians and Surgeons in 1901. Garrett's existence was unknown to the college until a subsequent Black woman graduate identified Garrett and pointed the way to her class picture. A crucial source of information about the existence and activities of women of color—often absent from official university histories—is the oral communications of other women. Archives photograph, Library of the Health Sciences, University of Illinois at Chicago.

12. Ruby E. C. Mason, dean of women from 1918 to 1923, established a hierarchy of rules and regulations which undermined both the university's egalitarian land-grant tradition and the tradition of women students' self-governance. Though she is not the most admirable representative of the office of dean of women, her tactics in dealing with the university president nevertheless make her worthy of feminist attention. *Illio Yearbook,* 1920.

13. Women in a food chemistry laboratory, 1890. Though women were enrolled in many science curricula, many more were channeled into domestic
science and other "female" curricula. Archives photograph.

14. Calling themselves the "Pioneer Women" of the University of Illinois College of Physicians and Surgeons, the first class of women in the medical school
in Chicago contributed an essay to the 1898 *Illini Women's Number*. "The fact
that there need be no discrimination of sex in science," they wrote, "has been
fully demonstrated." That same year, they formed the charter chapter of Nu
Sigma Phi, a medical society for women students and faculty. Its aim, wrote
founding member Hannah Huykill, was not only to be the first medical fraternity for women but to be above all "progressive." Archives photograph, Library
of the Health Sciences, University of Illinois at Chicago.

15. The Alma Mater, Still Standing. A joke among male undergraduates at the University of Illinois is that the Alma Mater sits down whenever a virgin walks by—"Ever seen her sit?" But feminists know that the Alma Mater won't sit down until sexism and discrimination against women come to an end. She's not sitting yet. Given the current political climate and the heavy weight of historical evidence of discrimination, women would do well in the years ahead to follow Mao's advice: Dig tunnels deep; store grain everywhere. Archives photograph, circa 1962.

The figure of "Dean Agnes Watson," who in this story spies on a fraternity house one Saturday night to see for herself whether the young men and women are keeping the regulation distance (six inches) between their bodies as they perform the latest campus dances, was based on a real dean of women named Ruby E. C. Mason; her five years in office from 1918 to 1923 marked an era of increasing administrative control that in many respects ran counter to the university's democratic land-grant tradition. Such control, in keeping with the conservatism of the times, exacerbated the differences in the student body I noted above. At the same time, Mason's experience emphasizes the tenuousness of any dean of women's authority and the special stresses for women administrators in "man-made" institutions.

Mason (Fig. 12) came to Illinois in the fall of 1918 from Indiana University with strong credentials and enthusiastic recommendations, but at Illinois she encountered difficulties almost at once. The Women's Residence Hall, completed at last but not yet ready to be occupied, left several hundred women students that fall scrambling for a place to live. Mason's initial actions did nothing to appease their anger at the administration. Though she blandly told a local newspaper interviewer that she sought to encourage "a sane and democratic social life" among the women students with "greater supervision of study lists and activities," she quickly laid down a series of repressive rules and regulations.[58] She outlawed the shimmy (the most daring and popular of campus dances), placed restrictions on dating, reversed several decisions made by the women students' self-government organization, strictly enforced chaperonage rules, and took unpopular stands on a number of issues which were at once declared to be none of her business.

These actions did not sit well with the women students whose growing rebellion went public in the spring of 1919. An editorial in the *Daily Illini*, like other campus publications largely dominated by the fraternities and sororities, argued that the rule restricting women's dating was "unjust and unfounded and will [in consequence] be disregarded." Accusing Mason and the administration of believing that "University of Illinois students are children," another editorial called her interference in student social life "prudish and childishly insane." "The Dean [of Men] has put the idea into her head that Illinois is a wicked place, too wicked for decent people to associate in—so she is trying to reform us. This is an insult and an outrage."[59] So Mason early on took a hard line against the flappers (the "bad girls"); at the same time, it was unclear for whom she was to speak, for she also mistrusted the Women's Group System and the independent students (the "good girls") it represented.

This in itself was of no particular concern to the administration. Indeed, Mason's views and actions struck a deeply sympathetic chord with those of moralistic, conservative president David Kinley, who applauded her "high ideals and splendid principles" against the "lower standards and looser regulations" of her detractors.[60] Still, Kinley was at last forced to pay attention to the continuing complaints he heard; in addition, despite their philosophical compatibilities, Kinley and Mason differed widely in administrative style. Mason's moral standards did not entirely make up for the disorganized way she ran her office. Their first encounter on this subject was to be prophetic in its inconclusiveness. In the spring of 1920, following additional public and private criticism from students, Kinley conveyed directly to her the charges that she was inefficient, strict, and tactless; her response thanked him for his frankness: "One who is not my friend," she wrote, "would not have said to me what you did," and went on to express confidence that the future would be different.[61] Kinley was not reassured, and over the next several weeks personally conducted an inquiry into her performance. He collected opinions from Dean Tommy Arkle Clark, the well-entrenched and powerful dean of men, from faculty and administrative staff including Isabel Bevier and Louise Freer, and from women students identified by Dean Clark and others. These informants were asked not only to comment on Dean Mason's performance but also to recommend whether to keep her or let her go. In addition, Kinley wrote a frank letter to the president of Indiana University to reconfirm her positive performance there. Though no doubt he believed he was being both fair and discreet, he questioned at least twenty people directly or indirectly; what he told Dean Mason while the inquiry was going on isn't clear, but it seems unlikely that she was oblivious to it.

What is most striking about Kinley's inquiry is not its kangaroo court quality (reflected in other incidents during his administration as well[62]) but rather its use of individual women to document Mason's shortcomings and in doing so turn the women's community against itself. Though most informants were guardedly favorable in their recommendation that Mason "be kept," they were undoubtedly sensitized to Mason's difficulties by the very fact of an open inquiry and certainly alerted for trouble in the future; further, in addition to one apparent case of outright self-interest,[63] their responses on such matters as the rules about campus dancing highlighted existing differences among various campus factions over "campus morality." Thus Dean Clark noted in his own recommendation (a miniature masterpiece of hedged discourse which nonetheless supported Mason's being rehired), "I feel sure that the better class of girls and the more conservative will not disapprove of her retainment here."[64]

The decision to rehire Mason did not foster confidence in her nor clarify the question of whom she was to speak for; Kinley's inquiry, moreover, clearly usurped her authority and further solidified her image as the male administration's puppet. Though subtle, there is also the hint in some of the accusations against her that she was not quite normal in her persecution of dating, dancing, and other heterosexual activities. The *Illio Yearbook* that spring was brutal in its description of "Ruby's Adventures in Wonderland": "Ruby was beginning to get tired of Indiana University since, having subdued all culprits there was nothing more for her to do." Arriving at Illinois, Ruby comes face to face with the sinful ways of sorority life. In horror, she blacklists all sororities and posts a list of ten commandments in several likely locations including the Woman's Building:

> Thou must not pull the eye-brows.
> Thou shalt not wear spit-curls.
> Thou must resemble high-brows
> Instead of chorus girls.
> Thou must wear low-heeled shoes,
> Thy nails thou must not shine,
> Thou must not whistle, me-oh my!
> Or else I shall resign.
> Best not laugh dance or sing or join a sorority.
> And if you're good Perhaps you could
>   become a dean like me.[65]

Here Mason is cast not only as the enemy of heterosexuality but as the opponent of social freedom. The sorority women (espousing fashion, make-up, laughter, dancing, and general high spirits) see themselves as the standard-bearers of modern progress and freedom in opposition to "high-brows," other "good girls," and deans. Had Mason strived to build a community of women with priorities different from those of the sorority leaders, she might have been more successful. Instead, students resented her not simply for her moralistic positions but also for the tactics she used to subvert the established processes of women's self-governance. By imposing rules and regulations, she created a hierarchy that undermined a tradition of democratic decision-making. One of her acts, for example, was to revise the constitution of the Woman's League so that its "object shall be to cooperate with the Council on Administration in the regulation of all matters pertaining to the student life of the women of the University."[66] This was perceived as radically changing the Women's League from a broadly representative organization to a hierarchical system in which a favored few were taken under the wing of the dean of women and used to enforce her policies. Mason, it was believed, in turn enforced the policies of the administration.

Interestingly, this was never entirely the case. If Andrew Draper's strategy for dealing with Violet Jayne's concerns can be said to have consisted of pervasive evasion and inattention, Kinley's handling of Ruby Mason, in dramatic contrast, involved increasingly explicit but consistently unsuccessful attempts to tell her what to do. A kind of administrator's administrator who kept detailed files and thrived on paperwork, Kinley was adept at creating documentation which would serve his own purposes, and his correspondence to Ruby Mason is marked by phrases that seem to be written to establish a record of fair play: "I want to repeat what I said to you the other evening." "I am writing this . . . simply that there may not be any misunderstanding," "My movements are so uncertain that I am dropping you this note instead of trying to make an appointment." In one sense, Ruby Mason was no match for these polished discursive tactics and seems to have been ill-equipped to return them in kind. She never challenged or addressed Kinley's charges, or created an alternative record which told her side of the story. She never adopted Violet Jayne's "feminine" communication strategies, nor did she tell Kinley bluntly to leave the management of her office to her. On the other hand, given the fact that Kinley considered firing her as early as 1920 but didn't actually manage it until 1923, Mason's tactics must in some sense be considered successful. Indeed, there is something almost magnificent in her eventual ability to baffle and enrage the cool Kinley simply by responding in "unprofessional" and thus to him utterly inexplicable ways. In June 1920, for example, Kinley had his executive clerk forward to Mason the notice of a position for a dean of women at the University of Manitoba with the request that she refer it to anyone appropriate; a form of needling still in use today (for example by department heads who feel like rattling assistant professors up for tenure), the job opportunity seems to have unsettled Mason. It certainly muddied her communications with Kinley, who wrote ironically to a colleague (at this point he could still be ironic) that "she would like to accept but would like to stay here (I mean just what I say)."[67]

The upshot was that Mason stayed. The following spring, Kinley reappointed her for the 1921–22 academic year and even, "after long consideration and with some reluctance," gave her the salary of $4,500 per year that she had requested; in communicating this decision to her, Kinley took the opportunity to document, in two-and-a-half single-spaced pages, a number of her failings, particularly the "poor business practices" of her office.[68] This letter stimulated an uncharacteristically prompt reply from Mason, who wrote by return post that Kinley's reluctance to approve her salary "has stung me to the quick, for much as I have needed the money I have coveted more your good will and approval." She continued by hoping for his guidance in the future and, again, concluded by expressing confidence that things would improve. Kinley appears to have thought he was at last on the track of an effective management strategy, for he responded briefly and quite cordially that he was sorry to have hurt her but "plainness is necessary": "I could not write otherwise than I did without stultifying myself and misleading you."[69]

Things did not improve. Although the 1921–22 year passed without apparent incident, there is no evidence that Mason made any changes, and in the spring and summer of 1922, Kinley once again had to wrestle with the problems of her office, the terms of her reappointment, and other difficulties. By reappointment time in the spring of 1923, Kinley had made up his mind that she had to go, and he wrote to tell her so. After noting the "pretty widespread discontent" of her years in office and reminding her that "four years ago I interposed against a movement to prevent your reappointment" (a somewhat self-serving interpretation of the inquiry), he noted that widespread student complaints had continued; "under the circumstances," he concluded, with "disappointment" and "sorrow," "I feel it necessary . . . to advise you urgently that it would be better for you and for us if you could secure another position next year. It distresses me greatly to have to write this, and to say it."[70]

After his years of equivocation and ambivalence, Kinley must have been greatly relieved to put a final decision in writing at last. He was, then, doubtless unsettled to learn when he next spoke with Mason that she seemed not to have grasped the implications of his letter. He wrote her at once, "After reflecting again on the whole matter in the light of our conversation the other day and in order to avoid misunderstanding, I am writing to say that your name will not be included in my recommendations for reappointment after the expiration of your present term." Mason's response, dated four days later, is one line long: "I am writing to acknowledge the receipt of your letter of April 20." Whether this was denial or a deliberate refusal to seal her own fate in writing is unclear, but a month later she submitted detailed recommendations for the 1923–24 academic year which covered personnel, the reorganization of the office, and, finally, her own salary. Quite possibly fearing that he might have to have her bodily removed from the office, Kinley merely acknowledged her "favor" to him in sharing with him her recommendations about the office, then called attention to his earlier letter and its decision. At some point during the summer, he wrote Mason a final time to request that she let the university handle personnel decisions regarding the dean of women's office.[71]

Ruby Mason left Urbana for her home in Canada in August 1923, but she did not go altogether quietly. According to Filbey's account of the history of the deans of women, "Ruby Mason destroyed all the records of the Office of the Deans of Women and departed, never to be heard from again."[72] This is half the story. She did leave her Illinois office in disarray, but she did not disappear; rather, she became the first dean of women at the University of Western Ontario in London, Canada, a position she held from 1923 to 1932. Following an illness of several years, she died in Stratford, Ontario, in 1942.[73]

At a coeducational university, a large number of male administrators exist and are judged successful or unsuccessful according to the performance of their assigned responsibilities.[74] In contrast, the very few women in comparable administrative roles are frequently hired because of their sex, usually an insufficient but often a necessary condition of their employment. With sex thus taking precedence over other qualifications, the job description may in fact come to depend on constructions of "woman" and "femininity." Ironically, it is sex which is then scrutinized, questioned, and used to challenge job legitimacy and performance. Though a standard feature of administrative line positions is the dual loyalty they demand to those above and below in the hierarchy, the difficulties women encounter as they attempt to represent or act on behalf of other women argue forcefully that antagonistic pressures are both systemic and multiply determined.

Ruby Mason is a good example, for her case illustrates the coincidence of the particular and the general. Her failure at Illinois, preceded and followed by successful experiences elsewhere, can in part be traced to the incompatibility of her moralistic outlook with the liberal view of coeducational opportunities and commitment to self-governing social life represented by the sororities and women student leaders. In addition, her administrative abilities were perhaps better suited to a smaller school. Certainly her inefficiency and other "poor business practices" were increasingly intolerable to the tidy Kinley. By the students she was perceived as rigid, a "despot," and "childishly insane."[75] She policed heterosexuality without building a woman-centered community as an alternative. All these concrete problems contributed to her difficulties, but just as an argument over a carpet is really an argument about other things, the fate of individual women administrators is multiply determined. The fact is that Ruby Mason's experience was by no means unique. Like other deans of women, the particulars of her job performance unfolded against a backdrop of profound unease about women in positions of authority. Though she showed herself willing to enforce the attitudes and practices of the university administration, this was no protection in the end. Indeed, the fact that she had lost the confidence of the women students was used against her. Encouraged to police them, she was faulted for alienating them. Had she not monitored them, she would have been faulted for indulging them; had she built a loyal constituency, this too would have signaled danger to the administration.

The lack of a supportive environment was the case not only for the deans of women of Violet Jayne's and Ruby Mason's day. A hostile environment is experienced today by many women administrators— department heads, deans, and directors of women's studies programs.[76] Feminist scholars may also face difficulties, for the ambivalences and contradictions surrounding women's administrative roles herald those encountered by women faculty during the past fifteen years in their academic departments and disciplines.[77] Considerable evidence, in fact, makes clear that despite gains and progress, the academic environment remains a "chilly climate" for women.[78]

A variety of institutional practices act to make the academic environment inhospitable and alienating and to diminish, individually or collectively, women's authority and voice. Terms like sexism, racism, classism, anti-Semitism, and homophobia enact themselves on a day-to-day basis in a variety of concrete petty tyrannies. Space is one example, as it has been historically.[79] Although women are rarely barred today from particular classrooms or curricula, they are still sometimes excluded from spaces to which their professional credentials entitle them. Women in such traditionally male fields as medicine, for example, may still find hospital dressing rooms, lounges, restrooms, and sleeping spaces set up to accommodate male students and physicians only. As recently as 1983, a major public university interviewed job candidates at a private club which does not admit women. The allocation of financial resources—salaries, raises, fellowships, scholarships, grants, and funding for women's studies programs—remains a potent form of institutional control in which inequities for women persist.[80] At many schools, notably in the South, rules and regulations still differentiate women from men and split the women's community into "good girls" and "bad girls." Though sexual harassment legislation in principle affords protection to women in their place of work or study, the application of these regulations remains painful and problematic. Further, the ubiquitous conditions upon which sexual harassment regulations are based continue to challenge women's right to a hospitable environment. The job description also remains a virtual black hole for institutional control, generating multiple and often contradictory directions for the feminist scholar. Similarly, the director of women's studies, asked to be simultaneous advocate and "manager" of women, carries out a dual role that is often confusing and contradictory. In addition, most jobs still assume a conventional work week in which such necessities as child care remain the problem and responsibility of the individual (usually female) parent, not of the institution. Communication is yet another institutional practice which seems to contribute to women's experience of the academy as alienating.[81]

Why should this be so? One explanation is that women's gains in the nineteenth century and again in the twentieth challenge traditional assumptions about sexual difference; an array of personal behaviors and institutional controls then become desirable resources for marking and reemphasizing differences based on sex, for re-sexualizing women in the academy.[82]

President Andrew Draper and his successors sought deans of

women who were not outspoken feminists and who would not repeatedly land in "hot water." Not coincidentally, they were relatively
successful in meeting the first objective, for even suffragists like Violet
Jayne saw how the wind was blowing in central Illinois and fairly
ingeniously disguised their sympathies by translating them into seemingly neutral institutional programs like the Watcheka League. But
again and again, the deans of women at Illinois ended up in "hot
water." Close inspection suggests that this was rarely the fault of the
women in question. On the presumed grounds that any woman was
automatically qualified for the position, deans of women were sometimes appointed with inappropriate skills, commitments, or credentials;
one such dean was reportedly a drug addict, another had no interests
but her own research. In other cases, personal claims conflicted with
institutional and social mores. The well-liked and respected Louisa Allen—who combined "a trained mind with a warm heart"—was ha-
rassed for a year following her marriage to John Gregory in 1878, a
time when women scholars still married at their peril. Violet Jayne
resigned before marrying a faculty member and thus escaped public
humiliation in such forums as the student newspaper. Lily Kollack,
somewhat later, conducted her romance less discreetly and lost her job
in consequence. Even deans with no hint of romance were rumored to
be romantically or sexually involved with their chief administrative
officers (university president, governor, etc.), as though no woman
could achieve administrative authority on her own merits but only by
"buying" her position with sexual favors. In still other cases, it seems
precisely their outstanding qualifications and leadership talents that
caused these women to come into conflict with the administration. This
was true at other institutions as well, and over the years various strategies evolved for dealing with "unsatisfactory" deans of women. Several
cases became notorious: in some cases, they were fired outright (usually
by letter and/or while they were on leave) or their jobs were abolished;
in other cases, they were assigned demeaning responsibilities, moved
into closets, or otherwise subjected to unacceptable working conditions. In these ways, many outstanding women in academic administration were, in the words of one present-day male university administrator, "defanged and declawed."[83]

The existence of these patterns, however, should not delude us into
embracing a monolithic notion of "women." Our growing knowledge
of women's institutional history suggests that in reality women have

many simultaneous identities and experiences, and that these are multiply determined. Similarity and difference, moreover, are created through given *contexts,* not through the existence of fixed categories. Thus a Black woman English professor may be committed simultaneously to Chaucer, social change, and child care; she may chair a committee in which her knowledge of Roberts' Rules of Order is more immediately relevant than her status as a female (though the latter may shape the former); her scholarly article published in *PMLA* may or may not be a piece of feminist scholarship. In front of a classroom, she may less frequently enact an identity as a Black teacher (for example in speech patterns) than when she is talking informally with Black students. Of course I am not arguing that these identities do not interact but rather that their complexity has not yet registered on institutions (and numerous institutionalized individuals) for whom the categories "female," "feminine," and "feminist" continue to function like binary switches which override other data. That the word "woman" seems to trigger a more or less limited number of associations stems in part from ongoing discussions of "woman's true nature," discussions which have flourished in the academy. A final look at the past will illuminate the continuing presence of essentialism.

Scholarship and Woman's Place

> I thought I had never seen so flat and so muddy a place: no trees, no hills, no boundaries of any kind. This lack of boundaries, physical and mental, the open-mindedness of the authorities and their willingness to try experiments, indeed their desire to do so, opened up a whole new world for me.
>
>   Isabel Bevier, describing the University of
>   Illinois in 1900[84]

To create a women's community at Illinois, Violet Jayne worked with women students to edit and produce a special issue of the student paper. Writings in the *Illini Women's Number* (March 11, 1898) testify to her efforts and, in their buoyant optimism, to a faith in the land-grant spirit and its promised "lack of boundaries" for women. These student essays make clear that by the turn of the century coeducation at Illinois had touched virtually every curriculum area, including medicine, pharmacy, and architecture, but they also speak to the notion that the union of "learning and labor" benefits all women, not just those with professional goals (Fig. 13). Thus the essay by a woman in architecture distinguished the career-oriented woman from the homemaker but envisioned science and learning as fundamental to both roles. These women students are eager daughters of Alma Mater, trustingly confident that they will be granted a portion of her abundance. "The fact that there need be no discrimination of sex in science," wrote the women in medicine, "has been fully demonstrated" (Fig. 14).

Of course the *Illini Women's Number* did not grow out of a vacuum but rather was part of a tradition of commentary on the significance of the land-grant university for women. Katherine Kennard, an Illinois graduate and feminist whose clever groundwork in the 1890s contributed to the establishment of the Department of Household Science, had written in 1891 that "science is the hand maid of home culture no less than the hand maid of agriculture."[85] The university's fruitfulness for women was similarly praised in *Co-ed,* Olive Deane Hormel's 1926 tribute to the University of Illinois' academic ideals: "Sue . . . looked up with a dreamy light in her eyes to tell them quite casually her 'real ideas' as to a future in Architecture. . . . Women lived in houses more than men did—women ought to plan them. . . . Houses with personality—and real beauty. . . . And only women knew how to make them really practical. . . ."[86]

Isabel Bevier, who headed Household Science at Illinois (and appears in *Co-Ed*), spoke articulately of her sense of collegiality in the land-grant enterprise:

> In the early days of my own work, I very soon learned to distinguish whether the passing visitor, of whom there were many, belonged to the Land-grant College or to the traditional classical school, by the response which they made to my statement: "We are working at the problems of the home from the scientific basis." The man from the Land-grant College said: "Yes, the home opens up a very interesting field for the application of science." The man from the classical school looked at me a little questioningly and said: "Yes, yes,—are we a little late for breakfast? Are the biscuits gone?" In other words, the former understood my language.[87]

Thus the university at this time was in many respects a fruitful environment for women. These spirited and self-confident statements are grounded not only in convictions of equality, both as to women's ability and to the worth of their endeavors, not only in the notion of a theorized practice as an encompassing and particularly relevant educational philosophy, but also in perceptions that the coeducational setting offered a hospitable and generous community for intellectual development.

President Draper mistrusted the theoretical aspects of domestic science and attempted to have it seen merely as a practical means toward staffing his lunch room; like many men, he resisted the notion of women as intellectual beings and found the notion of their intellectual development troubling. The growing reality of coeducation did not entirely prevent the older and deeper questions from continuing to be argued: What is women's higher education *for?* Are women capable of being educated? Should women be educated at all? At the same time that women were perceiving science as the "hand maid" to their vision of the future, their opponents were marshaling "scientific" arguments against them. Strategies for the scientific control of women were numerous, and carried special weight within academic institutions.

Like President Draper's arguments for not furnishing the Woman's Parlor, like judgments that a particular dean of women was unsatisfactory, arguments for not educating women shifted to exploit or demolish prevailing ideas and goals. During the nineteenth century, higher education was out of reach for most of the working class, female or male; but as middle-class women increasingly sought access to colleges and universities, physicians, scientists, and other authorities argued that such intellectual over-stimulation could terminate their menstrual periods, cause atrophy and other damage to the reproductive organs, and produce unhealthy babies. Besides, their brains were different, rendering them incapable of abstract, objective, or original thought. Some argued that their brains were smaller and softer. (This argument was flawed because the critical ratio of brain weight to body weight gave women proportionally the larger brain.) Others argued that the frontal lobes, then thought to be the location of the intellect, were more developed in men. (When at the turn of the century the experts situated the intellect in the parietal lobes, they decided women actually had larger frontal lobes.) Some scientists concluded that women showed greater variability (that is, deviation from physical and psychological norms) and were thus more unstable, inferior creatures. (After Darwin argued that variation from the norm was linked to evolutionary progress, biologists and anatomy experts began to suggest that males actually showed more

variation from the norm.) Such "scientific" declarations bolstered arguments that women's intellectual and scholarly aspirations were probably dangerous and certainly futile.[88] Black women were subjected to
racial as well as sexual mythologies; according to prevailing stereotypes, they were, as one historian has put it, "allegedly approaching
extinction and possessing the mental capacity of an anthropoid ape";
they thus faced an even more formidable array of obstacles than did
white middle-class women. Longstanding commitments to education
within the Black community helped make their progress possible.[89]

Earlier, at schools for ladies, women's education continued to
reflect the notion of separate spheres. Women followed what was
clearly a "ladies" curriculum: a little foreign language, domestic instruction, and decorative sewing. The more ambitious schools founded
by such women as Emma Willard and Catharine Beecher reflected an
awareness that their programs, if they were to succeed, must on the one
hand have requirements as strict as those of men's schools, but on the
other hand encourage womanly behavior in word, action, and dress.
(So, for example, landscape painting might be considered unsuitable
because it required unladylike shoes and tramping around out-of-
doors.)[90] These new schools accepted the notion of "woman's place"
but had a new vision of what that place should be like. Women should
be full and enlightened participants in household affairs, not ornamen-
tal lilies. By the late nineteenth century, leaders in women's education
like M. Carey Thomas of Bryn Mawr, Anna Julia Cooper of Oberlin
and Washington, D.C., and Marion Talbot of the University of Chicago
were urging that women be educated "as thinking beings and not as
females."[91] Though coeducation was a matter of economic necessity for
many institutions because male enrollments had dropped radically as a
result of the Civil War (the University of Michigan reluctantly adopted
coeducation in 1870, for example, under pressure from the state legislature), women rapidly took advantage of the openings and the undergraduate enrollment of women grew steadily at many coeducational
schools including the University of Illinois. Further, enrollment figures
at the turn of the century indicated that women were winning the right
to study most of the subjects men studied.

What happened over the next several decades was an astonishing
reversal of these trends. Each advance into new territory brought
women in contact with new barriers, often in the form of new
"scientific" accounts of women's "true nature." Higher education in-

stitutions themselves took the lead in discriminating against women graduates. Though colleges and universities might become coeducational, very few became coeducat*ing* by hiring women for their own faculties.[92] Even when, by 1920, women were earning almost half of the undergraduate and one-third of the graduate degrees, they were not accepted as intellectuals who were capable of teaching men; thus in 1921, women held 4 percent of the professorships at coeducational institutions and 68 percent of them at women's colleges. (As Margaret Rossiter notes, it is ironic that the women's colleges were initially established to produce mothers of more enlightened sons, and instead produced generations of educated, erudite, and often remarkable scholars who were considered unfit to educate sons—and had nowhere to go but where they came from, the women's colleges.)[93]

The fortunes of academic women have always been linked simultaneously to economic conditions on the one hand and to the existence of feminist activity on the other. Accordingly, as men's enrollments stabilized just after the turn of the century, as professional competition mounted in a number of fields, and as the feminist movement narrowed to focus increasingly on suffrage, a move toward "professionalization" in many academic fields led to the reinstatement of restricted enrollments for women, tighter admissions standards, and the closing of many women's schools.[94] These closings deprived women of an important power base in hard times, and left them subject to discriminatory decision-making by male experts and authorities that was often harmful to their interests. Though the promise that women would be "a part, never apart" was used to dismantle separate structures for women, their undemarcated assimilation into male institutions was not what occurred; rather, women remained a marked class, subject to decisions and restrictions over which they had no control, and with few alternative structures through which they could pursue their educational and professional aspirations. Except in "women's disciplines" like domestic science and nursing, women were repeatedly subjected to common law court decisions that hampered their educational progress. Although these women's disciplines provided thousands of women with satisfying professional lives, they also, as Charlotte Conable and Margaret Rossiter have noted, drained off female competition from the professional mainstream.[95] Through a systematic structuring of power and rewards, women's labor in such fields as laboratory science was rendered virtually invisible. Unexplained, unwritten admissions policies restricted their access to many fields. If they were able to complete degree programs, they were often barred from advanced study, internships, apprenticeships, membership in professional and scholarly societies, and employment.[96] Here, again, Black women faced barriers that were even sturdier and more seamless. Their opportunities for development were almost exclusively in the Black community, and specifically in all-Black institutions.[97] Likewise, when white women did find professional employment, it was rarely in institutions judged to be "first rate"—a judgment synonymous with "white male" (i.e., selected men's or coeducational colleges and universities). When women did obtain positions at high quality institutions, they were confined to lower ranks and systematically exploited.[98]

These conditions remained in effect until the activism, public hearings, and legislation of the 1960s and 1970s initiated slow and painful efforts toward challenge and change. This history of systematic, *routine* oppression of women was thus profoundly embedded in academic life until quite recently, and even today, despite some change, the patterns of the past imprint themselves on the present.[99] Nowhere is vigilance more needed than in the identification and evaluation of intellectual and scientific arguments about "woman's nature," arguments which are by no means confined to the nineteenth century. Claims for a universal "maternal instinct," medical and psychiatric accounts of female development, hypotheses about women's "raging hormones," "objective" tests which imply that healthy adults are those who accept existing sex roles—all these arguments have been used in the twentieth-century United States to challenge women's right to intellectual and professional equality. Though we hear fewer crude arguments today about the negative effects of brain stimulation on the uterus, sociobiology is one currently fashionable field where "scientific" theory and research generate essentialist arguments that define and limit "women's nature," now intertwined within the genetic structure of DNA.[100] Feminist scholarship is critically important in challenging the overt content of such arguments and in demonstrating the ways in which scholarship is repeatedly harnessed to ideology as a mechanism for representation and control.[101]

Feminist scholarship, with roots outside the academy and potential for self-conscious transformation, can also show us how male-dominated traditions have monopolized the power of definition. It is as though women were locked into a conversation in which men asked all the questions, dictating (as questions do) that women's contributions must consist only of reactions and responses. Traditional scholarship thus reproduces and reinforces patterns of male-female interaction found in the larger society. Feminist scholarship, in asking its own questions, can function to reverse what has been a largely unilateral power of definition.

The Tasks of Feminist Scholarship: Reclaiming Alma Mater

It's cold as hell out here—and as lonely.

> Black woman faculty member at a large midwestern university.[102]

As practitioners of lesbian studies, we must remain apart; our scholarship cannot flourish in isolation from our communities. The freedom to create our own culture has been too painfully won to be entrusted to university sanction or control.

> Margaret Cruikshank[103]

In the top three professional ranks combined, women earned an average of 19 percent less than their male colleagues in academic year 1982–83. . . . The data showed that the higher the rank, the greater was the gap between the earnings of male and female faculty members.[104]

For more than a decade, gatherings of feminist scholars and other academic women have featured both a text and a subtext. The text involves the intellectual business of feminist teaching and scholarship: questions of theory and methodology, of the interdisciplinary nature of feminist scholarship and women's studies, and of the links between curriculum, pedagogy, and research. The subtext involves the conditions of our institutionalization. Here we discuss ways of establishing, preserving, and expanding our bases of support in the form of women's studies programs, status of women committees, women's caucuses, graduate programs, journals, faculty appointments, library resources, and seminar programs. We share information on the tenure and promotion process, news about jobs, and details of child care. We discuss legislation and litigation; we follow grievance proceedings, tenure and promotion hearings, and notorious cases. We compare notes on departments and disciplines, their treatment of women, and their hospitality to feminism and feminist scholarship. We discuss participation in the life of the university: teaching, advising, writing, publishing, serving on committees. We look for ways to make bridges among women despite differences of class, color, education, rank, position, and politics. We seek generalizations about the ways we've found to survive and thrive. This subtext glosses the business of being women in the academy, a man-made institution whose political and social conditions, along with those of the feminist movement, constitute the foundation for feminist scholarship within the academy. Women's continual subtextual talk attempts the impossible task of mediating between these two different sites, enabling us sometimes to elude disciplinary and other constraints and meet as members of what we might call Alma Mater's sorority.

This brief history of women at the University of Illinois suggests that feminist scholarship can help illuminate a number of issues in this regard. One issue involves what we are talking about when we talk about "women." Even in its earliest notions of women, for example, the university was pragmatic and flexible, with the result that the very definition process was highly unstable. Women were faulted first one way, then another, but always excluded from positions of authority; one result was that while the university grudgingly became coeduca*tional* it never became coeduca*ting;* thus we call it an institution made by men, not by women. Note that this formulation, like the phrase "Alma Mater's sorority," entails a contradiction, for it argues that the category "women" is crucial even while, as I have suggested above, it obscures equally crucial multiplicities. The tasks of feminist scholarship are simultaneously to render visible and to call into question what we know about women. In this sense it is a form of consciousness-raising, encompassing both articulation and self-critique.

It is also a form of vigilance. Despite gains in past years, women continue to lag behind men on most standard measures of academic and professional advancement. Thus Joanne Spencer Kantrowitz calls the Alma Mater "a woman of ill repute."[105] In January 1970, the Women's Equity Action League filed, under Executive Order 11246, the first charge of sex discrimination against an institution. In the decade since, sex discrimination charges have been filed against many additional institutions and hundreds of pages of congressional testimony have been taken, yet not one penny of federal money has been withdrawn on the basis of sex inequities. Reports on women's progress are typically titled "The Long Uphill Climb" and "But We Shall Persist." Despite women's successes, in the academy the old rule holds: the higher the rank, the fewer the women. Staring into the needle's eye, feminist scholars are

pressed to institutionalize their insights and perspectives. When they do
not, tenure and promotion committees continue to compare feminist
scholarship unfavorably to traditional scholarship (which they do not
call men's studies) and dismiss it as political (and therefore subjective),
emotional (and therefore unscholarly), unconventional in its methodologies and conclusions (and therefore discountable), conventional in
its methodologies and conclusions (and therefore unoriginal), and
oriented toward women (and therefore biased or trivial). Notwith-
standing such judgments, feminist scholarship as an enterprise is flour-
ishing. Such contradictions make the Alma Mater, whose duality I
suggested at the opening of this essay, an appropriate emblem for
women at the present time (Fig. 15).

An important task of feminist scholarship is to identify and expli-
cate these contradictions by examining the academy itself. One clear
project is to continue to monitor and assess women's status in academic
settings and interpret their institutional experiences.[106] In a variety of
concrete ways an academic institution's day-to-day practices can be
said to be "male," yet the woman academic is inevitably positioned
within the academy as a female: she is identified as such statistically, her
activities and behavior may be sex-linked in several ways, and she will
often be perceived and evaluated as a female. Many studies, for example, show that on the whole the classrooms of women teachers are
friendlier, livelier, and create an atmosphere in which students actively
participate in the learning process; to the degree that a teacher is judged
to teach in this way she is simultaneously judged to be less competent in
her discipline. The performance of women is affected by yet does not in
turn affect the existing values and structures of the institution.[107] To
take another example: child care continues to be treated by many institutions as the "problem" of the (usually female) individual rather
than as an institution's way of adapting to an increasingly heterogeneous workforce which includes working mothers, single parents, and
dual career households. Recognition of this new reality would mark
child care as the institution's clear responsibility. Instead, like Andrew
Draper and the carpet for the Woman's Parlor, the institutional response to child care is to deny institutional responsibility; solutions
depend on an individual parent's ingenuity and pocketbook, an individual boss's good will, and on the factors that exist on an individual
campus to facilitate or hinder the establishment of rational child care
arrangements.[108]

Another project of feminist scholarship is to identify and challenge the way that political, ideological, and biological arguments of patriarchal origin are used to construct and maintain sexual hierarchies. Several "scientific" examples have been noted. Another example is the pervasive definition of women's academic contributions and intellectual productions as non-theoretical or insignificant, thus distancing women from key sites where meaning is generated (e.g., writing, publishing, producing theory) and instead linking them to practical and material productions—teaching, advising, and committee work.[109]

Feminist scholarship plays a key role in recounting and interpreting the history of women and academic institutions and in exploring the "complex strategies women [have] used to pursue their interests in the face of consistent opposition."[110] Not only does such scholarship render visible what has remained largely invisible in male-oriented histories, establishing women's presence within academic institutions, it illuminates links between material and ideological conditions. "Woman," as I have said, is a complex category, women's situations are diverse and multiply-determined, and local conditions both enact and reinforce larger social and historical trends. Part of women's story is told through enrollments, salaries, degrees granted, hiring, tenure, promotion, and other statistical measures, but the story also unfolds in a university's day-to-day practices and uses of language. Within institutional prose, meanings accumulate over time and are codified and institutionalized with specific and broad implications for women. Such meanings influence ideological renderings of women's significance in any given context as well as the flow of resources to women's projects and interests. To gain a theoretical understanding of the process by which concrete linguistic events interact with institutional policy is another important task of feminist scholarship.[111]

Feminist scholarship, then, is a crucial means for studying the academy itself.[112] A growing body of research aims at detailing the complexity of the relationships between women and academic institutions and illuminating the ways in which we are and simultaneously are not female in a wide variety of daily practices. Some of the fundamental paradoxes of coeducation arise out of this very multiplicity of selves. The project of feminist scholarship needs to include an examination of this multiplicity and the institutional structures in which it is enacted. Thus historical and current relationships between education and sexuality (e.g., between coeducation, heterosexuality, and heterosexism) might profitably be examined.[113] We need to provide continuing theoretical grounding for women's studies programs and for relationships to women's programs outside the academy. The inevitable controversy in women's studies over separatism versus assimilation (expressed by the Cruikshank quotation at the opening of this section) reproduces controversies about coeducation itself.[114] Finally, feminist research promises to make visible the experience of specific women and groups of women within the academy and place these experiences within a larger political context.[115]

In this essay I have tried to document and illuminate the relationship between women and the University of Illinois at Urbana-Champaign between 1890 and 1925. Through the scrutiny and interpretation of historical information and specific discursive practices, I have examined some of the ways in which notions of "woman" acquired meaning during this period. In many cases, institutional authorities drew upon prevailing notions of women yet showed considerable flexibility and ingenuity in reconstructing these notions to suit their changing needs. Conditions for women at any given moment were determined by a variety of factors, with local decisions enacting and reconstituting broader social and historical developments (this is clear in the very notion of "coeducation," an educational vision in which both sexes are to be educated equally but which is often enacted locally as a series of management strategies whereby one sex is assimilated to the ways of the other). Feminist scholarship, I conclude, is beginning to be used to critique and influence the academy's structural and methodological practices. Feminist scholarship potentially embodies a theoretical challenge to the academy's traditional division of labor, to its hierarchy of values, and to its exclusion of women from the realms where theory and policy are generated.[116]

Notes

1. Miriam Beard, "Woman Springs from Allegory to Life," *New York Times*, circa 1920; rpt. in *Women: Their Changing Roles*, ed. Elizabeth Janeway (New York: Arno Press, 1973), p. 146.

2. Jessie Bernard, *Academic Women* (New York: New American Library, 1964), p. 1.

3. *Daily Illini*, June 12, 1929. The land-grant union of learning and labor was formally commemorated in an 1868 anthem written by Regent Gregory for

the university's inaugural ceremonies and set to music by Chicago composer George F. Root:

> O'er homes of the millions, o'er fields of rich toil,
> Thy science shall shine as the sun shines on soil,
> And Learning and Labor—fit head for fit hand—
> Shall crown with twin glories our broad prairie land.

Richard Gordon Moores, *Fields of Rich Toil: The Development of the University of Illinois College of Agriculture* (Urbana: University of Illinois Press, 1970), pp. 21–22.

4. Alma Mater photograph file, Record Series 39/2/20, University of Illinois Archives. Maynard Brichford, University archivist, suggested to me the probability that the fur boa was incompatible with the university's representation as a land-grant institution.

5. Catharine R. Stimpson, ed., *Discrimination against Women* (New York: R. R. Bowker, 1973).

6. Katherine Kennard to Charles H. Shamel, Oct. 15, 1891, Charles H. Shamel Papers, RS 26/20/3, University of Illinois Archives.

7. Winton U. Solberg, *The University of Illinois 1867–1894* (Urbana: University of Illinois Press, 1968), p. 364. Mary Loise Filbey comments on the inaccuracy of this description: "Women were not restricted from the other University buildings—but the men *were* restricted from the Woman's Building." "Early History of the Deans of Women, University of Illinois, 1897–1923," typescript, 1969, Filbey Family Papers, RS 41/20/38, University of Illinois Archives, p. 46.

8. The naming of the Woman's Building is discussed in Filbey, "History of the Deans of Women." The practice of naming buildings after anyone, male or female, is relatively recent at Illinois; academic buildings are nevertheless named for Isabel Bevier, founder of domestic science, and for Louise Freer, who developed women's athletics.

9. Henry Seidel Canby, *Alma Mater: the Gothic Age of the American College* (New York: Farrar & Rinehart, 1936), p. 166. Canby continues: "Women in the academy society grew salty, eccentric, many-angled in character; or prudish, dry, fussy, and self-indulgent; or, transcending the limitations of their sex, sublimated their difficulties into an amenity of real culture. They were never passionate—at least in public" (pp. 166–67). "Women in the academy" also denotes faculty wives.

10. Joanne Spencer Kantrowitz, "Paying Your Dues, Part-time," in *Rocking the Boat: Academic Women and Academic Processes,* ed. Gloria DeSole and Leonore Hoffman (New York: Modern Language Association, 1981), p. 15. Jessie Bernard, in *Academic Women,* writes: "It is curious, and worth a moment's consideration, that even schools with no women on their faculties are symbolized as cherishing mothers. Even where there are women on the faculties, not they but a mystical female—Alma Mater—nourishes and disciplines and shapes her charges. . . . Students of symbolism could undoubtedly explain why

it is that colleges and universities are pictured as females. It is not immediately obvious" (p. 1).

11. Olive Deane Hormel, *Co-Ed* (New York: Charles Scribner's Sons, 1926), p. 222. Hormel graduated from the University of Illinois in 1916. See n. 55.

12. Isabel Bevier, "The Land-Grant Colleges and the Education of Women," An Address Given on the Occasion of the Semicentennial Celebration of Ohio State University, Oct. 14, 1920, p. 5, University of Illinois Archives.

13. Dorothy Day, *The Long Loneliness: The Autobiography of Dorothy Day* (New York: Harper, 1952), p. 50. Day was a student at the University of Illinois from 1914 to 1916. See also William D. Miller, *Dorothy Day: A Biography* (San Francisco: Harper & Row, 1982), pp. 31–47.

14. Allan Nevins, *Illinois* (New York: Oxford University Press, 1917), p. 68. Gregory, of course, echoed national sentiment that "coeducation, a particularly American innovation in higher education, was considered by many to be an experiment fraught with peril to women, men, and educational institutions." Charlotte Williams Conable, *Women at Cornell* (Ithaca: Cornell University Press, 1977), p. 7.

15. Women at the University of Illinois are discussed in Margaret Rossiter, " 'Women's Work' in Science 1880–1910," *Isis* 71, no. 258 (1980): 391–98, as well as in her *Women Scientists in America: Struggles and Strategies to 1940* (Baltimore: The Johns Hopkins University Press, 1982). See also Filbey, "History of the Deans of Women"; Karl Max Grisso, "David Kinley, 1861–1944: The Career of the Fifth President of the University of Illinois" (Ph.D. dissertation, University of Illinois at Urbana-Champaign, 1980); Moores, *Fields of Rich Toil;* Nevins, *Illinois;* Solberg, *University of Illinois 1867–1894;* Carl Stephens, "Manuscript History of the University of Illinois," RS 26/1/21, University of Illinois Archives. Women at a comparable midwestern university during this period are discussed in Ellen D. Langill, "Women at Wisconsin: 1909–1939," in *University Women: A Series of Essays,* ed. Marian J. Swoboda and Audrey J. Roberts (Madison: Office of Women, 1980), vol. 1, pp. 11–30.

Discussions of women in U.S. higher education include Bettina Aptheker, "Quest for Dignity: Black Women in the Professions, 1865–1900," in *Women's Legacy: Essays on Race, Sex, and Class in American History* (Amherst: University of Massachusetts Press, 1982), pp. 89–110; Jessie Bernard, *Academic Women;* Constance M. Carroll, "Three's a Crowd: The Dilemma of the Black Woman in Higher Education," in *But Some of Us Are Brave,* ed. Gloria T. Hull, Patricia Bell Scott, and Barbara Smith (Old Westbury, N.Y.: The Feminist Press, 1982), pp. 115–28; Conable, *Women at Cornell;* Margaret Cruikshank, ed., *Lesbian Studies Present and Future* (Old Westbury, N.Y.: The Feminist Press, 1982); Marion Vera Cuthbert, *Education and Marginality: A Study of the Negro College Graduate* (New York: Columbia University Press, 1942); Patricia Albjerg Graham, "Expansion and Exclusion: A History of Women in American Higher Education," *Signs: Journal of Women in Culture and Society* 3, no. 4 (1978): 759–73; Lillian Faderman, *Surpassing the Love of Men* (New

York: William Morrow, 1981), pp. 178–230; Eleanor Flexner, *Century of Struggle: The Woman's Rights Movement in the United States* (New York: Atheneum, 1968); Nancy Hoffman, *Woman's "True" Profession: Voices from the History of Teaching* (Old Westbury, N.Y.: The Feminist Press, 1981); Linda Nicholson, "Women and Schooling," *Educational Theory* 30, no. 3 (Summer 1980): 225–33; Jeanne Noble, *The Negro Woman's College Education* (New York: Columbia Teachers College Press, 1956); Florence Read, *The Story of Spelman College* (Princeton: Princeton University Press, 1961); Pamela Roby, "Women and American Higher Education," *Annals of the American Academy of Political and Social Science* 404 (1972): 118–39; Rosalind Rosenberg, *Beyond Separate Spheres: Intellectual Roots of Modern Feminism* (New Haven: Yale University Press, 1982); Adele Simmons, "Education and Ideology in Nineteenth-Century America: The Response of Educational Institutions to the Changing Role of Women," in *Liberating Women's History: Theoretical and Critical Essays,* ed. Berenice A. Carroll (Urbana: University of Illinois Press, 1976), pp. 115–26; Virginia Shadron, Eleanor Hinton Hoytt, Margaret Parsons, Barbara B. Reitt, Beverly Guy Sheftall, Jacqueline Zalumas, and Darlene R. Roth, "The Historical Perspective: A Bibliographical Essay," in *Stepping Off the Pedestal: Academic Women in the South,* ed. Patricia A. Stringer and Irene Thompson (New York: Modern Language Association, 1982), pp. 145–68; Phyllis Stock, *Better Than Rubies: A History of Women's Education* (New York: G. P. Putnam's, 1978); Marian J. Swoboda and Audrey J. Roberts, eds., *University Women: A Series of Essays,* 3 vols.; Anna Mary Wells, *Miss Marks and Miss Woolley* (Boston: Houghton Mifflin, 1978).

16. Violet DeLille Jayne to Andrew Sloan Draper, June 9, 1899, Faculty Correspondence (1894–1904), RS 2/4/2, Box 5, University of Illinois Archives.

17. Draper to Jayne, June 21, 1899. *Draper Letterbooks* (1894–1904), RS 2/4/3, Box 3, University of Illinois Archives. Compare the account of the narrator of Charlotte Perkins Gilman's 1892 story *The Yellow Wallpaper,* reporting that her husband refuses to let her have her bedroom repapered: "He said that after the wall-paper was changed it would be the heavy bedstead, and then the barred windows, and then the gate at the head of the stairs, and so on" (Old Westbury, N.Y.: The Feminist Press, 1973), p. 14.

18. Jayne to Draper, June 26, 1901, Faculty Correspondence (1894–1904), RS 2/4/2, Box 5, University of Illinois Archives.

19. *Twenty-first Report to the Board of Trustees of the University of Illinois* (Urbana, 1899), p. 107. The Squirrel Park episode was probably as galling to many male faculty and administrators as it undoubtedly was to Violet Jayne. David Kinley, for example, then dean of the Graduate College, was during this period trying to obtain basic classroom furnishings (blackboards and chairs instead of backless benches, and so on) and saw Draper's Squirrel Park as further evidence of his anti-academic bias (Karl Max Grisso, personal communication).

20. Jayne to Draper, June 24, 1903, Faculty Correspondence (1894–1904), RS 2/4/2, Box 9, University of Illinois Archives.

21. Lucy Flower was the first woman elected to state office in Illinois.

"Though feminist sentiment had helped bring her to state office, she herself was a political conservative who opposed unlimited suffrage for women, believing that the illiterate and uneducated of both sexes should be excluded from the election rolls." J. David Hoeveler, Jr., in *Notable American Women,* ed. Edward T. James (Cambridge, Mass.: Belknap Press of Harvard University Press, 1971), p. 636. Her actions on behalf of women at the University of Illinois nevertheless were unequivocal, shrewd, and crucial. On the general subject of women trustees, see Mary Ellen S. Capek, "Women Trustees, or 'Would You Not Be More Comfortable on the Sofa?' " Draft manuscript for the Russell Sage Task Force on Women in Higher Education (1983).

22. Filbey, "History of the Deans of Women," pp. 13–15.

23. Draper to Flower, Sept. 15, 1898, *Draper Letterbooks* (1894–1904), RS 2/4/3, Box 4.

24. Draper to Flower, Apr. 24, 1899, *Draper Letterbooks* (1894–1904), RS 2/4/3, Box 5.

25. See Estelle Freedman, "Separatism as Strategy: Female Institution Building and American Feminism, 1870–1930," *Feminist Studies* 5, no. 3 (Fall 1979): 512–29; Conable, *Women at Cornell;* Rosenberg, *Beyond Separate Spheres;* Mary Roth Walsh, *Doctors Wanted: Women Need Not Apply* (New Haven: Yale University Press, 1977).

26. Lois Seyster Montross, "Girls Who Pet," in Lois Seyster Montross and Lynn Montross, *Town and Gown* (New York: George H. Doran, 1923), p. 113. Lois Montross graduated in 1919 from the University of Illinois at Urbana-Champaign. See n. 53.

27. Hormel, *Co-Ed,* p. 224.

28. Notes, Meeting of Colored Persons to Discuss a House for Suggested Colored Girls for Next Year, 1923–24, Colored Women, 1923–40, Dean of Students/Dean of Women file, RS 41/3/1, Box 4.

29. Stock, *Better Than Rubies,* pp. 222–23; Graham, "Expansion and Exclusion." Graham traces the evolution of higher educational institutions from a pre–Civil War period of prescribed and monolithic classical education to the crucial period of advancement for women between 1875 and 1925 when "a strikingly heterogeneous array of acceptable and praiseworthy institutions existed in America" (p. 761) to the post-1925 emergence of the research university when once again a monolithic model and single sanctioned standard prevailed. See also Bernard, *Academic Women,* and Laurence R. Veysey, *The Emergence of the American University* (Chicago: University of Chicago Press, 1965).

At the University of Illinois, women made up 9 percent of the student body (24 out of 278) in 1870–71. By 1900–1901, their numbers had increased to 19 percent (467 out of 2,505). The figure jumped in 1920–21 to 25 percent (1,983 out of 7,879), a percentage that remained relatively stable despite numerical increases until the 1970s, when growth began again: in 1970–71, 35 percent of the students were women, or 11,978 out of 34,018.

Discussing the arrival of women as non-traditional students during the nineteenth century, Jo Ann Fley points out that "one could legitimately argue that the very first non-traditional student in American higher education was the American Indian. Harvard, William and Mary, and Dartmouth all had the purpose of educating and Christianizing native Indians among their original charter purposes and developed curricula for Indian students almost immediately after their foundings. An important area for further research is the response of the colonial colleges to this group of non-traditional students." "Documentary History of Student Personnel: Background and Introduction to Documents 1636–1919," draft manuscript, p. 9.

30. Hormel, *Co-Ed,* pp. 231, 228–29.

31. Lois Seyster Montross, "Peter Warshaw," in Montross and Montross, *Town and Gown,* p. 42.

32. Montross, "Peter Warshaw," in Montross and Montross, *Town and Gown,* pp. 51–52.

33. Hormel, *Co-Ed,* p. 271.

34. Grisso, "David Kinley, 1861–1944," pp. 331, 332.

35. Just one example is the long friendship between Dean Maria Leonard and Dr. Maude Lee Etheredge, commemorated in Etheredge's booklet about Leonard printed circa 1978 (n.p., n.d.). Leonard was dean of women at Illinois from 1923 to 1946, about the same period that Etheredge headed the Women's Health Service on campus; they lived together from 1929 until Leonard's death in 1976.

36. "Four Faculty Women," University of Illinois Archives Exhibit, Nov. 1980.

37. *Illini Women's Number,* Mar. 11, 1898. Filbey, "History of the Deans of Women," writes that "the use of the name 'Watcheka' is symbolic of the spirit and pride that Violet Jayne was attempting to create among the Illinae. It comes from an old legend of the Indian tribe of the Illini who were supposedly attacked and plundered by the Dakotas. Watcheka was the beautiful and fearless daughter of the Chief of the Illini. When the braves rejected her plan for revenging the Dakotas because they thought it too hazardous, Watcheka secretly and silently led the other squaws in the dark night. They slipped across the river, surprising the Dakotas and putting them to flight. Their courageous example led the braves to take heart and follow them" (p. 21).

38. Stephens, "Manuscript History of the University of Illinois," Chapter 9. Margaret Hollett, a graduate student during the period 1910–13, described in detail the evolution of the self-governance system in a letter to the historian Allan Nevins. Carl Stephens Papers, RS 26/1/20, Box 13, University of Illinois Archives.

39. Stephens, "Manuscript History of the University of Illinois," Chapter 2; Moores, *Fields of Rich Toil,* p. 186. When Laura J. Huelster became head of physical education in 1949, she found that the singular and plural were used interchangeably in speech and on documents; it is she who learned from the university's architect the original rationale for the singular usage "Woman's Building." At her instigation, the university president declared the name of the

Women's Building to be "an administrative matter" and authorized her to resolve the dilemma; because she felt that the name "Women's Building" had come to make more sense, she changed all the singulars to plurals. Laura J. Huelster, personal communication.

40. Montross, "Peter Warshaw," in Montross and Montross, *Town and Gown*, p. 22.

41. Stephens, "Manuscript History of the University of Illinois," Chapter 9; Grisso, "David Kinley, 1861–1944," pp. 590–600. Kinley helped start up and furnish the Alpha Omega Alpha house out of his personal resources. About 1915, Dorothy Day wrote of her best friend at the University of Illinois, "in spite of brilliant scholarship and an outstanding personality, good looks and wealth, she was not invited to join any sorority. It was my first contact with anti-Semitism." *The Long Loneliness*, p. 48. As a result of such discrimination, two Jewish sororities formed in the 1920s as well.

42. Day, *The Long Loneliness*, p. 42.

43. *Illinois Magazine* 5 (Dec. 1913), p. 187; Stephens, "Manuscript History of the University of Illinois," Chapter 9.

44. University of Michigan Board of Regents 1858, cited in Fley, "Documentary History of Student Personnel," p. 10.

45. Filbey, "History of the Deans of Women," p. 11.

46. Gertrude S. Martin, "The Position of the Dean of Women," *Journal of the Association of Collegiate Alumnae*, ser. 4, no. 2 (1911), pp. 65–78, cited by Jo Ann Fley, "Gertrude S. Martin: Defining Ideals and Bridging Generations," *Journal of NAWDAC* (Spring 1979), p. 45.

47. Filbey, "History of the Deans of Women," p. 8.

48. *Nineteenth Report of the Board of Trustees* (Urbana, 1897), p. 64.

49. Filbey, "History of the Deans of Women"; Grisso, "David Kinley, 1861–1944," p. 618. University of Illinois administrators were not alone in their confusion over the position of dean of women. When Evelyn Wight Allan arrived at Stanford, the president sent her to a member of the Board of Trustees to learn her duties; when she told the trustee she was the new dean of women, he exclaimed in disbelief, "The devil you are!" and was as baffled as the president about her job responsibilities. Fley, "Gertrude S. Martin," p. 43. For many years, the history of the deans of women was thought too trivial to study, and early writings on the subject, like Lois Kimball Mathews's *The Dean of Women* (Cambridge, Mass.: Riverside Press, 1915), were ignored. What most institutional authorities did understand was discipline, which one dean of women described in 1929 as "the most distasteful and unpleasant and discouraging duty" of the office. Jo Ann Fley, "Changing Approaches to Discipline and Student Personnel Work," *Journal of NAWDAC* (Spring 1964), pp. 105–13. At the coeducational institution, the dean of women was expected to keep disciplinary matters firmly under control, an expectation that Dean Mary Bidwell Breed mocked in 1908: "When things get to a certain point—usually when something happens to remind people of the Garden of Eden—the university appoints a Dean of Women, whose powers seem to consist in persuading the

unpersuadable and in making water run up hill." Jo Ann Fley and George R. Jaramillo, "Mary Bidwell Breed: The Educator as Dean," *Journal of NAWDAC* (Winter 1979), p. 48. See also Marion Talbot, *The Education of Women* (Chicago: University of Chicago Press, 1910); Marion Talbot and Lois Kimball Mathews Rosenberry, *The History of the American Association of University Women, 1881–1931* (Boston: Houghton Mifflin, 1931); Marion Talbot, *More than Lore: Reminiscences of Marion Talbot* (Chicago: University of Chicago Press, 1936).

50. Etheredge, "Dean Maria Leonard," p. 17.

51. Jo Ann Fley, "Miriam A. Sheldon," *Weeds: the University of Illinois Women's Week Magazine* (Champaign: Andromeda, 1973), pp. 29–30. In 1967, while Sheldon was still dean of women, the position was precipitously abolished by the university administration on the grounds that special efforts on behalf of women were no longer needed. Ironically or coincidentally, this occurred at the very moment in history when questions of women's rights, interests, and abilities were to be raised with startling new vehemence.

52. Filbey, "History of the Deans of Women," p. 78.

53. Despite President Kinley's distaste for it, *Town and Gown* was praised enthusiastically by others. Carl Van Doren called it "the most entertaining and satisfactory volume of college stories this country has produced," and another reviewer said it "may be regarded as doing for the coeducational universities of the middle west what *This Side of Paradise* did a few years ago for Princeton." Stephens, "Manuscript History of the University of Illinois," Chapter 9.

54. *Town and Gown* emphasizes the deep chasm that separated the fraternity and sorority students from the independents who didn't belong and suggests that the significant campus activities were dominated by the Greek contingent. The division is noted in Stephens's "Manuscript History of the University of Illinois," which quotes an *Illinois Magazine* complaint in the early 1920s that the student body consisted of a "small half-amused half-cynical group of critics and a large placid group of indifferent vegetables" (Chapter 9, p. 37). Beginning in 1929 with the stock market crash, things changed: the independents got organized and took over campus elections, produced newspapers, and engaged in activism; the Greek system declined for many decades.

55. Although *Co-Ed* is a more conventional book than *Town and Gown*, concluding with its protagonist Lucia on the verge of marriage to a university graduate in agriculture, it addresses a number of interesting issues including the exclusiveness of sorority rushing, premarital sex, abortion (an episode in which a woman student almost dies), a love affair between a woman student and a married professor, and the intellectual and professional development of women.

56. Day, *The Long Loneliness*, p. 44.

57. Lynn Montross, "Bass Drums," in Montross and Montross, *Town and Gown*, p. 185.

58. Champaign-Urbana *Courier*, Mar. 4, 1919.

59. *Daily Illini*, Apr. 9, May 20, 1919.

60. David Kinley to Florence R. Curtis, May 26, 1919, Kinley Correspon-

dence, 1919–30, RS 2/5/3, Box 183, University of Illinois Archives. On May 21, 1919, responding to the *Daily Illini* criticism of Mason, Curtis had written Kinley a strong letter in Mason's defense.

61. Ruby E. C. Mason to David Kinley, Mar. 2, 1920, Kinley Correspondence, 1919–30, RS 2/6/1, Box 15, University of Illinois Archives.

62. In the view of many faculty, the Kinley administration was flawed by "overcentralization and overregulation." Kinley's infamous rule against smoking caused the faculty to be ridiculed by their peers at other institutions. It was also believed that Kinley, acting through Dean of Men Tommy Arkle Clark, spied on faculty and kept secret records of their activities. Grisso, "David Kinley, 1861–1944," pp. 570–74.

63. The most negative report was forwarded to Kinley by an alumnae advisor named Helene Doty whose letter concludes: "I filed formal application with Professor Weston for the Economics department position here—and I really wish I would get it. I think all things considered—from what you said too—I will be better off here than elsewhere. You are so generous in your attention to my problems and I do appreciate it." Helene Doty to Kinley, Mar. 30, 1920, Kinley Correspondence 1919–30, RS 2/6/1, Box 15, University of Illinois Archives. There is no evidence that Doty, an assistant in chemistry, obtained a position in economics.

64. Tommy Arkle Clark to Kinley, Mar. 29, 1920, Kinley Correspondence, 1919–30, RS 2/6/1, Box 15, University of Illinois Archives. Clark's support was perhaps not disinterested. Not only was he in sympathy with Kinley's conservative views on campus social life but also he had clashed publicly with the outspoken Lois Mathews on the subject of women deans and may well have found the less extroverted Ruby Mason a greatly preferable type. Jo Ann Fley, "Regulation of Student Conduct and Legal Implications," in *College Student Personnel: Readings and Bibliographies,* ed. Laurine E. Fitzgerald, Walter F. Johnson, and Willa Norris (Boston: Houghton Mifflin, 1970). Clark's paternalism embodied the notion of *in loco parentis,* and, as this verse suggests, often obscured the very existence of a dean of women:

> Oh, the dean of men and women
> At dear old Illinois
> Is a father to the girls
> And a mother to the boys.
> He looks out for their morals
> Especially after dark,
> Our matriarchal, patriarchal
> Thomas Arkle Clark.

Quoted by Lex Peterson, Champaign-Urbana *News-Gazette,* Apr. 3, 1983. See also Jo Ann Fley, "Thomas Arkle Clark: Patriarch and Dean from Illinois," *Journal of NAWDAC* (Spring 1978), pp. 120–23.

65. *Illio Yearbook,* 1920, p. 462.

66. Ruby Mason, 1920–21 Report, Office of Dean of Student Personnel,

Dean of Students/Dean of Women file, RS 41/3/1, University of Illinois Archives.

67. Kinley to C. R. Richards, July 31, 1920, Kinley Correspondence, 1919–30, RS 2/6/1, Box 19, University of Illinois Archives.

68. Kinley to Mason, August 3, 1921, Kinley Correspondence, 1919–30, RS 2/6/1, Box 41, University of Illinois Archives. Characteristically, he cites an additional failing of Mason's to explain why he is writing this to her at all: "I had rather taken it for granted, in view of my letter of last summer, that you would approach me on the subject. However, since we did not talk it over, it seems worth while to write somewhat fully." By this point, Kinley's exasperation was still tinged with disbelief. Complaining that her secretary lacked tact and judgment, for example, he commented, "Indeed, I myself at one time went to see you and was told that you were too busy to see me, although I wanted to have you join me with a party of people that were inspecting your building. I took them through myself, and while going up the stairs near your office, the young woman called to me and asked if I wanted to see you then; but I did not."

69. Kinley-Mason correspondence, Aug. 7, Sept. 12, 1921, Kinley Correspondence, 1919–30, RS 2/6/1, Box 41.

70. Kinley to Mason, Mar. 20, 1923, Kinley Correspondence, 1919–30, RS 2/6/1, Box 85.

71. Kinley-Mason correspondence, Apr. 20/24, May 22/25, June 30, 1923, Kinley Correspondence, 1919–30, RS 2/6/1, Box 85.

72. Filbey, "History of the Deans of Women," p. 59. Her information about Mason's destruction of the records came from Miriam A. Sheldon, dean of women at Illinois from 1948 to 1968 (with corroboration from others); much of Filbey's history had to be reconstructed from alternative sources. Though some attempts to trace Mason after she left Illinois apparently failed, faculty records in the archives (RS 26/4/1) include annual updates of her address in Canada and note her death in 1942.

73. During this time, she seems to have reproduced the elements of women students' life at Illinois: she organized a women's student government; introduced sororities; established Alpha House, the first women's residence hall, initially operating it in her own home; and developed a number of undergraduate women's organizations. John R. W. Gwynne-Timothy, *Western's First Century* (London, Ontario: University of Western Ontario, 1978), pp. 732–34; James J. Talman and Ruth Davis Talman, *"Western"—1878–1953* (London, Ontario: University of Western Ontario, 1953), pp. 117–18.

74. This is not, of course, to say that male administrators are not also judged according to complex and sometimes capricious factors but rather to emphasize the point that "maleness" is not the gold standard against which their performance is weighed.

75. Filbey, "History of the Deans of Women," p. 91.

76. See, for example, Suzanne Perry, "Women Administrators Say They Still Battle to Win Acceptance from Male Colleagues," *Chronicle of Higher Education* (Mar. 30, 1983).

77. Bernice Sandler, "Women on Campus: A Ten-Year Retrospective," *Association of American Colleges Project on the Status and Education of Women* 26 (Spring 1980); DeSole and Hoffman, eds., *Rocking the Boat;* Jane W. Loeb and Marianne A. Ferber, "Representation, Performance, and Status of Women on the Faculty at the Urbana-Champaign Campus of the University of Illinois," in *Academic Women on the Move,* ed. Alice Rossi and Ann Calderwood (New York: Russell Sage Foundation, 1973); Jane W. Loeb, Marianne A. Ferber, and Helen M. Lowry, "The Effectiveness of Affirmative Action for Women," *Journal of Higher Education* 49, no. 3 (1978): 218–30. Roby, "Women and American Higher Education," describes the university as a "competitive, egocentric, entrepreneurial and stereotypically masculine culture."

78. Roberta M. Hall with the assistance of Bernice Sandler, "The Classroom Climate: A Chilly One for Women," *Project on the Status and Education of Women,* 1982.

79. Conable, *Women at Cornell,* describes the battle over whether the student union building was to have a separate entrance for women (it did). Walsh, *Doctors Wanted,* cites the case of Alice Hamilton, pioneer of industrial medicine; one condition for her appointment to the faculty of the Harvard Medical School was her agreement never to march on the commencement platform with the other faculty. For many years at the University of Illinois, women were not permitted to use the righthand staircase of the main academic building (and restrooms on campus were racially segregated until 1946).

80. See, for example, Sandler, "Women on Campus."

81. See Paula A. Treichler and Cheris Kramarae, "Women's Talk in the Ivory Tower," *Communication Quarterly* 31, no. 2 (Spring 1983): 118–32.

82. Catharine A. MacKinnon argues that as women move increasingly into traditionally male jobs, sexual harassment functions to re-sexualize them, *Sexual Harassment of Working Women: A Case for Sex Discrimination* (New Haven: Yale University Press, 1979). It is possible that the not uncommon accusation that feminist activists are "lesbians" is another tactic for representing women in what are deemed by the accusers to be sexual (as well as insulting) terms. Women's attentive deconstruction of these terms continues to be an important counter-tactic.

83. Verbal report of a statement made at an informal committee meeting at the University of Illinois in the 1970s.

84. Isabel Bevier, describing her first visit to the University of Illinois in 1900, "The History of Home Economics at University of Illinois, 1900–1921," typewritten manuscript, Home Economics Library, University of Illinois, 1935.

85. Katherine Kennard, letter to the editor of the *Farmer's Review* (Nov. 30, 1891). Charles H. Shamel Papers, RS 26/20/3, University of Illinois Archives.

86. Hormel, *Co-Ed,* pp. 237–38.

87. Bevier, "Land-Grant Colleges." Elsewhere, Bevier commented on the naming of the Department of Household Science, a task assigned to her, Dean Eugene Davenport, and Professor Thomas Burrill. "The three of us wanted

science as the basis and the scientific approach to the subject, but it was Dean Davenport who said, 'I believe there will be some day a science of the household. Let's get ready for it and develop it.' So the child was named 'Household Science' and thus due warning was given that neither a cooking school nor a milliner's shop was being opened in the University." "The History of Home Economics at University of Illinois, 1900–1921." One might compare discussions of the naming of "women's studies" and its alternatives.

88. Feminist observations on this subject include Pauline Bart, "Biological Determinism and Sexism: Is It All in the Ovaries?" in *Biology as a Social Weapon*, ed. The Ann Arbor Science for the People Collective (Minneapolis: Burgess Publishing, 1977), pp. 69–83; Jessie Bernard, *Sex Differences: An Overview*, Module 26 (n.p., MSS Modular Publications, 1973); Barbara Ehren-reich and Deirdre English, *For Her Own Good: One Hundred and Fifty Years of the Experts' Advice to Women* (Garden City, N.Y.: Anchor, 1979), pp. 126–28; Stephanie Shields, "Functionalism, Darwinism, and the Psychology of Women: A Study in Social Myth," *American Psychologist* 30 (1975): 739–54. David Gelman (with others), "Just How the Sexes Differ," *Newsweek* (May 18, 1981), pp. 72–83, summarizes past and present views succinctly.

89. Bettina Aptheker, "Quest for Dignity," p. 96. The quotation summarizes the implications suggested by racist and white supremacist "scientific" writings of this period. See also Flexner, *Century of Struggle*, pp. 127–30.

90. Sara Delamont and Lorna Duffin, *The Nineteenth-Century Woman: Her Cultural and Physical World* (London: Croom and Helm, 1978), p. 145.

91. Marion Talbot, 1902, quoted in Rosenberg, *Beyond Separate Spheres*, p. 48. Anna Julia Cooper, who graduated from Oberlin in 1884 (one of the first Black women to earn a college degree), described her Alma Mater's pioneering decision—"adopted with fear and trembling by the good fathers"—to admit women to a special "Ladies' Course" in 1833: "The girls came, and there was no upheaval. They performed their tasks moderately and intelligently. Once in a while one or two were found choosing the gentlemen's course. Still no collapse; and the dear, careful, scrupulous, frightened old professors were just getting their hearts out of their throats and preparing to draw one good free breath, when they found they would have to change the names of those courses; for there were as many ladies in the gentlemen's course as in the ladies', and a distinctively Ladies' Course, inferior in scope and aim to the regular classical course, did not and could not exist." *A Voice from the South* (Xenia, Ohio, 1892), rpt. in *Black Women in Nineteenth-Century American Life*, ed. Bert James Loewenberg and Ruth Bogin (University Park: Pennsylvania State University Press, 1976), p. 319. M. Carey Thomas, who went on to become president of Bryn Mawr (1894–1922), called her coeducational experience at Cornell a "fiery ordeal," but the only way to demonstrate at that time that women could excel academically. Conable, *Women at Cornell*, p. 20.

92. University of Illinois alumnae and other advocates for women petitioned the Board of Trustees in 1892 to make the university a "Co-educating as well as a Co-educational institution" by appointing women to the faculty and making them full professors. Solberg, *University of Illinois 1867–1894*, p. 351.

93. Rossiter, *Women Scientists in America.*

94. Joan Jacobs Brumberg and Nancy Tomes, "Women in the Professions: A Research Agenda for American Historians," *Review in American History* (June, 1982), pp. 275–96.

95. See, for example, Barbara J. Harris, *Beyond Her Sphere: Women in the Professions in American History* (London: Greenwood Press, 1978), pp. 110–16 and Conable, *Women at Cornell,* pp. 114–15. Rossiter, " 'Women's Work,' " notes that women entering graduate training during the period of scientific expansion at the turn of the century were counseled to enter home economics, the only field where they could hope to become full professors, department chairs, or deans at coeducational institutions. Women who entered the other sciences could expect chiefly to find positions as technicians or research associates in the laboratories of established (and progressive) male scientists; they were not expected to set up labs and direct investigations on their own. "Thus a segregated, low-status, almost invisible kind of 'women's work' offered a harmonious way to incorporate the newcomers into the scientific labor force in ways that divided the ever-expanding labor, but withheld the ever more precious recognition. A pattern had been set for the twentieth century" (p. 398). It was noted during the discrimination hearings of 1970 that the presence of a majority of women in a profession lowers its "property value." *Discrimination Against Women: Hearing before the Special Subcommittee on Education and Labor,* House of Representatives, 91st Congress, 2nd sess., on Section 805 of HR 16098 (1970), p. 251.

96. Discrimination against women in the medical profession is one example. During the nineteenth century, when many women were actively engaged in medical practice and competing with male physicians for patient populations and professional prestige, male members of the profession not uncommonly referred to women physicians as "unnatural," "loathsome and disgusting," and "the third sex"; such labeling, accompanied by concrete discriminatory practices, sought to lessen women's legitimacy and professional appeal; Walsh, *Doctors Wanted,* p. 140. See also Paul Starr, *The Social Transformation of American Medicine* (New York: Basic Books, 1983) and Carroll Smith-Rosenberg and Charles Rosenberg, "The Female Animal: Medical and Biological Views of Woman and Her Role in Nineteenth-Century America," *Journal of American History* 60 (Sept. 1973): 332–56. To preserve the status quo some male physicians told themselves repeatedly over the decades that just as "cheap money drives dear money out of circulation . . . the weaker sex drives out the stronger." Walsh, *Doctors Wanted,* p. 201, quoting from the Boston *Transcript,* about 1910.

By the turn of the century, when women were beginning to gain access to medical schools and to the specialized knowledge they offered, highly specific "scientific" arguments were marshaled to bolster the view that women could not be trained to be physicians. "It is impossible to make a doctor out of a woman," a trustee of Northwestern University told the press when the women's medical college was closed in 1902; "women cannot grasp the chemical and pharmaceutical work, the intricacies of surgery, or the minute work of anatomy." Patricia Spain Ward, "Aren't Women Smart Enough to be Doctors?" paper presented at the conference Women and Wellness, Northwestern University, 1980, p. 15. See also Helen MacKnight Doyle, *Doctor Nellie* (Mammoth Lakes, Calif.: Genny Smith Books, 1983 [1934]), pp. 237–315.

In *Doctors Wanted*, Walsh documents the medical profession's continued attempts to bar women from county, state, and national medical societies and the laborious reasoning used to deny them commissions during World War I and other professional rights and privileges. "Scientific" reasons were used to block women's entrance into internship programs and to channel women into certain fields within medicine over others. A 1902 editorial in the *Journal of the American Medical Association* argued that "without going into the psychophysical nature of women as such, it will perhaps be generally granted that women are, on the average, more emotional, more formally unreasoning, more unmechanical, physically weaker, yet stronger in sympathy than are men." This granted, the editorial continued, it is obvious that women should not go into surgery or other fields where "a critical case demands independent action and fearless judgment." To refute such claims, women physicians patiently and repeatedly documented evidence and counter-arguments: an early example is Sarah H. Stevenson, *The Physiology of Woman, Embracing Girlhood, Maternity and Mature Age* (Chicago: Thomas Cushing, 1881); more recent efforts are documented in Dorothy Rosenthal Mandelbaum, "Women in Medicine," *Signs* 4, no. 1 (Autumn 1978): 136–45, and Sandra Chaff, Ruth Haimbach, Carol Fenichel, and Nina Woodside, eds., *Women in Medicine: An Annotated Bibliography of the Literature on Women Physicians* (Metuchen, N.J.: Scarecrow Press, 1977). The obstacles women physicians faced during the bleak period from approximately 1920 on are vividly summarized in a series of articles published during 1926 and 1927 in the *Women's Medical Journal* by the physician Bertha Van Hoosen. By the time Dr. Frances S. Norris testified at the 1970 congressional hearing, medical schools had established what she called "a long, dishonorable tradition of discrimination against women," in *Discrimination against Women: Hearing before the Special Subcommittee on Education and Labor,* House of Representatives, 91st Congress, 2nd Sess., on Section 805 of HR 16098 (1970), p. 519.

97. Bettina Aptheker, "Quest for Dignity," in *Woman's Legacy,* writes that discrimination against Black women in the professional world "was so intense that their names were frequently erased from historical records which otherwise noted the work of Black men or white women" (p. 96); see also Flexner, *Century of Struggle.*

98. Representative is the story of Dr. Alice Hamilton's experience at Harvard. Walsh, *Doctors Wanted,* pp. 211–12.

99. Stimpson, ed., *Discrimination against Women.*

100. See, for example, Ethel Tobach and Betty Rosoff, eds., *Genes and Gender,* 4 vols. (Staten Island, N.Y.: The Gordian Press, 1978–83), a series that grew out of a conference designed to critique and counter views of women

derived from sociobiology; see also Janet Sayers, *Biological Politics: Feminist and Anti-Feminist Perspectives* (New York: Tavistock, 1982).

101. Examples are Donna J. Haraway, "In the Beginning Was the Word: The Genesis of Biological Theory," *Signs* 6, no. 3 (Winter 1981): 469–81; Mary E. Payer, "Is Traditional Scholarship Value Free? Toward a Critical Theory," in *The Scholar and the Feminist IV: Connecting Theory, Practice, and Values* (New York: The Women's Center, Barnard College, 1977); Hilary Rose, "Hand, Brain, and Heart: A Feminist Epistemology for the Natural Sciences," *Signs* 9, no. 2 (Autumn 1983): 73–90.

102. Quoted by Gloria T. Hull and Barbara Smith, "The Politics of Black Women's Studies," in *But Some of Us Are Brave,* ed. Hull, Scott, and Smith, p. xxiv.

103. Margaret Cruikshank, introduction, *Lesbian Studies,* ed. Cruikshank, p. xiv.

104. Bernice Resnick Sandler, ed., "On Campus With Women," *Project on the Status and Education of Women* 13, no. 4 (Spring 1984): 10, reporting statistics collected from over 2,700 colleges and universities by the National Center for Education Statistics.

105. Joanne Spencer Kantrowitz, "Paying Your Dues, Part-time," in *Rocking the Boat,* ed. DeSole and Hoftman, p. 15.

106. Scholarly collections that illuminate women's current status in academic institutions include DeSole and Hoffman, eds., *Rocking the Boat;* Florence Howe, ed., *Women and the Power to Change* (New York: McGraw-Hill, 1975); Rossi and Calderwood, eds., *Academic Women on the Move;* Stringer and Thompson, eds., *Stepping Off the Pedestal;* Swoboda and Roberts, eds., *University Women; Women on Campus: The Unfinished Liberation* (New Rochelle, N.Y.: *Change,* 1975). Statistical information is collected by the Association of American Colleges, Project on the Status and Education of Women, 1818 R St. N.W., Washington, D.C., 20009.

107. Treichler and Kramarae, "Women's Talk in the Ivory Tower," and Arlie Russell Hochschild, "Inside the Clockwork of Male Careers," in *Women and the Power to Change,* ed. Florence Howe, pp. 47–80.

108. University president David Kinley helped fund the Black sorority house out of his own pocket; this personal generosity and good will short-circuited the issue of institutional responsibility. The institutional role in child care is discussed in "Campus Child Care: A Challenge for the 80's," *Project on the Status and Education of Women,* Field Evaluation Draft, May 1980; Rhoda M. Gilinsky, "Day Care Finds a Home on Campus," New York *Times,* Jan. 9, 1983; Barbara S. Kraft, "Day-Care Programs Take Hold on Campuses," *Chronicle of Higher Education,* Feb. 15, 1984; Paula A. Treichler, "No Sex in Science: Women at the University of Illinois College of Medicine, 1898–1982," paper presented at the University of Illinois College of Medicine Centennial, Chicago, June, 1982.

109. Berenice A. Carroll, "The Politics of 'Originality': Women and the Class System of the Intellect," paper presented at the Unit for Criticism and Interpretive Theory Colloquium, University of Illinois at Urbana-Champaign,

Apr. 1983; Paula A. Treichler, "Teaching Feminist Theory," in *Theory in the Classroom*, ed. Cary Nelson (Urbana: University of Illinois Press, forthcoming).

110. Brumberg and Tomes, "Women in the Professions," p. 284.

111. Efforts to prove institutional discrimination often involve the assembling of documents which are of considerable linguistic interest in this respect. Marlene Dixon's brilliant *Things Which Are Done in Secret* (Montreal: Black Rose, 1977) presents the actual documents of a tenure case. See also Phyllis Rackin, "Not by Lawyers Alone: Ten Practical Lessons for Academic Litigants," in *Rocking the Boat*, ed. DeSole and Hoffman, and Stimpson, ed., *Discrimination against Women*, for examples.

112. Brumberg and Tomes, "Women in the Professions," believe that the class consciousness of the women's liberation movement has discouraged the study of academic women because they are relatively privileged; they suggest several promising research directions.

113. Examples include Bernard, *Academic Women*; H. Patricia Hynes, "Toward a Laboratory of One's Own: Lesbians in Science," in *Lesbian Studies*, ed. Cruikshank, pp. 174–78; Adrienne Rich, "Compulsory Heterosexuality and Lesbian Existence," *Signs* 5, no. 4 (Summer 1980): 631–60, and "Toward a Woman-Centered University," in *On Lies, Secrets, and Silence* (New York: W. W. Norton), pp. 125–55; Dale Spender, ed., *Men's Studies Modified* (London: Pergamon, 1981).

114. This issue is widely and intensely discussed. See, for example, Roisin Battel, Renate Duelli Klein, Catherine Moorhouse, and Christine Zmroczek, *So Far, So Good—So What? Women's Studies in the U.K.*, *Women's Studies International Forum* 6, no. 3 (1983); Gloria Bowles, ed., *Strategies for Women's Studies in the 80s*, *Women's Studies International Forum* 7, no. 3, 1984; Zoe Ingalls, "Women's Colleges Show Renewed Vigor After Long, Painful Self-Examination," *Chronicle of Higher Education* 29, no. 3 (Sept. 12, 1984): 1; Treichler, "Teaching Feminist Theory," in *Theory in the Classroom*, ed. Cary Nelson.

115. Sources cited throughout this essay document the institutional experience of specific groups of women. The argument that such information is crucial to our theoretical understanding of "women's experience" is made in Shadron et al., "The Historical Perspective," in *Stepping Off the Pedestal*, ed. Stringer and Thompson; Brumberg and Tomes, "Women in the Professions"; Cruikshank, ed., *Lesbian Studies*; Rich, "Compulsory Heterosexuality."

116. See, for example, Angela McRobbie, "The Politics of Feminist Research: Between Talk, Text and Action," *Feminist Review* 12 (Oct. 1982): 46–57. See also Stuart Hall, "Cultural Studies and the Centre: Some Problematics and Problems," in *Culture, Media, Language*, ed. Stuart Hall, Dorothy Hobson, Andrew Lowe, and Paul Willis (London: Hutchinson, 1980), pp. 15–47.

The Alma Mater statue of Columbia University, sculpted by Daniel Chester French, graces the steps leading to Low Library. Photo courtesy of the Columbia Public Information Office.

Section 2. On Language

Questions about language are increasingly central to the theory and practice of feminist scholarship. How does language figure in scholarly practice? Is it language, rather than content, that makes our enterprise feminist? How are theory, culture, and academic traditions encoded in language? If language is riddled with male-dominated assumptions, whose voice speaks in feminist writing? What theoretical grounding enables us to explore these questions? What can and cannot be said?

The papers in this section explore the nature of feminist discourse, including academic feminist discourse, and attempt to sort out some of the features that complicate and challenge our attempts to speak and write as feminist scholars. Carol Thomas Neely raises issues based on her experience as a feminist Shakespeare critic, a field of literary study that is, she writes, "symbiotically intertwined with patriarchal literature." Feminist criticism, for Neely, is not defined by its methodology but rather by its ideology: "feminist critics are feminists." Thus the internal dialogue is between the trained Shakespeare scholar and the necessarily ideological feminist critic who must, between them, determine what "story" is to be told. That this is territory to be delicately negotiated is reflected, perhaps, in the essay's own metaphors: feminist critics, she writes, are "acutely conscious of the dangers of being boxed in or locked out"; they become "supple escape artists." Posing lesbian separatism as a potential alternative to the compromises and contradictions of her own critical enterprise, she suggests that this "purer feminism" creates its own contradictions.

Cary Nelson, with the self-reflexivity that characterizes his own tradition of contemporary critical theory, asks, "How does a man begin to write about feminist criticism?" Outlining a number of ongoing theoretical projects in contemporary criticism, he focuses particularly on the feminist claim that language is inherently phallocentric and explores the theoretical grounds on which such a claim might be tested. Positioning himself with those feminists who valorize difference, Nelson argues that the "distancing myth of female otherness" offers a fruitful ground for genuinely radical discourse, and explores a notion of semiosis based on a male-female differentiation.

Gayatri Chakravorty Spivak, whose theoretical work has turned increasingly to the problems of entwining feminist discourse simultaneously with other bodies of theory, and with feminism in the third world, defines the central problem of literature and literary theory as "not knowing"; this is what sets literary texts off from other discourses. Feminism, she argues, has the potential to undo disciplinary subdivisions of labor. Spivak has always been interested in rewriting the major male texts, specifically Freudian and Marxist, to incorporate the notion of woman in a central and fundamental way. She now seeks, further, a discourse in which dialogue between "First World" and "Third World" feminists may occur. In the process, she weaves herself in and out of her own texts in a kind of autobiographical critical narrative.

Tey Diana Rebolledo describes the explosion of writing by Chicanas over the last several years: "The Chicana writer is being recognized not as part of a marginalized exotic literature but as a fully integrated and important part of the creative experience." Tracing the directions of this writing, its current themes and preoccupations, Rebolledo suggests the complexity of simultaneous links to a Mexican-American heritage and to contemporary feminism, to a Latin American poetic tradition and to a tradition of American female poetics. The language of these writings combines English with Spanish, formal speech with slang, traditional with experimental structures, negotiating linguistically and often self-consciously among these multiple traditions.

Sally McConnell-Ginet, a linguist, reviews the impact feminist scholarship and linguistics have had on each other. She suggests on the one hand the ways in which feminism requires us to ask basic questions about language and to embed our answers firmly within the social context of language; on the other hand, she indicates those theoretical precepts of linguistics as a field which make it impervious or inhospitable to the feminist challenge. She goes on to distinguish the academic feminist from the feminist scholar: the first, a feminist who is also an academic, does not necessarily bring feminism into her field of study; the feminist scholar, however, finds feminism and scholarly investigation mutually informing.

Marsha Houston Stanback points to a gap in women's studies and Black studies research which leaves us with minimal understanding of the speech and language behavior of working class, Black, and other minority women. Because Black women have historically been active in *both* domestic and public activities, linguistic analyses relevant to white middle-class women may be of limited value in analyzing Black women's speech. This is a theoretically significant claim because of the degree to which feminist research, primarily based on observations of white women's speech, makes judgments and conclusions about "women and language" which may be quite invalid for all women.

Feminist Criticism in Motion

Carol Thomas Neely

> It is impossible to *define* a feminine practice of writing, and this is an impossibility that will remain, for this practice can never be theorized, enclosed, coded—which doesn't mean that it doesn't exist.[1]
>
> Hélène Cixous

Although I have great difficulty defining feminist criticism, I know that it exists because I see others doing it and I am doing it myself. This essay, part of an ongoing attempt to understand, clarify, and enlarge what we are doing, is presented here in a form designed to reflect its development. For me, the process of definition began in the fall of 1977 when Carolyn Ruth Swift, Gayle Greene, and I started to write an introduction to our anthology, *The Woman's Part: Feminist Criticism of Shakespeare*. An offshoot of that introduction, the earliest version of Part 1 of this essay, was presented at a feminist scholarship conference at the University of Illinois in February 1978. A revised version of Part 1 was presented to a special session, "Feminist Criticism of Shakespeare," at the annual meeting of the Modern Language Association of America in December 1978, and with further revisions was published as "Feminist Modes of Shakespearean Criticism: Compensatory, Justificatory, and Transformational," in the first of two issues of *Women's Studies* devoted to feminist criticism of Shakespeare (Volume 9, no. 1 [1981]). Part 2 of this essay was written for presentation at the Feminist Studies in Literature Conference at the University of Minnesota in October 1981, and shows the influence of my return to teaching and broader immersion in women's studies. Part 2 allows conflicts to surface which were submerged in the rhetoric of implied progress and potential reconciliation of Part 1. Adrienne Rich's keynote address at that conference, "Toward a More Feminist Criticism," enlarged my perspective further and engendered additional revisions. In order to keep the sense of movement and re-vision, I have left the parts of the essay relatively unchanged while using the notes to place my remarks within the context of more recent developments in the communal enterprise of feminist criticism. I am grateful to the occasions and publications which gave this essay space to grow, and to the numerous organizers, editors, readers, participants, and audiences who have contributed to it.[2]

The poles of the essay—theory and practice, scholarship and teaching, power and victimization, reconciliation and opposition, separatism and assimilation—have parallels in much other feminist theory and practice. The conclusion shares with recent feminist writing an emphasis on self-division, difference, and opposition, and a hope that the exploration of conflicts will produce not paralysis but continued movement.[3]

Part 1. Theory and Practice:
Fall 1977–Summer 1980

Feminist criticism is, somewhat disturbingly, a creature of lack, more easily defined by what it is not than by what it is. I would insist at the outset, however, that its very amorphousness helps generate the flexibility and self-consciousness which are its strengths. Unlike, for example, new criticism or historical criticism, it is not a methodology and does not presuppose one; feminist critics employ many methods. This criticism does, however, presuppose an ideology—feminist critics are feminists—but the ideology itself escapes definition and the relation between the ideology and the criticism is a loose and problematic one. Feminism is only now in the process of creating and defining itself; therefore, feminist criticism, unlike Marxist or Freudian criticism, lacks the core theoretical texts—the law of the father—from which concepts and methodology might be derived. Feminist critics need not have read de Beauvoir, Millett, Mitchell, Daly, Chodorow, Barrett, Rich, or any other specific text; those who have read them do not necessarily make much direct or explicit use of them in their criticism.[4] Feminist critics may be Marxist or psychoanalytic, further complicating although also enriching the ideological basis of the approach. Feminist criticism of

Shakespeare, furthermore, lacks a unique subject matter. Women's history and women's sociology open up new areas for research just as some feminist critics, especially of later periods of literature, discover comparable new data as they unearth lost woman writers, retrieve lesbian existence, formulate a female literary history, or analyze female style. But the women in Shakespeare, or in Chaucer, Spenser, or Milton, however often they have been minimized, stereotyped, or misunderstood, have never been entirely lost. Feminist critics, moreover, do not necessarily focus only on women; they examine men, relations between the sexes, the cultural and political structures which influence these relations. But so do other sorts of critics.

Nor does it seem that feminist criticism can be defined by its unique style, except perhaps negatively. Its style is intended to be non-sexist; it refuses to degrade women and does not wish to prescribe behavioral norms for them. It may tend to employ what might be called reverse sexism, attacking and stereotyping male characters and male critics; predictable as this rhetoric may be, it is neither a necessary nor a sufficient determinant of feminist critical style. More positively, French feminists have been calling for women to create a uniquely female style, compounded from and celebrating their association with the body, the emotions, and the unconscious, with fluidity, darkness, and madness.[5] But even if women can inscribe in their critical writing the traces of their otherness, they may, in doing so, trap themselves. The traits bred of marginality should not and will not be maintained intact as women move to place themselves at the center of discourse.

The French feminists' valuing of woman-as-other points to a dilemma central to feminism and to much feminist criticism, including that of Shakespeare. By declaring themselves feminists, women reanimate the binary opposition between the sexes which is the source of their oppression; the very analysis of and reaction against this oppression creates inevitable dependence on it. All attempts to eradicate the traditional sex-role stereotypes fail to evade their structure or their power. Feminist critics may try to conflate them, pursuing an elusive notion of androgyny, but this concept does not seem to have proved generally useful either as a theoretical paradigm or as a critical tool. Feminist critics may try to reverse the conventional stereotypes, representing female characters as active, powerful, and rational, and male characters as passive, weak, and unhinged. Or, like the French feminists, they may retain them, weighted differently, and celebrate female qualities formerly devalued: emotion, concreteness, tenderness, and nurturing. Still, the force of the conventional stereotypes determines the shape of each of these projects; the projects themselves may impose new rigidities, and the basic asymmetry of the genders is not eliminated.[6]

Practicing feminist critics, acutely conscious of the dangers of being boxed in or locked out, demonstrate remarkable ability to break out of the impasse described. Because they do not have a ready-made method, ideology, subject, or style, they must constantly reassess and alter what they do. Feminist critics must be supple escape artists, but feminist criticism is, thanks to them, alive, well, and in motion. Some aspects of this motion are visible in three modes of feminist criticism of Shakespeare.

I call these modes compensatory, justificatory, and transformational criticism; these somewhat ungainly terms suggest the nature of the modes, the assumptions underlying them, the material they examine, and their function. This abstract model is, of course, oversimplified, and makes overly sharp distinctions among three modes that are not incompatible in theory or in practice. The model is not intended to be either historical or evaluative. The third mode is not precisely a synthesis of or transcendence of the first two, which will not and should not wither away, but as I read feminist criticism of Shakespeare, and other feminist criticism as well, I think that I perceive some movement toward the third, more inclusive mode. My model is indebted to and parallels the three-stage models of feminist history propounded by Joan Kelly and Gerda Lerner. In their analyses, feminist history moves from "compensatory" history (the study of "women worthies," achievers, by male standards, in a male world) to "contribution" history (the study of women's contribution to and oppression by patriarchal society) to the history of "the social relations of the sexes" (the study of the relative position of men and women in historical periods).[7]

The first mode, compensatory criticism, declares women characters or authors worthy of and in need of a new kind of attention. It is embodied in the notion, "Images of Women in Literature," the title of numerous pioneering women's studies courses.[8] In Shakespeare criticism, this first mode focuses on powerful, prominent women, on Kate and the disguised heroines of comedy, Portia, Rosalind, Viola, on Lady Macbeth and Cleopatra; on Marina, Perdita, and Hermione in the late romances. It restores to such women their virtues, their complexity, and their power, compensating for traditional criticism which has minimized or stereotyped them. Kate's shrewishness is seen not as a flaw but as a mark of intelligence and independence and a necessary defense against her situation. Cleopatra is given her due as the heroic center of her play. Weaker or more peripheral women are rescued and given new characterizations; Desdemona's spirit and strength are emphasized, and Ophelia's madness is viewed not as charming or passive, but as revelatory. In her mad scenes, she boldly presents to the court of Elsinore images of its own corruption and of the virtues it has renounced.[9]

As feminist critics, seeking positive role models, engage in this essential and exciting compensatory project, some of its difficulties become apparent. The heroines tend to be viewed in a partial vacuum, unnaturally isolated from the rest of the play, the Shakespearean canon, and the culture in which that canon is rooted. Thus the process by which the women are singled out for attention, the characteristics attributed to them, and the framework within which they are valued become suspect, vulnerable to objections of ahistoricity and wishful thinking and, what is worse, subject to contamination by the sex-role stereotypes of the culture in which the criticism exists and which it is reacting against. We see this contamination more easily in our foremothers than in ourselves. Anna Jameson, writing in the early nineteenth century, praises Shakespeare's heroines for their intellect and spirit, but she insists always that these are tempered by softness and is defensive about their bold language and overt expressions of sexuality.[10] Agnes Mure MacKenzie, an avowed feminist writing in the early twentieth century, generally applauds female frankness and boldness but reveals the influence of her culture's norms for appropriate female behavior in her harsh criticism of Helena's participation in the bed trick in *All's Well that Ends Well,* a crucial plot element Jameson never mentions in her discussion of the heroine.[11] Contemporary critics, myself included, may admire too much the assertiveness of the bed trick, while ignoring its duplicitous or demeaning aspects. Influenced by their own battles for equality, feminist critics may overcompensate and attribute inappropriately or too enthusiastically to women characters qualities traditionally admired in men: power, aggressiveness, wit, and sexual boldness. Reversing but not discarding the conventional stereotypes, they may compromise both their interpretations and their feminism. The mode also may find it difficult to deal with women who are not heroines and with the men who are important to all of Shakespeare's women, whether powerful or powerless.

Thus the first mode helps generate the second mode, justificatory criticism, which acknowledges the existence in Shakespeare's plays and in his culture of the traditional dichotomy, the stereotyping of women, and the constraints of patriarchy. This mode has the effect of justifying, or at least of accounting for, the limitations of some women characters and the limiting conceptions of women held by male characters. In the justificatory mode, feminist critics of Shakespeare explore the place of all women, heroines and especially victims, in the male-defined and male-dominated world of the plays, showing how their roles are circumscribed by political, economic, familial, and psychological structures. They may draw on varied analyses of patriarchal society by historians like Lawrence Stone or anthropologists like Claude Lévi-Strauss.[12] Such criticism explores themes, political structures, and historical background as they interact with character; it traces beyond the confines of particular plays the dominance-subordination relations of rulers and subjects, husbands and wives, fathers and daughters.

In this mode, critics find that even strong or rebellious women are defined or controlled by patriarchal imperatives. Women like Gertrude and Lady Macbeth, conventionally viewed as lustful or domineering, are seen as subordinated to and acting in the service of the patriarchal culture which has shaped them. Cressida's infidelity to Troilus is not ignored or defended but explained as the result of her role as an object defined, controlled, and exchanged by men, and totally dependent on them. Even the powerful heroines of the comedies, it is noted, eventually remove their disguises and declare their submission to their husbands: "To you I give myself for I am yours," a subdued Rosalind, no longer in male disguise, vows to both father and husband in the last scene of *As You Like It* as the concluding marriages alleviate male rivalry and renew patriarchal structures. The more extreme and thoroughgoing submissiveness of a woman like Ophelia is explained as a function of her role as an object of male admonition, manipulation, and brutal control; her father and brother lecture her on chastity and regulate her behavior, Claudius sets her up as a decoy, and Hamlet, reinforcing earlier lessons, calls her a whore and orders her to a nunnery, projecting onto her his anxiety about his mother's sexuality.[13] Although justificatory criticism acknowledges, with compensatory criticism, that particular women in the plays challenge male actions, attitudes, and values, it points out that nowhere do women withdraw their allegiance from men, act apart from men, or alter patriarchal structures. At the end of the comedies, the women take their places within these structures which are thus perpetuated; at the end of the tragedies, they have been sacrificed—or have sacrificed themselves—to them.

As the first mode has difficulty defining the characteristics of the heroines without reverting to sex role stereotypes, the second mode has difficulty assessing patriarchy's varied quality and weight from play to play without falsely stereotyping or rigidifying it. Justificatory critics differ over whether Shakespeare defends patriarchal structures, attacks them, or merely represents them.[14] Such criticism may be led to portray the structures as more monolithic or oppressive than they are, to minimize both the freedom of action of individual women within them and the part such women play in determining their shape; the result may be depressing, and also unbalanced.[15]

The third mode does not take powerful women as its point of entry into the text as compensatory criticism does, or oppressive structures as justificatory criticism does. Instead, it examines the multiple interactions between the commanding heroines and the confining culture, the two pervasive and antithetical features of Shakespeare's plays. It asks, to borrow terms from a feminist anthropologist, not simply what women do or what is done to them, but what meaning these actions have and how this meaning is related to gender.[16] I term this mode transformational. Its subject is the mutually transforming roles and attitudes of men and women in individual plays and the transformation of these roles throughout the canon. Its goal is not only to compensate for or to justify the treatment of women characters by traditional criticism but to transform that criticism, to shift its ground and alter its vision of Shakespeare.

Critics in this mode interrogate the relations between male idealization of and degradation of women, between women as heroines and women as victims, between the patriarchal text and the matriarchal subtext. Some critics explore how male idealization of women in the comedies serves to alleviate the heroes' anxieties about sex, as do the disguises of the heroines and their ultimate submission to men in marriage. Others show how male misogyny in the tragedies is a defense against male fears of feminization and powerlessness and, ironically, brings about the very loss of potency which men fear. Critics examine the mutual accommodation of female power with sexuality and patriarchal control in plays as diverse as *The Taming of the Shrew, King Lear,* and the late romances.[17] They delineate in Shakespeare a female subculture, examining its interactions with and influence on the dominant male culture. In other plays, they find men assuming the nurturing activities of women, thus decreasing their dependence on them.[18] A central focus is the examination of the relationship between gender roles and generic structures.[19]

Perhaps I have dreamed the third mode. At any rate, my perspective on it is not detached enough for its limitations to be fully apparent. One problem is obviously the sheer difficulty of intertwining all the strands in the text, and outside of it, without falling back on the old paradigms and stereotypes or merely reversing them. Feminist critics must find new ways to talk about gender roles. A second problem is what to do with the parts of plays which are not resonant to feminist analysis. A final problem is that, as feminist criticism of Shakespeare enlarges its perspective, both its subject matter and style become still more amorphous and perhaps therefore less political, less definably feminist. If so, it may eventually be absorbed back into the mainstream of Shakespearean criticism. Before this can happen, it must alter the location of that channel.

In order to indulge my passion for practical criticism and to suggest the nature of the final mode, I will look for a moment at *Hamlet,* employing the strategies of a third mode critic to place Ophelia's movement from submissive daughter to mad prophet in its wider contexts. Ophelia is perhaps not simply driven to madness but freed for it by Hamlet's rejection of her and subsequent disappearance, by her father's death, Laertes' absence, and Claudius's indifference. The madness, however, incorporates the earlier pressures on her: the desired and forbidden loss of chastity, the virtues hypocritically enjoined, and the corruption perceived. Even if not fully comprehended by the other characters, the madness influences them. It magnifies Laertes' obsession with revenge, driving him to become Claudius's tool as Ophelia was before him. It draws from Gertrude an uncoerced acknowledgment of her own guilt. The death in which Ophelia's madness culminates repurifies her for Hamlet, freeing him to love her and to achieve his own revenge. This solitary death by drowning, outside the castle walls, mermaidlike at home in the water, completes Ophelia's separation from her roles as daughter, sweetheart, subject, and from the literal and metaphorical poison which kills the others in the play. The borderline suicide prefigures Gertrude's later death when, disobeying Claudius's command, she drinks from the poisoned cup, thus withdrawing from the wifely role she has acquiesced in throughout. The two women break their ties with the corrupt roles and values of Elsinore as Laertes and Hamlet, returning to the castle to seek revenge, move toward accommodation with these values. Killing each other, they bring to the throne—with Hamlet's explicit approval—Fortinbras, the strong man, whose passionate, simplistic embrace of violence and of his father's quarrels throughout the play suggests that, while the chain of "casual slaughters" which began with the murder of Hamlet senior may be given a veneer of military heroism, it will not be ended. The womanless world of the end of *Hamlet,* perhaps cleansed, but more obviously debilitated, has affinities with the similarly all-male, similarly shrunken worlds surviving at the conclusions of *Othello, Macbeth, King Lear,* and *Antony and Cleopatra.* At the end of the play, Hamlet asks Horatio to stay alive to "tell his story": "report me and my cause aright / To the unsatisfied." As a feminist critic, I must tell Ophelia's story and retell Hamlet's in relation to it; I must interpret these desolate womanless endings and reinterpret my relation to them.

Part 2. The Personal and the Political: Spring 1981–Summer 1982

I must also reinterpret my own theory and practice and tell my own story. Looking back on my earlier discussion, I can see that it, like much other feminist description and despite my disclaimers, implies a thesis/ antithesis/higher synthesis model in which feminist writing progresses toward increasing inclusiveness, integration, reconciliation, and transcendence. These models create a kind of *Bildungsroman* for feminist criticism; in its happy ending, feminist critics reintegrate their life and work, revitalize the academy, reorder their students' priorities, and transform the world, ushering in what one critic aptly dubbed "the peaceable kingdom."[20]

The contours of this peaceable kingdom are not so clear to me anymore. Instead, I find myself confronted with conflicts in feminist theory, feminist criticism, feminist pedagogy, and in my own feminism that seem irresolvable and require uneasy compromises. I find, at the start, a gap between the insufficiency of feminist literary theory—which I often find merely pragmatic, narrowly prescriptive, unjustifiably ro-

mantic, or impenetrably theoretical—and the many, vigorous, un-
categorizable examples of feminist criticism that proliferate chaotically,
energetically, illuminatingly everywhere.

Within the domain of practical criticism, I also find a division, a
professional and critical hiatus between feminist critics who deal with
male authors in the traditional canon—Chaucer, Spenser, Shakespeare,
Milton—and the larger, better-known group of feminist critics who
deal with women authors, mostly from the nineteenth and twentieth
centuries. The concerns and even the existence of the first group seem to
go largely unacknowledged in many of the best-known discussions of
feminist criticism, which often focus on issues not relevant to feminist
analysis of traditional male authors, on, for example, the nature of a
female aesthetic, the female literary tradition, or the reshaping of the
canon. This tendency is evident, for example, in the typical and influential reviews of literary criticism over the years in *Signs,* all of which
deemphasize or ignore altogether the first group and focus on the work
of the second. Both types of feminist critics would benefit from communication with each other and from questions raised about whether
both employ the same strategies, have the same problems and goals, can
be served by the same models, and are engaged in the same enterprise or
in equally valid enterprises. Feminist critics of traditional male authors
can assess the degree to which their female characters are stereotypical
or transcend stereotypes, the extent to which they are universal or
narrowly conceived, by setting them against writers in a female tradition; they would benefit from the discovery and analysis of that tradition. Critics working with women authors can better understand these
writers' indebtedness to the male tradition as well as to the female
tradition, their uses and transformations of it, if they understand that
tradition anew with the help of feminist critics' re-interpretations of it.[21]

Recent work by lesbian feminists and feminist women of color has
illuminated deeper and more dangerous divisions within feminism and
feminist criticism. These critics document the eradication or distortion
of the experience and literature of lesbians and women of color in the
theory and practice of white, academic, middle-class, heterosexual
feminists, in, for example, the *Signs* reviews and most of the essays
already cited. We are reminded of our potential and actual complicity in
the patriarchal structures in which we participate and alerted to the
extent of our own women-blindness. But these critics argue, too, for the
possibility of making fruitful use of acknowledged differences.[22] They

begin the difficult task of defining a Black feminist criticism and a lesbian feminist criticism, preparing the ground for the creation of a wider and more genuinely feminist criticism which embraces both.[23]

Another difficult problem is what part men can, will, and should play in the generation of feminist criticism. While the anthology of feminist criticism of Shakespeare which I co-edited includes essays by men, and while I have assumed and argued that feminist criticism is a matter of perspective, not gender, that men as well as women can and should do it, lately I find myself wondering whether in fact male feminist critics are doing the same thing I am, or whether they should be. Do not the assumptions of socially conditioned asymmetry and binary opposition between the sexes which underlie feminism imply that the concerns, the angle of vision, and the tone of male feminists will be radically different from that of female feminists? If this is true, what are the differences and what follows from them? Do female feminists have the right, or the gall, to accuse the men who are most in sympathy with them of importing into *their* "feminist" criticism some of the attitudes and assumptions that feminists most need to abandon? I think that they do, for the ensuing dialogue could be mutually illuminating.

When a male colleague asked me to comment on a draft of a paper describing the stages he had gone through in his nine years of taking feminism seriously, I found myself annoyed at what I saw as his self-indulgent exasperation at what he termed "Feminism's Limited Understanding of Men," at his finding the "moral will" of "most feminists" "almost brutal in its refusal to acknowledge the complexity of male feelings and motives." He denied the self-indulgence but understood my irritation. Another male colleague, in a draft of a paper for a feminist criticism of Shakespeare session, wrote: "In facilitating the co-existence of nurturant and sexual femininity with reaffirmed manhood, death serves a function analogous to that of 'the mother's part.' . . . The three terms, maternal nurture, sexual engagement, and death are interchangeable elements, each one posing a deep threat to individual autonomy." When I pointed out his romantic, nostalgic commitment to rigidly polarized sex-role stereotypes of nurturant femininity and heroic manhood, he altered his language if not his idea and placed this commitment explicitly in Shakespeare's and Freud's imaginations. When I read a draft of Cary Nelson's essay for this volume, "Envoys of Otherness," I characterized his tone throughout as "relentlessly assertive, phallocentric, and patronizing." His admonition that "feminist critics should pursue their project to its end; they should become envoys of otherness" prompted me to respond, "I don't want to be an envoy; I want to be king." His response was to add a self-consciously apologetic introduction to the essay. These interchanges raised questions for me about whether similar or identical statements made by female feminist critics would seem as self-indulgent, romantic, or patronizing. Should male feminists perhaps concern themselves exclusively with male experience, with male consciousness-raising, inverting the project of female feminists? Or is this merely to recapitulate the women-blindness of patriarchy? Should their focus, too, be on women?

This question raises in yet another way the more general one of what the content of feminist criticism should be, and here, too, a conflict emerges. Perhaps this criticism should focus on female experience as Cheri Register urges in her *Signs* review: "If we define our task as the illumination of female experience, whatever that might be, and are prepared to deal with any resultant political implications, we can afford to leave our questions open-ended."[24] Or perhaps it should focus on male power as Annette Kolodny implies: "What unites and repeatedly invigorates feminist literary criticism, then, is neither dogma nor method but . . . an acute and impassioned attentiveness to the ways in which primarily male structures of power are inscribed (or encoded) within our literary inheritance; [and] the consequences of that encoding for women."[25] These positions are not, of course, incompatible since, as the quotations suggest, "female experience" is encoded with the effects of male power, and male power is studied by feminists with the purpose of examining its "consequences" for women. But the articulation of each approach reveals problems with the other. "Female experience" as manifested by authors of what gender, what class, what color is to be our province? Once the "consequences" of male power are clear—are they not clear already—should these continue to be documented?

Further, in practical terms, feminists in their reserach and teaching must stress one or the other. They must think about trivial but necessary issues such as whether a feminist critic worthy of the name can teach or write about *Julius Caesar* and not discuss Calpurnia and Portia. Should she write or teach the play and only talk about these two minor characters? Should she stop teaching *Julius Caesar* and replace it with another of Shakespeare's works where female characters and female experience are prominent? My responses to these questions, and to the larger one of whether we should teach Shakespeare at all, are subtly (and self-interestedly) inconsistent and compromised. I want to be a feminist and a Shakespearean, to teach Shakespeare and Women's Literature. In my writing on Shakespeare, I try to give the experience of women characters more than equal attention to compensate for their neglect and because so little has been written about them. In Women in Literature courses, I explore female experience including as wide a range of it as my own knowledge will permit. In my Shakespeare classes, I give women and men, female experience and male power, the attention their place in the play seems to demand, devoting attention to Ophelia and Gertrude, but more to Hamlet, about whom, it might be thought, more than enough has been said already.

But by whom? Not by my undergraduate non-majors in Women in Literature courses, not by my undergraduate majors, not even by those of my graduate students who come into an M.A. program with little background in literature. This raises the question of the different contexts in which feminist criticism takes place and the effect of this context on its shape. Feminist criticism, as I practice it, has grown out of, reacts against, and is symbiotically intertwined with patriarchal literature, patriarchal culture, and a patriarchal literary tradition. The "compensatory," "justificatory," and "transformational" modes of criticism described above have emerged in relation to those patriarchal traditions. Can they be useful in teaching students who, although they have grown up within patriarchy and absorbed its imperatives, have no traditions, literary or critical, to react against? Can students who have never had contact with a male aesthetic and the literature embodying it understand in the way that we do the nature and the implications of a female aesthetic? Does it make sense to teach Gertrude and Ophelia to students who have never looked at Hamlet; to present to the token male students in Women in Literature courses a host of male characters who are marginal, caricatured, stereotyped, and victimized? Is this reverse sexism and, if it is, can it be justified? Such questions raise a larger question of feminism's changing relation to the culture at large and the different strategies appropriate to different stages of its history. Most of us white, middle-aged, middle-class feminist critics have taken as our motto and experienced for ourselves Adrienne Rich's generative concept of "re-vision—the act of looking back, of seeing with fresh eyes, of entering an old text from a new critical direction." This re-vision has been for many of us, in her words, "an act of survival."[26] But does feminist criticism necessarily involve re-vision—dramatic revulsion from patriarchal notions and from one's own pre-feminist past—or can it start from scratch? Can it supply a competing vision that does not assume the priority of its entrenched competitor? Will the criticism which emerges from younger critics nurtured from the start on feminism, feminist criticism, and women's literature look like ours? Will it be as regenerative for them as ours has been for us? Will they find in our work a tradition on which to build? Or is our legacy to them merely a set of already outworn conventions (for example, the requisite exposé of the sexism of all prior critics) which will require, in their turn, revision? Will they repeat our movement through these three modes, or will they begin in the third mode and move on?

Lately it has seemed to me that re-vision has not brought about and cannot bring about the hoped-for integration of life and art, of criticism and pedagogy, of the self, or, at least, that this integration has been more painful than I had foreseen. Writing and teaching had been for me, in Adrienne Rich's exact formulation, the place where I "lived as no-one's mother" and no one's wife or daughter, where I "existed as myself" freed from female roles.[27] To be a feminist critic, and, even more, to be a feminist teacher, is to be committed to manifesting one's participation in those roles, to be forced to bring the conflicts of one's life into the center of writing and teaching, and in this way to exacerbate them. While doing so, the feminist teacher is aware, especially in Women in Literature courses, that she is serving as a role model for female students in areas that range far beyond the criticism of literary texts. Thus I find myself having to decide daily whether it is ideologically or pedagogically appropriate or psychologically possible to present myself as oppressed victim, as ruthless achiever, as nurturing mother, as superwoman, or whether it is better to reveal the hidden and disintegrated self beneath the roles—feminist critic as hysteric, perhaps—the madwoman out of the attic and expected to function sanely in the world.

The final and most radical challenge to the peaceable kingdom (which is perhaps an equally idealistic resolution of conflicts spawned by it) is provided by lesbian feminist separatists, most cogently for me in the work of Adrienne Rich and Marilyn Frye.[28] Rich argues that "compulsory heterosexuality" is the root of patriarchal oppression and defines a "lesbian continuum" which resists this oppression. Frye takes the erasure of lesbians from social and ontological reality as symbolic of the erasure of all women in heterosexual society and argues that to achieve re-vision fully, genuinely to be "women-seers," women must withdraw from all of the forms of heterosexuality, from fathers and sons, husbands and lovers, male friends and colleagues, male institutions and traditions, even, I suppose, from Hamlet and Shakespeare. This position has extraordinary coherence, clarity, purity, and power, but its impracticality is staggering, and even to begin to attempt such a withdrawal would result, as I see it, in a more limited, if less conflict-ridden, world; it is a price I am not willing to pay. I wonder if feminist criticism would not pay a large price, too, for the resolution of *its* conflicts. It has been nurtured by its reaction against the heterosexual order, by its continuing tensions with it, and by the transformations, however small, it has wrought within that order. As lesbian feminists remind us, though, it may be crippling to depend too much or too long on that damaging source of nurture and action. The lesbian perspective starkly illuminates my own divided and compromised and impure feminism, but it also illuminates the compromise of myself that this purer feminism would lead to.

All of these conflicts in feminist criticism and feminism raise in different ways, and the last most dramatically, the question of whether feminists should advocate separation from the dominant culture or assimilation to it. Both options pose threats. Feminism and feminist criticism must sustain an autonomy which cannot be allowed to be co-opted by the promise that its conflicts with patriarchal culture will be transcended, but feminism must not risk becoming isolated and detached from a male order left thereby to develop on its own without opposition, for this order will touch women's lives. Hence, I would argue for both separation and assimilation, for the movement as a whole and for individuals within it. I see both as necessary personal, critical, pedagogical, and political strategies. I advocate supporting lesbian *and* heterosexual feminists, female *and* male feminists, white feminists *and* feminists of color, teaching authors of all sexes, races, and classes, paying attention to female experience *and* male power, analyzing the patriarchal tradition *and* the history of female resistance to it, allowing the self-confidence and self-knowledge engendered by relationships with women to provide the ground from which to encounter and know men. Neither side of these dichotomies should be abandoned; the tensions between them must be acknowledged, exposed, analyzed, exploited, and endured.[29] Transformation is not imminent. No peaceable kingdom this.

Notes

1. "The Laugh of the Medusa," trans. Keith Cohen and Paula Cohen in *New French Feminisms,* ed. Elaine Marks and Isabelle de Courtivron (Amherst: University of Massachusetts Press, 1980), p. 253.

2. I am especially indebted to my co-editors, Carolyn Ruth Swift and Gayle Greene, and to Margaret Dickie and Cary Nelson, commentators on my paper at the University of Illinois Feminist Scholarship Conference. My discussion of the three modes of feminist criticism of Shakespeare was made possible by the numerous feminist critics who submitted essays to the anthology and to sessions I have chaired as well as by the acknowledged publications. I would also like to thank Paula Treichler for bombarding me with more bibliography, photocopied articles, criticisms, and inspired suggestions than I have been able to assimilate.

3. Muriel Dimen, in "Theory From The Inside Out, Or Process is Our Most Important Product," in mimeographed proceedings of The Second Sex—Thirty Years Later: Commemorative Conference on Feminist Theory, September 27–29, 1979, pp. 57–63, argues for the value of process and indeterminancy in feminist theory: "Only human interaction which values process as much as product can respect and cross the gaps between self and other, different social groups, and Nature and Culture" (p. 62).

4. Simone de Beauvoir, *The Second Sex,* trans. and ed. H. M. Parshley (New York: Bantam, 1961); Kate Millett, *Sexual Politics* (New York: Doubleday, 1970); Juliet Mitchell, *Women's Estate* (New York: Pantheon, 1972), and *Psychoanalysis and Feminism* (New York: Pantheon, 1974); Mary Daly, *Beyond God the Father: Toward a Philosophy of Women's Liberation* (Boston: Beacon, 1973), and *Gyn/Ecology: The Metaethics of Radical Feminism* (Boston: Beacon, 1978); Nancy Chodorow, *The Reproduction of Mothering* (Berkeley: University of California Press, 1978); Michèle Barrett, *Women's Oppression Today: Problems in Marxist Feminist Analysis* (New York: Schocken, 1981); Adrienne Rich, *Of Woman Born: Motherhood as Institution and Experience* (New York: W. W. Norton, 1976), and *On Lies, Secrets, and Silence: Selected Prose: 1966–78* (New York: W. W. Norton, 1979).

5. For an introduction to French writing on women's style, see the translated selections by Xavière Gauthier, Julia Kristeva, Marguerite Duras, Chantal Chawaf, and Madeleine Gagnon, pp. 159–80, and Hélène Cixous, "Laugh of the Medusa," pp. 245–64 in *New French Feminisms,* ed. Marks and de Courtivron, and Luce Irigaray, "When Our Lips Speak Together," *Signs* 6, no. 1 (Autumn 1980): 66–79. American critics likewise make claims for a unique female style. In a *Critical Inquiry* issue on "Writing and Sexual Difference," 8, no. 2 (Winter 1981), Elaine Showalter, in "Feminist Criticism in the Wilderness," calls women's writing "a double-voiced discourse" (p. 201), and Mary Jacobus in "The Question of Language: Men of Maxims and *The Mill on the Floss,*" says that it is "multiple, duplicitous, unreliable, and resistant to binary oppositions" (p. 210).

6. The concept of *écriture féminine* (along with that of *fémininité* which

provides the basis for it) has been criticized for its theoretical murkiness, its tendency to reiterate conventional patriarchal notions of gender polarization, and its divorce from social analysis and political action. For detailed criticisms see "Variations on Common Themes," pp. 212–30 in *New French Feminisms,* ed. Marks and de Courtivron; Ann Rosalind Jones, "Writing the Body: Toward an Understanding of *L'Écriture Féminine,*" esp. pp. 252–60, and Hélène Vivienne Wenzel, "The Text as Body/Politics: An Appreciation of Monique Wittig's Writings in Context," 264–88, both in *Feminist Studies* 7, no. 2 (Summer 1981).

7. *Conceptual Frameworks in Women's History* (mimeographed conference papers, Bronxville, N.Y.: Sarah Lawrence Publications, 1976). The terms "compensatory" and "contribution" history are employed by Gerda Lerner in her essay, "Placing Women in U.S. History: Definitions and Challenges" (also published in *Feminist Studies* 3, nos. 1–2, [Fall 1975]: 5–14), as is the term "women worthies," which she takes from Natalie Zemon Davis. The phrase "social relations of the sexes" is used by Joan Kelly in her contribution, "Notes on Women in the Renaissance and Renaissance Historiography"; she derives it and the model it describes from Juliet Mitchell's *Women's Estate.* For a more recent discussion of and debate about developments in women's history, see Ellen DuBois, Mari Jo Buhle, Temma Kaplan, Gerda Lerner, and Carroll Smith-Rosenberg, "Politics and Culture in Women's History: A Symposium," *Feminist Studies* 6, no. 1 (Spring 1980): 26–64.

8. The first anthology of feminist criticism was Susan Cornillion's *Images of Women in Fiction* (Bowling Green, Ohio: Bowling Green University Popular Press, 1972).

9. See Coppélia Kahn, "*The Taming of the Shrew:* Shakespeare's Mirror of Marriage," in *The Authority of Experience,* ed. Arlyn Diamond and Lee Edwards (Amherst: University of Massachusetts Press, 1977), pp. 84–100; L. T. Fitz, "Egyptian Queens and Male Reviewers: Sexist Attitudes in *Antony and Cleopatra* Criticism," *Shakespeare Quarterly* 28 (1977): 297–316; S. N. Garner, "Shakespeare's Desdemona," *Shakespeare Studies* 9 (1976): 233–52; Joan Larsen Klein, "Angels and Ministers of Grace: *Hamlet* IV, v–vii," *Allegorica* 1, no. 2 (1976): 156–76. Juliet Dusinberre's *Shakespeare and the Nature of Women* (New York: Barnes and Noble, 1975), with its claim that the drama of Shakespeare and his contemporaries is "feminist in sympathy" (p. 5), embodies both the strengths and difficulties of this approach. More recently, Irene Dash, *Wooing, Wedding, and Power: The Women in Shakespeare's Plays* (New York: Columbia University Press, 1981), focuses on the strength and complexity of Shakespeare's women and the ways in which these characteristics are manifested or curtailed in productions of the plays.

10. *Shakespeare's Heroines: Characteristics of Women* (London: Ernest Nister, 1835), pp. 23, 25, 54–55, 76, and passim.

11. *The Women in Shakespeare's Plays* (London: Heinemann, 1924; rpt. Folcroft, Pa.: Folcroft Library Edition, 1973), pp. 48–51.

12. Lawrence Stone, *The Crisis of the Aristocracy, 1558–1641* (Oxford: Clarendon, 1965), and *The Family, Sex and Marriage in England 1500–1800*

(New York: Harper and Row, 1977); Claude Lévi-Strauss, *The Elementary Structures of Kinship* (Boston: Beacon Press, 1949), and *Structural Anthropology* (New York: Anchor Books, 1967).

13. In *The Woman's Part: Feminist Criticism of Shakespeare*, ed. Carolyn Ruth Swift Lenz, Gayle Greene, and Carol Thomas Neely (Urbana: University of Illinois Press, 1980), see Rebecca Smith, " 'A Heart Cleft in Twain': The Dilemma of Shakespeare's Gertrude," pp. 194–210; Joan Larsen Klein, "Lady Macbeth: 'Infirm of purpose,' " pp. 240–55; Gayle Greene, "Shakespeare's Cressida: 'A kind of self,' " pp. 133–40; and Clara Claiborne Park, "As We Like It: How a Girl Can Be Smart and Still Popular," pp. 100–116. On *As You Like It* see Louis Adrian Montrose, " 'The Place of a Brother' in *As You Like It:* Social Process and Comic Form," *Shakespeare Quarterly* 32 (1981): 28–53. On Ophelia, see David Leverenz, "The Woman in Hamlet: An Inter-personal View," *Signs* 4, no. 2 (Winter 1978): 291–308, rpt. in *Representing Shakespeare: New Psychoanalytic Essays*, ed. Murray M. Schwartz and Coppélia Kahn (Baltimore, Md.: Johns Hopkins University Press, 1980).

14. For a discussion of Shakespeare's relation to patriarchy, see the introduction to *The Woman's Part*, ed. Lenz, Greene, Neely, pp. 5–6. For an extended analysis of the operations of patriarchy in Shakespeare, see Coppélia Kahn, *Man's Estate: Masculine Identity in Shakespeare* (Berkeley: University of California Press, 1981).

15. This parallels the larger problem which worries feminist theory and analysis of how to acknowledge the oppressive structures which confine women without perpetuating victimization, how to comprehend women's power and women's resistance without exaggerating or romanticizing them.

16. Michelle Rosaldo, "The Use and Abuse of Anthropology: Reflections on Feminism and Cross-Cultural Understanding," *Signs* 5, no. 3 (Spring 1980): 389–417. Rosaldo urges feminist anthropologists to undertake explorations which seem remarkably parallel to those which Lerner and Kelly advocate for feminist historians, and to those which I see in third mode Shakespeare critics. She suggests that anthropologists might transcend both universalizing tendencies that imply that male dominance is a biologically inevitable universal, and romanticizing tendencies that examine women's lives in isolation from those of men, by searching out the meanings gender-related activities have in particular cultures:

> It now appears to me that woman's place in human social life is not in any direct sense a product of the things she does (or even less a function of what, biologically, she is) but of the meaning her activities acquire through concrete social interactions. And the significances women assign to the activities of their lives are things that we can only grasp through an analysis of the relationships that women forge, the social contexts they (along with men) create—and within which they are defined. Gender in all human groups must, then, be understood in political and social terms, with reference not to biological

constraints but instead to local and specific forms of social relationship and, in particular, of social inequality (p. 400).

17. On idealization see Richard P. Wheeler, *Shakespeare's Development and the Problem Comedies: Turn and Counter-Turn* (Berkeley: University of California Press, 1981), pp. 45–57, 167–79. On misogyny see Madelon Gohlke, " 'I wooed thee with my sword': Shakespeare's Tragic Paradigms," in *The Woman's Part,* ed. Lenz, Greene, Neely, pp. 150–70, and Kahn, *Man's Estate,* pp. 151–92. On accommodation see Marianne Novy, "Patriarchy and Play in *The Taming of the Shrew,*" *English Literary Renaissance* 9 (1979): 264–80, and "Patriarchy, Mutuality, and Forgiveness in *King Lear,*" *Southern Humanities Review* 13 (1979): 281–92; and Charles Frey, " 'O sacred, shadowy, cold, and constant queen': Shakespeare's Imperiled and Chastening Daughters of Romance," in *The Woman's Part,* ed. Lenz, Greene, Neely, pp. 295–313.

18. On female subculture see Carole McKewin, "Counsels of Gall and Grace: Intimate Conversations between Women in Shakespeare's Plays," in *The Woman's Part,* ed. Lenz, Greene, Neely, pp. 117–32. See also Peter Erickson, "Sexual Politics and the Social Structure in *As You Like It,*" *Massachusetts Review* 23, no. 1 (Spring 1982): 65–83; Marianne Novy, "Transformed Concepts of Manhood in the Romances," in *Love's Argument: Gender Relations in Shakespeare* (Chapel Hill: University of North Carolina Press, 1985).

19. This approach is exemplified in the papers written for the seminar "Gender and Genre: Feminist Approaches" at the International Shakespeare Congress at Stratford-Upon-Avon, England, Aug. 1981, and is found in two recent books devoted to an examination of woman as other in Shakespeare which see the genders as polarized in conventional ways in the plays and make distinctions between the role of women in comedy, tragedy, and history: Marilyn French, *Shakespeare's Division of Nature* (New York: Summit Books, Simon and Schuster, 1981), and Linda Bamber, *Comic Women Tragic Men: A Study of Gender and Genre in Shakespeare* (Stanford: Stanford University Press, 1982). Bamber's book illuminates the characters, the plays, and the issues more than French's does.

20. I am indebted to Cary Nelson for this description of the model presented in the first version of the first part of this essay. That model has affinities with the development delineated and the goals advocated in a number of other pieces of feminist writing and criticism contemporary with it; with Elaine Showalter's description of feminine, feminist, and female novels (in *A Literature of their Own: British Women Novelists from Brontë to Lessing* [Princeton, N.J.: Princeton University Press, 1977]); with Barbara Gelpi's colonial paradigm which posits a four-stage development of American women's poetry from 1) denial of victimization to 2) acknowledgment of victimization to 3) anger to 4) transcendence into full personhood (Gelpi's paper, "A Common Language: The American Woman Poet," first published in 1976, is reprinted in *Shakespeare's Sisters: Feminist Essays on Women Poets,* ed. Sandra M. Gilbert and Susan Gubar [Bloomington: Indiana University Press, 1979], pp. 269–79); with the adaptation of Gelpi's paradigm by Cheri Register to describe the de-

velopment of feminist criticism in her literary criticism review, *Signs* 6, no. 2 (Winter 1980): 268–82; with Annette Kolodny's call for a "playful pluralism" which will regenerate the academy and reorder the world in "Dancing through the Minefield: Some Observations on the Theory, Practice, and Politics of a Feminist Literary Criticism," *Feminist Studies* 6, no. 1 (Spring 1980): 1–25. Although these writers do not represent the whole range of feminist criticism, and although they do not intend their paradigms as rigid ones, the discussions all embody a sense of progression toward integration and transformation.

French feminists have likewise delineated a three-stage movement toward liberation in which the three stages are both simultaneous and progressive. Their millenial third stage envisages not reconciliation but a radical elimination of the roots of social and personal gender polarization. See the analysis of "Femininity, Femininitude and Feminism: the Three 'Moments' of the Battle" in "Variations on Common Themes," *New French Feminisms*, ed. Marks and de Courtivron, pp. 225–27, and Julia Kristeva's discussion in "Women's Time," *Signs* 7, no. 1 (Autumn 1981), pp. 13–35, of the three "generations" or "attitudes" of women. "In this third attitude, which I strongly advocate—which I imagine?—the very dichotomy man/woman as an opposition between the two rival entities may be understood as belonging to *metaphysics*. . . . What I mean is, first of all, the demassification of the problematic of *difference*. . . . And this not in the name of some reconciliation . . . but in order that the struggle, the implacable difference, the violence be conceived in the very place where it operates with the maximum intransigence, in other words, in personal and sexual identity itself, so as to make it disintegrate in its very nucleus" (pp. 33–34).

21. The reviews of literary criticism in *Signs* 1, no. 2 (Winter 1975): 435–60, by Elaine Showalter; 2, no. 2 (Winter 1976): 404–21, by Annette Kolodny; 4, no. 3 (Spring 1979): 514–27, by Sydney Janet Kaplan; and 6, no. 2 (Winter 1980): 268–82, by Cheri Register focus chiefly on criticism (and biography) of women writers and on nineteenth- and twentieth-century literature. The absence of more than an occasional reference to feminist criticism of, for example, Chaucer, Spenser, Shakespeare, Milton, or Pope may perhaps be accounted for by the enormous amount of material to be covered in the essays, the fact that the first three reviewers do their own work in the nineteenth and twentieth centuries, and by the dearth, at that time, of book-length studies of earlier periods.

Theoretical discussions of feminist criticism likewise tend to assume its focus on women writers—without exactly acknowledging or arguing for this position. For example, Annis Pratt, "The New Feminist Criticism," *College English* 32 (May 1971): 872–78, finds that the main task of feminist criticism is to identify and analyze "feminist" and "feminine" works and hence focuses on nineteenth- and twentieth-century fiction by women or by male novelists overtly concerned with "feminist" issues. Annette Kolodny begins her essay, "Some Notes on Defining 'A Feminist Literary Criticism,'" *Critical Inquiry* 2, no. 1 (Autumn 1975): 75–92, by saying that feminist criticism is loosely defined as "(1) any criticism written by a woman, no matter what the subject; (2) any criticism written by a woman about a man's book which treats that book from a 'political' or 'feminist' perspective; and (3) any criticism written by a woman about a woman's book or about female authors in general," but she immediately narrows the focus of her discussion to those critics engaged in the "still more ambitious task" of discovering and defining a unique female style (p. 75). Both essays are reprinted in *Feminist Criticism: Essays on Theory, Poetry and Prose,* ed. Cheryl L. Brown and Karen Olson (Metuchen, N.J.: Scarecrow Press, 1978). Twenty of the twenty-one essays of practical criticism in the volume focus on women writers. Similarly, Elaine Showalter in "Feminist Criticism in the Wilderness" urges that feminist critics become *"gynocritics,"* taking women's writing as their primary subject.

On the other hand, Diamond's and Edwards's anthology, *The Authority of Experience,* both in its foreword and in an essay by Marcia Landry, "The Silent Woman: Towards a Feminist Critique," argues that feminists must reexamine their literary heritage as well as enlarge it, and includes essays on writers from Chaucer to Hemingway. Annette Kolodny's "Dancing through the Minefield" notes that male as well as female authors have been "subjected to new feminist scrutiny" (p. 3). *Critical Inquiry's* issue on "Writing and Sexual Difference," 8, no. 2 (Winter 1982) declares "the notion of difference" (p. 173) as a new focus of feminist criticism and explores various aspects of difference: the relationship of female writing to the male tradition (Mary Jacobus, "The Question of Language," Margaret Homans, "Eliot, Wordsworth, and the Scenes of the Sisters' Instruction," Susan Gubar, " 'The Blank Page' and the Issues of Female Creativity"); the uses of women in male texts (Nancy J. Vickers, "Diana Described: Scattered Woman and Scattered Rhyme," Froma I. Zeitlin, "Travesties of Gender and Genre in Aristophanes' *Thesmophoriazousae*"); the infiltration of female power in male creations (Nina Auerbach, "Magi and Maidens: The Romance of the Victorian Freud," Annette Kolodny, "Turning the Lens on 'The Panther Captivity': A Feminist Exercise in Practical Criticism").

22. See Audre Lorde, "An Open Letter to Mary Daly," and "The Master's Tools Will Never Dismantle the Master's House," in *This Bridge Called My Back: Writings by Radical Women of Color,* ed. Cherríe Moraga and Gloria Anzaldúa (Watertown, Mass.: Persephone Press, 1981), pp. 94–101, and "The Uses of Anger," in *Women's Studies Quarterly* 9, no. 3 (Fall 1981): 7–10. In the same issue of *Women's Studies Quarterly* see Adrienne Rich, "Disobedience is what NWSA is Potentially About," pp. 4–6. See also Rich's "Disloyal to Civilization: Feminism, Racism, and Gynophobia," in Rich, *On Lies, Secrets, and Silence,* pp. 275–310.

23. On lesbian feminist criticism see Elaine Marks, "Lesbian Intertextualities," in *Homosexualities and French Literature,* ed. George Stambolian and Elaine Marks (Ithaca, N.Y.: Cornell University Press, 1979), pp. 353–77; Lillian Faderman, *Surpassing the Love of Men: Romantic Friendship and Love between Women from the Renaissance to the Present* (New York: William Morrow and Co., 1981); Catharine R. Stimpson, "Zero Degree Deviancy: The Lesbian Novel in English," *Critical Inquiry* 8, no. 2 (Winter 1981): 363–79;

Bonnie Zimmerman, "What has Never Been: An Overview of Lesbian Feminist Literary Criticism," *Feminist Studies* 7, no. 3 (Fall 1981): 451–75. On Black feminist criticism, see Barbara Smith, "Toward a Black Feminist Criticism," and Lorraine Bethel, " 'This Infinity of Conscious Pain': Zora Neale Hurston and the Black Female Literary Tradition," in *But Some of Us are Brave: Black Women's Studies,* ed. Gloria T. Hull, Patricia Bell Scott, and Barbara Smith (Old Westbury, N.Y.: The Feminist Press, 1982) pp. 157–75, 176–88; Norma Alarcón, "Chicana's Feminist Literature: A Re-Vision Through Malintzin/or Malintzin: Putting Flesh Back on the Object," in *This Bridge Called My Back,* ed. Moraga and Anzaldúa, 182–90.

24. Register, Review Essay, p. 282.

25. Kolodny, "Dancing through the Minefield," p. 20.

26. *On Lies, Secrets, and Silence,* p. 35.

27. *Of Woman Born,* p. 30.

28. Adrienne Rich, "Compulsory Heterosexuality and Lesbian Existence," *Signs* 5, no. 4 (Summer 1980): 631–60, and responses to it by Ann Ferguson, Jacquelyn N. Zita, and Kathryn Pyne Addelson in *Signs* 7, no. 1 (Autumn 1981): 158–99; Marilyn Frye, "To Be and Be Seen: Metaphysical Misogyny," *Sinister Wisdom* 17 (1981): 57–70.

29. I am arguing for the sort of comparative analysis outlined by Myra Jehlen who, in "Archimedes and the Paradox of Feminist Criticism," *Signs* 6, no. 4 (Summer 1981): 575–601, advocates that feminist critics, from their special vantage point on the frontier where female territory joins the male domain, re-examine everything, that they focus especially on juxtapositions, contradictions, and "confrontations" which erupt along that troubled border in order to illuminate the countries on both sides of it. Conflicts are the focus of other recent feminist criticism as well. Rich's recent work emphasizes conflicts with patriarchy and among women. Conflicts among women are the subject of Audre Lorde's essays cited in n. 22 and of other essays in *This Bridge Called My Back,* ed. Moraga and Anzaldúa. Internal conflicts are the focus of Susan Griffith, "The Way of All Ideology," *Signs* 7, no. 3 (Spring 1982): 641–60.

Envoys of Otherness:
Difference and Continuity
in Feminist Criticism

Cary Nelson

How does a man begin to write about feminist criticism? Several personae are readily available: the benign paterfamilias, the cornered rat, the condescending authority, the defender of the sacred, the guilty supplicant. None of these is very appealing, especially since whatever anxiety and defensiveness I feel in beginning to write about the subject is countered by my conviction that feminist criticism has been one of the most successful and revolutionary enterprises of the past decade. Nevertheless, each of these personae no doubt makes at least a fleeting appearance here. For men to acknowledge the difficulties we have in writing about feminist criticism does not do away with those difficulties. What follows is the result not only of an awareness of the problematics of my voice (and some uneasiness about it) but also of an effort to think through both the internal potential of feminist theoretical writing and its challenge to other bodies of theory.[1] I would like first to review some of the possibilities and the difficulties built into any effort to encourage a more reflective and self-conscious feminist critical practice. Then I will concentrate on what is, I believe, one of the major and most problematic features of feminist theory—the claim that the language we have inherited is inherently patriarchal or phallocentric.

Feminist critics since the 1970s have regularly been calling for greater theoretical self-awareness and sophistication in their field. More recently, the quantity and visibility of explicitly theoretical feminist criticism has increased at an extraordinary rate. From my own perspective, these developments are important for several reasons. Theoretical reflection and argument have enriched an intellectual movement that is already uniquely vital and productive. Furthermore, feminist criticism opens a particularly appropriate space within which to reconsider how critical discourse is generally constituted and constrained. Thus any feminist reconsideration of the status and aims of critical practice reflects on and challenges not feminist criticism alone but the whole range of critical languages.

Not all feminists are comfortable with writing that emphasizes abstract argument and theoretical reflection, but theoretical writing has nonetheless clearly become an important part of the feminist critical enterprise. In 1975 Elaine Showalter was able to argue that feminist scholars have been "stubbornly empirical; they have generated relatively little theory and abstraction."[2] Even at the time, Showalter's generalization was more valid for America than for Europe. Moreover, in the mid-1970s several American feminist journals began to publish theoretical criticism.[3] Now there are a considerable number of American critics doing innovative feminist theoretical work. In literary studies, for example, one thinks, among others, of Shoshana Felman, Jane Gallop, Annette Kolodny, and Gayatri Chakravorty Spivak.[4] In the general area of language and culture, Mary Daly is particularly important. Nonetheless, there remains significant resistance to theoretical reflection both here and in Europe. As Elaine Marks has emphasized, the avoidance of theory is often quite intentional, since "many women who refer to themselves as radical . . . are convinced that the will to theory is the most pernicious of male activities."[5]

An explicit stand against theoretical discourse is itself a theoretical position. Indeed, it is reasonable to argue that no interpretive practice can be free of theoretical assumptions and implications. Within feminist criticism, an antitheoretical position is especially difficult to maintain. Although there is already a substantial tradition of feminist scholarship—a tradition that generates considerable political and psychological support, as well as certain discursive constraints, for its advocates— feminist criticism remains an activity intensely animated alternately by moments of self-doubt and epiphany. Thus, it is difficult to address feminist concerns without some political, personal, and methodological reflection. Even those feminist critics who eschew theoretical writing depend on the polemical and theoretical writing of their feminist predecessors. Despite any efforts to naturalize feminist criticism within traditional academic disciplines, the possibility of writing or even conceiving of feminist scholarship will remain a product of political action and theoretical writing outside academia. The feminist movement, in short, has made feminist scholarship possible, and the politics and theory of the movement remain constitutive for scholarship. Finally, it is feminist critical writing, as writing, that manifests problems, stresses, and ambitions that are unavoidably theoretical. The self-reflection that precedes the decision to try to produce a disinterested but still feminist scholarly prose—the political and professional alienation that often accompanies the effort to gain institutional approval for it, the polemicism that either surfaces or is repressed in feminist scholarship, and the whole effort to create a discursive space for a new group of writers—in all these features of a feminist practice, the points of likely theoretical difficulty for feminist writers are foregrounded.

In 1975 Elaine Showalter attempted to account for the disjunction between political self-consciousness and the relative lack, at least at that time, of powerful theoretical criticism in America by arguing that feminist criticism is "more coherent as an ideology than as a methodology."[6] This remains a suggestive formulation, but it needs qualification. Any attempt to segregate discourse so as to label some of its moments "ideological," "methodological," "theoretical," and "empirical" is immensely problematic. As I suggest above, polemical texts that argue against existing scholarly traditions and for new directions in criticism are shaped by important theoretical assumptions. The most stubbornly empirical texts are themselves constituted ideologically. The method that distinguishes a particular practice can never be decisively separated from the practice as a whole. The very confidence, articulated either with satisfaction or as a complaint, that there exists criticism that is "stubbornly empirical" reflects the positivist assumptions of much conservative, male American scholarship, assumptions that feminist scholarship has often worked very effectively to challenge.

Showalter's judgment reflects the familiar conviction that ideology, theory, and disinterested empirical research are three quite separate kinds of writing. This conviction, still widespread both here and abroad, enables many traditional critics to argue that, while their work is ideologically neutral, feminist work is ideologically contaminated and consequently unsound. Instead of supporting what is, in effect, an ideologically motivated defense of ideological neutrality, feminist critics clearly have more to gain intellectually by confronting their own ideology and working to identify the ideology of traditional scholarship, as Judith Fetterley and others have tried to do.[7] The same logic applies to efforts to avoid theoretical writing or to deny the theoretical component of one's own research. Far from resisting a destructive patriarchal impulse, a feminist rejection of theory merely duplicates a longstanding bias in the male-dominated academy.

Theoretical self-reflection is always partial. All of us function within historical limits determined by our discipline and culture. Despite the most well intentioned efforts at self-reflection, despite substantial alienation from the disciplinary conventions we want to criticize, we can only recognize and write certain things at particular times. Challenging the complacent distinction between theory and application will not eliminate it. In this historical moment, then, all of us will continue to write and think in relation to an uncritical, unexamined division between theory and practice. In order to criticize that distinction, for example, I must also, alas, reinscribe it within the territory of contemporary theory. The distinction provides me with a reason to write and thus partly shapes my enterprise, yet the determining power of distinctions like this is actually much greater. Depending on what our own historical perspective brings into prominence or makes invisible, we will still view certain passages as more theoretical than others. Certain texts, certain moments, will appear to be ideological, while others will seem altogether naturalized. There is no definitive way to overcome the historically based categorization of various styles and modes of writing. We can only work to call them into question, remembering that the decision about which discourses to label "theoretical" or "ideological" is itself historically and ideologically determined.

Arguing that feminist criticism, despite its considerable diversity, displays complete ideological consistency, requires a careful foregrounding of only certain elements of feminist discourse. The claim for ideological consistency, whether mounted by the left or the right, gives determining power to certain phrases and sentences, while de-emphasizing or entirely ignoring others. It is more accurate to argue that there are no nonideological sentences, no nonideological moments, in either feminist or any other form of criticism. What ideological harmony there is in the field exists in part because both assumptions and actual practices potentially in opposition to one another have been left largely unexplored or unacknowledged. The reasons for that silence about implicit conflicts are essentially political. To the extent that it has bracketed out differences, feminist criticism has created an atmosphere of mutual support and encouragement, an atmosphere tolerant of a variety its practitioners have cannily often not examined too closely. (As it begins to acknowledge differences, it multiplies them, for difference, as the French have helped to show us, is not a stable chart of distinctions.) Similarly, by appearing to be ideologically unified, the feminist movement can be more politically effective within the general culture. Within feminist criticism, ideological unity makes for more powerful efforts to re-territorialize the traditional scholarly disciplines, yet the ideological coherence in feminist criticism exists primarily in the atmosphere of shared urgency that precedes and partly motivates critical writing. Where it does not exist is in the total range of practices actually represented in feminist books and essays, unless those critical texts are themselves filtered through a selective ideological reading.

This is not to say that many feminist critical texts do not display numerous elements in common: a much more detailed and sympathetic attention to women's roles in texts and social practices; a critical, rather than unthinking or approving, attitude toward the repression, idealization, stereotyping, trivialization, degradation, and destruction of women; an effort to amplify the phenomenology of women's experience; an analysis of the nature of women's writing; a general reconsideration of the historical meaning and future potential of the concepts of femaleness and maleness. Such intentions and interests do help to generate critical texts and do remain partly constitutive of them. As soon as we locate these aims in actual practices, however, their differences become inescapable. Consider a critical reading of female stereotyping from the perspective of a critic who accepts the nuclear family and heterosexuality as the norm, as opposed to a critic who is a politically active lesbian. Consider an interpretation of female sexuality by a critic who takes sexuality to be a site for fantasy and role playing as opposed to an interpretation by a critic who takes sexuality to be a sacred zone where individuals acknowledge, share, and honor each other's coherent subjectivity. These issues are currently subjecting the feminist movement to considerable stress, but feminist texts include many other equally diverse and competing ideological differences.[8]

Feminist texts merit reading and evaluation in terms of their entire verbal specificity, a specificity whose immense range attests to the varying constituents of all critical discourses: the ideologies, methodologies, objects of study, disciplinary constraints, socially and professionally coded languages, and individual psychological motivations that leave their traces in criticism. The minute choices feminist critics make, sentence by sentence, phrase by phrase, as they work to control, use, subvert, or transform a received and perhaps phallocentrically contaminated language, are each themselves significant. These choices diverge from one another, cutting off certain possibilities and calling forth others. Such verbal decisions exist in dialogue with possible and actual decisions by other feminist critics; together, they establish a field of play and conflict, supporting and rejecting various alternatives. Thus, Showalter and others correctly argue that no one methodology could represent what is an extraordinarily diversified field. Feminist scholars are unlikely to repeat the ill-fated search for a single, universal method in American studies, a quest that was in any case as much a product of that moment in critical history as an expression of the cultural fantasies of a particular field. Yet we do not have the happy, liberal diversity Showalter describes, nor are we likely to see many instances of the "playful pluralism" Annette Kolodny has called for, "responsive to the possibilities of multiple critical schools and methods, but captive of none."⁹ Many of us, myself included, would like to achieve that kind of voice, but it may well be that in the history of criticism we have only one successful instance of this self-consciously plural critical writing: the work Roland Barthes did in the last decade of his life.

Different methodologies do have important and quite different uses within feminist criticism. A phenomenological feminism provides an intuitive, metaphorically reactive, texturally rich response to female characters and to the style of women writers. Developed into its more radical incarnations in the various versions of *l'écriture féminine,* phenomenology offers a new feminist semiosis, a rewriting of the connotative field in which we read and write. A Marxist feminism helps to identify the economics of woman's repression and containment, although sexist practices deeply ingrained in the discourses of particular periods are likely to require research as ambitious as that Foucault outlines in *The Archeology of Knowledge* if their structural place in a culture is to be well understood. So long as a rapprochement between these different alternatives remains part of an anticipated project, these methodologies may seem compatible and complementary. When one actually writes in the service of one of these methods, their differences become more real. The Marxist may decide that the phenomenologist's responsiveness to female characters is a pastoral escapism that supports existing power structures. The phenomenologist may conclude that the Marxist's description of the power structured into male-female relations ignores or even depreciates the actual verbal texture of a character or an entire work. These differences are inherited from the larger field of criticism; in cutting through that field for its own self-definition, feminism cannot fail to duplicate them, but feminism is neither simply an alternative to all other competing methodologies nor one methodology among others. It is a redefinition of the entire territory of critical writing, one in which existing methodological competition is necessarily renewed but with the terms of the competition rewritten in the context of feminist concerns. As Jane Gallop has written, feminist writing "is the child of two parents . . . the feminist critic in her inheritance from both feminism and criticism lives the at once enabling and disabling tension of a difference within."[10] One of the advantages of analyzing feminist criticism is that existing methodological differences are both highlighted and challenged, in part because feminist critics are led to read and react to one another's work by their assumptions about a shared ideology, whereupon some discover that they reject or even cannot understand a colleague's discourse.

Rather than hope for the emergence of a new, communal pluralism, feminist critics are beginning to exploit these differences.[11] This process should prove more interesting and productive if it proceeds not merely by way of the simple labels I have offered in the previous paragraph, but by way of the detailed readings of individual feminist texts. If feminist criticism is given careful and elaborate reading, then the partial ideologies feminists have in common may make it possible for their actual ideological and methodological differences to exist in more intricately competitive dialogue with each other. Unlike the world of patriarchal scholarship, they may avoid turning their differences into programs of silence and exclusion. At least within feminist criticism, phenomenological, psychoanalytic, Marxist, and semiotic critics may be able to interact with each other, something at which the rest of us have not been overly adept. We should not, however, expect that this interaction will take the form of something like Jürgen Habermas's ideal speech situation. It may well not go beyond identifying exemplary and historically necessary differences and misrepresentations. In the process, a conflicted but more richly reflective kind of critical writing may emerge.

There is yet another reason, however, why individual feminist

writers will want to draw on the collective reflection and support that
the larger enterprise of feminist criticism offers. More than most critics,
who are guaranteed the kind of institutional and discursive encouragement they need in order to ignore the inherent contradictions in their
work, feminist critics are likely to recognize how their aims are subverted by the process of writing. Writing is a praxis that co-opts the
willed ideology we bring to it. Just as no discourse can be wholly and
independently structuralist, Marxist, or New Critical, so no discourse
can be altogether feminist. To the extent that their interests are revolutionary, whether the revolution is disciplinary or societal, feminist
critics are called (and can call to each other) to note the failure of their
enterprise. Feminist criticism has a special imperative because of the
very frustration of its larger aims, aims it is uniquely willing to entertain
openly, because of the impossibility of writing a prose that is altogether
feminist, to ask what its critical languages in fact are. What are, what
should be, and what can be, the languages of feminist criticism? From
what vantage points does it speak? With what traditions is it entwined?
What domains does it seek to represent?[12] The fatefulness of all discourse is to be taken up in the already existing codes of the language, to
become what an author may not wish it to be.

This problem is one women have described in fiction, poetry, and
criticism: "In the interstices of language," Adrienne Rich writes, "lie
powerful secrets of the culture"—"the power of the fathers has been
difficult to grasp because it permeates everything, even the language in
which we try to describe it."[13] As Tillie Olsen puts it, the language is
saturated with "male rule; male ownership; our secondariness; our
exclusion."[14] Thus the issue is not only that particular usages (like the
generic pronoun) privilege male authority and sexuality, though feminist writers have been very effective in identifying such usages, but also
that a global indictment may be justified: language as a whole may be
"a symbolic system closely tied to a patriarchal social structure."[15] The
argument, presumably, would not be that language is a neutral structure that simply happens to serve or reflect the recurrent system of
patriarchal values. Language would be seen as a product of patriarchal
history; patriarchy would be woven into all our existing texts and into
all the discursive options we have available to us. Language, in effect,
would be seen as constituted by its history of articulating an infinite
number of distinctions based on the assumption of male superiority. At
that point, language would no longer be merely pervasively patri-

archical; it would be intrinsically so, making the problem of remediation immensely more difficult. In its most economical version, the whole signifying function could be said to center on sexual difference; patriarchal discourse becomes phallocentric.

This vision is perhaps the greatest challenge feminist criticism poses for Western culture, yet it is also the most severe challenge to the writing of feminist criticism. So far, however, the claim that all of our discourse is intrinsically patriarchal or phallocentric, while supported by much argument and by telling examples, remains generally unproven.[16] The work to demonstrate that it is more than a claim will take many years. We can, however, provisionally suggest some of the ways in which the claim might be analyzed.

Is language, including both the network of connotation we have inherited from the past and the range of usages we have available to us in the present, inherently patriarchal or phallocentric? Feminist critics have shown that both particular usages and major elements of certain entire discourses disparage women and privilege male authority and male sexuality. Often those discourses constitute and maintain institutions that extend the effects of this kind of linguistic bias through the culture. To sustain a more general claim about language, however, we need a model both more basic and more pervasive than that suggested by the most dramatically gender-marked diction and biases of particular discourses. As a first step, we need a way of analyzing individual texts as sexually differentiated and perhaps phallocentric in all of their manifestations. Locating a few sexually biased phrases in a complex text, an approach that Sandra Gilbert and Susan Gubar sometimes employ in *The Madwoman in the Attic* and "Alphabet Soup," will not be enough either to describe or to indict its entire practice.[17] Calling a text phallocentric on the basis of scant evidence risks making the charge appear either trivial or melodramatic. That is not to say that even minimal evidence is not important. It can point the way toward further indications of a text's assumptions, and even a few ill-chosen phrases can seriously affect a text's impact. Nonetheless, if phallocentrism is so deeply a part of our writing, we need a way of thinking about the concept that lets us see its impact on all of the linguistic features of a text.

The term phallocentric itself makes it necessary to consider using Lacan's definition of the phallus as both the primary signifier and the sign of an unachievable identity. It is possible that a broad sense of linguistic differences could be based on a model negotiating between the presence and absence of the phallus—Barthes has very nearly offered us one in *S/Z*—but I believe we will be better served at present by a model whose terminology is more neutral.[18] That initial neutrality will facilitate the substitutions necessary in dealing with a wide variety of writing practices.

We might begin with the following proposition: that language, and hence culture as a whole, is a network of power relations organized, stratified, structured, ranked as a series of oppositions reproducing the opposition male/female. One can easily make lists that exemplify this organization: masculine/feminine; active/passive; presence/absence; validated/excluded; success/failure; superior/inferior; primary/secondary; independent/dependent; unity/multiplicity; organized/scattered; intellect/imagination; logical/illogical; defined/undefined; dependable/capricious; head/heart; mind/body; subject/object; penis/vagina; firm/soft; sky/earth; day/night; air/water; form/matter; transcendence/immurement; culture/nature; logos/pathos. Many critics have made this kind of effort, and others will no doubt continue to do so; this list borrows a number of pairs from Simone de Beauvoir, Hélène Cixous, Michèle Le Doeuff, and Adrienne Rich.[19] Yet as soon as we consider the connotative history of these terms or test the various pairs for congruence, such lists begin to disintegrate. First, the sexual identity of the members of some of these pairs is intrinsically culture-bound, unstable, and reversible. Indeed the sexual status of any word can be ambiguated, disambiguated, or altered by its context. The opposition active/passive deteriorates when we remember that the history of civil disobedience teaches us that passivity can be a very substantial action. Few poets would calmly accept the parallel valuation of the oppositions superior/inferior and intellect/imagination. The ship that we conventionally name after a woman can also, within another symbolic system, become a penis that cleaves the female sea.

We will not, therefore, prove the thesis that language is phallocentric by dividing the dictionary into two lists headed by "male" and "female." On a smaller scale, however, lists like these can be informative, since they suggest at once the pervasiveness and the variation or flexibility in sexual differentiation. To make that procedure useful, then, we need to emphasize its difficulties. It is not merely that the composition of the lists changes culturally and historically, but also that the composition of the lists is never at any moment fixed. Yet this conclusion does not disprove the hypothesis that language for us is constituted as a series of oppositions reproducing the opposition male/female. An opposition need not be unchanging or even momentarily fixed in order for it to be constitutive and determining.

The key claim is not that the substitutions for the opposition male/female are set and determinable, but that the opposition itself is inescapable. The notion that any discursive performance *reproduces* this opposition needs to be amplified with a sense of textual diversity. Every utterance, we may say, reproduces the opposition male/female in that it openly or secretly seeks out or evades those terms. An individual instance of language, we may say, traverses and is traversed by the opposition male/female whether by imitation, assertion, avoidance, or denial. There is a boundary, a dividing line, that every effort at verbal differentiation crosses and thereby inscribes within itself. It is a mobile, uncertain dividing line that can be exploited, denounced, or joyously affirmed, but however often we call attention to its mode of operation we cannot free ourselves of its recurrence. Male/female, female/male: within the limits of our culture and our personalities, the terms are subject to continuing transformation, but they are always with us. The argument about the constitutive, informing role of sexual opposition, then, needs to be grounded in the claim that male/female is the minimal irreducible unit of discourse. To say that every discursive moment inscribes within itself and reproduces the paradigmatic form male/female is thus to say that every apparently unitary sign signifies only by way of this difference.

I am not suggesting that all differentiation, all assertion, each affirmation and negation, simply be reduced to the terms male and female. That project would merely reintroduce the naive distortion of the Freudianism that sought a penis in every convex object and a vagina in every concave one. Like this formulaic reduction to a single binary opposition, the analysis of discourse in terms of the distinction male/female is useless if it ignores the instability and the evasiveness of a constitutive sexual differentiation. There is no primary, original, decisive, comprehensive distinction between maleness and femaleness to which all further differentiation can refer, though there are any number of theories and myths about what such a distinction might be. We may need to think of this distinction as one that any discursive practice simultaneously desires and fears, one that every verbal distinction alludes to and evades at the same time. Paradoxically, therefore, we can neither fix this distinction nor escape it.

We can begin to apply this rather problematic claim to textual analysis by looking at the value judgments, the overtly binary diction, and eventually all the distinctions and assertions within a given writing practice in the context of how it constructs and draws on relationships between maleness and femaleness. We can then describe a varied field of oppositions pointing to and even contradicting a text's particular vision of sexual difference. The attitudes conveyed will always be part of a diverse and, to varying degrees, mobile field of differences. This field of differences will have considerable textual specificity; the opposition male/female should thus be used to organize and identify the specificity of particular textual practices, not to obliterate them. Finally, it may be possible to show that any utterance, any discursive decision or choice, occurs in part as a relation to a text's constitutive vision of maleness and femaleness.

A brief example will be useful here. Sartre has been faulted of late for depicting an intermediate state between being and nothingness with a series of tropes that link sliminess with femaleness: "What mode of being is symbolized by the slimy [*visqueux*]? . . . Slime is the agony of water. . . . Nothing testifies more clearly to its ambiguous character as a 'substance in between two states' than the slowness with which the slimy melts into itself. . . . It is a soft, yielding action, a moist and feminine sucking, it lives obscurely under my fingers, and I sense it like a dizziness; it draws me to it as the bottom of a precipice might draw me. . . . Slime is the revenge of the In-itself. A sickly-sweet, feminine revenge. . . ."[20]

These passages occur within an analysis of how psychological values come to be associated with physical substances. Rather appalling references to femaleness occur several times; though they are not the center of the discussion, their inclusion in this chain of substitutions is startling and requires careful and aggressive evaluation in the light not only of *Being and Nothingness* but of Sartre's other works as well. Taken out of context, passages like those above may lead us to conclude that Sartre identifies women with values conventionally debased in the West, values which Sartre also finds repugnant. Yet even within *Being and Nothingness,* the distribution of valorized and rejected conditions of being fails to match the list of conventional sex-linked oppositions cited earlier. Sartre's negative picture of the world outside us, for example, embodies qualities traditionally associated with masculinity: hardness and self-sufficiency. Conversely, Sartre considers human consciousness to be always empty and insufficient, qualities Western culture typically fears and identifies with women.[21] Rather than reject those qualities, however, he suggests that an authentic consciousness might recognize that we are constituted as emptiness. These considerations do not eliminate the impact of Sartre's use of the feminine within his series of tropes describing sliminess and its dangerous temptations. The association of femaleness with liquid and engulfing matter, evident both in *Being and Nothingness* and in some of Sartre's fiction, does dramatically sexualize Sartre's binarism and does justify a reading of Sartre's affirmative and negative impulses in terms of sexual differentiations. Yet such a reading will have to account for Sartre's detailed rearrangement and rereading of the sexual valuations conventional in our culture, since his image of how persons develop includes a positive analysis of many qualities conventionally considered female. His attitude toward men and women is thus far more complex than the now notorious passages quoted above would imply.

It seems clear what this brief discussion suggests about the analysis of phallocentricity: that particular discourses are structured by oppositions that are analogous to and even often overtly grounded in images of sexual differentiation, but that complex discourses create a gestalt of various oppositions that can be unpredictable and both complementary and contradictory. At once determining and determined, the culture's catalog of binary oppositions will be radically redistributed in complex texts. We can trace a series of associations through such a field of oppositions, but the results will be more accurate if we realize the pathways are multiple and the resultant map of associations is often fluid and three-dimensional. We can go further in the case of particular discourses, such as Sartre's, if we are willing to analyze each distinction in a text as simultaneously deferred throughout and coalescing within such a pattern of associations. Each distinction, then, is a transformation of a sexual differentiation in an endless process of substitution.

One of the most challenging arguments that could be raised against either such readings of particular texts or the general project of analyzing discourse in terms of its sexual binarism is one that is, perhaps, least likely to be voiced, since it threatens not only the feminist project but also interpretive argument throughout the humanities and social sciences. The argument would run this way. A critic who interprets a text thoroughly in these terms would be subject to the charge that the interpretive model accounted for all of the text only because that is what interpretive activity *always* does. A coherent, reasonably consistent discourse can always be overlaid with a comparably consistent reading. One would have proven that the text could be read in this way but not that it was written this way; one would have demonstrated, so the argument would run, nothing definitive about the text's inherent character. There is reason for feminist critics to address this problem directly, for the answer will in its own way encourage the sort of self-aware writing that can undermine patriarchal discursive structures. The critic would answer, in effect, that the charge is just, but that criticism is concerned not with proving how a text was written but with influencing how it will be read.[22] Given the immense resistance to feminist readings that expose biases and logical contradictions in texts that are either revered or uncritically assumed to be neutral, even demonstrating that texts can be read as pervasively sexually differentiated is significant. But that is not the only thing to be gained. The power that criticism seeks over texts is always the power to rewrite them, to direct their connotative effect in such a way that we will never again be able to read them as we did before. At that point, in the aftermath of a powerful reading, it seems that the text was always constituted as it has now been newly interpreted. With much criticism, such a perceptual change may seem an inconsequential victory, but feminist criticism can radically restructure not only the codes by which we read texts but the codes by which we read our social life as well. The text in question, the discourse being analyzed, the social institution being reread, is always, most persuasively in its very specificity, a vehicle for a representative cultural commentary. As with other methods the West often resists, such as Marxist or psychoanalytic, a successful reading challenges how we read our culture and ourselves. Far more directly than most forms of criticism, feminist criticism questions the semiotics of the ideologies of our historical moment. The challenge of a vigorous feminist reading is always implicitly the one Rilke voiced in a context where a different sexual politics was at stake: "You must change your life."[23]

The pressure toward change comes in part from recognizing hierarchies achieved in all binary structures. This is the element of my initial proposition that is perhaps most important to the women and men who

live out the consequences of a language structured by sexual difference—that such oppositions may always manifest a relationship of
dominance and power. Derrida argues that in any occurrence of a
binary pair, one term is always privileged; one term is always the master, one term the slave. If he is correct, then no existing language can
simply be disinterestedly gender-centric; one gender will dominate.
Thus to say, as I did above, that any binary relationship is intrinsically
reversible does not mean that in a given social formation such a reversal
can actually be carried out. It is often the case that the reversal cannot
even be thought. Male and female are only neutral structural categories
in principle. There will be nothing neutral about them in any text,
including the text you are reading, just as there is nothing neutral about
them in our culture. Civilization has much invested in trying to maintain a stable, consistent, hierarchical relationship between the terms
"male" and "female." The possibility that sexual binarism is pervasive
and irreducible leads us to consider the further possibility that a power
relationship is negotiated and codified in every instance of discourse,
not only discourse that is overtly marked for gender but all discourse.
This need not suggest that power is a more fundamental, more primary
and more determining, reality than sexuality, but rather that power is
an omnipresent consequence of all binarism, and that our culture has
privileged sexual binarism in ways both open and covert. For us, the
dualities of power—strong/weak, dominant/submissive—cannot be entirely separated from the duality of maleness and femaleness. Moreover,
as Foucault has convincingly argued, power cannot merely be characterized as oppression, prohibition, and interdiction; power induces, encourages, and structures certain forms of productivity. The dualities of
power energize and solicit our language and our social life. Sexual
differentiation and hierarchization, we can argue, at once restrict and
facilitate the production of discourse.

Yet is a hierarchical binarism intrinsically phallocentric? There are
two clear routes of argument. We can say, as Adrienne Rich sometimes
does, that the very existence of binary mechanisms is intrinsically phallocentric, that binarism in general is thus the historical product of many
centuries of male dominance. Or we can say that only the repeated
dominance of "male" over "female" throughout Western history makes
the present condition of language inherently phallocentric, that our
history has privileged *particular* binary values. These are not merely
abstract propositions, for they imply very different directions for schol-

arly research and radically different programs for achieving social change.

I want to suggest that the first argument may be impossibly contradictory and that the second, conversely, offers a number of possibilities for productive work. The first argument generally proceeds by pointing out that binarism is an intrinsically antagonistic, disputative, conflictual mode of operation; it leads inevitably to attempts for dominance and control. Yet much of the structuralist research of the last twenty-five years suggests that all culture, indeed all thought, is binary. Lévi-Strauss in particular has tried to show that not only rationalistic or scientific thought but all thought is binary. Feminist discourse therefore cannot proceed outside binarism. If Lévi-Strauss is correct that all thought, even primitive and non-Western thought, is binary, and if those feminists who believe that binarism is inherently phallocentric are correct, then feminism is confronted with an impossible problem. Its main recourse would be to a Derridean position that only through the disruptive use of phallocentric, binary rhetoric can one undermine binary thinking. Feminist politics is not, however, likely to be satisfied with the limited, ironic victories possible through the kind of Derridean play that self-consciously tries to maintain a dialogue with its own phallocentricity. Feminism aims in the end to do away with phallocentrism, at least within feminist writing itself, and possibly elsewhere as well. Thus it may be more useful for feminists to argue that not all binarism is phallocentric but only binarism of a certain sort, the sort we now have as our historical inheritance. Indeed, no existing feminist writing operates outside binarism. As Barthes and Kristeva have argued, though, a mobile, plural, playful binarism is a considerable threat to the particular complex of hierarchies by which contemporary power is maintained.

The relationship between stable, determined meaning and a more open, unpredictable play of signification has, itself, been characterized with terms that merit inclusion in the chain of substitutions for male and female: denotation/connotation. Denotation involves the effort to control and specify meaning. It operates, for Western cultures, within that field of related oppositions that are themselves representations and deferrals of the stereotypical attributes of maleness and femaleness: denotation/connotation; dependable/capricious; organized/scattered; logical/illogical or emotive. Because maintaining the structures of power depends on the strict control of meaning (by encouraging specific parameters of connotation so that words may seem merely to denote), connotation as a general process has come to represent a loss of control, the failure of denotative law to prescribe how discourse shall signify. If we view the series of oppositions above as a Bachelardian phenomenology of denotation and connotation, then we can say that connotation for the West evokes the free play of the female materiality of the signifier. It suggests what Umberto Eco calls unlimited semiosis.[24] If connotation is given free rein, a possibility our culture both fears and desires, language will seem capable of its own independent, generative activity, a kind of sheerly material production outside the domain of consciousness.

Perhaps the patriarchal terror of and wish for a sheerly material verbal production—a writing whose substance is self-generating, indifferent to the demands of a willed intelligence—is invoked quite specifically by the French effort to "speak the female":

> More so than men who are coaxed toward social success, toward sublimation, women are body. More body, hence more writing . . . woman overturns the "personal" . . . secretly, silently deep down inside, she grows and multiplies . . . unselfishly, body without end, without appendage, without principle "parts". . . . This doesn't mean that she's an undifferentiated magma, but that she doesn't lord it over her body or her desire. . . . She lets the other language speak—the language of 1,000 tongues which knows neither enclosure or death.[25]

The chief characteristic of the language Cixous calls for is its material connotativeness. The response of the patriarchy to this connotative eruption is to try to impose the spiritual law of denotation, an imposition that can never be wholly effective, since denotative law can only be articulated in language with its own connotative effect. The battle, variously comic and tragic, is unending. Bound into the binary contest between maleness and femaleness, between transcendence and immurement, phallocentric intentionality melodramatically sets itself the spiritual task of redeeming discourse from its female materiality. Intentionality spiritualizes language, or so phallocentric thought would dream, directing its signification toward form and away from matter.

There are two quite different but equally radical operations that can be performed on this culturally determined, hierarchical relationship between denotation and connotation. One can demonstrate, as Derrida has done, that the hierarchical relationship between the two terms is always unstable and self-contradictory, thereby undermining the means by which power inscribes its values and is itself inscribed within a particular system of differences. Derrida himself has only recently begun to make practical political use of these methods in his work; others, of course, can recognize their utility for still more radical projects.[26] Alternatively, as Hélène Cixous and Luce Irigaray have done, one can intensify many of those very differences the culture has specified but reverse the conventions of valorization.

This move within French feminist theory, a move with several points of similarity with Mary Daly's work in this country, has been deeply and unnecessarily, if inevitably, misunderstood. Because the different versions of *l'écriture féminine* set out deliberately to valorize some of the metaphors for a female otherness that have facilitated woman's oppression, the movement may appear from a distance to be a frightening product of sexist binarism. There are several reasons why this is anything but the case. The *locus classicus* of the analysis of woman as other is itself French; Simone de Beauvoir's 1949 *The Second Sex* and the lead article in the first issue of de Beauvoir's *Questions Féministes* include a critique of the effort to "speak the female" in all its difference and otherness. I believe both the editorial collective of *Questions Féministes* and the American feminists who reject *l'écriture féminine* may misunderstand its various writing practices.

At one level, as one vector of power, the effort to speak the female is an effort to introduce certain new verbal practices, and thus certain new verbal options, into the play and warfare of discourses. Why then the attacks on *l'écriture féminine?* In part, I believe, the problem comes from a failure to make a conceptual division between two aims, modes, motives, or imperatives of all interpretive writing, all discourse. I would call them the tautological and dialogical imperatives of discourse. The tautological imperative aims for a radical kind of self-sufficiency and exclusivity; I am, it would claim, the only discourse there is. The dialogical imperative, conversely, writes itself out as a conversation, variously supportive and competitive, with other discourses; I am, it would claim, only the weaving together of all these other voices. Of course these moments are not really separate. The dialogical mode can offer itself as the ideal form of writing, suggesting thereby that it should dominate other ways of writing. The tautological mode will be undercut by its intertextual constitution, by the other voices we can hear within its assertion of priority.

Nonetheless, these two modes are worth distinguishing, particularly in the response to and analysis of critical positions. Some of the attacks on *l'écriture féminine* read as if only the tautological mode were on view. As I shall try briefly to show, however, this kind of writing is necessarily responsive to and inscribed with other voices. For it not to be so inscribed, it would have to come from a world without patriarchy and without a more socially active feminism. That is not to say that it lacks a will to conquer, absorb, and replace other kinds of writing. All writing has such motives. It is rather to say that it cannot actually do so; moreover, it is to say that its dialogical character is an inescapable part of what it is. All the varieties of feminist writing are in dialogue both with one another and with non-feminist discourses. A fair analysis of any one feminist practice requires that we describe its tautological and its dialogical imperatives.

It is helpful, and historically appropriate, to begin this analysis with *The Second Sex*, which remains an elegant statement of how verbal difference can help sustain social oppression. *L'écriture féminine* explodes those same stable, complacent binarisms in another way, by so deepening and extending the connotative force of female otherness as to make it a genuine and unpredictable power within discourse. Nothing in *l'écriture féminine* precludes social action and the continuing demand for equality.[27] Its aim is to *change the language* by entering new writing practices into the field of discourses. Even the effort to change the language, moreover, includes multiple referential functions. The very pressure toward a self-referential, tautological language is inescapably contaminated, if you will, by all the other forms of referentiality. As Derrida demonstrates, self-*reference* installs a contradictory moment of difference within identity. Even without this move, however, it is fair to argue that referentiality is an inescapable feature of linguisticality itself. This is not necessarily to say that language always refers to a non-linguistic material world outside itself; rather, referentiality is coded into the connotative web of the language. Whatever else it may be, referentiality is one of language's internal effects. Thus, even in analyzing *l'écriture féminine* as a series of self-contained writing practices, the issue of referentiality remains pertinent, problematic, and an appropriate concern. To treat *l'écriture féminine* as merely externally referential would, nonetheless, be an unfair reduction of its enterprise.

A detailed analysis of the work of writers like Cixous and Irigaray would require a book, not a section of an essay, but some brief comments will suggest how their work fits into this argument. In the economy of the West's sexual codes, Irigaray writes, the feminine is defined "as nothing other than the complement, the other side, or the negative side, of the masculine."[28] Male sexuality is the model of formal completion and full presence; female sexuality is "a flaw, a hole," for a woman's "sex organ represents the horror of having nothing to see."[29] Irigaray begins to meditate on this conventionalized image of female emptiness, so as to turn it into a fluid form of presence: "There is no abyss. For us, depth does not mean a chasm. . . . Our depth is the density of our body, in touch 'all' over."[30] Valorizing the very images associated with female otherness, she produces new claims and connotative language that are unstably polemical and ecstatic, threatening, and playful: "Woman finds pleasure precisely in this incompleteness of the form of her sex organs, which is why it retouches itself indefinitely."[31] A woman's "sex is composed of two lips which embrace continually."[32] Femaleness is thus admired in a radical version of all those impulses and states of being phallocentric culture has feared and rejected:

> But *woman has sex organs just about everywhere.* . . . "She" is indefinitely other in herself. That is undoubtedly the reason she is called temperamental, incomprehensible, perturbed, capricious—not to mention her language in which "she" goes off in all directions and in which "he" is unable to discern the coherence of any meaning. . . . One must listen to her differently in order to hear an *"other meaning" which is constantly in the process of weaving itself.* . . . [Women] do not experience the same interiority that you do and which perhaps you mistakenly presume they share. "Within themselves" means *in the privacy of this silent, multiple, diffuse tact.*[33]

Even in these brief quotations, it is clear that Irigaray's effort to valorize a radical female otherness has two characteristics: first, it remains within the binary system of phallocentric thought; second, this deflationary observation is in no way a sufficient description of the specific texture and achievement of Irigaray's prose. For although she writes against the norm that privileges the phallus, and although her prose thus depends in part on the logic of a negative theology, many of its specific textual moments are utterly surprising and unpredictable.

The element of negation in Irigaray's work takes a number of forms. First, the monolithic quality of phallocentrism is defined negatively and rejected: "Let them have oneness, with its prerogatives, its domination, its solipsisms."[34] Then female relations are defined affirmatively as phallocentrism's opposite: "Between us, there are no owners and no purchasers, no determinable objects and no prices."[35] Indeed, female language is partly described as a reversal of and response to phallocentric logic; it "diverts the linearity of a project . . . disconcerts fidelity to only one discourse."[36] Finally, she enters the effort to "speak the female": "*Woman has sex organs just about everywhere . . .* 'she' goes off in all directions." Here too, however, the binarism of differing from phallocentrism remains. Both Irigaray's critique of "the dominant phallic economy" and her argument that female sexuality is multiple, unlike the oppositional and proprietary sexuality of phallocentrism, reflect the logic of a negative theology; nonetheless, this effort to write within a plural femaleness achieves a vision of female sexuality that phallocentric discourse has never offered us.

The same two-fold discourse, a rhetoric rejecting conventional sexuality and a rhetoric attempting a new plural sexual textuality, occurs in the work of Hélène Cixous and Monique Wittig. The difference between the two kinds of writing is apparent if one compares the more polemical passages in Wittig's *Les Guérillères* with the experimental writing in *The Lesbian Body*. Wittig says that the feminist movement has proved capable of producing "texts in a context of total rupture with masculine culture, texts written by women exclusively for women, careless of male approval."[37] It is doubtful whether this claim can be entirely credited. Writing which is reactive to and antagonistic toward masculine culture can never be entirely independent of it. Moreover, as Kristeva has often pointed out, though not to universal agreement, plural feminist writing grows out of the experiments of modernist and post-modernist writing. Writers like Barthes and Derrida have attempted an equally plural "female" writing. As with Irigaray, the two kinds of writing are often inseparable, the merely polemical and reactive infiltrating the newer plural textuality. These qualifications should not prevent us from recognizing that Wittig's texts record her effort to accomplish that goal. That effort, like Irigaray's to "speak the female," is almost as extraordinary as we might imagine her success might be. She goes on to say of *The Lesbian Body* that "the body of the text subsumes all the words of the female body. . . . The fascination for writing the never previously written and the fascination for the unattained body proceed from the same desire." This ambition and desire to write what has never been written, to incarnate in a discourse the whole of an otherness that has paradoxically at once been excluded and debased in Western culture, runs through women's literature and stands as well as the key challenge for feminist criticism. Can feminist critics, using a language permeated by the history of phallocentric discourse, contain, represent, or even allude to a world until now denied to all of us? Some critics, Adrienne Rich, Hélène Cixous, and Luce Irigaray among others, argue that feminist writers can take over the language of male writers and reconceive it. Whether or not this is actually possible, we need not doubt the value of the attempt to do so. No stronger need to demonstrate that the subject can be constituted in its discourse exists than the need for self-expression manifested in women writers and feminist critics. No more telling evidence exists to show us that the subject, however belittled and transcended by the powerful and independent regularities of discourse, does indeed leave its traces there. Can it be that women writers are, in some substantial way, less fully constituted in their discourse than men, at least to the extent that the received language of phallocentricism cannot adequately present a female identity? Or is it rather that men are culturally, discursively, deluded into assuming that their language is at the service of their subjectivity? If women writers, responding to their sense of alienation and exclusion, see themselves as representatives, emissaries, of the obverse of Western culture, they may succeed in dramatizing more clearly than before the mix of the original and the fateful in the expressiveness of language.[38] If so, then there is no better context in which to discuss, not only for women but for all of us, the relation between the subject and its discourse.

Nietzsche opens the preface to *Beyond Good and Evil* with the famous sentence, "Supposing truth is a woman—what then?" With different motivations, that may as well be the general question repeatedly posed in feminist criticism, however overly ambitious it may seem as a characterization of much more narrowly focused feminist scholarship. In an essay meditating on Nietzsche's aphorisms on women, Derrida writes that truth, if a woman, is an endless, unfathomable otherness that can engulf and distort "all vestige of essentiality, of identity, of property."[39] Derrida, of course, is engaging not only the role of the trope of femaleness in philosophy but also in his own discourse and in his own sexual anxieties. Feminist critics can thus be expected to have quite different images of the otherness they seek to express. But their project does lead there, from the careful observation of women's identity and voice in literature and society, to a recognition of how particular discursive traditions and entire cultures are dependent on a distancing myth of female otherness, and finally to a desire to make that otherness intricately present. A certain continuity, then, an entelechial principle, runs through the whole spectrum of feminist criticisms; from the "stubbornly empirical" to *l'écriture féminine,* there is a revolutionary pressure for vision and change toward which all the different feminisms contribute. Of course Western culture has ways of rendering that role within its own hegemony: idealized, romanticized, exoticized, otherness would remain powerless; women working in the margins of our order would bring back extraordinary and enticing images to the men in power at the center. Yet as I write that feminist criticism works to make a radical otherness intricately present, it is not, in any case, a desire for mastery that I feel. It is uncertainty, risk, and perhaps a desire to be personally changed in ways it seems I will not change myself. Yet it is hardly for me or for the benefit of men in general that feminist criticism should both retain and enlarge its subversive purpose. In the service of the inner logic of their enterprise, feminist critics should pursue their project to its end; as writers, they should become the envoys of otherness.[40]

Notes

1. At least I think these are my motivations, though it would be irresponsible of me to ignore Gayatri Chakravorty Spivak's quite devastating localization of the will to power: "Why is it that male critics in search of a cause find in feminist criticism their best hope? Perhaps, because, unlike the race and class situations, where academic people are not likely to get much of a hearing, the women's struggle is one they can support 'from the inside.' Feminism in its academic inceptions is accessible and subject to correction by authoritative men. . . ." "The Politics of Interpretations," *Critical Inquiry* 9 (1982): 278.

2. Elaine Showalter, "Literary Criticism," *Signs* 1 (1975): 436. Also see Showalter's "Feminist Criticism in the Wilderness," *Critical Inquiry* 8 (1981): 179–205.

3. The mid-point of the 1970s was an important year for feminist theory. *Signs* published its first issue in 1975. That was also the year when *Diacritics* published its important special issue *Textual Politics/Feminist Criticism.*

4. This list embodies a preference that I should clarify—a preference for those critics who situate feminist theory in relation to the other major theoretical movements of our moment. This effort is, of course, hardly a passive or subservient one since it involves aggressive rereadings and critiques of alternative models. Yet it does require citing, sometimes approvingly, criticism by men, an activity that some feminists may argue amounts to subjecting feminist practice to the will of the fathers. "If neofeminist thought in France seems to have ground to a halt," writes Christiane Makward, "it is because it has continued to feed on the discourse of the masters." "To Be or Not to Be . . . A Feminist Speaker," in *The Future of Difference,* ed. Hester Eisenstein and Alice Jardine, (Boston: G. K. Hall, 1980), p. 102. One can respond by arguing that some of the fathers have worked both to call their own authority into question and to weaken the hold of phallocentrism on discourse in general. It is true, though, that a broad range of citations alters the nature of feminist textuality. Such a range of citations threatens feminism's independent and local character, something Foucault, defining the characteristics of all local discourses, describes as "an autonomous, noncentralized kind of theoretical production, one that is to say whose validity is not dependent on the approval of the established régimes of thought," in *Power/Knowledge: Selected Interviews and Other Writings 1972–1977,* ed. Colin Gordon (New York: Pantheon, 1980), p. 81.

5. Elaine Marks, "Why This Book?" in *New French Feminisms,* ed. Elaine Marks and Isabelle de Courtivron (Amherst: University of Massachusetts Press, 1980), p. xi.

6. Showalter, "Literary Criticism," p. 437.

7. See Fetterley, *The Resisting Reader: A Feminist Approach to American Fiction* (Bloomington: Indiana University Press, 1978).

8. For some excellent analyses of the ideological underpinnings of some of the more conservative feminist positions on sexuality see *Heresies* 3, no. 4 (1981), and Jean Bethke Elshtain, "The Victim Syndrome: A Troubling Turn in Feminism," *The Progressive* (June 1982), pp. 42–47.

9. Annette Kolodny, "Dancing Through the Minefield: Some Observations on the Theory, Practice, and Politics of a Feminist Literary Criticism," *Feminist Studies* 6, no. 1 (1980): p. 19.

10. Jane Gallop, "*Writing and Sexual Difference:* The Difference Within," *Critical Inquiry* 8 (1981): 804.

11. See Carol Neely's essay, "Feminist Criticism in Motion," in the present collection; it is divided into two parts, the first part expressing some hope for a new feminism synthesizing differences, the second part instead opting for knowledge of the differences themselves.

12. According to Jean Bethke Elshtain: "The nature and meaning of feminist discourse itself must be a subject for critical inquiry. What sort of language, public and private, do feminists propose that women speak?" "Feminist Discourse and Its Discontents: Language, Power, and Meaning," *Signs* 7 (1982): 605.

13. Adrienne Rich, *Of Woman Born: Motherhood as Experience and Institution* (New York: Norton, 1976) pp. 249, 57–58.

14. Tillie Olsen, *Silences* (New York: Delacorte Press/Seymour Lawrence, 1978), p. 240.

15. Cheris Kramer, Barrie Thorne, and Nancy Henley, "Perspectives on Language and Communication," *Signs* 3 (1978): p. 646.

16. At issue here, in part, is what would constitute sufficient evidence. For an extensive survey of the existing literature—from the perspective of one who believes the evidence is sufficient—see Dale Spender, *Man Made Language* (London: Routledge, 1980). For an ambitious, verbally inventive exploration of both the evidence and the issues see Mary Daly, *Gyn/Ecology: The Metaethics of Radical Feminism* (Boston: Beacon Press, 1978).

17. See Sandra M. Gilbert and Susan Gubar, *The Madwoman in the Attic: The Woman Writer and the Nineteenth-Century Literary Imagination* (New Haven: Yale, 1979). "Alphabet Soup" will be the introduction to their companion volume on twentieth-century literature.

18. Part of the problem with using the phallus to describe the presence and absence of a privileged instance of signification is that there is really no way to make a decisive distinction between the male organ and its generalized discursive symbolism. In *The Language of Psycho-analysis* (1967), trans. Donald Nicholson-Smith (New York: Norton, 1973), J. Laplanche and J.-B. Pontalis similarly suggest that there is reason to doubt the "wisdom of setting up a radical distinction between penis and phallus in psycho-analytic terminology" (p. 314).

19. See Simone de Beauvoir, *The Second Sex*, trans. H. M. Parshley (N.Y.: Knopf, 1953); Hélène Cixous, "Sorties," in *New French Feminisms*, ed. Marks and de Courtivron, pp. 90–98; "The Laugh of the Medusa," *Signs* 1 (1976): 875–93, reprinted in *New French Feminisms*, ed. Marks and de Courtivron, pp. 245–64; Adrienne Rich, *Of Woman Born* and *On Lies, Secrets, and Silence: Selected Prose 1966–1978* (New York: Norton, 1979); Michèle Le Doeuff, "Women and Philosophy," *Radical Philosophy* 17 (1977): 2–12.

20. Jean-Paul Sartre, *Being and Nothingness* (1943), trans. Hazel E. Barnes (New York: Philosophical Library, 1956), pp. 607, 609. For feminist critiques of Sartre see Margery Collins and Christine Pierce, "Holes and Slime: Sexism in Sartre's Psychoanalysis," *The Philosophical Forum* 5 (1973–74), pp. 112–27; Naomi Green, "Sartre, Sexuality, and *The Second Sex*," Philosophy and Literature 4 (1980): 199–211; Peggy Holland, "Jean-Paul Sartre as a NO to Women," *Sinister Wisdom*, no. 6 (1978): 72–79; Dorothy Kaufmann McCall, "Simone de Beauvoir, *The Second Sex*, and Jean-Paul Sartre," *Signs* 5 (1979): 209–23.

21. In accepting the state of nothingness, Sartre would have us take full responsibility for whatever we fill the moment with; for Sartre one cannot simply refuse that responsibility. There is considerable evidence in Sartre's *Saint Genet* (1952) that he thinks of masculinity and femininity not only as human genders but also as qualities essential to both men and women.

22. For detailed discussion of related issues see Stanley Fish, *Is There a Text in This Class? The Authority of Interpretive Communities* (Cambridge, Mass.: Harvard University Press, 1980).

23. "You must change your life" translates the last line of Rilke's "Archaic Torso of Apollo."

24. See Umberto Eco, *A Theory of Semiotics* (Bloomington: Indiana University Press, 1976).

25. Hélène Cixous, "The Laugh of the Medusa," in *New French Feminisms*, ed. Marks and de Courtivron, pp. 257, 258, 259, 260.

26. For the first extended analysis of these issues see Michael Ryan, *Marxism and Deconstruction: A Critical Articulation* (Baltimore: Johns Hopkins, 1982).

27. See, for example, Luce Irigaray's detailed insistence on the importance of social action in "Woman's Exile: Interview with Luce Irigaray," *Ideology and Consciousness* no. 1 (1977): 62–76.

28. Irigaray, "Woman's Exile," p. 63.

29. Irigaray, "This Sex Which Is Not One," *New French Feminisms*, ed. Marks and de Courtivron, p. 101.

30. Irigaray, "When Our Lips Speak Together," *Signs* 6 (1980): 75.

31. Irigaray, "This Sex Which Is Not One," p. 101.

32. Ibid., p. 100.

33. Ibid., p. 103.

34. Irigaray, "When Our Lips Speak Together," p. 71.

35. Ibid., p. 76.

36. Irigaray, "This Sex Which Is Not One," p. 104. Also see Irigaray's "When the Goods Get Together," *New French Feminisms*, ed. Marks and de Courtivron, pp. 107–10, and her "And the One Doesn't Stir without the Other," *Signs* 7 (1981): 60–67. Irigaray's most important feminist works are *Speculum de l'autre femme* (Paris: Minuit, 1974), *Ce sexe qui n'en est pas un* (Paris: Minuit, 1977), and *Amante marine: de Friedrich Nietzsche* (Paris: Minuit, 1980). A portion of *Amante marine* is translated, with introduction and notes, as "Veiled Lips," *Mississippi Review* 33 (Winter–Spring, 1983): 93–131. For introductions to and commentaries on her work see Diana Adlam and Couze Venn, "Introduction to Irigaray," *Ideology and Consciousness* no. 1 (1977), pp. 57–61; Carolyn Burke, "Introduction to Luce Irigaray's 'When Our Lips Speak Together,' " *Signs* 6 (1980): 66–68; Shoshana Felman "Women and Madness: The Critical Phallacy," *Diacritics* 5, no. 4 (1975): 2–10; Monique Plaza, " 'Phallomorphic Power' and The Psychology of 'Woman,' " *Ideology and Consciousness* no. 4 (1978), pp. 4–36; Elizabeth L. Berg, "The Third Woman," *Diacritics* 12, no. 2 (1982): 11–20; and Jane Gallop, *The Daughter's Seduction: Feminism and Psychoanalysis* (Ithaca: Cornell, 1982). Plaza faults Irigaray for valorizing an ahistorical, idealized, unchanging feminine essence, though Berg argues that "the difficulty of Irigaray's enterprise stems from her sensitivity to the dangers of falling back into an economy of representation where the woman would be given one more image, proposed as the 'true' image, and thereby recuperated and redefined in necessarily phallocentric terms" (p. 17). In response to Plaza's critique one must also say that the epithet "Idealist!" has become one of the more empty and unreflective rhetorical gestures in

contemporary criticism. There are idealist moments in all discourse; one can work to be partly conscious and critical of them, but no discourse is free of idealism. Whether one sees Irigaray as idealist or not, a related issue is that of whether she intends her practice to be an actual representation of the female body. In sympathy with Jane Gallop's excellent essay on representation in Irigaray, "Quand nos lèvres s'écrivent: Irigaray's Body Politic," *Romantic Review* 74, no. 1 (1983): 77–83, I would argue that Irigaray's work is first of all a writing practice and therefore a transformation of *discourse* about the body, not an effort to describe or represent. One can find passages in Irigaray that explicitly reject representation; however, as Gallop argues, this does not do away with the fact that representation and the material body are a continual issue in Irigaray's writing, one that cannot be easily resolved or reduced. Her writing, in its effort to speak the body in a radically new way, also serves to disturb the bodily images we bring to the text; but she is not engaged in a naive representational project. Indeed, if we want to deal with her work's representational challenge, we have to direct her full textuality, not merely her most scandalous moments, toward the physical body we may think we know apart from language. Meagan Morris, in "A-mazing Grace: Notes on Mary Daly's Poetics," *Intervention* no. 16 (1982): 70–92, brings these issues full circle, arguing that Irigaray's "image of a woman's two open lips is not presented as a form discovered in nature which is appropriate to an existing female language, but rather as a *metaphor-addressed-to*" (p. 87). She considers Irigaray's language, in its textual specificity and rigor, as a political intervention. "In calling Irigaray's work a Rhetoric, I mean that hers is primarily a politics of *address:* adroitness, subtlety, but above all a double labour of both direct and indirect engagement with the master-thinkers of phallocracy on the one hand, and with the political and symbolic struggles of women on the other" (p. 87).

37. Monique Wittig, *The Lesbian Body* (1973), trans. David Le Vay (1975; rpt., New York: Avon, 1976), p. ix.

38. For research with important implications for the study of the struggle women writers have had with their connotative inheritance see Paula A. Treichler, "The Construction of Ambiguity in *The Awakening:* A Linguistic Analysis," in *Women and Language in Literature and Society,* ed. Sally McConnell-Ginet, Ruth Borker, and Nelly Furman (New York: Praeger, 1980), pp. 239–57, and Treichler, " 'Trapped Like a Trap In A Trap': Verbal Subversion in Dorothy Parker," *Language and Style* 13, no. 4 (1980): 46–61.

39. Jacques Derrida, *Eperons: Nietzsche's Styles* (Venice: Corboe Fiore, 1976), p. 43.

40. This last sentence clearly requires a clarifying note. "To tell feminists that they 'should' be envoys of otherness," one of my colleagues writes, "is at once to foreground the traditional view of women as other, women in a special demarcated sphere, and to require that woman, if she is to do well, must do well by staying in her sphere. What lurks behind this recommendation is the refusal to contemplate the fact that women may *not* be other, that women may actually be 'the same.' That this thought is far more fearful to (some) men than the idea

that women have a 'separate but equal' mission is hardly surprising. . . . My feminist project is precisely to insist that I am a self not an other, and to refuse to join any club that says I can join so long as I continue to play the role of outsider." In reply, I need to emphasize that although I am urging a certain discursive commitment (one with personal and social effects) I am not presuming to prescribe the essential personal identities of women. Feminist criticism may help us to recognize that we are *all* "other," that identity is only difference, never a secure and complacent sameness. The discursive commitment I urge, moreover, is one either explicit or implicit in the wide range of existing feminist writing practices. As it has been written in the last decade, otherness seems less a controlled and demarcated identity than a liberating and unpredictable discursive force. As Muriel Dimen writes, women can "transform the qualities which come from that Other place inside Culture to which we have been historically assigned. . . . The situation is dialectical: Our place, historically or culturally fashioned as other than human, is yet in the guts of each culture. A theory from within strikes at the culture as if from the outside, because we are defined as Other than it. . . . We will create change from within." "Theory From the Inside Out, or Process is Our Most Important Product," paper presented at The Second Sex—A Commemorative Conference on Feminist Theory, New York, 1979.

Feminism and Critical Theory

Gayatri Chakravorty Spivak

What has been the itinerary of my thinking during the past few years about the relationships among feminism, Marxism, psychoanalysis, and deconstruction? The issues have been of interest to many people, and the configurations of these fields continue to change. I will not engage here with the various lines of thought that have constituted this change, but will try instead to mark and reflect upon the way these developments have been inscribed in my own work. The first section of the essay is a version of a talk I gave several years ago. The second section represents a reflection on that earlier work. The third section is an intermediate moment. The fourth section inhabits something like the present.

1

I cannot speak of feminism in general. I speak of what I do as a woman within literary criticism. My own definition as a woman is very simple: it rests on the word "man" as used in the texts that provide the foundation for the corner of the literary criticism establishment that I inhabit. You might say at this point, defining the word "woman" as resting on the word "man" is a reactionary position. Should I not carve out an independent definition for myself as a woman? Here I must repeat some deconstructive lessons learned over the past decade that I often repeat. One, no rigorous definition of anything is ultimately possible, so that if one wants to, one could go on deconstructing the opposition between man and woman, and finally show that it is a binary opposition that displaces itself.[1] Therefore, "as a deconstructivist," I cannot recommend that kind of dichotomy at all, yet, I feel that definitions are necessary in order to keep us going, to allow us to take a stand. The only way that I can see myself making definitions is in a provisional and polemical one: I construct my definition as a woman not in terms of a woman's putative essence but in terms of words currently in use. "Man" is such a word in common usage. Not *a* word, but *the* word. I therefore fix my glance upon this word even as I question the enterprise of redefining the premises of any theory.

In the broadest possible sense, most critical theory in my part of the academic establishment (Lacan, Derrida, Foucault, the last Barthes) sees the text as that area of the discourse of the human sciences—in the United States called the humanities—in which the *problem* of the discourse of the human sciences is made available. Whereas in other kinds of discourses there is a move toward the final truth of a situation, literature, even within this argument, displays that the truth of a human situation *is* the itinerary of not being able to find it. In the general discourse of the humanities, there is a sort of search for solutions, whereas in literary discourse there is a playing out of the problem as the solution, if you like.

The problem of human discourse is generally seen as articulating itself in the play of, in terms of, three shifting "concepts": language, world, and consciousness. We know no world that is not organized as a language, we operate with no other consciousness but one structured as a language—languages that we cannot possess, for we are operated by those languages as well. The category of language, then, embraces the categories of world and consciousness even as it is determined by them. Strictly speaking, since we are questioning the human being's control over the production of language, the figure that will serve us better is writing, for there the absence of the producer and receiver is taken for granted. A safe figure, seemingly outside of the language-(speech)-writing opposition, is the text—a weave of knowing and not-knowing which is what knowing is. (This organizing principle—language, writing, or text—might itself be a way of holding at bay a randomness incongruent with consciousness.)

The theoreticians of textuality read Marx as a theorist of the world (history and society), as a text of the forces of labor and production-circulation-distribution, and Freud as a theorist of the self, as a text of consciousness and the unconscious. This human textuality can be seen not only *as* world and self, *as* the representation of a world in terms of a self at play with other selves and generating this representation, but also *in* the world and self, all implicated in an "intertextuality." It should be clear from this that such a concept of textuality does not mean a reduction of the world to linguistic texts, books, or a tradition composed of books, criticism in the narrow sense, and teaching.

I am not, then, speaking about Marxist or psychoanalytic criticism as a reductive enterprise which diagnoses the scenario in every book in terms of where it would fit into a Marxist or a psychoanalytical canon. To my way of thinking, the discourse of the literary text is part of a general configuration of textuality, a placing forth of the solution as the unavailability of a unified solution to a unified or homogeneous, generating or receiving, consciousness. This unavailability is often not confronted. It is dodged and the problem apparently solved, in terms perhaps of unifying concepts like "man," the universal contours of a sex-, race-, class-transcendent consciousness as the generating, generated, and receiving consciousness of the text.

I could have broached Marx and Freud more easily. I wanted to say all of the above because, in general, in the literary critical establishment here, those two are seen as reductive models. Now, although nonreductive methods are implicit in both of them, Marx and Freud do also seem to argue in terms of a mode of evidence and demonstration. They seem to bring forth evidence from the world of man or man's self, and thus prove certain kinds of truths about world and self. I would risk saying that their descriptions of world and self are based on inadequate evidence. In terms of this conviction, I would like to fix upon the idea of alienation in Marx, and the idea of normality and health in Freud.

One way of moving into Marx is in terms of use-value, exchange-value, and surplus-value. Marx's notion of use-value is that which pertains to a thing as it is directly consumed by an agent. Its exchange-value (after the emergence of the money form) does not relate to its direct fulfillment of a specific need, but is rather assessed in terms of what it can be exchanged for in either labor-power or money. In this process of abstracting through exchange, by making the worker work longer than necessary for subsistence wages or by means of labor-saving machinery, the buyer of the laborer's work gets more (in exchange) than the worker needs for his subsistence while he makes the thing.[2] This "more-worth" (in German, literally, *Mehrwert*) is surplus-value.

One could indefinitely allegorize the relationship of woman within this particular triad—use, exchange, and surplus—by suggesting that woman in the traditional social situation produces more than she is getting in terms of her subsistence, and therefore is a continual source of the production of surpluses, *for* the man who owns her, or *by* the man for the capitalist who owns *his* labor-power. Apart from the fact that the mode of production of housework is not, strictly speaking, capitalist, such an analysis is paradoxical. The contemporary woman, when she seeks financial compensation for housework, seeks the abstraction of use-value into exchange-value. The situation of the domestic workplace is not one of "pure exchange." The Marxian exigency would make us ask at least two questions: What is the use-value of unremunerated woman's work for husband or family? Is the willing insertion into the wage structure a curse or a blessing? How should we fight the idea, universally accepted by men, that wages are the only mark of value-producing work? (Not, I think, through the slogan "Housework is beautiful.") What would be the implications of denying women entry into the capitalist economy? Radical feminism can here learn a cautionary lesson from Lenin's capitulation to capitalism.

These are important questions, but they do not necessarily broaden Marxist theory from a feminist point of view. For our purpose, the idea of externalization *(EntäuBerung/VeräuBerung)* or alienation *(Entfremdung)* is of greater interest. Within the capitalist system, the labor process externalizes itself and the worker as commodities. Upon this idea of the fracturing of the human being's relationship to himself and his work as commodities rests the ethical charge of Marx's argument.[3]

I would argue that, in terms of the physical, emotional, legal, custodial, and sentimental situation of the woman's product, the child, this picture of the human relationship to production, labor, and property is incomplete. The possession of a tangible place of production in the womb situates the woman as an agent in any theory of production. Marx's dialectics of externalization-alienation followed by fetish formation is inadequate because one fundamental human relationship to a product and labor is not taken into account.[4]

This does not mean that, if the Marxian account of externalization-alienation were rewritten from a feminist perspective, the special interest of childbirth, childbearing, and childrearing would be inserted. It seems that the entire problematic of sexuality, rather than remaining caught within arguments about overt sociosexual politics, would be fully broached.

Having said this, I would reemphasize the need to interpret reproduction within a Marxian problematic.[5]

In both so-called matrilineal and patrilineal societies the legal possession of the child is an inalienable fact of the property right of the man
who "produces" the child.[6] In terms of this legal possession, the common custodial definition, that women are much more nurturing of children, might be seen as a dissimulated reactionary gesture. The man
retains legal property rights over the product of a woman's body. On
each separate occasion, the custodial decision is a sentimental questioning of man's right. The current struggle over abortion rights has foregrounded this unacknowledged agenda.

In order not simply to make an exception to man's legal right, or to
add a footnote from a feminist perspective to the Marxist text, we must
engage and correct the theory of production and alienation upon which
the Marxist text is based and with which it functions. As I suggested
above, such Marxist feminism works on an analogy with use-value,
exchange-value, and surplus-value relationships. Marx's own writings
on women and children seek to alleviate their condition in terms of a
desexualized labor force.[7] If there were the kind of rewriting that I am
proposing, it would be harder to sketch out the rules of economy and
social ethics; in fact, to an extent, deconstruction as the questioning of
essential definitions would operate if one were to see that in Marx there
is a moment of major transgression where rules for humanity and criticism of societies are based on inadequate evidence. Marx's texts, including *Capital,* presuppose an ethical theory: alienation of labor must
be undone because it undermines the agency of the subject in his work
and his property. I would like to suggest that if the nature and history of
alienation, labor, and the production of property are reexamined in
terms of women's work and childbirth, it can lead us to a reading of
Marx beyond Marx.

One way of moving into Freud is in terms of his notion of the
nature of pain as the deferment of pleasure, especially the later Freud
who wrote *Beyond the Pleasure Principle.*[8] Freud's spectacular mechanics of imagined, anticipated, and avoided pain write the subject's
history and theory, and constantly broach the never-quite-defined concept of normality: anxiety, inhibition, paranoia, schizophrenia, melan-
choly, mourning. I would like to suggest that in the womb, a tangible
place of production, there is the possibility that pain exists *within* the

concepts of normality and productivity. (This is not to sentimentalize the pain of childbirth.) The problematizing of the phenomenal identity of pleasure and unpleasure should not be operated only through the logic of repression. The opposition pleasure-pain is questioned in the physiological "normality" of woman.

If one were to look at the never-quite-defined concepts of normality and health that run through and are submerged in Freud's texts, one would have to redefine the nature of pain. Pain does not operate in the same way in men and in women. Once again, this deconstructive move will make it much harder to devise the rules.

Freud's best-known determinant of femininity is penis-envy. The most crucial text of this argument is the essay on femininity in the *New Introductory Lectures*.[9] There, Freud begins to argue that the little girl is a little boy before she discovers sex. As Luce Irigaray and others have shown, Freud does not take the womb into account.[10] Our mood, since we carry the womb as well as being carried by it, should be corrective.[11] We might chart the itinerary of womb-envy in the production of a theory of consciousness: the idea of the womb as a place of production is avoided both in Marx and in Freud. (There are exceptions to such a generalization, especially among American neo-Freudians such as Erich Fromm. I am speaking here about invariable presuppositions, even among such exceptions.) In Freud, the genital stage is preeminently phallic, not clitoral or vaginal. This particular gap in Freud is significant. The hysteron remains the place which constitutes only the text of hysteria. Everywhere there is a nonconfrontation of the idea of the womb as a workshop, except to produce a surrogate penis. Our task in rewriting the text of Freud is not so much to declare the idea of penis-envy rejectable, but to make available the idea of a womb-envy as something that interacts with the idea of penis-envy to determine human sexuality and the production of society.[12]

These are some questions that may be asked of the Freudian and Marxist "grounds" or theoretical "bases" that operate our ideas of world and self. We might want to ignore them altogether and say that the business of literary criticism is neither your gender (such a suggestion seems hopelessly dated) nor the theories of revolution or psychoanalysis. Criticism must remain resolutely neuter and practical. One should not mistake the grounds out of which the ideas of world and self are produced with the business of the appreciation of the literary text. If one looks closely, one will see that, whether one diagnoses the names or not, certain kinds of thoughts are presupposed by the notions of world and consciousness of the most "practical" critic. Part of the feminist enterprise might well be to provide "evidence" so that these great male texts do not become great adversaries, or models from whom we take our ideas and then revise or reassess them. These texts must be rewritten so that there is new material for the grasping of the production and determination of literature within the general production and determination of consciousness and society. After all, the people who produce literature, male and female, are also moved by general ideas of world and consciousness to which they cannot give a name.

If we continue to work in this way, the common currency of the understanding of society will change. I think that kind of change, the coining of new money, is necessary. I certainly believe that such work is supplemented by research into women's writing and research into the conditions of women in the past. The kind of work I have outlined would infiltrate the male academy and redo the terms of our understanding of the context and substance of literature as part of the human enterprise.

2

What seems missing in these earlier remarks is the dimension of race. Today I would see my work as the developing of a reading method that is sensitive to gender, race, and class. The earlier remarks would apply indirectly to the development of class-sensitive and directly to the development of gender-sensitive readings.

In the matter of race-sensitive analyses, the chief problem of American feminist criticism is its identification of racism as such with the constitution of racism in America. Thus, today I see the object of investigation to be not only the history of "Third World Women" or their testimony but also the production, through the great European theories, often by way of literature, of the colonial object. As long as American feminists understand "history" as a positivistic empiricism that scorns "theory" and therefore remains ignorant of its own, the "Third World" as its object of study will remain constituted by those hegemonic First World intellectual practices.[13]

My attitude toward Freud today involves a broader critique of his entire project. It is a critique not only of Freud's masculism but of nuclear-familial psychoanalytical theories of the constitution of the sexed subject. Such a critique extends to alternative scenarios to Freud that keep to the nuclear parent-child model, as it does to the offer of Greek mythical alternatives to Oedipus as the regulative type-case of the model itself, as it does to the romantic notion that an extended family, especially a community of women, would necessarily cure the ills of the nuclear family. My concern with the production of colonial discourse thus touches my critique of Freud as well as most Western feminist challenges to Freud. The extended or corporate family is a socioeconomic (indeed, on occasion political) organization which makes sexual constitution irreducibly complicit with historical and political economy.[14] To learn to read that way is to understand that the literature of the world, itself accessible only to a few, is not tied by the concrete universals of a network of archetypes—a theory that was entailed by the consolidation of a political excuse—but by a textuality of material-ideological-psycho-sexual production. This articulation sharpens a general presupposition of my earlier remarks.

Pursuing these considerations, I proposed recently an analysis of "the discourse of the clitoris."[15] The reactions to that proposal have been interesting in the context I discuss above. A certain response from American lesbian feminists can be represented by the following quotation: "In this open-ended definition of phallus/semination as organically *omnipotent* the only recourse is to name the clitoris as orgasmically phallic and to call the uterus the reproductive extension of the phallus. . . . You must stop thinking of yourself privileged as a heterosexual woman."[16] Because of its physiologistic orientation, the first part of this objection sees my naming of the clitoris as a repetition of Freud's situating of it as a "little penis." To the second part of the objection I customarily respond: "You're right, and one cannot know how far one succeeds. Yet, the effort to put First World lesbianism in its place is not necessarily reducible to pride in female heterosexuality." Other uses of my suggestion, both supportive and adverse, have also reduced the discourse of the clitoris to a physiological fantasy. In the interest of the broadening scope of my critique, I should like to reemphasize that the clitoris, even as I acknowledge and honor its irreducible physiological effect, is, in this reading, also a short-hand for women's excess in all areas of production and practice, an excess which must be brought under control to keep business going as usual.[17]

My attitude toward Marxism now recognizes the historical antagonism between Marxism and feminism, *on both sides*. Hardcore Marxism at best dismisses and at worst patronizes the importance of women's struggle. On the other hand, not only the history of European feminism in its opposition to Bolshevik and Social Democrat women, but the conflict between the suffrage movement and the union movement in this country must be taken into account. This historical problem will not be solved by saying that we need more than an analysis of capitalism to understand male dominance, or that the sexual division of labor as the primary determinant is already given in the texts of Marx. I prefer the work that sees that the "essential truth" of Marxism or feminism cannot be separated from its history. My present work relates this to the ideological development of the theory of the imagination in the eighteenth, nineteenth, and twentieth centuries. I am interested in class analysis of families as it is being practiced by, among others, Eleanor Fox-Genovese, Heidi Hartman, Nancy Hartsock, and Annette Kuhn. I am myself bent upon reading the text of international feminism as operated by the production and realization of surplus-value. My own earlier concern with the specific theme of reproductive (non) alienation seems to me today to be heavily enough touched by a nuclear-familial hysterocentrism to be open to the critique of psychoanalytic feminism that I suggest above.

On the other hand, if sexual reproduction is seen as the production of a product by an irreducibly determinate means (conjunction of semination-ovulation), in an irreducibly determinate mode (heterogeneous combination of domestic and politico-civil economy), entailing a minimal variation of social relations, then two original Marxist categories would be put into question: use-value as the measure of communist production and absolute surplus-value as the motor of primitive (capitalist) accumulation. For the first: the child, although not a commodity, is also not produced for immediate and adequate consumption or direct exchange. For the second: the premise that the difference between subsistence-wage and labor-power's potential of production is the origin of original accumulation can only be advanced if reproduction is seen as identical with subsistence; in fact, the reproduction and maintenance of children would make heterogeneous the original calculation in terms of something like the slow displacement of value from fixed capital to commodity.[18] These insights take the critique of wage-labor in unexpected directions.

When I earlier touched upon the relationship between wage-theory and "women's work," I had not yet read the autonomist arguments about wage and work as best developed in the work of Antonio Negri.[19] Exigencies of work and limitations of scholarship and experience permitting, I would like next to study the relationship between domestic and political economies in order to establish the subversive power of "women's work" in models in the construction of a "revolutionary subject." Negri sees this possibility in the inevitable consumerism that socialized capitalism must nurture. Commodity consumption, even as it realizes surplus-value as profit, does not itself produce value and therefore persistently exacerbates crisis.[20] It is through reversing and displacing this tendency within consumerism, Negri suggests, that the "revolutionary subject" can be released. Mainstream English Marxists sometimes think that such an upheaval can be brought about by political interventionist teaching of literature. Some French intellectuals think this tendency is inherent in the "pagan tradition," which pluralizes the now-defunct narratives of social justice still endorsed by traditional Marxists in a post-industrial world. In contrast, I now argue as follows:

> It is women's work that has continuously survived within not only the varieties of capitalism but other historical and geographical modes of production. The economic, political, ideological, and legal heterogeneity of the relationship between the definitive mode of production and race- and class-differentiated women's and wives' work is abundantly recorded. . . . Rather than the refusal to work of the freed Jamaican slaves in 1834, which is cited by Marx as the only example of zero-work, quickly recuperated by imperialist maneuvers, it is the long history of women's work which is a sustained example of zero-work: work not only outside of wage-work, but, *in one way or another*, "outside" of the definitive modes of production. The displacement required here is a transvaluation, an uncatastrophic *im*-plosion of the search for validation via the circuit of productivity. Rather than a miniaturized and thus controlled metaphor for civil society and the state, the power of the *oikos*, domestic economy, can be used as the model of the foreign body unwittingly nurtured by the *polis*.[21]

With psychoanalytic feminism, then, an invocation of history and politics leads us back to the place of psychoanalysis in colonialism.

With Marxist feminism, an invocation of the economic text foregrounds the operations of the New Imperialism. The discourse of race has come to claim its importance in this way in my work.

I am still moved by the reversal-displacement morphology of deconstruction, crediting the asymmetry of the "interest" of the historical moment. Investigating the hidden ethico-political agenda of differentiations constitutive of knowledge and judgment interests me even more. It is also the deconstructive view that keeps me resisting an essentialist freezing of the concepts of gender, race, and class. I look rather at the repeated agenda of the situational production of those concepts and our complicity in such a production. This aspect of deconstruction will not allow the establishment of a hegemonic "global theory" of feminism.

Over the last few years, however, I have also begun to see that, rather than deconstruction simply opening a way for feminists, the figure and discourse of women opened the way for Derrida as well. His incipient discourse of woman surfaced in *Spurs* (first published as "La Question du Style" in 1975), which also articulates the thematics of "interest" crucial to political deconstruction.[22] This study marks his move from the critical deconstruction of phallocentrism to "affirmative" deconstruction (Derrida's phrase). It is at this point that Derrida's work seems to become less interesting for Marxism.[23] The early Derrida can certainly be shown to be useful for feminist practice, but why is it that, when he writes under the sign of woman, as it were, that his work becomes solipsistic and marginal? What is it in the history of that sign that allows this to happen? I will hold this question until the end of this essay.

3

In 1979–80, concerns of race and class were beginning to invade my mind. What follows is in some sense a check list of quotations from Margaret Drabble's *The Waterfall* that shows the uneasy presence of those concerns.[24] Reading literature "well" is in itself a questionable good and can indeed be sometimes productive of harm and "aesthetic" apathy within its ideological framing. My suggestion is to use literature, with a feminist perspective, as a "nonexpository" theory of practice.

Drabble has a version of "the best education" in the Western world: a First Class in English from Oxford. The tradition of academic radicalism in England is strong. Drabble was at Oxford when the prestigious journal *New Left Review* was being organized. I am not adverse to a bit of simple biographical detail: I began to re-read *The Waterfall* with these things in mind as well as the worrying thoughts about sex, race, and class.

Like many woman writers, Drabble creates an extreme situation, to answer, presumably, the question "Why does love happen?" In place of the mainstream objectification and idolization of the loved person, she situates her protagonist, Jane, in the most inaccessible privacy—at the moment of birthing, alone by choice. Lucy, her cousin, and James, Lucy's husband, take turns watching over her in the empty house as she regains her strength. *The Waterfall* is the story of Jane's love affair with James. In place of a legalized or merely possessive ardor toward the product of his own body, Drabble gives to James the problem of relating to the birthing woman through the birth of "another man's child." Jane looks and smells dreadful. There is blood and sweat on the crumpled sheets. And yet "love" happens. Drabble slows language down excruciatingly as Jane records how, wonders why. It is possible that Drabble is taking up the challenge of feminine "passivity" and making it the tool of analytic strength. Many answers emerge. I will quote two, to show how provisional and self-suspending Jane can be:

> I loved him inevitably, of necessity. Anyone could have fore-seen it, given those facts: a lonely woman, in an empty world. Surely I would have loved anyone who might have shown me kindness. . . . But of course it's not true, it could not have been anyone else. . . . I know that it was not inevitable: it was a miracle. . . . What I deserved was what I had made: solitude, or a repetition of pain. What I received was grace. Grace and miracles. I don't much care for my terminology. Though at least it lacks that most disastrous concept, the concept of free will. Perhaps I could make a religion that denied free will, that placed God in his true place, arbitrary, carelessly kind, idly malicious, intermittently attentive, and himself subject, as Zeus was, to necessity. Necessity is my God. Necessity lays with me when James did [pp. 49–50].

And, in another place, the "opposite" answer—random contingencies:

> I loved James because he was what I had never had: because he belonged to my cousin: because he was kind to his own child: because he looked unkind: because I saw his naked

wrists against a striped tea towel once, seven years ago. Because he addressed me an intimate question upon a beach on
Christmas Day. Because he helped himself to a drink when I
did not dare to accept the offer of one. Because he was not
serious, because his parents lived in South Kensington and
were mysteriously depraved. Ah, perfect love. For these reasons, was it, that I lay there, drowned was it, drowned or
stranded, waiting for him, waiting to die and drown there, in
the oceans of our flowing bodies, in the white sea of that
strange familiar bed [p. 67].

If the argument for necessity is arrived at by slippery happenstance from
thought to thought, each item on this list of contingencies has a plausibility far from random.

She considers the problem of making women rivals in terms of the
man who possesses them. There is a peculiar agreement between Lucy
and herself before the affair begins:

I wonder why people marry? Lucy continued, in a tone of such
academic flatness that the topic seemed robbed of any danger.
I don't know, said Jane, with equal calm. . . . So arbitrary,
really, said Lucy, spreading butter on the toast. It would be
nice, said Jane, to think there were reasons. . . . Do you think
so? said Lucy. Sometimes I prefer to think we are victims. . . .
If there were a reason, said Jane, one would be all the more a
victim. She paused, thought, ate a mouthful of the toast. I am
wounded, therefore I bleed. I am human, therefore I suffer.
Those aren't reasons you're describing, said Lucy. . . . And
from upstairs the baby's cry reached them—thin, wailing, des-
perate. Hearing it, the two women looked at each other, and
for some reason smiled [pp. 26–27].

This, of course, is no overt agreement, but simply a hint that the "reason" for female bonding has something to do with a baby's cry. For
example, Jane records her own deliberate part in deceiving Lucy this
way: "I forgot Lucy. I did not think of her—or only occasionally, lying
awake at night *as the baby cried,* I would think of her, with pangs of
irrelevant inquiry, pangs endured not by me and in me, but at a distance, pangs as sorrowful and irrelevant as another person's pain"
[p. 48; italics mine].

Jane records inconclusively her gut reaction to the supposed natural connection between parent and child: "Blood is blood, and it is not good enough to say that children are for the motherly, as Brecht said, for there are many ways of unmothering a woman, or unfathering a man. . . . And yet, how can I deny that it gave me pleasure to see James hold her in his arms for me? The man I loved and the child to whom I had given birth" [p. 48].

The loose ending of the book also makes Jane's story an extreme case. Is this love going to last, prove itself to be "true," and bring Jane security and Jane and James happiness? Or is it resolutely "liberated," overprotesting its own impermanence, and thus falling in with the times? Neither. The melodramatic and satisfactory ending, the accident which might have killed James, does not in fact do so. It merely reveals all to Lucy, does not end the book, and reduces all to a humdrum kind of double life.

These are not bad answers: necessity if all fails, or perhaps random contingency; an attempt not to rivalize women; blood bonds between mothers and daughters; love free of social security. The problem for a reader like me is that the entire questioning is carried on in what I can only see as a privileged atmosphere. I am not saying, of course, that Jane is Drabble (although that, too, is true in a complicated way). I am saying that Drabble considers the story of so privileged a woman the most worth telling. Not the well-bred lady of pulp fiction, but an impossible princess who mentions in one passing sentence toward the beginning of the book that her poems are read on the BBC.

It is not that Drabble does not want to rest her probing and sensitive fingers on the problem of class, if not race. The account of Jane's family's class prejudice is incisively told. Her father is headmaster of a public school.

> There was one child I shall always remember, a small thin child . . . whose father, he proudly told us, was standing as Labour Candidate for a hopeless seat in an imminent General Election. My father teased him unmercifully, asking questions that the poor child could not begin to answer, making elaborate and hideous semantic jokes about the fruits of labour, throwing in familiar references to prominent Tories that were quite wasted on such . . . tender ears; and the poor child sat there, staring at his roast beef . . . turning redder and redder, and trying, pathetically, sycophantically, to smile. I hated my father at that instant [pp. 56–57].

Yet Drabble's Jane is made to share the lightest touch of her parents' prejudice. The part I have elided is a mocking reference to the child's large red ears. For her the most important issue remains sexual deprivation, sexual choice. *The Waterfall,* the name of a card trick, is also the name of Jane's orgasms, James's gift to her.

But perhaps Drabble is ironic when she creates so class-bound and yet so analytic a Jane? It is a possibility, of course, but Jane's identification with the author of the narrative makes this doubtful. If there is irony to be generated here, it must come, as they say, from "outside the book."

Rather than imposing my irony, I attempt to find the figure of Jane as narrator helpful. Drabble manipulates her to examine the conditions of production and determination of microstructural heterosexual attitudes within her chosen enclosure. This enclosure is important because it is from here that rules come. Jane is made to realize that there are no fixed new rules in the book, not as yet. First World feminists are up against that fact, every day. This should not become an excuse but should remain a delicate responsibility: "If I need a morality, I will create one: a new ladder, a new virtue. If I need to understand what I am doing, if I cannot act without my own approbation—and I must act, I have changed, I am no longer capable of inaction—then I will invent a morality that condones me. Though by doing so, I risk condemning all that I have been" [pp. 52–53].

If the cautions of deconstruction are heeded—the contingency that the desire to "understand" and "change" are as much symptomatic as they are revolutionary—merely to fill in the void with rules will spoil the case again, for women as for human beings. We must strive moment by moment to practice a taxonomy of different forms of understanding, different forms of change, dependent perhaps upon resemblance and seeming substitutability—figuration—rather than on the self-identical category of truth:

> Because it's obvious that I haven't told the truth, about myself and James. How could I? Why, more significantly, should I? . . . Of the truth, I haven't told enough. I flinched at the conclusion and can even see in my hesitance a virtue: it is dishonest, it is inartistic, but it is a virtue, such discretion, in the moral world of love. . . . The names of qualities are interchangeable: vice, virtue: redemption, corruption: courage, weakness: and hence the confusion of abstraction, the prolif-

eration of aphorism and paradox. In the human world, perhaps there are merely likenesses. . . . The qualities, they
depended on the supposed true end of life. . . . Salvation,
damnation. . . . I do not know which of these two James
represented. Hysterical terms, maybe: religious terms, yet
again. But then life is a serious matter, and it is not merely
hysteria that acknowledges this fact: for men as well as
women have been known to acknowledge it. I must make an
effort to comprehend it. I will take it all to pieces. I will resolve
it to parts, and then I will put it together again, I will reconstitute it in a form that I can accept, a fictitious form [pp. 46, 51,
52].

The categories by which one understands, the qualities of plus and
minus, are revealing themselves as arbitrary, situational. Drabble's
Jane's way out—to resolve and reconstitute life into an acceptable
fictional *form* that need not, perhaps, worry too much about the
categorical problems—seems, by itself, a classical privileging of the
aesthetic, for Drabble hints at the limits of self-interpretation through a
gesture that is accessible to the humanist academic. Within a fictional
form, she confides that the exigencies of a narrative's unity had not
allowed her to report the whole truth. She then changes from the third
person to first.

What can a literary critic do with this? Notice that the move is
absurdity twice compounded, since the discourse reflecting the constraints of fiction-making goes on then to fabricate another fictive text.
Notice further that the narrator who tells us about the impossibility of
truth-in-fiction—the classic privilege of metaphor—is a metaphor as
well.[25]

I should choose a simpler course. I should acknowledge this global
dismissal of any narrative speculation about the nature of truth and
then dismiss it in turn, since it might unwittingly suggest that there is
somewhere a way of speaking about truth in "truthful" language, that a
speaker can somewhere get rid of the structural unconscious and speak
without role playing. Having taken note of the frame, I will thus explain
the point Jane is making here and relate it to what, I suppose, the
critical view above would call "the anthropomorphic world": when one
takes a rational or aesthetic distance from oneself one gives oneself up
to the conveniently classifying macrostructures, a move dramatized by
Drabble's third-person narrator. By contrast, when one involves oneself

in the microstructural moments of practice that make possible and undermine every macrostructural theory, one falls, as it were, into the deep waters of a first person who recognizes the limits of understanding and change, indeed the precarious necessity of the micro- macro-opposition, yet is bound not to give up.

The risks of first-person narrative prove too much for Drabble's fictive Jane. She wants to plot her narrative in terms of the paradoxical category—"pure corrupted love"—that allows her to *make* a fiction rather than try, *in* fiction, to report on the unreliability of categories: "I want to get back to that schizoid third-person dialogue. I've one or two more sordid conditions to describe, and then I can get back there to that isolated world of pure corrupted love" [p. 130]. To return us to the detached and macrostructural third person narrative after exposing its limits could be an aesthetic allegory of deconstructive practice.

Thus Drabble fills the void of the female consciousness with meticulous and helpful articulation, though she seems thwarted in any serious presentation of the problems of race and class, and of the marginality of sex. She engages in that microstructural dystopia, the sexual situation in extremis, that begins to seem more and more a part of women's fiction. Even within those limitations, our motto cannot be Jane's "I prefer to suffer, I think"—the privatist cry of heroic liberal women; it might rather be the lesson of the scene of writing of *The Waterfall:* to return to the third person with its grounds mined under.

4

It is no doubt useful to decipher women's fiction in this way for feminist students and colleagues in American academia. I am less patient with literary texts today, even those produced by women. We must of course remind ourselves, our positivist feminist colleagues in charge of creating the discipline of women's studies, and our anxious students, that essentialism is a trap. It seems more important to learn to understand that the world's women do not all relate to the privileging of essence, especially through "fiction," or "literature," in quite the same way.

In Seoul, South Korea, in March 1982, 237 woman workers in a factory owned by Control Data, a Minnesota-based multinational corporation, struck over a demand for a wage raise. Six union leaders were dismissed and imprisoned. In July, the women took hostage two visiting

U.S. vice-presidents, demanding reinstatement of the union leaders. Control Data's main office was willing to release the women; the Korean government was reluctant. On July 16, the Korean male workers at the factory beat up the female workers and ended the dispute. Many of the women were injured and two suffered miscarriages.

To grasp this narrative's overdeterminations (the many telescoped lines—sometimes noncoherent, often contradictory, perhaps discontinuous—that allow us to determine the reference point of a single "event" or cluster of "events") would require a complicated analysis.[26] Here, too, I will give no more than a checklist of the overdeterminants. In the earlier stages of industrial capitalism, the colonies provided the raw materials so that the colonizing countries could develop their manufacturing industrial base. Indigenous production was thus crippled or destroyed. To minimize circulation time, industrial capitalism needed to establish due process, and such civilizing instruments as railways, postal services, and a uniformly graded system of education. This, together with the labor movements in the First World and the mechanisms of the welfare state, slowly made it imperative that manufacturing itself be carried out on the soil of the Third World, where labor can make many fewer demands, and the governments are mortgaged. In the case of the telecommunications industry, making old machinery obsolete at a more rapid pace than it takes to absorb its value in the commodity, this is particularly practical.

The incident that I recounted above, not at all uncommon in the multinational arena, complicates our assumptions about women's entry into the age of computers and the modernization of "women in development," especially in terms of our daily theorizing and practice. It should make us confront the discontinuities and contradictions in our assumptions about women's freedom to work outside the house, and the sustaining virtues of the working-class family. The fact that these workers were women was not merely because, like those Belgian lacemakers, oriental women have small and supple fingers. It is also because they are the true army of surplus labor. No one, including their men, will agitate for an adequate wage. In a two-job family, the man saves face if the woman makes less, even for a comparable job.

Does this make Third World men more sexist than David Rockefeller? The nativist argument that says "do not question Third World mores" is of course unexamined imperialism. There *is* something like an answer, which makes problematic the grounds upon which we base our own intellectual and political activities. No one can deny the dynamism and civilizing power of socialized capital. The irreducible search for greater production of surplus-value (dissimulated as, simply, "productivity") through technological advancement; the corresponding necessity to train a consumer who will need what is produced and thus help realize surplus-value as profit; the tax breaks associated with supporting humanist ideology through "corporate philanthropy"; all conspire to "civilize." These motives do not exist on a large scale in a comprador economy like that of South Korea, which is neither the necessary recipient nor the agent of socialized capital. The surplus-value is realized elsewhere. The nuclear family does not have a transcendent enobling power. The fact that ideology and the ideology of marriage have developed in the West since the English revolution of the seventeenth century has something like a relationship to the rise of meritocratic individualism.[27]

These possibilities overdetermine any generalization about universal parenting based on American, Western European, or laundered anthropological speculation.

Socialized capital kills by remote control. In this case, too, the American managers watched while the South Korean men decimated their women. The managers denied charges. One remark made by a member of Control Data management, as reported in *Multinational Monitor,* seemed symptomatic in its self-protective cruelty: "Although 'it's true' Chae lost her baby, 'this is not the first miscarriage she's had. She's had two before this.'"[28] However active in the production of civilization as a by-product, socialized capital has not moved far from the presuppositions of a slave mode of production. "In Roman theory, the agricultural slave was designated an *instrumentum vocale,* the speaking tool, one grade away from the livestock that constituted an *instrumentum semi-vocale,* and two from the implement which was an *instrumentum mutum.*"[29]

One of Control Data's radio commercials speaks of how its computers open the door to knowledge, at home or in the workplace, for men and women alike. The acronym of this computer system is PLATO. One might speculate that this noble name helps to dissimulate a quantitative and formula-permutational vision of knowledge as an instrument of efficiency and exploitation with an aura of the unique and subject-expressive wisdom at the very root of "democracy." The undoubted historical-symbolic value of the acronym PLATO shares in the effacement of class-history that is the project of "civilization" as such: "The slave mode of production which underlay Athenian civilization necessarily found its most pristine ideological expression in the privileged social stratum of the city, whose intellectual heights its surplus labour in the silent depths below the *polis* made possible."[30]

"Why is it," I asked above, "that when Derrida writes under the sign of woman his work becomes solipsistic and marginal?"

His discovery of the figure of woman is in terms of a critique of propriation—proper-ing, as in the proper name (patronymic) or property.[31] Suffice it to say here that, by thus differentiating himself from the phallocentric tradition under the aegis of a(n idealized) woman who is the "sign" of the indeterminate, of that which has im-propriety as its property, Derrida cannot think that the sign "woman" is indeterminate by virtue of its access to the tyranny of the text of the proper. It is this tyranny of the "proper"—in the sense of that which produces both property and the proper name of the patronymic—that I have called the suppression of the clitoris, and that the news item about Control Data illustrates.[32]

Derrida has written a magically orchestrated book—*La carte postale*—on philosophy as telecommunication (Control Data's business) using an absent, unnamed, and sexually indeterminate woman (Control Data's victim) as a vehicle, to reinterpret the relationship between Socrates and Plato (Control Data's acronym) taking it through Freud and beyond. The determination of that book is a parable of my argument. Here deconstruction becomes complicit with an essentialist bourgeois feminism. The following paragraph appeared recently in *Ms:* "Control Data is among those enlightened corporations that offer social-service leaves. . . . Kit Ketchum, former treasurer of Minnesota NOW, applied for and got a full year with pay to work at NOW's national office in Washington, D.C. She writes: 'I commend Control Data for their commitment to employing and promoting women. . . .' Why not suggest this to your employer?"[33] Bourgeois feminism, because of a blindness to the *multi*national theater, dissimulated by "clean" national practice and fostered by the dominant ideology, can participate in the tyranny of the proper and see in Control Data an extender of the Platonic mandate to women in general.

The dissimulation of political economy is in and by ideology. What is at work and can be used in that operation is at least the ideology of nation-states, nationalism, national liberation, ethnicity, and religion.

Feminism lives in the master-text as well as in the pores. It is not the determinant of the last instance. I think less easily of "changing the world" than in the past. I teach a small number of the holders of the can(n)on, male or female, feminist or masculist, how to read their own texts, as best I can.

Notes

1. For an explanation of this aspect of deconstruction, see Gayatri Chakravorty Spivak, "Translator's Preface" to Jacques Derrida, *Of Grammatology* (Baltimore: Johns Hopkins University Press, 1976).

2. It seems appropriate to note, by using a masculine pronoun, that Marx's standard worker is male.

3. I am not suggesting this by way of what Harry Braverman describes as "that favorite hobby horse of recent years which has been taken from Marx without the least understanding of its significance" in *Labor and Monopoly Capital: the Degradation of Work in the Twentieth Century* (New York and London: Monthly Review Press, 1974, pp. 27, 28). Simply put, alienation in Hegel is that structural emergence of negation which allows a thing to sublate itself. The worker's alienation from the product of his labor under capitalism is a particular case of alienation. Marx does not question its specifically *philosophical* justice. The revolutionary upheaval of this philosophical or morphological justice is, strictly speaking, also a harnessing of the principle of alienation, the negation of a negation. It is a mark of the individualistic ideology of liberalism that it understands alienation as *only* the pathetic predicament of the oppressed worker.

4. In this connection, we should note the metaphors of sexuality in *Capital*.

5. I remember with pleasure my encounter, at the initial presentation of this paper, with Mary O'Brien, who said she was working on precisely this issue, and who later produced the excellent book *The Politics of Reproduction* (London: Routledge and Kegan Paul, 1981). I should mention here that the suggestion that mother and daughter have "the same body" and therefore the female child experiences what amounts to an unalienated pre-Oedipality argues from an individualist-pathetic view of alienation and locates as *discovery* the essentialist *presuppositions* about the sexed body's identity. This reversal of Freud remains also a legitimation.

6. See Jack Goody, *Production and Reproduction: A Comparative Study of the Domestic Domain* (Cambridge: Cambridge University Press, 1976), and Maurice Godelier, "The Origins of Male Domination," *New Left Review* 127 (May/June 1981): 3–17.

7. Collected in *Karl Marx on Education, Women, and Children* (New York: Viking Press, 1977).

8. No feminist reading of this text is now complete without Jacques Derrida's "Spéculer—sur Freud," *La Carte postale: de Socrate à Freud et au-delà* (Paris: Aubier-Flammarion, 1980).

9. *The Standard Edition of the Complete Psychological Works of Sigmund Freud,* trans. James Strachey, et al. (London: Hogarth Press, 1964), vol. 22.

10. Luce Irigaray, "La tâche aveugle d'un vieux rêve de symmétrie," in *Speculum de l'autre femme* (Paris: Minuit, 1974).

11. I have moved, as I explain later, from womb-envy, still bound to the closed circle of coupling, to the suppression of the clitoris. The mediating moment would be the appropriation of the vagina, as in Derrida (see Gayatri Chakravorty Spivak, "Displacement and the Discourse of Women," in Mark Krupnick, ed., *Displacement: Derrida and After* (Bloomington: Indiana University Press, 1983).

12. One way to develop notions of womb-envy would be in speculation about a female fetish. If, by way of rather obvious historico-sexual determinations, the typical male fetish can be said to be the phallus, given to and taken away from the mother (Freud, "Fetishism," *Standard Edition,* trans. James Strachey, et al., vol. 21), then, the female imagination in search of a name from a revered sector of masculist culture might well fabricate a fetish that would operate the giving and taking away of a womb to a father. I have read Mary Shelley's *Frankenstein* in this way. The play between such a gesture and the Kantian socio-ethical framework of the novel makes it exemplary of the ideology of moral and practical imagination in the Western European literature of the nineteenth century. See Gayatri Chakravorty Spivak, "Feminism and a Critique of Imperialism," forthcoming in *Critical Inquiry.*

13. As I have repeatedly insisted, the limits of hegemonic ideology are larger than so-called individual consciousness and personal goodwill. Gayatri Chakravorty Spivak, "The Politics of Interpretations: A Response," *Critical Inquiry* 9, no. 1 (September 1982); "A Response to Annette Kolodny," forthcoming in *Signs.*

14. This critique should be distinguished from that of Gilles Deleuze and Felix Guattari, *Anti-Oedipus: Capitalism and Schizophrenia,* trans. Robert Hurley, et al. (New York: Viking Press, 1977), with which I am in general agreement. Those authors insist that the family-romance should be seen as inscribed within politico-economic domination and exploitation. My argument is that the family romance-effect should be situated within a larger familial formation.

15. "French Feminism in an International Frame," *Yale French Studies* 62 (1981).

16. Pat Rezabek, unpublished letter.

17. What in man exceeds the closed circle of coupling in sexual reproduction is the entire "public domain."

18. I understand Lise Vogel is currently developing this analysis. One could analogize directly, for example, with a passage such as Karl Marx, *Grun-*

drisse: Foundations of the Critique of Political Economy, trans. Martin Nicolaus (New York: Vintage Books, 1973), p. 710.

19. Antonio Negri, *Marx Beyond Marx,* trans. Harry Cleaver, et al. (New York: J. F. Bergen, 1984). For another perspective on a similar argument, see Jacques Donzelot, "Pleasure in Work," *I & C* 9 (Winter 1981–82).

20. An excellent elucidation of this mechanism is to be found in James O'Connor, "The Meaning of Crisis," *International Journal of Urban and Regional Research* 5, no. 3 (1981): 317–29.

21. Jean-Francois Lyotard, *Instructions païens* (Paris: Union générale d'éditions, 1978). Tony Bennett, *Formalism and Marxism* (London: Methuen, 1979), p. 145 and passim. Marx, *Grundrisse,* p. 326. The self-citation is from "Woman in Derrida," unpublished lecture, School of Criticism and Theory, Northwestern University, July 6, 1982.

22. See Gayatri Chakravorty Spivak, "Love Me, Love My Ombre, Elle," *Diacritics* (Winter 1984); pp. 19–36.

23. Michael Ryan, *Marxism and Deconstruction: A Critical Articulation* (Baltimore: Johns Hopkins University Press, 1982), p. xiv.

24. Margaret Drabble, *The Waterfall* (Harmondsworth: Penguin, 1971). Subsequent references are included in the text. Part of this reading has appeared in a slightly different form in *Union Seminary Quarterly Review* 35 (Fall–Winter 1979–80): 15–34.

25. As in Paul de Man's analysis of Proust in *Allegories of Reading: Figural Language in Rousseau, Nietzsche, Rilke, and Proust* (New Haven: Yale University Press, 1979), p. 18.

26. For definitions of "overdetermination," see Freud, *Standard Edition,* trans. James Strachey, et al., vol. 4, pp. 279–304; Louis Althusser, *For Marx,* trans. Ben Brewster (New York: Vintage Books, 1970), pp. 89–128.

27. See Gayatri Chakravorty Spivak, response, "Independent India: Women's India," forthcoming in a collection edited by Dilip Basu.

28. "Was Headquarters Responsible? Women Beat Up at Control Data, Korea," *Multinational Monitor* 3, no. 10 (September 1982): 16.

29. Perry Anderson, *Passages from Antiquity to Feudalism* (London: Verso Editions, 1978), pp. 24–25.

30. Ibid., pp. 39–40.

31. Spivak, "Love Me, Love My Ombre, Elle."

32. I have already made the point that "clitoris" here is not meant in a physiological sense alone. I had initially proposed it as the reinscription of a certain physiological emphasis on the clitoris in some varieties of French feminism. I use it as a name (close to a metonym) for women in excess of coupling-mothering. When this excess is in competition in the public domain, it is suppressed in one way or another. I can do no better than refer to the very end of my earlier essay, where I devise a list that makes the scope of the metonym explicit. "French Feminism," p. 184.

33. *Ms.* 10, no. 11 (May 1982): 30. In this connection, it is interesting to note how so gifted an educator as Jane Addams misjudged nascent socialized

capital. She was wrong, of course, about the impartiality of commerce: "In a certain sense commercialism itself, at least in its larger aspect, tends to educate the working man better than organized education does. Its interests are certainly world-wide and democratic, while it is absolutely undiscriminating as to country and creed, coming into contact with all climes and races. If this aspect of commercialism were utilized, it would in a measure counterbalance the tendency which results from the subdivision of labor" (*Democracy and Social Ethics*, Cambridge, Mass.: Harvard University Press, 1964), p. 216.

The Maturing of Chicana Poetry:
The Quiet Revolution of the 1980s

Tey Diana Rebolledo

Until the Chicano Renaissance of the 1960s, Mexican American women who were writing were almost always marginalized. Some have called it a heritage of silence. During the 1970s Chicana writers gradually began to assert their voices, if not always in mainstream American literature.[1] Some Chicana writers writing in the 1970s have been recognized, published, and circulated in journals such as *The Bilingual Review* and the *Revista Chicano-Riqueña*. Many women self-published or published in small presses: Angela de Hoyos with M. and A. Press, and Margarita Cota-Cárdenas with Scorpion Press are some well known examples.[2] Nevertheless, other fine poetry was scattered in literary journals and newspapers or published in chap books and was hard to find except in some Chicano Studies libraries. The net effect of the lack of publishing and distribution was that while some Chicana writers were fairly well known in the West and Southwest, most were writing in relative obscurity and were certainly unknown and unreviewed by mainstream presses and writers. Thus while *Chicano* writers were enjoying the flowering and acknowledgment of their writing, the women continued to write and publish where they could. Even in the early 1980s, Chicana poetry was referred to by some as "adobe poetry" or "tortilla poetry," alluding to early poems about the men making revolution while the women made coffee and prepared tortillas in the kitchen. "You Cramp My Style, Baby," by Lorna Dee Cervantes is an early example of the anger and bitterness felt by Chicana writers as they felt used and abused by their men.

143

> You cramp my style, baby
> when you roll on top of me
> shouting, "Viva La Raza"
> at the top of your prick.[3]

Patronized, "You 'mija' 'mija'/'mija' me/until I can scream," and called a traitor, "Come on Malinche, gimme some more!" the Chicanas felt at the same time oppressed and neglected on all fronts.[4] They were particularly ignored by publishers, and critical inquiry into the nature of Chicana literature lagged behind. In a 1977 interview Rolando Hinojosa, a noted Chicano writer, was asked to name the works that in his opinion were milestones of Chicano literature, and he did not include any work by a woman. Similarly anthologies of Chicano literature included few works by women; anthologies of works by American women writers included no publications by Chicana women. *The Third Woman,* published in 1980 by Houghton Mifflin, was a notable exception to the rule, but then again, it focused solely on minority women writers of the United States.

In the last few years, however, there has been a virtual explosion and celebration of the Chicana experience. In part this is the result of energetic self-publishing by the Chicana writers themselves, in part the result of more attention being paid to the Chicanas by Chicano publishers, most notably the Bilingual Press and Arte Público Press. In 1984 the National Association of Chicano Studies Conference had as its theme "Las voces de la mujer" (the voices of women), and a great deal of new and exciting work has emerged from that conference. The Chicana writer is being recognized not as part of a marginalized exotic literature but as a fully integrated and important part of the creative experience. Literary critics working on Chicana writers are continuing to expand the critical vision of *la mujer Chicana.*[5]

Previously, most Chicana literature was poetry; more and more short stories, dramas, and novels are taking shape. There is also a great deal of interest in and research on the early periods of Chicano culture and its contribution to United States culture. At centers all over the West research into the past is being done. Arising from the Mexican Heritage Project at the Arizona Heritage Society in Tucson, a photographic exhibition and several books of photographs and oral histories of early Hispanic settlers have been published.[6] Great care was taken to include a large number of women, and we are able to analyze their lives from this perspective. Historians are also researching the lives of Hispanic women. A 1982 issue of the *New Mexico Historical Review* had a fascinating series of articles on early women in New Mexico.[7] In addition, to encourage young writers, there are literary contests being held annually for the best creative writing and literary reviews, and journals for beginning writers are being published in Santa Barbara, Tucson, El Paso, and other areas.

What does all this ferment, outpouring, and explosion of writings by Chicanas and interest in their work mean? At this moment Chicana literature is coming into its own. The angry writings arising from the bitterness of exclusion have diminished. Early Chicana writers such as Angela de Hoyos, Margarita Cota-Cárdenas, Lorna Dee Cervantes, and Bernica Zamora functioned as role models. With them in mind, more recent Chicana writers are turning to the task of exploring, defining, and refining their own voices. Beverly Silva, for example, thinks of Lorna Dee Cervantes when she writes, "Two hours between classes/ reading Lorna's poems/knowing again that literature heals the hunger and the pain."[8] Silent for too long, the excitement of discovering their ability and potential has turned into a quiet revolution of writing. They have heeded Cota-Cárdenas's call of the 1970s where she stated:

> busca tu nombre
> dentro de ti misma
> Chicana
> crea tu propia palabra
> tu esencia   TU
> . . .
> se homenaje a tu raza, crea tu propio cosmos
> CHICANA HERMANA MUJER
> Ahora actua por
> TI[9]

As if in response, Beverly Silva writes in "The Cactus"

> November sunshine floods my kitchen window.
> The plants thrive.
> The lemon tree bursts with ripe fruit.
> i measure the cactus.
> Five inches of new growth
> since that cold January afternoon
> i found it.
> Lone, spindly thing like all the life here
> on Second St.

uprooted and cast off in a corner of the alley
between Taconazo and my apartments.
i brought it home
laid wet paper towels on its roots
not knowing then
that almost nothing can kill a cactus.
i planted this dried up spike in a plastic pot
with dirt from the parking lot of this next door dance hall.
Taconazo dirt.

The cactus grows.
i eat nopalitos every morning with my breakfast.[10]

As Chicana literature matures and as one examines the corpus of texts, several trends emerge, not all of them necessarily new. Chicana poets are moving away from the type of strictly social commentaries about the oppression of the system and of the oppression of the male Machista tradition that occurred in the 1960s and early 1970s. That is not to say that they have abandoned social commentary altogether; it is just that social judgments are better integrated into the structure of poetic discourse, and are no less strong because they are well written. The themes of woman and independent feminist, perhaps more tolerant and less bitter toward the men in her life, appear in a more subtle way. María Inés Lagos-Pope in "A Space of Her Own" sees the Chicana writer as searching precisely for that space, as being in an "experience of being in-between, of being at a crossroads."[11]

It seems that the poets are turning to a personal, interior complex imagery to reflect on identity and conflict. They are reflecting on their heritage as a positive, integrating experience rather than as one that has separated and alienated them from society. Perhaps this is a direct result of the pride Chicanos have taken in their culture, literature, and traditions since the Chicano Renaissance. In their poetry, the Chicana writers comment on their relations with family and men, their place in society, their struggles and desires, their growing up. They laugh, they cry, they talk about domestic violence, they speak of their search for self and transcendence, they look for role models, they create role models, they explore ancient and new myths. They tend to focus on relations, their selves, their role as writers, the craft of poetry. They are ironic. What one constantly senses, though, is expectation, hope, and energy. It is as if the burst of creation has released a voice that has been seeking an

outlet for centuries. In the explosion of creativity, a new sense of hope
has been released. As Denise Chávez writes:

> Pomegranate tree
> bubble and burst[12]

This explosion has manifested itself in several directions.

1. *Growing up.* Story after story, poem after poem is concerned
with the maturation period of the writer. Different in many aspects
from that represented by men, growing up for the young women can
mean acknowledging or recognizing death, becoming different because
you have reached maturity as a woman and thus are sexually vulnerable, or coming into a sense of the limitation of the adult vis á vis the
freedom of the child. These young girls, in the description of their
maturation process, often sympathize with or hero worship a "rebel"
female member of the family who is viewed as having come into her
own. There is also a sense of self-possession in these poems not seen
before, an early example of which is Cota-Cárdenas's "Nostalgia":

> I thought then
> that I would like to be a nun with
> long white veil floating in the wind
> mounted on horseback like the actress María Felix
> riding riding off into
> a lovely cinema type sunset
> in the Convent of the Good Shepard
> we ate dark cornflakes
> wheaties with coffee and not milk and thus
> poor but pure we would get to be
> instant nuns
> the way I thought one could do everything
> like in the movies of the 1940's
> at the Motor-Vu.[13]

In contrast to these illusions and fantasy of childhood, Denise Chávez
writes,

> Worm child: That summer
> I killed insects
> with tiny grey rocks
> because I was lonely
> and hot.

P.D., my cousin,
whose mother was dying of cancer
sprayed them
dead
watched them
fall from walls
numbed,
noiseless.[14]

And Elena Guadalupe Rodríguez presents a picture of confidence and poise in "Trenza."

Intertwined
a mass of long
hair
forms a lasso
thick
      dark
            interminable
      and
            heavily
enriched
      with
            simplicity
      and
great
            care
is lavished
with a multicolor
rainbow
of intermingled
bows.
Freely
it falls
down
my shoulders
            or
down my back.
Each trenza gently
prances
with such
figurative
poise

<pre>
side
        to
              side
up
        and
              down
</pre>
as I steadily
make my
way.[15]

2. *Self-Identity*. Finding a space of one's own is certainly a central theme of Chicano writing in general and of Chicana poetry in particular. Although connected to the theme of growing up, it is different in that it concerns not the revisitation of childhood to see what has influenced or created the person of today, but rather a realistic vision of one's present, everyday life and needs and the necessity of finding an area which is truly one's own. When society or personal relations do not allow or recognize this need for acceptance as one is, then conflict ensues and the dilemma is examined by the poet. This search for self is exemplified by Beverly Silva in "not because i love literature less."

> but because i love life more
> i've left the University,
> that refuge for a stormy life,
> and i seek a new knowledge.
> For days i speak only Spanish
> or not at all.
>
>   . . .
>
> Not because i love literature less
> but because i love life more
> i'm content to sit here at this window
> waiting for the next chapter.[16]

Pat Mora examines the ambivalent feelings the Chicana has as she slips in and out of roles, across cultures and languages: her feelings of alienation, distance, and confusion as she sorts out who she is.

> Bi-lingual, Bi-cultural,
> able to slip from "How's life?"
> to "me'stan volviendo loca,"
> able to sit in a paneled office
> drafting memos in smooth English,
> able to order in fluent Spanish

at a Mexican restaurant,
American but hyphenated,
viewed by Anglos as perhaps exotic,
perhaps inferior, definitely different,
viewed by Mexicans as alien,
(their eyes say, "You may speak
Spanish but you're not like me")
an American to Mexicans
A Mexican to Americans
a handy token
sliding back and forth
between the fringes of both worlds
by smiling
by masking the discomfort
of being pre-judged
Bi-laterally.[17]

She also analyzes varying expectations of herself and her relationship to society as she grows older in "Sola."

I wanted to dance through life
with a tall-dark-handsome
who would choose me, s^{P}i$_n$
me, lead me past envying eyes
while I strained to match his steps,
my hands holding him.

At forty I dream of g l i d i n g

alone

on ice, to music no one else has heard

arms free[18]

3. *The Female Tradition.* This general category deals with relations with other women, particularly with female family members. Who you are is often mirrored in the eyes of your mother, sister, aunt, or *abuelita*. These women writers tend to look more toward female familial relationships for their self-reflection than toward men. Lorna Dee Cervantes certainly did this in her poem "Beneath the Shadow of the Freeway," and this tradition continues with Alma Villanueva, Denise Chávez, and Pat Mora. The emphasis of the oral tradition of stories, cooking recipes, and other verbal messages handed down by women in

the family is very strong. An excellent example of this emphasis is "Family Ties" by Pat Mora, written for Teresa McKenna, whose grandmother is the focus of the poem.

> Though I shop for designer jeans,
> uniforms make me smile.
> Chalk-white uniforms in store windows remind
> me of my grandmother who refused to learn English,
> who would laugh with the women from the canneries
> when they filled her small home with the smell of fish,
> filled her hands with crumpled dollars in exchange
> for the white garments piled in pale pink
> boxes throughout the house.
>
> My grandmother preferred to shop in grocery stores,
> preferred buying garlic, onion, chile, beans,
> to buying me gifts of frilly blouses and barettes,
> hers a life of cooking, cleaning, selling.
> But when I shyly showed my *abuelita*
> my good report card or recited the Pledge of Allegiance,
> my grandmother would smile and hand me a uniform,
> never the right size, but a gift,
> which I would add to the white stack
> at the bottom of my closet.[19]

Another example is Evangelina Vigil's poem "ser conforme," a universal expression of a daughter's relationship with her mother.

> my mother made me a beaded necklace
> a beaded ring
> and also a bracelet
> gypsy colors
> were the ones she used
> indio colors but
> fluorescent
>
> and I think to myself
> why is it that mothers always know
> what kinds of things their daughters like
> like when you were small and
> she'd come home with two new dresses
> one that you just loved
> but expensive and
> one that didn't strike

your fancy but was
cheaper[20]

4. *Search for myth and tradition*. There is a revival of Chicano and Indian traditions and myths as an integrative view of the future. In the early years of Chicana writing, mythic figures such as La Malinche, Aztec goddesses such as Coatlicue, and revolutionary heroines such as La Adelita were perhaps overused as symbolic figures of inspiration but also as symbols of cultural and social conflict, violence, and rape. Contemporary poets seem to focus on role models who display more cognitive skills, intuition, healing powers, and intelligence. One example in drama is the recent play by Estela Portillo Trambley on Sor Juana Inés de la Cruz.[21] Denise Chávez uses the Virgin of Guadalupe as an integrating figure, and Pat Mora focuses on Southwest traditions such as the *curandera* and the *bruja* integrating the source of their power, which comes from inner resources of strength and magic, to her own power in writing. She does this in "Curandera."

They think she lives alone
on the edge of town in a two-room house
where she moved when her husband died
at thirty-five of a gunshot wound
in the bed of another woman. The curandera
and house have aged together to the rhythm
of the desert.

She wakes early, lights candles before
her sacred statues, brews tea of yerbabuena.
She moves down her porch steps, rubs
cool morning sand into her hands, into her arms.
Like a large black bird, she feeds on
the desert, gathering herbs for her basket.

Her days are slow, days of grinding
dried snake into powder, of crushing
wild bees to mix with white wine.
And the townspeople come, hoping
to be touched by her ointments,
her hands, her prayers, her eyes.
She listens to their stories, and she listens
to the desert, always, to the desert.

By sunset she is tired. The wind

strokes the strands of long gray hair,
the smell of drying plants drifts
into her blood, the sun seeps
into her bones. She dozes
on her back porch. Rocking, rocking.

At night she cooks chopped cactus
and brews more tea. She brushes a layer
of sand from her bed, sand which covers
the table, stove, floor. She blows
the statues clean, the candles out.
Before sleeping, she listens to the message
of the owl and the coyote. She closes her eyes
and breathes with the mice and snake
and wind.[22]

5. *Focus on the image of the poet and the craft of poetry*. This is
not a new or recent trend but a continuing development from early
concerns of Cervantes, de Hoyos, and Zamora about the writer's image
of herself and her concern about her art.[23] Good writing as well as great
art continue to be overriding preoccupations for these women who use
poetry not only to examine their individual issues, conflicts, and concerns but to examine those central to Chicanos and Chicanas, men and
women, people everywhere. Luca Corpi, for example, describes the
anxiety of waiting for inspiration:

Like the seed that waits
for gentle rain
my thirsting poem is silent.
Its quietude scatters
inside me and I am frightened
by its withered whiteness.[24]

And, as Pat Mora writes,

Silent morning coolness, silence
ended by the scratching of rough
fingertips digging in the desert,
turquoise threads buried by the Indian
woman, buried to bribe the Earth.

Come, Mother. Guide my hands
to weave singing birds, flowers

rocking in the wind, to trap them
on my cloth with a web of thin threads.

Secretly I scratch a hole in the desert
by my home. I bury a ballpoint pen
and lined yellow paper. Like the Indian
I ask the Earth to smile on me, to croon
softly, to help me catch her music with words.[25]

6. *Social criticism*. Chicana poetry is, in many ways, a very direct, heartfelt poetry. The poet can never be separated from the world in which she lives, and must, of necessity, examine and evaluate it. The social criticism evident in the early days of the Chicano Renaissance continues: it examines prejudice, hate, and violence, yet the recent poetry does not reject the society from where the poet springs. There is energy and hope and expectation that society will change and that writing will help in the process of change. "South Sangamon" by Sandra Cisneros is a poem which examines the issue of family violence and wife abuse.

We wake up
and it's him
banging and banging
and the doorknob rattling open up.
His drunk cussing,
her name all over the hallway
and my name mixed in.
He yelling from the other side open
and she yelling from this side no.
A long time of this
and we say nothing
just hoping he'd get tired and go.
Then the big door shakes
like his big foot meant to break it.
Then quiet
so we figured he'd gone.
That day he punched her belly
the whole neighborhood watching
that was Tuesday.
So this time we lock it.
And just when we got those kids quiet,
and me. I shut my eyes again,

> she laughing,
> her cigarette lit,
> just then
> the big rock comes in.[26]

7. *The acceptance of the everyday life of women as being fit material for poetry.* Perhaps this has been what has helped the Chicana writer the most. When poetry could only be about "noble" subjects, causes, ideals, and revolutions in order to be meaningful, woman's voice was stifled because her life and her work seemed trivialized. Washing dishes and diapers; cleaning kitchens and bathrooms; looking after husbands and children; thinking about school and supper; rape, domestic violence, and handicapped sisters and brothers seemed to be subjects not fit for poetic exploration. The Chicana poetic tradition, which fits into the testimonial, confessional poetry used by both the Latin American poetic tradition (Alfonsina Storni, Rosario Castellanos) as well as the American female poetic tradition (Sylvia Plath) is exemplified by Cervantes, Cota-Cárdenas, Villanueva, and Zamora. It has been freed from the stifling necessity to speak on "grand" terms. We have come to understand that one can write about great ideals, expectations, and revolutions but that the fabric that is woven around our everyday lives and interiors is also significant for exploring meaning and universal concerns. Just as Sor Juana learned about science by watching eggs boil and mixtures being mixed in the kitchen, so can the problems of the world be explored in the everyday talk of children. An example would be Margarita Cota-Cárdenas's poem, "Dedicated to American Atomics."

> —Mommy,
> Dougie has radioactivity in his pee
> and his Daddy too.
> They got it in a neighbor's swimming pool
> and I heard it on T.V.
> —Can you see it?
> No, no, and it isn't any color.
> Well, what it does is,
> that it can make you sick see.
> Well, they don't know when.
> Yes, if you have too much,
> you might even vomit.[27]

8. *Expression of Sexuality.* A final and persistently strong trend in Chicana poetry is a direct, often erotic and certainly passionate expression of love and sexuality. These poets have a direct connection to life and its experiences and a deeply felt need to incorporate both mind and body into their poetry. This can be seen in Beverly Silva's poem "Two Brothers."

> One gives me kitchens
> & kids
> Everyday phone calls
> punctuality
> fixes faucets & toilets
> brings me coffee in bed.
>   the other slips in late at night
> not speaking
> peels me like a banana
> loves until dawn
> leaves making no promises.[28]

Another example of sensuality and eroticism is Mora's "Mielvirgen."

> In the slow afternoon heat she sits
> in the shade watching the bees,
> remembering sweet evenings
> of dipping her fingers into warm
> honey, smoothing it on his lips,
> licking it slowly with her tongue,
> hearing him laugh
>   then breathe harder
> slowly unbuttoning her
> blouse, rubbing his
> tongue on her sweet skin,
>   lips, honey, breasts
> buzzing
> like the bees she hears now,
> her eyes closed, her tongue sliding
> on her lips, remembering, remembering[29]

These are just some examples in the ways that Chicana poetry is evolving. It is evolving from the fine tradition established by early writers and continuing its search for meaning, definition and self. It has come a long way. What are the writers doing now? What will they do in the future? They will continue to invent, explore and explode. Miriam

Bornstein-Somoza is writing fine poems in English. Pat Mora and Denise Chávez are exploring the medium of children's literature. Margarita Cota-Cárdenas is writing a novel. Others also are defining, inventing, and reinventing their future by revaluing and revalidating the past, incorporating, rejecting, and creating it but using the traditions, oral and ideal; most of all, and most important, they are putting their future into words. The Quiet Revolution has finally arrived.

Notes

1. The term Mexican-American was generally used until the flowering of pride in race and ethnicity during the late 1960s when the term Chicano became one of common usage. Chicano is generic including both men and women, but can also refer only to males. Chicana refers specifically to women.

2. Margarita Cota-Cárdenas, ed., *Siete Poetas* (Tucson, Az.: Scorpion Press, 1978); Angela de Hoyos, M. and A. Editions, San Antonio, Texas; Bernice Zamora, *Restless Serpents* (Menlo Park, Ca.: Diseños Literarios, 1974).

3. Lorna Dee Cervantes, "You Cramp My Style, Baby," *Fuego de Aztlán* 1, no. 4 (1977); 40.

4. "Mija" is "mi hija" meaning my daughter, a term commonly used for young women. In this case an ironic one since the woman, his wife, is not equal to the man. *Malinche* was the Indian woman who translated and aided Cortez during the conquest of Mexico. She has come to symbolize the betrayer of *la raza*, the race. Chicana writers have been engaged in a revision of Malinche as a symbol, pointing out that she was a slave and had no control over her own destiny.

5. Some recent critical studies include the following: *Third Woman* II, 1, 1984, ed. Norma Alarcón includes articles by Justo S. Alarcón on Miriam Bornstein-Somoza; Naomi Lindstrom, "Four Representative Hispanic Women Poets of Central Texas"; Sylvia Lizárraga on Gina Valdés; Elizabeth J. Ordoñez, "The Concept of Cultural Identity in Chicana Poetry"; and Tey Diana Rebolledo on poetic inspiration in Chicana Poetry. Other critical studies include María Hererra Sobek, ed. *Beyond Stereotypes: Chicana Writers* (Binghamton, N.Y.: Bilingual Press, 1985); and Evangelina Vigil, ed. *Woman of Her Word: Hispanic Women Write* (Houston, Tx.: Arte Público Press, 1983).

6. Patricia Preciado Martin, *Images and Conversations: Mexican Americans Recall a Southwestern Past* (Tucson: University of Arizona Press, 1983). The Mexican Heritage Project, *Del Rancho al Barrio: The Mexican Legacy of Tucson.* (Tucson: Arizona Historical Society, 1983).

7. *New Mexico Historical Review*, 57:4, 1982. See also Janet A. Lecompt, "The Independent Women of Hispanic New Mexico, 1821–1846," *Western Historical Quarterly* 22 (Jan. 1981): 335–59.

8. Beverly Silva, *The Second St. Poems* (Ypsilanti, Mich.: Bilingual Press, 1983), p. 69.

9. Look for your name
inside your own self
Chicana
create your own word
your essence   you

   . . .

be a credit to your race   create your own cosmos
CHICANA   SISTER   WOMAN
  now   *act*   for
  yourself

Margarita Cota-Cárdenas, *Noches despertando in Conciencias* (Tucson: Scorpion Press, 1975) n.p.

10. Silva, *The Second St. Poems*, p. 36.

11. María Inés Lagos-Pope, "A Space of Her Own," Introduction in Silva, *The Second St. Poems*, p. 12.

12. Denise Chávez, unpublished poem.

13. Cota-Cárdenas, *Siete Poetas* (Tucson: Scorpion Press, 1978), p. 69.

14. Denise Chávez, unpublished poem.

15. Elena Guadalupe Rodríguez, *Morena* (Santa Barbara, Ca., n.p. 1980), p. 63.

16. Silva, *The Second St. Poems*, p. 37.

17. Pat Mora, *Chants* (Houston: Arte Público Press, 1984), p. 52.

18. Ibid., p. 44.

19. Ibid., p. 35.

20. Evangelina Vigil, *Revista Chicana Riqueña* X:1–2 (1982), 141.

21. Estela Portillo Trambley, *Sor Juana and Other Plays* (Ypsilanti, Mich.: Bilingual Press, 1983).

22. Mora, *Chants*, pp. 26–27.

23. Tey Diana Rebolledo, "Witches, Bitches and Midwives: The Shaping of Poetic Consciousness in Chicana Literature," in *The Chicano Struggle* (Binghamton, N.Y.: Bilingual Press, 1984), pp. 166–177.

24. Lucha Corpi, *Fireflight* (Oakland, Ca., n.p. 1976), p. 47.

25. Mora, *The Pawn Review* V, 54.

26. Sandra Cisneros, *Bad Boys* (San Jose, Ca.: Mango, 1980), n.p.

27. Cota-Cárdenas in Tey Diana Rebolledo, "The Bittersweet Nostalgia of Childhood in the Poetry of Margarita Cota-Cárdenas," *Frontiers* 5, no. 2 (1980): 35.

28. Silva, *The Second St. Poems*, p. 55.

29. Mora, *Chants*, p. 45.

Feminism in Linguistics

Sally McConnell-Ginet

Linguistics, the "science of language," has links to feminist scholarship that seem obvious to the non-linguist and rather obscure to the linguist. We might attribute this obscurity to the dominance of men in the profession, but many women and feminists in linguistics find themselves rather puzzled as well. This is not simply a question of sexism in linguistics, though it is certainly true that sexist examples abound in linguistics texts and journal articles and that linguists have focused on varieties of language that they themselves or people like them (i.e., an educated male elite) use.[1] More broadly, the question is this: how might linguistics contribute substantively to an understanding of women's experience? How might a feminist orientation illuminate those questions about language that led many of us into linguistic research? How has feminism begun to influence linguistic scholarship? Finally, perhaps most important, what further questions might a feminist linguistics explore?[2]

Disciplines are delineated not only by subject matter but also by methodology and theoretical orientation. On the first day of an introductory linguistics class and in the first chapter of our introductory linguistics texts, we say that linguistics is of great importance because language is central in human thought and in social interaction. The remainder of the course or text is then devoted to the study of language as an autonomous structured system whose use (in thought or social life) is beyond our scope. The focus on formal structures in isolation from their use reflects the important insight that linguistic systems can be elegantly described in terms that do not refer to the "extra-linguistic" context. By treating language on its own terms, linguists have been able to achieve a degree of theoretical rigor and descriptive precision unmatched by other behavioral and social sciences. Sloppiness has been excised by a strategy that abstracts linguistic forms from the sociocultural and psychological matrices in which they are embedded.

Many critics would say that rigor in linguistics has been achieved at the price of rigor mortis. The radical operation required to "isolate" the language system has killed it: formal rules and representations provide no insight into language as a human activity. The defense against this malpractice charge, of course, is to develop an account of the relation between abstract linguistic systems and the mental states and processes, social actions and cultural values, that infuse them with life. My own view is that the isolating strategy is the only viable first approach. It is extraordinarily unlikely that one could provide a revealing account of language uses and their relation to language users without distinguishing forms independently of the uses their users put them to. Certainly no one has. Yet the modular approach that explains complex phenomena as the product of interacting simpler systems does require that our simple modules be "connectable" and that their structures "support" the desired kinds of interaction. More specifically, an autonomous account of a linguistic system has done only part of the job of a theory of human language and linguistic communication.

Two approaches connect linguistics with feminist questions about human thought and action; each illustrates a mode of feminist scholarship conducted from the perspective of traditional disciplines. In the "applied" mode, disciplinary tools shed light on women in culture and society, on the place of gender in human thought and social structures. Linguistic scholarship here serves to inform feminism, and the need for interdisciplinary and collaborative research quickly becomes apparent.

In the "feedback" mode, linguistics is informed by feminism (and, ultimately, human experience). Insights and knowledge derived from women's lives and their analyses of sexism, male dominance, and related phenomena lead us to ask new questions about what language is like and how it works. For example, "telescopic" approaches to the study of language and the sexes, to adopt Barrie Thorne's label for this work, frequently suggest that men "control" language.[3] Since all speakers and all language systems are "equal" in the eyes of the Great Grammarian, it is initially difficult to know how such control could be exercised and what is meant by the claim. Although there is not an all-male legislative body directing our linguistic developments, it is nevertheless apparent that our vocabulary and various aspects of our accepted and expected ways of talking are indicative of male-centered perspectives and sexist biases.[4] Few linguists doubt that vocabulary somehow bears the imprint of (past and present) sociocultural values. None, however, has proposed an account of the mechanisms through which the semantic system of a language develops in response to its users' situationally specific notions of how the world is (or is feared or wished to be). Feminist observations make it imperative for linguistic theory to address this question and, more particularly, to consider how it is that the notions of some users are more successfully encoded than those of others.[5] I will return briefly in the final section to discussion of how feminist investigations and analyses can feed back into linguistics.

There are not really two separate "modes" of feminist scholarship, of course, since it is in trying to "apply" linguistics that feminists find their efforts "feeding back" to extend or transform the conceptual frameworks and research methods of the discipline. Application and theory must go hand in hand, just like the study of language uses and language structure. But the distinction is useful for talking about the focus and implications of current research.

Linguistics Applied in Feminist Scholarship

What tools can linguists offer feminist scholars for the study of language? First (and probably foremost), we can offer *precise formal characterizations of expressions speakers (and writers) use.* We describe language at a number of different structural levels: any aspect of linguistic form, ranging from the most minute details of sound patterning to the specifications of different levels of syntactic structure (connecting "deep" and "surface" hierarchical structuring of phrases via transformational rules), is potentially significant in an account of language and behavior.

What is meant by an utterance is not, however, specifiable with the same level of precision as its syntactic and phonological structure. Insofar as communicative significance depends on such strictly linguistic considerations as the particular semantic domain in which words occur or the syntactic relationships of words in a particular utterance, linguistic specifications of semantic structure are useful to feminist investigators. However, communicators draw on more than common knowledge of a vocabulary and syntax. Not only do they exploit what have been dubbed "mutual contextual beliefs,"[6] but in face-to-face communication their words are set in an intonational framework and accompanied by facial expressions, manual gestures, body postures and the like. Linguists do not agree on how to describe intonational structure nor on precisely how it is integrated into the syntactic and phonological systems of a language. Nonvocal gestures receive even less attention, since most linguists view them as independent accompaniments to the specialized language system (except, of course, in cases like American Sign Language). Nonetheless, what we convey to one another when we speak face-to-face clearly draws on a full range of expressive behaviors: both intonation and nonvocal gesture have been the subject of feminist discussion.[7] Thus it becomes imperative for investigators to develop analyses that permit us, for example, to describe the "same" intonational pattern as recurring in different communicative contexts (and superimposed on different sentence frames).

Second, linguistics offers some *methods and procedures for the collection and analysis of language uses.* Linguistic patterning often takes place below the level of conscious attention for members of the speech community. Although what people say about their language (about word meanings, for example, or relationships among sounds) is important for the linguist, it is not decisive. The linguist looks at data on actual language *use* as well as linguistic intuitions of speakers, and is trained in techniques that facilitate discovery of the abstract system(s) underlying speakers' language use. Working with informants (including oneself if the language under study is native to the investigator) in order to test explicit and detailed hypotheses about the language system is the classic method; it involves eliciting judgments about the sameness and difference of linguistic forms, "appropriateness" of forms to a context of use, and the like. More recently, linguists have extended these methods (not abandoning the familiar techniques but adding new procedures) in order to discover fine-grained regularities governing apparent irregularities in the data collected from different speakers in different contexts and to try to dissolve what William Labov calls the "Observer's Paradox."[8] The paradox arises because the investigator needs high-quality recordings of systematically-sampled actual language use, yet the process of careful observation affects (and distorts) the language used. Our job is to find ways to provide good data on speech in the social context without obscuring or distorting the effects of that context. There is no single technique that solves the problem, but the careful researcher uses a variety of techniques and kinds of data with the aim of canceling out the error inherent in any single approach. Work with isolated informants, although still important, is not sufficient because much systematicity in the community's language use can only be observed through detailed analysis of socially heterogeneous language users in situations other than the special one of interacting with a linguist.

Linguistic studies of language used by and about the sexes do not by themselves illuminate feminist concerns. The linguist's tools must be used in conjunction with other tools that help us identify language users' aims and purposes, the effects of language use on hearers (and readers), the sociocultural conventions governing particular kinds of speech events in particular settings, and similar phenomena. In other words, linguistics in feminist scholarship must be integrated into more general, cross-disciplinary investigations.

In applying linguistic tools, feminist scholars studying language have pursued three main themes: (1) language as a subtle indicator of social structure and cultural values; (2) language use as a significant factor both in maintaining and in transmitting male-centered values and views; (3) language change as a potential instrument for achieving the far-reaching social, cultural, and political changes envisioned by the women's movement.

Linguistic Indicators of Women's Experience in Society and Culture

Much careful work on language as an indicator of nonlinguistic phenomena has focused on speech varieties—that is, on the repertoires used by socially differentiated groups of speakers (women and men, for example) within a speech community—looking at frequency of use of alternative forms for saying the "same thing," what is called *linguistic variation*. Two related sorts of cases are easily accessible for systematic study: (1) communities with distinct codes or languages available and multilingual speakers who switch among them, and (2) communities that exhibit structured "sociolectal" variation in the use, for example, of alternative pronunciations, especially where such variation is indicative of ongoing change. In both sorts of situations, gender appears to interact with language use and/or evaluation. The major question behind all such research can be put simply: what leads people to adopt a particular variety of speech? We do not know what is indicated by a speaker's use of a particular variety unless we have some answer to the question of how she (or he) came to use that variety rather than some other of the community's options.

How one speaks, given options in the particular community's linguistic repertoire, can indicate any or all of the following four factors:

1. *Access.* This depends on formal education and on communicative frequency. How do the people to whom you talk most often speak? Which variants from the collective repertoire do you hear most often?

2. *Social bonds.* What do your friends, the people whom you turn to for social interaction, "talk like"? Here, quality or purpose rather than quantity of verbal interchange is emphasized.

3. *Social identity and status.* Speech differences may be maintained even where communication is frequent and personal ties exist if such differences mark distinctions that organize the life of the community. Gender identity may, for example, be marked verbally as a symbol of sexual difference.

4. *Utility.* Certain varieties of talk may be required for particular occupations or activities, the pool of marriage partners may be linked to the linguistic varieties, and so on. The instrumental value of particular varieties may differ for women and men because of their different occupational choices and options for social mobility.

All of these factors operate for both women and men, their relative weight depending on both social and psychological considerations. We need assume no inherent differences in the social psychology of the sexes but rather suppose both women and men to be rational social actors, whose choices reflect available information and likelihood of success. Information on how these factors operate in particular speech communities for women and men will help us understand speech differences and similarities.

Some examples will help. Patricia C. Nichols, reporting on a larger study of sociolectal variation in speech forms used in some South Carolina black communities, shows that differences between women and men in their use of Creole as opposed to "standard" variants are chiefly explained in terms of their differential social mobility. In one community, the better-paying jobs for women (teacher, clerk, etc.) required some facility in use of non-creole forms. Jobs held by men from this community were blue-collar occupations, not requiring any special linguistic skills. In that community, women used non-creole variants (representing innovations, a change from the traditional forms of the community) much more frequently than did men. In a nearby community where both women and men were relatively restricted in their occupational options, men were more likely than women (whose mobility was most restricted) to have some access to non-creole variants and to use them, thus exhibiting more "innovative" linguistic behavior.

Studies of code-switching show similar complexities in sex-differentiated patterning. Ann Farber and Susan Gal describe quite different bilingual situations. Farber studied the use of Cakchiquel, a local Mayan language, and Spanish in a Guatemalan village, finding Indian women much less likely to be fluent in Spanish than their male counterparts and less likely to admit to knowledge of Spanish even if they had it. Since Cakchiquel is the language of domestic life in the village, attempts to use Spanish are seen as forays from the domestic domain to which Indian women in the village have been traditionally confined. Men receive somewhat more formal education, though this is changing, and thus have more explicit instruction in Spanish. Spanish is essential for men's upward mobility, whereas for women, Spanish is associated with rejection of traditional Indian society and the women's roles associated with that society.

In Gal's study, the bilingual situation reflects long-term close contact of Hungarian- and German-speaking populations near the Austro-Hungarian border (within present-day Germany). Here, use of Hungarian is associated with peasant life, an option that women are more forcefully rejecting than men. Both sexes know each of the two languages, although some old peasant women are monolingual in Hungarian, reflecting their relatively lesser access to German as a result of limited schooling and restricted participation in non-domestic domains. Weighing industrial wage labor against small-scale farming, a Hungarian man may see certain advantages in the life of the farmer. For the young woman, however, industrial society offers clear advantages: life as a factory worker or as the wife of a worker is considerably more comfortable than the drudgery that falls to the wife in a farming household. Similar factors apparently explain the finding by Werner Leopold of women's greater use of standard German rather than local dialects as industrialization began to offer an attractive option to family-based agriculture, an option especially appealing to women, given the sexual division of labor operative in that society.[9]

Thus the linguistic map of a community may provide a signpost to

previously uncharted social phenomena. Once the investigator has considered the effects of access, social ties, identities and statuses, and
utility in the use of competing variants, shifts within a particular speaker's production will serve to indicate how that speaker assesses her (or
his) social and occupational options, what identities are being presented, and the like. Linguistic choices reflect the speakers' own social
analyses and thus provide one way to get at women's own perspective
on their lives, rather than relying on the categorizations developed by
androcentric social science, which is generally also biased toward the
distinctions that operate for a particular class, ethnic group, and cultural setting.[10]

In these cases, we are talking about variation whose main explanation is to be found in the existence of alternatives associated with different groups and situations within the speech community. Social meaning
is attached, for example, to the choice of a particular pronunciation of a
word or to the use of one language rather than another; the point at
issue is not the primary message but the secondary form its expression
takes. In contrast, some differences in language use arise from saying
something different in roughly equivalent communicative situations;
there are distinct *speech strategies* for "doing things with words." In
very similar circumstances, speakers can say something different (not
the same thing in different words) as they follow distinct courses of
verbal action in order to achieve their (often slightly different) social
and personal goals. The alternatives used in this case represent different
linguistic signaling elements or different structural arrangements of
such elements.

For example, if I need to know the time and believe you can provide me with that information, I might say:

(a) Hey, man. What time is it?
(b) Excuse me. What time do you have?
(c) Oh, sir. Do you have the time?
(d) I'm sorry to bother you, but could you please tell me what time
    it is?

And so on. Any fluent speaker of English is able to interpret any of these
utterances as a request for information and knows that the difference
among them is linked to the social relationships of the speaker and
addressee and the relative care being taken by the speaker to recognize
the addressee's possible inconvenience in complying with such a re-

quest. In (a) and (c), the forms used to attract the addressee's attention signal a male addressee; (a) also suggests a male addressor.

The same four factors that influence patterns of linguistic variation can also help determine preferred speech strategies: what one does when one is not paying special attention to speech choices. Thus precisely what *is* meant by saying certain things—making certain moves— may depend in part simply on social identity. Ruth Borker and Daniel Maltz have argued that American girls and boys, who spend much of their unstructured play time in single-sex groups, develop somewhat different preferred speech strategies and thus that the same acts in what look like equivalent contexts may have quite different significance. Failure of each sex to recognize these differences in their "habitual" speech strategizing can lead to communication breakdowns.[11]

A number of linguistic forms and constructions function primarily (sometimes in conjunction with other communicative functions) to mark social relations and how an action is to be interpreted—its significance, given the linguistic and extralinguistic context. Address forms, politeness particles, and what are sometimes called "indirect speech acts"—in (c) and (d) above the point is not what is "literally" conveyed—all function in this way. Mapping such linguistic forms can provide indexes of sexual stratification within the society and can illuminate the negotiating of social relations and status within particular interactions. It is often said that women are more polite in their speech, and many studies do find such results and explain them in terms of women's generally subordinate position. Yet as Penelope Brown (n. 10) shows, there are multiple reasons for choosing "polite" speech strategies, and important distinctions among kinds of politeness, and one must investigate in detail the functions of particular speech forms in a given linguistic community in order to see, in her phrase, "how and why" women are more polite.

Turning from a focus on women and men as speakers to women and men (and their relationships) as spoken of, we find additional evidence of sex-typing in the division of labor and in expected behavior as well as indications of past (and present) attitudes towards women and men. Here we find, among other things, studies of the vocabulary of sexism. Linguist Robin Lakoff has noted asymmetries in vocabulary; she points to the sexualization of many terms for referring to women (compare, for example, *master* and *mistress*) and the linguistic chivalry that extends an originally "elevated" term like *lady* to virtually all

contexts of female reference (compare *cleaning lady* with the nonoccur-
ring male parallel, *garbage gentleman*). She argues that the chivalry and
sexualization are linked: there is a need for euphemisms to use in certain contexts in lieu of the sexually explicit and degrading terms so
widely used.[12]

The methodological strategy underlying such analyses is consideration of oppositions within the means of expression available to
speakers and recognized by them. For example, most speakers do analyze *lady* as opposed to *woman, girl,* and possibly less neutral terms of
reference such as *broad* and *chick.* It is also, of course, opposed to
gentleman in some uses, to *fella* or *buddy* in others (as in the position
indicated by the parentheses: *Look here, ( ). I had the right of way.*).
The linguist looks at such oppositions or alternations as well as the
contexts of use, both linguistic and extra-linguistic, in order to assess
the "meaning" of linguistic forms. The major problem, of course, is that
the set of alternatives is not well defined nor is the range of linguistic
and social contexts in which forms occur determinate. Sometimes for
some speakers, *lady* is in opposition to *cunt.* For other speakers, the
term *cunt* is never used to refer to a female human nor seldom (if ever)
heard in such uses. Whose culture and whose conceptual world are we
inferring?

Similar problems arise in considering the significance of terminology and word histories. For example, though *virtue* is historically
linked with *virile* and indicates the ancient view that excluded women
from the moral community, this particular connection is probably no
longer operative for most speakers. On the other hand, *sissy* still con-
veys devaluation of women's behavior and activities so whether or not
speakers link it with *sister* does not matter in terms of their being able to
infer something about prevalent misogyny. A more recent example:
OTR comes from *on the rag,* an expression referring to menstruation
and used (by extension based on beliefs about menstruation and its
effects) to signify irritableness. Some speakers do not know the history
of *OTR* or of *on the rag;* for them, it simply means something like
"grouchy." Even where the history of an expression is transparent to
users, they may employ it in a use whose initial establishment depended
on views to which they themselves do not subscribe; for example a
correspondent to *Ms.* magazine noted Robin Lakoff's use of "left-
handed compliment."[13] Although the existence of this phrase eloquently
testifies to a prevalent distrust of left-handers and a preference for right-

handers (as does the asymmetry between *sinister* and *dextrous,* deriving from the terms designating left and right, respectively), it is now a "fixed" phrase. (Actually we need not suppose prejudice but simply the assumption of the right-handed majority's perspective on the relative worth of left and right.) This does not mean the expression is innocent of double messages; it simply indicates how a particular speaker may (perhaps unwittingly) convey messages about attitudes and values she (or he) does not share.

If, however, we can point to certain kinds of patterns in a particular speaker's language use, we may well uncover a complex of beliefs and feelings that were not evident before, and perhaps not consciously articulated. A point on the infamous "generic" *he* may help make this clear. Listening to a lecture on how to be a good teacher, I found myself attributing to the speaker the apparent intention to use *he* with sex-indefinite antecedents: *the good student, a conscientious professor,* and so on. Then when the speaker said, "When a student finally gathers courage to ask a question, don't intimidate her," he revealed a sex-linked stereotype of the timid student, a stereotype that he might have denied, sincerely but self-deceptively, if queried about it directly. Links of language to individual and general attitudes and values are complex, a complexity obscured by the indiscriminate use of such terms as "sexist language." We do not discover meanings only by consulting dictionaries but by looking at patterns of actual language use, the connections speakers make among linguistic forms, and similar evidence.[14]

Language as "Conservator" of Existing Values

Linguists have had relatively little to say about the role of language (use) in maintaining and transmitting male-centered values, and what they have offered about the role of linguistic change in social change is often either inadequate or plain wrong. Given, however, the value of patterns of language (use) for indicating social attitudes and values, it is not hard to see how those patterns become implicated in maintaining the power of the socially dominant group (in our own culture, males of the white upper-middle class). The members of the sociocultural group read and read again and thus attach renewed significance to the indicators they have created. In particular, the child entering the system becomes a "reader," an interpreter of the system into which she (or he) must fit. In addition, of course, we all receive subtle extra messages in addition to the not-so-subtle overt control exercised by the powerful in verbal exchanges. Because at least some uses of language *are* social actions, they do not simply indicate to us an independently existing social order but work to create that order and maintain it.

Language as Instrument for Social Change

Thus changes in language can be part of social change. To the extent that language functions to make knowledge and experience public, it is important for feminists to arrive at some consensus on ways of articulating new insights that derive from woman's knowledge and experience. Sometimes new lexical items are helpful: labels like *sexism* and *male chauvinism,* for example, tie feminist analyses of women's oppression and exclusion from the mainstream to analyses of such related phenomena as racism and superpatriotism.[15] This provides a framework for analysis and investigation that may ultimately illuminate our understanding of women's position, perhaps eventually transforming the original framework in light of what we come to know about sexual differentiation and stratification in different sociocultural and historical settings.

Terms of address and reference shift as women (and men) adopt different social positions and roles. Changed patterns of address and reference play a role in changing views of options and roles, since they indicate alternative social maps. It is true that we can not suppose that words alone will win the war, but no feminist was ever so deceived. A determined male chauvinist may scrupulously use *chairperson,* generally with strong stress on the second part of the compound to say, "What a good boy am I," whereas many a committed feminist slips into the familiar *chairman,* with an unstressed suffix that does not sound like the independent form *man.* The linguist cannot predict the fate of particular attempts to change patterns of language use (and thus, ultimately, the system underlying those patterns). What the linguist can do and has frequently failed at is provide a careful analysis of present usage and an account of the likeliest directions of change, given the present system AND given the present attitudes, beliefs, values of those who would participate in propagating the changes launched. Speakers can then make individual choices (perhaps with benefit of collective strategizing) in order to maximize chances of advancing their goals.

It is sometimes suggested that women change their speech styles and strategies in order to improve their chances of achieving desired ends. Assertiveness training, for example, teaches people certain so-called assertive communicative devices to employ in particular situations.[16] Women do sometimes fall into a nonassertive trap by, for example, letting strategies of politeness and indirection become so habitual that they are used even when not suited to the situation or the speaker's aims.[17] It also may well be useful to look closely at one's own language use to discover the sorts of attitudes and beliefs one may be unintentionally communicating, the ways in which one submits or defers without really intending such action. Nonetheless, precisely because there may be, and usually are, multiple functions assigned to a single form and thus competing explanations of particular usages, women must beware of falling into another trap: reading themselves according to a male-centered view of how people "should" behave, and what is indicated when they don't behave that way.

Toward a Feminist Theory of Language

Language is central in human life because it connects the individual mind and its stock of experience with a social and cultural order which embodies the evidence of others' perceptions, interpretations, thoughts, and beliefs. Variety among languages serves to demarcate social groupings, to mark identity, to build social structures. The conventional linguistic view of language as a system sealed off from the public world and from other psychological systems is inadequate to account for the feedback that relates language, mind, and society.

To combat views of the inherent superiority of the Indo-European languages, twentieth-century linguists have tended to accept the twin principles of linguistic optimism and linguistic egalitarianism:

1. Principle of linguistic optimism: all linguistic systems are ideally suited to meet the expressive and communicative needs of their users.

2. Principle of linguistic egalitarianism: language users have equal access to the resources of their language, equal facility in deploying them, and equal status as users and interpreters.

We needn't return to the belief that God thinks in Greek to object to this ostrich-like view of how languages serve their speakers' needs. It was always recognized that (1) might not hold at all times: a supplementary principle held that the linguistic system lagged somewhat behind the social system but eventually—without anyone's giving the matter any conscious thought—the linguistic system "caught up."

These principles relate to two other principles implicit in most linguistic theories:

3. Principle of autonomous semantics: semantic/conceptual structures exist independently of their linguistic encoding.

4. Principle of marginality of the lexicon: changes in productive and/or receptive lexical repertoires do not significantly change linguistic competence. Lexical creation and shift and extension of existing lexical resources to new uses are seen as essentially non-linguistic.

Detailed examination of the actual facts of language use forces us to abandon these and related dogmas.

It is not that feminist scholarship has shown us what form an adequate linguistic theory must take. Rather feminist scholarship shows us that the conventional approaches to the description of linguistic structures are inadequate. Recent investigations of "linguistic pragmatics"—the contribution to "meaning" of speech acts, language users, and contexts—move toward restoring language to the sociocultural context from which we extracted it for analysis. Cognitive theories, with attention to perceptual strategies, for example, are beginning to reconnect language with its mental environment. If linguists pay attention to the interrelationships among language, thought, and sociocultural systems that feminist scholarship is uncovering, we may be pushed to revise our theories of language, perhaps eventually to make precise and explicit the insights long ago hinted at by the linguist and anthropologist Edward Sapir. Sapir flirts with the four principles I just gave, noting also the value of language as an index to the culture of those who speak it and enunciating the view that "the form of language is the form of thought." I don't know whether Sapir would have considered himself a feminist; I do know that the most careful study of sex-based differences in speech prior to the relatively recent upsurge of attention was his "Male and Female Forms of Speech in Yana," succeeded by research of some of his students.[18]

What kinds of theories and research programs might a "feminist linguistics" develop? As I have already indicated, we badly need a plausible account of the mechanisms through which language use, e.g., speech situated in face-to-face interactions, affects the language system. Such a theory must answer to the evidence from careful documentation of ongoing language change; detailed studies of patterns of pronoun usage, for example, could be important in helping us understand how changes occur. Studies should sample a variety of social contexts and attend to interactional phenomena as well as to the speech output of individuals. More generally, we need a closer look at the give and take between speaker and hearer, at how "meaning" evolves, for example, during discourse.[19] More attention must be paid to the influence of contextual factors other than gender if we are to understand how gender interacts with such factors. I hypothesized that children draw some wrong inferences from what they hear, that this is a way language "slows" or "impedes" social change; such hypotheses need to be tested. The growing interest in single-sex speech interactions, e.g., talk in women's "consciousness-raising" groups,[20] must be studied in some detail if one is to assess the significance of data from cross-sex conversation. And so on.

I would stress, however, that theory and observation have to develop in tandem. Stacks of cassettes and reams of text are of little value in the absence of well-articulated explanatory frameworks. Theories, of course, need to be subjected to empirical tests, but theory-free observation does not exist, and feminist scholars need to articulate explicit theoretical frameworks to guide our observations toward potentially illuminating phenomena. This is especially vital since otherwise we are unlikely to make any advance in understanding beyond the impoverished conceptual frameworks we inherit from the long tradition of male-dominated scholarship. This doesn't mean starting *de novo*—were that possible—but rather following the painstaking process of revising and re-forming theories and methods in order to trans-form scholarship.[21]

When is an academic feminist a feminist scholar? When scholarship informs feminism and feminism informs scholarship.

Notes

1. These and related points have been illustrated and discussed in numbers of papers and talks, e.g., Julia Penelope Stanley, "Chomsky's 'Ideal' Native Speaker: Sexism in Synchronic Linguistics," paper given at the Women and Language Forum, Modern Language Association Annual Meeting, Dec. 1978; Patricia C. Nichols, "Women in Their Speech Communities," in *Women and Language in Literature and Society*, ed. Sally McConnell-Ginet, Ruth A. Borker, and Nelly Furman (New York: Praeger, 1980), pp. 140–49.

2. My "Linguistics in a Feminist Context," paper given at the Women and

Language Forum, Modern Language Association Annual Meeting, Dec. 1978, and "The Origins of Sexist Language in Discourse," in *Discourses in Reading and Linguistics,* ed. Sheila J. White and Virginia Teller (New York: Annals of the New York Academy of Science, vol. 433, 1984), pp. 123–36, deal most explicitly with these issues. The questions posed, however, underlie most of my research in this area.

3. Barrie Thorne talks of "telescopic" views of language and feminism, which she opposes to "microscopic" views. "Language and Social Stratification," paper given at the Feminist Scholarship Conference, University of Illinois, Urbana-Champaign, 1978.

4. Muriel Schulz, "The Semantic Derogation of Women," in *Language and Sex: Difference and Dominance,* ed. Barrie Thorne and Nancy Henley (Rowley, Mass.: Newbury House Publishers, 1975), pp. 64–75, documents some of the impact of sexism on the history of English vocabulary. Interesting articles dealing with this topic can also be found in *Sexism and Language,* ed. Alleen Pace Nilsen, Haig Bosmajian, H. Lee Gershuny, and Julia P. Stanley [now Julia Penelope] (Urbana, Ill.: National Council of Teachers of English, 1977); *Sexist Language,* ed. Mary Vetterling-Braggin (Totowa, N.J.: Littlefield, Adams, 1981). Casey Miller and Kate Swift, *Words and Women* (New York: Doubleday, 1977), is a clear discussion for a general audience. Although the literature on apparent sexism in the vocabulary is quite extensive, there are few discussions of syntactic signals of language users' sexism; see, however, Finn Tschudi, "Gender Stereotypes Reflected in Asymmetric Similarities in Language," paper given at the Gender, Androgyny, and Language Session, American Psychological Association Annual Meeting, Aug. 1979.

5. Cheris Kramarae, "Proprietors of Language," in *Women and Language,* ed. McConnell-Ginet, Borker, and Furman, pp. 58–68, and Maija S. Blaubergs, "An Analysis of Classic Arguments Against Changing Sexist Language," in *The Voices and Words of Women and Men,* ed. Cheris Kramarae (Oxford: Pergamon Press, 1980), pp. 135–48, discuss the social psychology of responses to feminist-inspired changes in language use. Wendy Martyna, "Psychology of the Generic Masculine," in *Women and Language,* ed. McConnell-Ginet, Borker, and Furman, pp. 69–78, provides solid empirical evidence that gender-differentiated patterns of comprehension and production exist. Such investigations offer valuable data and analyses against which linguistic hypotheses of mechanisms of language change and its relation to social processes must be tested.

6. See Kent Bach and Robert M. Harnish, *Linguistic Communication and Speech Acts* (Cambridge, Mass.: MIT Press, 1979) for interesting discussion of certain aspects of how this works.

7. See Sally McConnell-Ginet, "Intonation in a Man's World," *Signs* 3 (1978): 541–59; a revised and updated version appears in *Language, Gender and Society,* ed. Barrie Thorne, Cheris Kramarae, and Nancy Henley (Rowley, Mass.: Newbury House, 1983). See also Carole Edelsky, "Question Intonation and Sex Roles," *Language in Society* 8 (1979): 15–32. Nancy Henley, *Body Politics: Power, Sex, and Nonverbal Communication* (Englewood Cliffs, N.J.:

Prentice-Hall, 1977) is an illuminating study of nonverbal communication from a feminist perspective.

8. Labov has discussed this issue in a number of publications. The most accessible account is probably "The Study of Language in Its Social Context," *Sociolinguistic Patterns* (Philadelphia: University of Pennsylvania Press, 1972), pp. 183–259. The "Observer's Paradox" is formulated on p. 209.

9. The work discussed in the text is to be found in Anne Farber, "Language Choice and Sex Roles in Highland Guatemala," paper given at the Symposium on Language and Sex Roles, Annual Meeting of the American Anthropological Association, 1974; Susan Gal, "Peasant Men Can't Get Wives: Language Change and Sex Roles in a Bilingual Community," *Language in Society* 7 (1978): 1–16; Werner F. Leopold, "The Decline of German Dialects," *Word* 15 (1959): 130–53.

10. Penelope Brown develops and illustrates in detail the point about women's language usage giving a "woman's-eye" view of social options in "How and Why Are Women More Polite: Some Evidence from a Mayan Community," in *Women and Language,* ed. McConnell-Ginet, Borker, and Furman, pp. 111–36. In the same volume, Nichols, "Women in their Speech Communities," notes that most sociolinguistic studies have assumed that a woman's social status derives from that of some man (husband or father), an assumption that not only places single adult women in a no-woman's land but also distorts social status and roles of women who do happen to be part of a family unit including a male "head-of-household." Detailed analysis of language usage of women and men in the same household frequently makes it impossible to maintain this assumption. Individual women have a social identity that may be quite distinct from that of the men with whom they live; this fact seems blatantly obvious but detailed analysis of their speech provides evidence that the skeptical sociolinguist would find hard to ignore.

11. Daniel N. Maltz and Ruth A. Borker, "A Cultural Approach to Male-Female Miscommunication," in *Communication, Language, and Social Identity,* ed. John J. Gumperz (New York: Cambridge University Press, 1982), pp. 195–216. They note especially the evidence in Marjorie H. Goodwin, "Directive-Response Sequences in Girls' and Boys' Task Activities," in *Women and Language,* ed. McConnell-Ginet, Borker, and Furman, pp. 157–73. McConnell-Ginet, "Intonation in a Man's World," suggests that intonational choices may hold different significance in some cases for women and for men—and that men project their interpretation onto women's choices, sometimes refusing to acknowledge the possibility of alternative analyses.

12. Lakoff's work has received considerable attention and is more widely known among linguists than some of the related materials mentioned in n. 4. Most of the work mentioned in that note assumes *contra* Lakoff that such linguistic facts are not only indicative but also constitutive of sexism in society. I draw my examples from Robin Lakoff, *Language and Woman's Place* (New York: Harper Torchbook, 1975).

13. The correspondent was replying to "You are What You Say," *Ms.*

(July 1974), pp. 65–67; letter from Megan D. Price, Fair Haven, Vt., *Ms.* (Nov. 1974), p. 8.

14. Of course, lexicographers can sometimes provide us with useful data on actual uses and thus helpful guides to meaning. However, it is important to bear in mind that lexicography is no less a male-dominated profession than linguistics. Wendy Martyna (see n. 5) abundantly demonstrates that competing conventions of usage exist in the speech community: dictionaries and grammars are more likely to overlook women's interpretations and patterns of production than men's, I suspect.

15. See Marilyn Frye, "Male Chauvinism: A Conceptual Analysis," in *Philosophy and Sex,* ed. Robert Baker and Frederick Elliston (Buffalo: Prometheus, 1976), pp. 65–79, for an illustration of the intellectual fruits such neologisms can bear.

16. Nancy Henley, "Assertiveness Training: Making the Political Personal," paper given at the Society for the Study of Social Problems, Boston, Aug. 1979, provides a sharp feminist critique of assertiveness training programs.

17. Paula A. Treichler, "Verbal Subversions in Dorothy Parker: 'trapped like a trap in a trap,'" *Language and Style* 11, no. 4 (Fall 1980): 48–61, beautifully evokes this kind of "entrapment" history.

18. "Male and Female Forms of Speech in Yana" first appeared in *Donum Natalicium Schrijnen,* ed. St. W. J. Teeuwen, (Nijmegan-Utrecht, 1929), pp. 79–85; it is reprinted in *Selected Writings of Edward Sapir in Language, Culture, and Personality,* ed. David G. Mandelbaum (Berkeley: University of Calif. Press, 1949), pp. 206–12. This volume contains many interesting papers by Sapir. Sapir's student Mary Haas wrote another of the classic papers on sex-based differences in language use, "Men's and Women's Speech in Koasati," *Language* 20 (1944): 142–49, reprinted in *Language in Culture and Society,* ed. Dell Hymes (New York: Harper and Row, 1964), pp. 228–33.

19. I am working on an account of linguistic meaning and its relation to language-in-use that will, I hope, shed some light on these issues. That study, *The Construction of Meaning,* is highly theoretical, however, and these phenomena require careful and detailed empirical investigation as well. In "The Origin of Sexist Language in Discourse," I argue that conventionalization of conversational implicature is a central mechanism of semantic change, that power and privilege make it easier successfully to implicate one's own perspective, and thus that it is more likely not only that men's perspectives get "encoded" but also that such "encoding" could happen without women's "assenting" to the views so expressed.

20. See Susan Kalčik, ". . . like Ann's gynecologist or the time I was almost raped," *Journal of American Folklore* 88 (1975): 3–11; Naomi Scheman, "Anger and the Politics of Naming," in *Women and Language,* ed. McConnell-Ginet, Borker, and Furman, pp. 174–87.

21. Some have thought feminist linguists were discarding all "traditional" linguistic theory; see Mary-Louise Kean, "Comment on 'Intonation in a Man's World,'" and my "Reply to Kean," *Signs* 5 (1980): 367–72.

Language and Black Woman's Place: Evidence from the Black Middle Class[1]

Marsha Houston Stanback

A black woman describes her youthful search for an acceptable image of womanhood: "I remember reflecting on images . . . I felt like I was picking bits and pieces from different lives and trying to put . . . [them] together, but not really coming up with *me;* I didn't see *me* in the picture."[2] She might well have been describing black women's search for coherent images of themselves in the contemporary literature on language and gender.

During much of the previous decade, the belief that sexism created a common ground of communicative experiences for all women influenced many language and gender scholars to ignore the social class and subcultural differences among female speakers. Much of the published research on the speech and language use of women shows a bias toward the communicative experiences of white, middle-class women. In fact, our fund of information concerning middle-class white women's speech and language behavior has been greatly enriched during the past ten years, while that concerning working class, black, and other minority women has remained comparatively impoverished.

A similar situation exists in black communication research. Research on the Black English Vernacular (BEV) has so often focused on male interaction networks[3] that scholars have tended to regard black men as the more proficient users of dialect structure, and to consider vernacular speech events to be the exclusive province of men.[4] In short, neither contemporary research on language and gender nor that on black communication coherently describes black women's communicative experiences.

One researcher has noted that scholars in most disciplines have tended to overlook black women. Black women's experiences, needs, and realities have been "assumed to be identical with those of blacks and women in general."[5] Yet much contemporary scholarship has demonstrated that "the realities of black women depart in marked, fundamental ways from those of both white women and black men."[6]

Of course language and gender scholars now acknowledge that the female communicative experience is not everywhere the same, and they encourage "more research" regarding the communication of non-white and/or non-middle-class women.[7] The amount of published research on minority women's speech leads one to conclude that relatively few scholars are actually engaged in such research. In an earlier essay, I urged more studies focused specifically on black women's communication.[8] I suggested that such research be based on a re-framing of the central issues of language and gender research in light of black women's unique cultural and communicative experiences. The need for more research on black women's speech still exists. I will extend my earlier arguments regarding differences between black and white women's cultural and communicative experiences by summarizing some of my own recent findings regarding black middle-class women's speech.

The research findings that I will summarize here are drawn from a larger empirical study of variations in college-educated, socioeconomically middle class black and white women's speech in three different conversational contexts.[9] Both the black and white participants in the study varied their use of features associated with women's speech[10] in response to changing conversational contexts; the black women were also bi-dialectal and, therefore, simultaneously varied their use of certain Black English Vernacular (BEV) features as well.[11]

One implication of these findings is important to note at the outset of this discussion. The BEV is often misconceived as spoken only by the least educated, least affluent black people. Educated, middle-class blacks are often thought of—and often think of themselves—as speaking Mainstream American English (MAE)[12] exclusively, never the BEV, particularly if they have infrequent face-to-face contacts with other blacks. Yet most black adults, regardless of their current educational or economic status, learned to speak in black communities where the BEV was spoken to some extent by their peers and/or their parents, and where they developed some level of proficiency in speaking the dialect themselves.[13] More important, in black speech communities, speakers are enculturated into a uniquely black set of communication norms, attitudes, and expectations. The communication behavior of the participants in my study, particularly their alternation between MAE and BEV, is a significant indication that black middle-class speakers continue to apply communication norms and expectations learned in black speech communities when their interactions are no longer confined exclusively to those communities.[14] The necessity for understanding black culture as an essential part of the situational context of black women's speech is emphasized by educated, middle-class black women's retention and use of communication norms and behaviors learned in black cultural contexts.

The concept of communication as socially and culturally situated action is central to my discussion of black middle-class women's speech.[15] Nichols best summarized the dangers of ignoring the sociocultural contexts in which women develop and use language. She pointed out that while there may be common patterns in women's lives and in women's speech across diverse social and cultural groups, "women are members first and foremost of their own small speech communities, and it is in the daily context of their lives as speaking members of a larger group that their language must be examined."[16] Adequate explanations of black women's speech demand the realization that black women are both black *and* female speakers. In other words, adequate explanations of black women's speech must be grounded in clear conceptions of black cultural definitions of women's roles and women's speech.

Two influences on black cultural attitudes and expectations regarding women's speech—black women's tradition of work outside the home and black people's general ambivalence toward their own and white cultural forms[17]—will establish a context for black women's communicative development and language use which differs substantially from the context experienced by white women. Scholars emphasize a clear asymmetry between men's and women's relationships to the language in white middle-class American speech communities; in black American communities, however, gender differences in speech are seldom clear-cut and straightforward. There is a tension between male-female communicative parity and male-female communicative asymmetry in black American culture which results in black community norms for appropriate women's speech and language behavior that are more complex than those of socioeconomically similar white speech communities. Black women's tradition of work outside the home seems to create pressure toward male-female communicative parity; on the other hand, black people's recognition that their cultural tendency toward male-female communicative equality deviates from the traditions of the majority (white) culture seems to create pressure toward communicative asymmetry.

The "Second Shift": Women and Work in the Black Community

Scholars have most often considered gender differences in speech to result from the distinct separation of male and female work roles suggested by Rosaldo.[18] Kramarae explains, "Women perceive the world differently from men because of women's different experiences and activities rooted in the division of labor."[19] The usual argument is that women's unique perception of the world is shaped by their activities in the "domestic sphere" or, more important, by their near-exclusion from activities in the "public sphere." The unique perception of the world created by women's restricted social roles is realized in their speech. In traditional white middle-class American culture, for example, the ideal woman is exclusively a homemaker and mother; as a speaker, she is docile, self-effacing, and tentative, particularly when compared to the men of her culture. In short, scholars most often explain women's speech by referring to their repertoire of social roles.

Scholars also note that a young girl's speech and language development may be influenced as much by her culture's *expectations* regarding the social roles women *should* play as by the repertoire of social roles she may actually acquire as an adult. The historically prevailing white middle-class cultural expectation that women will be active primarily in the domestic sphere has influenced mainstream cultural norms regarding women's speech and language behavior: ". . . women are *expected* to have different interests and different roles, hold different types of conversations and react differently to other people" than are men.[20] Lakoff argues that mainstream women are socialized to communicate as less powerful social actors than are men.[21] Kramer suggests that because women are socialized as Lakoff describes, they "learn to control their speech to help convey the impression that they are living in the background."[22]

These generally accepted arguments regarding gender differences in the speech of middle-class whites are of only limited value in explaining differences in middle-class black men and women's speech. The distinct division between male and female spheres of activity, on which the arguments are based, has never been prevalent in black speech communities. While there are certainly differences between black male and female social roles based on women's primacy in the care of children and home, the boundary between the "domestic" and "public" spheres has always been more permeable for black than white women.[23]

It is important to remember that both black men and women were brought to the United States as workers. They shared equally in the labor as well as the oppression of slavery. The black woman's heritage from slavery—and its aftermath of poverty and racism—is a *tradition* of work outside the home. Historically, even if a black woman was married and her husband employed, her economic survival, and certainly the achievement or maintenance of middle-class economic status, required her to work.[24] Although most black women have worked in so-called female jobs (e.g., domestic servants, teachers, nurses, social workers), their tradition of work has created a perception of womanhood that starkly contrasts to white perceptions: the responsible, financially independent woman who assumes a strong role in the family has always been considered the norm rather than the exception.[25] In her study of black adolescent girls, Ladner found the strong, economically autonomous, family-oriented woman to be the prevailing image of womanhood. Two other acceptable images were the upwardly mobile, middle-class career woman and the sexually free, "laissez-faire" model of womanhood. All three images accepted by Ladner's participants involved "a sense of self-reliance, strength, and autonomy . . . an attitude that women can do whatever a man does."[26]

In summary, if we explain the typical black middle-class woman's speech by pointing to the repertoire of roles she derives from the social division of labor in her community, as is most often done in the literature on women's speech, then our explanation must include her tradition of working a "second shift"—of historically operating in both the domestic and public spheres.[27] Once we understand the typical black middle-class woman's historic dual roles as worker and homemaker, we understand that the domestic sphere/public sphere dichotomy is of limited value in analyzing and explaining her communication.

Instead, it is more useful to inquire how black women's activities in both spheres—or, at least, the cultural expectation that women will be active in both spheres—influences community definitions of womanhood and community norms for women's communication. Two qualities of black women's communication which have been discussed previously in the literature may be considered to be related to their tradition of working a "second shift." First, black women have been described as generally outspoken and self-assertive speakers.[28] One may speculate that just as there is a reciprocity between the traditional white middle-class woman's confinement to the domestic sphere and her self-effacing speech style,[29] there is also a reciprocity between the black middle-class woman's tradition of work, her perception of herself as an autonomous individual, and her outspoken style of speaking.

A second, related quality of black women's communication, which seems to be the consequence of the cultural expectation that both men and women will participate in the public sphere, is what some scholars have described as black women's tendency to verbally "contend" with black men. Several scholars have attributed the absence of black male dominance in the male-female encounters they observed to black female contentiousness.[30] Other researchers have suggested that black men and women communicate more nearly as equals than do white men and women because of blacks' more nearly equal social roles.[31] Women who communicate as equals with men may appear contentious, dominant, or even "verbally castrating" to researchers who are accustomed to encountering more submissive female speakers.

While I would not argue that there is absolute communicative equality between black women and men, I suggest that there is a fundamental tendency toward male-female communicative parity in black culture which starkly contrasts to the tendency toward communicative asymmetry which scholars emphasize for white women and men. The black tendency toward communicative parity is most striking when one examines black men and women's use of Black English Vernacular. Several researchers have found that black women are as proficient in using features of the BEV as black men.[32]

One BEV feature which has been used to illustrate both black women's alleged contentiousness and their communicative equality is "signifying."[33] Geneva Smitherman defines "signifying" as the "verbal art of insult in which a speaker humorously puts down, talks about, needles—that is signifies on—the listener"; it is "a culturally approved way of talking about somebody—usually through verbal indirection."[34]

In the following example, Ted is the object of everyone's "signification" (in the transcribed interactions that follow, an asterisk[*]marks the feature under discussion, bracketed utterances are spoken concurrently, and an equals sign[=]marks continuing speech):

> Jean: So what is the ideal woman, Ted?
> *Marv: Testify, Ted; tell-the-truth-tell-the-truth-tell-the-truth!
> *Jean: Knee deep! Lift your pocketbook, Rose, [it's gettin']
>   knee deep.
> All: (Laughter)
> Jean: (To Ted) Go 'head.
> Ted: No, no the reason I was listenin' was that, now I
>   know—
> *Jean: Get
>   the

shit-shovel. (Laughs) Go 'head, Ted.[35]

In my research, I use the term "smart talk" to include "signifying" and other BEV features (e.g., braggadocio, loud-talking[36]) which comprise the black woman's most outspoken communicative style:

> Rose: . . . so I just told [my husband], 'Don't EVER get . . .
>   [to your father's house] and pull this kinda bull on
>   me! Y'know, you don't help do this,   you don't help
>   to do that =
> *Jean: Utuh,   don't
>   try that!
>
> Rose: = cause I will EMBARRASS you!

A brief explanation of how the women in the study used "smart talk" will support my contention that black men and women tend to communicate as equals.

The black women whom I studied used "smart talk" in a manner consistent with Smitherman's definition of "signifying," as an indirect, humorous means to express strong negative feelings about a person, action, or event:

> Jean: . . . when we finally got here and got our apartment,
>   and stuff, y'know, and I prepared the food, and I'd
>   fixed MY plate and sat down started eatin'
> All: (Laughter)
> *Rose: (With sweet sarcasm) 'Aren't you gonna eat, Honey?'

Jean: [He would] want me to WAIT on him!
*Rose: (As above) 'Get it while it's hot!'

Like so much of black communication, "smart talk" is a blend of opposites.[37] It is outspoken yet indirect; it is humorous in tone but serious in intent. "Smart talk" includes not only the humorous turn of phrase which is easily represented on the printed page (as in the examples above), but also emotions and attitudes toward the object of criticism, expressed through subtle intonation shifts and other paralinguistic cues too complex and varied to represent adequately here. The emotional content emphasizes the seriousness of the criticism underlying the overt humor of "smart talk."

As the examples above indicate, the black women whom I have studied were competent users of "smart talk." In general, they tended to use "smart talk" more frequently in conversations with other black people, whether men or women, and less frequently in conversations with whites.

The overall proficiency in using "smart talk" demonstrated by the black middle-class women whom I studied provides one sort of evidence regarding male-female communicative parity, evidence that black women are as competent as black men in using black speech events. The participants' consistent use of "smart talk" with other blacks regardless of their gender provides a second sort of evidence of black male-female communicative parity, evidence that black women use their most outspoken speech register in certain conversations with other black men as well as with other black women.

"Double Consciousness": Black Culture as Sub-Culture

The foregoing discussion of "smart talk," black women's most outspoken communication style, indicates that there are black communicative norms which permit a greater degree of male-female expressive parity than the literature describes for white women and men. But the traditional black image of womanhood and the general tendency toward male-female expressive parity belies the ambivalence which many black people often feel toward such evidence of gender equality within the culture. Let us examine that ambivalence.

Black middle-class women's speech is influenced both by the cultural expectation that they will be proficient users of the BEV and by black cultural constraints on their use of certain BEV features. The constraints are the result of black awareness of differences between their own and the communicative norms of the majority culture— "double consciousness." "Double consciousness" may be a more powerful influence on the speech of black middle-class women than on other communities of black women. Historically, the black middle class has been aware of what Staples calls a unique position in American society: its cultural ties to the masses of black folk and its economic similarity to middle-class whites.[38] Contemporary black middle-class women often reside or socialize in black social contexts and work in white social contexts (or vice versa). Moving between the two cultures undoubtedly heightens one's awareness of communicative differences and, quite possibly, one's ambivalence toward the communicative norms of one or both cultures.

Black America is not an autonomous culture; rather, it is one of the coexisting cultures that make up U.S. society. As a result, both black culture and black communication are eclectic systems. Influences on both include West African cultures and languages, the slave heritage, racism, the traditional black church, mainstream (white, Euro-American) cultures and languages.[39]

Since the turn of the century, analysts of black life and culture have recognized black people's ambivalent relationships to their own and white cultural forms. W. E. B. Du Bois first described these relationships and labeled them "double consciousness": ". . . the Negro is a sort of seventh son, born with a veil and gifted with second-sight in this American world—a world which yields him no true self-consciousness, but only lets him see himself through the revelation of the other world. It is a peculiar sensation this *double consciousness,* this sense of always measuring one's soul by the tape of a world that looks on in amused contempt and pity. One ever feels his twoness—an American, a Negro. . . ."[40] In his study of a working-class black community, Hannerz found that the sort of double consciousness described by Du Bois presented difficulties for making decisions about actions and for evaluating actions: "This awareness of two cultures . . . is one of the major features of ghetto [black] life and outlook. It is an awareness which easily leads to conflicts and contradictions even as one acts according to one model or another. If one tries to act according to the mainstream model, the rewards may . . . be small because of the ghetto dweller's ascribed social position; if one accepts the ghetto model, one is aware of one's deviation from the dominant culture of American society."[41] Folb found a similar "ambivalence toward their blackness and their people" among the teenaged blacks she studied.[42]

Hannerz notes that double consciousness often leads blacks to accept an action as a practical necessity (for example, female out-spokenness), while regarding its opposite as a more desirable ideal (for example, female reticence).[43] This juxtaposition of practical and ideal behaviors which results from double consciousness has particular implications for black women's communication. Although the traditional black view of women as the communicative and social equals of men is part of the black cultural value system, it does not seem to be regarded as the ideal situation by many black men and women. For example, one scholar notes that black women's tradition of work has given them an image of being "beasts of burden," a decidedly "unfeminine" image.[44] Another scholar suggests that because black women are often perceived as unfeminine by whites, they must forge an identity for themselves "as women" in interracial encounters,[45] presumably by demonstrating their similarities to traditional mainstream women.

Folb points out that the black women in the community which she studied reported experiencing more situational constraints on their use of black vernacular speech than the men reported. For example, women who "cursed" (swore) or frequently "signified" on male peers earned the unflattering reputation of being "hard mouths" rather than "ladies" (i.e., ideal females).[46] If the numerous ethnographies of black male in-teraction networks are accurate, black men experience few such situa-tional constraints, particularly in regard to "signifying" and other BEV speech events.[47] The black man's use of "signifying" and other vernacu-lar speech events has been described in the literature as the means for establishing his "rep" as a "man-of-words" (i.e., an ideal male).[48]

Folb's findings suggest that double consciousness operates in rela-tion to judgments of black women's speech. Despite communicative norms which permit greater expressive parity between black men and women than between whites, black speech communities tend to define their men by their verbal prowess and their women by their verbal propriety in much the same manner as white speech communities.

The communication of the women whom I studied showed evi-dence of more subtle constraints on black women's speech than those pointed out by Folb. The most striking evidence of communicative asymmetry was the black women's greater silence in their conversation with the black men, demonstrated by their lower total speaking turn times and fewer backchannels.[49] The women spoke approximately half as much in their conversation with the black men as they did in conversation with other women. Indeed, the black women may be said to have retreated to the background of the conversation with the black men.

The black women's use of the call and response backchannel provides an example of their general retreat to the background of the cross-gender conversation. Call and response is a backchannel utterance in the black style:

>   Rose: . . . And if you—if you were a doctor, [my God you
>   were =
>   *Jean: Oh, chi::ile!
>   Rose   = you—you could do everything . . .

Call and response is one means by which black speakers create what some scholars have described as a uniquely black conversational form in which "there is no sharp line between performers or communicators and audience, for virtually everyone is performing and everyone is listening."[50] Call and response allows ongoing oral participation by all participants in a conversation without losing sight of the turn-taking process. Thus, call and response signals one's role as a "participant" in the conversation rather than as a mere "spectator":

>   Rose: . . . and I always felt I never wanted to get married
>   because I said, 'Is this the way it is?'   and then =
>   *Jean: Fuhget it!
>   Rose: = you know, you see so much you don't like . . .

The generally lower frequencies of call and response used by the black women in the cross-gender conversation suggest a tendency toward asymmetry in black male-female communication. The women assumed or were relegated to more spectator than participant roles in the cross-gender conversation than in the conversations with other women. One woman stated during a post-conversation interview that she "wanted to hear what the men had to say" on the topics discussed during the conversation with them, so she probably "listened more" than she had during the conversations with the women. Another woman commented that before the conversation with the men, she was afraid that the men would expect the women "to sit in the background . . . and let them give the opinions," and she observed that during the conversation the men often did not seem to include the women in their talk: "I found that the guys were talking to each other . . . they would look at each other looking for approval as opposed to the whole scope of us."[51]

The lower total speaking turn times and less frequent use of back-channels, including call and response, by the black women in my study are evidence of their willing or unwilling retreat to the background of conversations with black men. Such a retreat indicates a tendency toward communicative asymmetry in black male-female communication.

Middle-class black women's communicative experiences within their own cultural group form a striking contrast to those of middle-class white women. White women are often described in the literature as unskilled in using certain features of mainstream speech because of their confinement to domestic roles. Black women are described as proficient in using the full range of black communicative features, but as experiencing situational constraints which black men do not experience. For both groups of women, the outcome is a degree of communicative asymmetry. One should not forget, however, that the genesis of communicative asymmetry in the two communities is different: in white America, communicative asymmetry between the genders results from a historic, rigid division of labor according to gender; in black America, it is more the result of a historic unwillingness to accept certain black cultural behaviors as ideal.

Conclusion

A basic premise of women's communication research is that communication theories and models must account for the influence of gender on speech. Black communication research is based on the similar premise that communication theories must account for the influence of culture on speech. The contrast between the sociocultural contexts of white and black women's speech should indicate the advantages of attending to both culture and gender when making generalizations about women's speech. Attending to the varied sociocultural contexts in which women speak enables scholars to provide more comprehensive descriptions of the speech of specific communities of women. More important, attending to the sociocultural contexts of women's speech facilitates the development of more comprehensive theories regarding the general relationship between language and gender, theories which can account for diversity in the general category of women's speech.

Notes

1. My title is derived from that of Robin Lakoff, *Language and Woman's Place* (New York: Harper and Row, 1975). I thank Prof. Fern L. Johnson, University of Massachusetts, and Prof. Patricia Nichols, San Jose State University, for their comments on earlier versions of this paper.

2. Quoted from audio-taped conversational data gathered by the author; see also note 35.

3. See for examples, Roger D. Abrahams, *Deep Down in the Jungle: Negro Narrative Folklore from the Streets of Philadelphia* (Hatboro, Pa.: Folklore Associates, 1963); E. Liebow, *Talley's Corner: A Study of Negro Street-corner Men* (Boston: Little Brown, 1967); Ulf Hannerz, *Soulside: Inquiries into Ghetto Culture and Community* (New York: Columbia University Press, 1969); William Labov, *Language in the Inner City: Studies in the Black English Vernacular* (Philadelphia: University of Pennsylvania Press, 1972); Thomas Kochman, "Toward an Ethnography of Black American Speech Behavior," in his *Rappin' and Stylin' Out: Communication in Urban Black America* (Urbana: University of Illinois Press, 1972), pp. 241–64; T. Garner, "Playing the Dozens: Folklore as Strategies for Living," *Quarterly Journal of Speech* 69, no. 1 (1983): 47–57.

4. Edith Folb, *Runnin' Down Some Lines: The Language and Culture of Black Teenagers* (Cambridge, Mass.: Harvard University Press, 1980), pp. 193–94, 225; Nancy Faires Conklin, "Perspectives on the Dialects of Women," paper presented to American Dialect Society (1973), quoted in Barrie Thorne and Nancy Henley, *Language and Sex: Difference and Dominance* (Rowley, Mass.: Newbury House, 1975), p. 11.

5. W. R. Allen, "Family Roles, Occupational Statuses, and Achievement Orientations among Black Women in the U.S.," *Signs* 4 (1979): 670.

6. Ibid. See further evidence for Allen's assertion in Bonnie Thornton Dill, "The Dialectics of Black Womanhood," *Signs* 4 (1979), 543–71; Gloria I. Joseph and Jill Lewis, *Common Differences: Conflicts in Black and White Feminist Perspectives* (Garden City, N.Y.: Anchor, 1981); Bell Hooks, *Ain't I a Woman: Black Women and Feminism* (Boston: South End Press, 1981); Gloria T. Hull, Patricia Bell Scott, and Barbara Smith, eds., *But Some of Us Are Brave: Black Women's Studies* (Old Westbury, N.Y.: Feminist Press, 1982).

7. Barrie Thorne, Cheris Kramarae, and Nancy Henley, eds., *Language, Gender, and Society* (Rowley, Mass.: Newbury House, 1983), pp. 16–17.

8. Marsha Houston Stanback, "Language and Black Woman's Place: Toward a Description of Black Women's Communication," paper presented to the Speech Communication Association, Louisville, Ky., 1982.

9. The study examined the speech of two black and two white middle-class women during three informal conversations with their close acquaintances. In the first conversation each pair of participants talked with two women acquaintances from their own cultural group (i.e., black or white women); in the second conversation participants talked with two women acquaintances from the other cultural group; and in the third, participants talked with men acquaintances from their own cultural group.

10. Previous research on language and gender suggested the following features associated with women's speech which were examined in the study: hedges (e.g., I guess, I think, you know, like); intensifiers (e.g., only, always, so); tag questions (e.g., "Most of the schools were integrated, *right?*"); reinforcing backchannels (e.g., umhmm, yes, right).

11. The BEV was examined in a manner suggested by Geneva Smitherman, *Talkin' and Testifyin': The Language of Black America* (Boston: Houghton-Mifflin, 1977) as a system of structural features (phonology, lexico-grammar, syntax) and functional features (semantics, rhetoric, speech events). Features examined were the omission of the phonemes [I], [r], [g], and [d]; use of words and expressions from the black lexicon; use of invariant "be," copula deletion, uninflected third person singular of regular verbs, pleonastic subject, and substitutions of "it" for "there" and "got" for "have"; use of smart talk, marking, call and response, and narrative sequencing.

12. The term "Mainstream American English" was suggested by J. Wofford, "Ebonics: A Legitimate System of Oral Communication," *Journal of Black Studies* 9 (1979): 368. It is a very general designation, referring to the American English dialect which is most often spoken and accepted as "correct" by formally educated white Americans, i. e., it is the prestige dialect in the United States. I prefer the term "Mainstream American English" to the more common "Standard English" which suggests a written "standard" that omits essential features of spoken dialect (e.g., phonology, paralanguage, speech events) and, thus, is not an appropriate parallel to the Black English Vernacular.

13. Wofford, p. 368; H. Seymour and C. Seymour, "The Symbolism of Ebonics: I'd Rather Switch than Fight," *Journal of Black Studies* 9 (1979): 367–82.

14. Joshua Fishman's distinction between an "experiential" and a "referential" speech community is useful here; *The Sociology of Language* (Rowley, Mass.: Newbury House, 1972), pp. 23–28. Even if the physical boundaries of a black community no longer define a black woman's communicative experiences, she may continue to share "interests, views, and allegiances" with black people; that is, the black community in which she grew up or black American culture, in general, may continue to function as a referential speech community for her.

15. Dell Hymes, "Models of the Interaction of Language and Social Life," in *Directions in Sociolinguistics,* ed. John J. Gumperz and Dell Hymes (New York: Holt, Rinehart and Winston, 1972), p. 4; W. S. Hall and Roy O. Freedle, *Culture and Language: The Black American Experience* (Washington, D.C.: Hemisphere, 1975), p. 3; M. A. K. Halliday, *Language as Social Semiotic: The*

Interpretation of Language and Meaning (Baltimore: University Park Press, 1978), p. 23.

16. Patricia Nichols, "Women in their Speech Communities," in *Women and Language in Literature and Society,* ed. Sally McConnell-Ginet, Ruth Borker, and Nelly Furman (New York: Praeger, 1980), p. 140.

17. In this discussion, the terms "black" and "white" refer to different cultural rather than racial groups. Although generalizations about middle-class black and white women speakers should be qualified by the understanding that neither group is internally homogenous, there are common assumptions about women's speech within each culture—and contrasting assumptions between the two cultures—that have been demonstrated in previous research and are further supported by the data summarized here.

18. Michelle Z. Rosaldo, "Woman, Culture, and Society: A Theoretical Overview," in *Woman, Culture, and Society,* ed. Michelle Z. Rosaldo and Louise Lamphere (Stanford: Stanford University Press, 1974), pp. 17–18.

19. Cheris Kramarae, *Women and Men Speaking,* (Rowley, Mass.: Newbury House, 1981), p. 3.

20. Robin Lakoff, *Language and Woman's Place,* p. 62, my emphasis.

21. Ibid., pp. 2–8.

22. Cheris Kramer [Cheris Kramarae], "Women's Speech: Separate but Unequal?" *Quarterly Journal of Speech* 60, no. 1 (1974): p. 20.

23. Michelle Wallace, *Black Macho and the Myth of the Superwoman* (New York: Dial, 1978), pp. 22–24; L. W. Myers, *Black Women: Do They Cope Better?* (Englewood Cliffs, N.J.: Prentice Hall, 1980), p. 17; Dill, "Dialectics of Black Womanhood," pp. 548–53.

24. J. Noble, *Beautiful, Also, Are the Souls of My Black Sisters: A History of the Black Woman in America* (Englewood Cliffs, N.J.: Prentice Hall, 1978), pp. 123–25.

25. See discussions of black male and female family roles in Joyce Ladner, *Tomorrow's Tomorrow: The Black Woman* (Garden City, N.J.: Doubleday-Anchor, 1971); Robert Staples, *The Black Woman in America: Sex, Marriage and the Family* (Chicago: Nelson Hall, 1973); and Dill, "Dialectics of Black Womanhood," pp. 544–57.

26. Ladner, *Tomorrow's Tomorrow,* p. 127.

27. J. Cole, "Women in Cuba: The Revolution Within the Revolution," in *Comparative Perspectives of Third World Women,* ed. B. Lindsay (New York: Praeger, 1979), p. 172.

28. For examples see Roger Abrahams, "Negotiating Respect: Patterns of Presentation among Black Women," *Journal of American Folklore* 88, no. 347 (1975): 58–80; Staples, *Black Woman in America,* pp. 11, 30, 107; Liebow, *Talley's Corner,* pp. 102–60; Folb, *Runnin' Down Some Lines,* 146–48.

29. Kramarae, *Women and Men Speaking,* p. 3.

30. Abrahams, "Negotiating Respect," pp. 66, 73–77; Liebow, *Talley's Corner,* pp. 102–60.

31. Folb, *Runnin' Down Some Lines,* pp. 132–63.

32. See Claudia Mitchell-Kernan's discussion of black women's use of

"signifying" in *Language Behavior in a Black Urban Community,* Monographs of the Language Behavior Laboratory no. 2 (Berkeley: University of California, 1971), pp. 128–40; Folb's discussion on black teenage women's vernacular vocabulary, pp. 193–200; Stanback's discussion of black women's use of BEV grammar, syntax, and speech events ("Code-Switching in Black Women's Speech" [Ph.D., dissertation, University of Massachusetts, 1983], pp. 133–85).

33. Mitchell-Kernan, *Language Behavior in a Black Urban Community,* pp. 128–40; Abrahams, "Negotiating Respect," pp. 73–77; Folb, *Runnin' Down Some Lines,* pp. 196–98.

34. Smitherman, *Talkin' and Testifyin',* pp. 118–19.

35. All conversational exerpts are taken from verbatim written transcriptions of audio-taped conversations among middle-class black women. Excerpts are recorded according to the system developed by Jefferson and reported in Harvey Sacks, E. Schlegloff, and Gail Jefferson, "A Simplest Systematics of Turn-Taking for Conversation," *Language* 50 (1974): 696–735. Asterisks (*) indicate the feature being illustrated.

36. Smitherman defines braggadocio as talk designed to "convey the image of an omnipotent, fearless being, capable of doing the undoable" (p. 97). Mitchell-Kernan defines "loud-talking" as an utterance "which by virtue of its volume permits hearers other than the addressee, and is objectionable because of this." "Signifying, loud-talking, and marking," in *Rappin' and Stylin' Out,* ed. Kochman.

37. M. K. Asante [A. L. Smith], "Markings of an African Concept of Rhetoric," in his *Language, Communication, and Rhetoric in Black America* (New York: Harper and Row, 1972), pp. 367–69.

38. Staples, *Black Woman in America,* p. 43.

39. Smitherman, *Talkin' and Testifyin',* pp. 1–15; Hall and Freedle, *Culture and Language,* pp. 13–17.

40. W. E. B. DuBois, *The Souls of Black Folk* (1903; rpt., *Three Negro Classics,* New York: Avon Books, 1965), pp. 214–15.

41. Hannerz, *Soulside,* p. 102.

42. Folb, *Runnin' Down Some Lines,* p. xxiii.

43. Ulf Hannerz, "What Ghetto Males are Like: Another Look," in *Afro-American Anthropology: Contemporary Perspectives,* ed. N. E. Whitten and J. F. Szwed (New York: Free Press, 1970), p. 322.

44. J. C. Noble, quoted in Dill, "Dialectics of Black Womanhood," p. 553.

45. D. Pennington, "Black American Women: Strategies for Integration," paper presented to the International Communication Association, Philadelphia, Pa., 1979, p. 2.

46. Folb, *Runnin' Down Some Lines,* pp. 195–96.

47. For example, Abrahams, *Deep Down in the Jungle;* Liebow, *Talley's Corner;* Hannerz, *Soulside;* Labov, *Language in the Inner City;* Kochman, *Rappin' and Stylin' Out;* and Garner, "Playing the Dozens."

48. Roger Abrahams, "Black Views of Language Use: Rules of Decorum,

Conflict, and Men-of-Words," in *Current Trends in Language,* ed. N. Johnson (Cambridge, Mass.: Winthrop, 1976), pp. 189–94.

49. S. Duncan, Jr. ("Some Signals and Rules for Taking Speaking Turns in Conversations," *Journal of Personality and Social Psychology* 23 [1972]: 283–92) defines a backchannel as any brief utterance which does not constitute a speaking turn or an attempt to claim a speaking turn, but encourages the speaker currently holding the floor to continue his or her turn.

50. Smitherman, *Talkin' and Testifyin',* p. 108.

51. Stanback, *Code-Switching,* p. 177.

3

BARNARD GREEK GAMES

THIS STATUE IS PRESENTED TO THE COLLEGE
BY THE CLASS OF 1905, FOUNDER OF THE GAMES
TO COMMEMORATE THE TWENTY-FIFTH ANNIVERSARY
OF THEIR ESTABLISHMENT IN 1930

A statue of the Greek goddess Athena was presented to Barnard College by the Class of 1905 that founded the Barnard Greek Games to commemorate the college's twenty-fifth anniversary. Photo courtesy of the Barnard Alumnae Office.

Section 3. On Boundaries

Feminist scholars are creating new meanings for the term "disinterested" scholarship. Traditionally, the term has meant "neutral" scholarship, employing a presumed detachment in a carefully controlled search for answers to impersonal questions.

Paradigms in each discipline do change, but a premium is placed on "disinterested" scholarship and authoritative male voices. Feminist scholars violate traditional academic decorum when they make explicit not only their concern but their outrage at social conditions, acknowledge personal and social change as goals, value women's work done outside the academy as well as inside, express and value affect as a legitimate part of inquiry, and deal with issues of value, information, and techniques that borrow from many disciplines. That is, they are *interested* scholars.

The papers in this section are written on and about boundaries. Bobbie Anthony-Perez examines the ways academic boundaries have been used to separate black and white women; in an extensive review of the literature, she documents clear parallels between racist and sexist practices in education. The mutual history she exposes illustrates connections important to feminist efforts to effect change in the academy and out.

Edna Bay works in a field where the boundaries between "disinterested" scholarship, "disinterested policy," and vested interests break down. Western, male-centered research is used as the basis for policies that handicap Third World women in Africa. She would break down the boundary between the past and present and let historical events and concepts infuse current efforts by African women to gain more economic and political power.

Theories about women are incomplete, in part, because they are based on individual factors such as psyche, class, sex, literature, language, and history, derived from individual disciplines. Arlyn Diamond believes that a diverse intellectual community is of critical importance to the scholarly feminist enterprise; unless rooted in this community, it "runs the risk of becoming too vulnerable to attack from outside or too sterile to nourish the action which should be its fruit." We can learn to borrow, reevaluate, and confront the information and analytic frameworks from many disciplines (while recognizing that the research differs in level and unit of analysis) and escape, perhaps, the present failure of many individual disciplines to acknowledge, understand, or address the realities of social change.

Interdisciplinary Studies and a Feminist Community

Arlyn Diamond

Although most of us in women's studies have been thinking and talking for a long time about the need to be interdisciplinary, we have not found it easy to define an interdisciplinary methodology, or describe the routes to it. Trained within particular disciplines, our energies absorbed by the struggle to create new courses and programs in institutions designed to keep us locked into narrowly defined intellectual boxes called departments, we have been unable easily or speedily to transform our modes of thought. I consider myself typical of my generation of faculty in the ignorance and enthusiasm with which I agreed to coordinate a seminar for women's studies faculty which was supposed to help make us "interdisciplinary." The seminar, which was funded by the Wellesley Mellon Fellowship Program, was boldly entitled, "Introduction to Methodology in the Humanities and Social Sciences." Participants were members of the Five College Consortium: Smith, Amherst, Mount Holyoke, Hampshire College, and the University of Massachusetts. For me, at least, the entire experience was a great success, not because I can now claim that I have mastered an interdisciplinary approach, but because what happened gave me a much better idea of why such an approach is difficult, and of how it might liberate scholarship and inform it with new sense of purpose and energy.

About fifteen of us, all with conventional doctorates earned for the most part in the 1960s, all of whom had taught women's studies for several years, met weekly. A number of disciplines were represented, although not as many as we would have liked. We included people in psychology, political science, economics, English, French, education,

art history, sports studies, and religion. We badly needed anthropologists and more historians. Not surprisingly, given the sociology of
graduate study and notions of what the female mind is best suited for,
we were overloaded with literary critics, and some of us felt very guilty
about it.

Once we started, we realized how little we knew about what our
colleagues in other fields actually did. I had always thought that psychologists studied the unconscious; in fact, they studied rats. Those of
us in literature, who spent a lot of time talking about whether or not a
poem was good, and why, had to explain our concern to skeptical social
scientists. Humanists among us felt apologetic about our lack of power;
social scientists felt defensive about their abuse of power. Our mutual
astonishment at each other's assumptions was not always flattering, but
it was enlightening and made clear how much we had been ghettoized.
The substantive differences between our ways of thinking about problems clearly could not be bridged, except on the most superficial level,
without sustained effort.

All five schools represented in the seminar were located within a
ten-mile radius, and many of us had already worked together. The
nature and development of women's studies in the United States made it
inevitable that most of us had had experience with women's consciousness-raising groups, and various political movements of the late
1960s—the peace movement, civil rights movement, and radical political groups. We defined ourselves as feminists, although our definition
of the term was deliberately left as open as possible. Thanks to our
shared experiences within the academy, with attempts at social change,
and with small, intense groups, we were able to work together in ways
that more conventionally academic groups could not have. We were
also able to clarify very quickly some fundamental principles in regard
to the purposes of the seminar, principles which were essential to our
feminism. What we were doing was not an end in itself; the ultimate
goal of our work was social change. We were willing to acknowledge
that the need for this change was for us personal and strongly felt, and
we did not want to disguise the force of our personal investment in
change, and in the study of women, but use it. A second and related
goal was that we always intended to make clear the connection between
theory and practice. We were looking for an intellectual form which
would express our values. We wanted to find ways of combining so-

called rational discourse with human emotions and experiences. That is, our commitment to feminism meant a commitment to and awareness of the interplay between the personal and the political, and the analogous interplay between substance and style, not just in social relationships but in our own work as well. We were in women's studies in part because we had come to recognize that the formal, impersonal authoritative stance of most scholarship was not only sterile but a mask for a partial, biased view of reality which was incapable of acknowledging its own bias. What passed for detachment we knew, as outsiders, was merely another way of consolidating power. We sought a more honest and, therefore, potentially more effective methodology, a methodology which could discover, rather than cover over, the deepest questions.

How to make our goals work in the classroom, in writing, and in research was a problem which naturally we never solved, just as we never solved the problem of how to describe for others our interdisciplinary methodology in a way which would permit them to share our results without duplicating our efforts. Originally, I, like many, had thought that the equation before me was fairly clear: one English professor plus a list of readings in history or psychology equals one interdisciplinary scholar. I quickly learned that my initial concept of the task was much too shallow. Neither by sharing bibliographies nor by sharing approaches to a common problem, important and stimulating as those techniques were, could we learn to think in genuinely new ways, since the seminar discussions forced us to admit that all the bits we eagerly incorporated were attached to the same old mental structures.

Searching for a way into our mutual proceedings, we decided to begin by analyzing intellectually, as best we could, the nature of the dilemma we faced. This meant a series of individual statements describing what we did within our own fields, what we wanted to do in them, and how they needed to change in order to allow us to do what we wanted. Since we had been writing and teaching about women in these fields already, we did not find it difficult to articulate our dissatisfactions. We were almost all, it seems, involved with disciplines which ignored women, or distorted the nature of their lives, which valued the "hard" over the "soft," the abstract over the concrete, the mask of objectivity and omniscience over the open avowal of a human presence behind the lecture or the study or the article. Above all, our teachers and colleagues claimed to be disinterested, which was the most outrageous claim of all.

At this point, we found books and articles on the concept of ideology and sociology of knowledge useful. They offered a framework for our discussions of the connection between methodology and ideology, although of course not in terms of women's studies, while our own statements particularized the way the connection was made in our own fields. To admit to an ideology was not easy for some of us, for, after all, we have the same training as our "neutral" colleagues. Nonetheless, I think the admission was a necessary first step out of the ranks of so-called liberal scholars, with all their claims.

Our reading list as the semester continued was wide-ranging, even eccentric.[1] It was determined by the interests of the people in the seminar, and by our search for works whose methodology and subject-matter seemed to offer possible solutions to the problems with which we were struggling. Thus, in the course of a semester, we read sociologists, psychologists, economists, historians, film critics, and poets. We were not so much interested in specific knowledge as in ways of thinking which were both imaginative and rigorous. What mattered was not our choice of texts but the kinds of questions we brought to them. Is this true? What proofs does it offer us? Does it take account of the relationship between author and work, work and audience, audience and the world in which we actually live? Does it open up new views of women's lives and place in the world? Does it offer us a powerful vision? These were crude and idealistic questions, but they were important to us. What we found was that there were people, not necessarily in women's studies, who could help us, although as often by their failures as by their successes. A sociologist who talked about genes, for example, we thought confused superficial knowledge with fundamental understanding, and suggested to us that the profound awareness which comes from specialization is still necessary, as long as it is not identified with the compartmentalization of knowledge and the separation of study and context which we all deplored. The psychological study with profound implications was written in a language and tone accessible only to the most dedicated specialist. We began to get a clearer and clearer notion of what it was we rejected, and hoped for, in the works we read.

As I describe this, I suspect it all sounds very satisfactory. The trouble with this account of our work, however, is that I am now giving an illusory form to what was often formless, chaotic, even painful, and of course this was one of the problems we faced continually. A public presentation requires an ordering and shaping of material which is inevitably tidier and more limited than the ideas or experiences it is meant to express. Poets can sometimes fuse order and chaos, but I assure you that our seminar's endeavors were by no means as obvious and easy as I am making them sound. We were frequently confused and frustrated and angry at our own and others' obtuseness. Still, we kept coming back each week, because we had known from the beginning, after years of teaching women's studies and working in various politically committed groups, that our failures were inevitable, and that we had to keep working to develop the trust and openness which would free us to express our own ideas and feelings, and listen to those of our colleagues. Had we tried to rise above our conflicts as academic decorum requires, or waited to speak until we were sure we could speak with grace and authority, as academic status requires, we would have denied our initial commitment to the possibilities of an intellectual community based on the compelling need to unite personal and political, work and self. We insulted each other and called up to apologize, and met for dinner and tried to understand points of view which seemed crazy or ignorant or threatening. Sometimes we succeeded.

We had been driven to women's studies because there, it seemed, we could bridge the gaps in our lives. Our style was the expression of our beliefs and of the difficulties of our enterprise. Some of us felt that we were too impersonal, too chary about bringing our private lives into the room. Some of us felt that to do so would be too risky. Had we more time, we might have been able to be even more open. Had we less time, and a less stable group, or a less experienced one, I suspect we could not have done as much as we did, or felt so willing to come out from behind our intellectual barricades. I do not want to give the impression here that we were good pluralists, finding all ideas equally valuable out of the kind of tolerance which is based on fundamental unwillingness to take responsibility for the power of ideas. We took ideas very seriously. We were tolerant out of respect for each other as human beings, out of distaste for an aggressive, self-aggrandizing style of debate, and out of an awareness that we were all still exploring and could not afford to close our minds. There were real differences of opinion in the group and they were not dissolved in a bath of universal anti-intellectual good will, although they were not unaffected by our interchange either.

In retrospect, I can identify some of the sources of some of our problems. One was language. We not only lacked a common language, but we found intellectual language in general, as it is commonly used, inadequate to deal with the synthesis of reason and emotion which we felt we wanted. The more highly trained we were the more we relied upon a vocabulary which was depersonalized and esoteric, and which got in the way of our attempts to cross disciplinary boundaries. As a result, language itself quickly became one of our basic concerns.

Another handicap was our ambivalent relationship with our own fields and educational institutions. Our degrees were the badge of our faith in the life of the mind as it has been defined in prestigious graduate schools. We had started out with the belief that what we were doing was good, true, and important, but for all of us that belief had become tarnished. As feminists, we found the forms and substance of our disciplines inadequate theoretically and methodologically, and corrupt in the ways in which power was wielded within them. Some of us were successful professionally, in spite of our unconventionality and our sex, others had only marginal positions, or none at all, in the profession they had spent years training for. The seminar's research assistant, an undergraduate women's studies major, was amazed at the intensity of our love-hate bonds with higher education. Having rejected the false claims to objectivity and purity made in all our disciplines, we were never sure how much else we might have to reject. At any given moment, somebody wanted to drop out and forget that she had ever believed in the potential value of scholarship, somebody else (often me) clung with obstinate faith to the same potential, and somebody else wondered if we weren't wasting our time trying to develop theories in a rapidly disintegrating world. What we were attacking was what we were once a part of, and had invested in heavily, so that we were not always fair to ourselves or to each other. At the same time, it grew clear that our ongoing analysis of what was wrong with what was being studied and taught, and why, could coalesce into a sense of what the next tasks for women's studies might be.

A third source of difficulty was that all the theories we had for dealing with women as a subject were incomplete. In fact, we could not even decide, we decided, what a woman is: biological fact or social construct or historical experience. We agreed that we needed to find a way of comprehending women in terms of class, race, the historical moment, individual psyche, etc., and of perceiving each factor separately and simultaneously. Various disciplines had ways of describing certain facets of human existence, but none had succeeded in combining them in a way which we found totally satisfactory, especially in terms of women. Because of our training, we kept being trapped into thinking that one description must be more valid than another, that statistics were better than a novel, or that sociobiology or philosophy or radical economics could subsume all our categories. Too much of what labeled itself as women's studies seemed to us caught in the same trap, without our advantage, if one can call feeling trapped an advantage, of knowing it was a trap. I copied out a sentence from Lucien Goldmann's *The Human Sciences and Philosophy* which seemed to capture our dilemma. He says cheerfully that "in the human sciences the progress of knowledge proceeds from the abstract to the concrete through a continual oscillation between the whole and its parts."[2] Yes—but how, I wonder, does one grasp a continual oscillation, when one is part of the flux and cannot be sure which is a whole and which a part. The tensions we accepted as theoretically and methodologically necessary were in practice often impossible to balance, since to talk about women is to talk about all of human life in ways which are disturbingly unfamiliar, and to discover that which we would rather not know.

The closest we came to defining ways of focusing our understanding of the phenomena/material represented by women's studies was in our consensus that the explanations we sought were social on the one hand, and intrapsychic on the other. Feminist scholarship for us had to be able to describe social forces and processes, yet no social theories seemed to us sufficient to account for the power and consistency of sexual differentiation. Modes of production change, but in every culture we have ever known the female has always been the "other." The more we read and discussed, the more central the irrational response to the idea of the female seemed in human life, even in those areas ostensibly far removed from any concern with gender.

We had almost all brought to the seminar a particular attachment to one or the other of these modes of inquiry—social or psychic—and a particular regard for one or more of the theories associated with them. One woman, trying to capture what she found most remarkable about the group, said she had never in her life been in a room with so many

Marxists in it. Particularly in our early discussions of ideology, and our sense of the vital significance of class and of the material conditions in which women live, we were heavily influenced by Marxist concepts, and the methodology we found most sympathetic owed much to the notion of the dialectic, but like others we found that Marxist theory as it is currently framed leaves out too much essential to a full consideration of women's issues. As Marxists, Jungians, and Freudians, categories which for the most part described our past allegiances and interests, we found plenty of agreement on what we were asking questions about—for example, hatred of women, the role of the family, the power of mothering—and we very consciously avoided pitting one system against another. I think we all felt that if we were to make use of new ideas and knowledge without falling prey to the simplicity of ignorance or the certainty of doctrinaire wisdom, we had to learn to accept our differences for the time being.

Two of our most successful meetings were with Jean Baker Miller, the author of *Towards A New Psychology of Women,* and Dorothy Dinnerstein, author of *The Mermaid and the Minotaur.* Both women were interested in the role of the unconscious, but unlike most traditional Freudians they wanted to use their knowledge of psychology, and of the central role of mothering in human life, as a way of understanding why social change is desirable and inevitable. Sharing our questions about methodology and goals with women whose work we respected and who saw what they did as part of an ongoing intellectual project fueled by their commitment to feminism and to an ideal of human transformation and integration was enormously energizing for us. We were reminded that, after all, the feminist search for an authentic intellectual voice is a collective task, which expands as we work at it, and gets more exciting as it expands and as we share it. Individualistic scholarship, isolated from other scholars and from a real world, can never in the long run become truly interdisciplinary. We may grapple with particular projects on our own, but if we ignore the fact that we are part of a community, whether or not formalized as in our seminar, we will lack the nourishment we need to destroy old fallacies and build new truths. Our isolation and our narrowness are not individual failures but symptoms of what is wrong with the conventional learning which has distorted the world.

Our seminar for me was an invaluable experience, although I could not neatly encapsulate its significance. I have discussed what we did not do, what we rejected, and what we feared, out of the certain knowledge that every single member of the seminar would have a different version of what went on, and why it was so important. I have also described our crises of confidence and doubts because too often these are disregarded as irrelevant. For us, they were relevant, because they were part of what it means to do women's studies now, just as our enthusiasm and conviction that what we were attempting mattered a great deal are also part of women's studies, a women's studies informed by feminist values. Genuine intellectual community is so rare, and so hard to achieve in an individualistic, competitive academy that it is only in areas like women's studies, where the need to go beyond the borders of any discipline is not mere fashion but part of a larger demand for change, personal and social, that it can be achieved, and then only by a long, arduous, and self-conscious process.

Afterword

Looking back at our seminar now, I can see that its successes and failures were not just ours. The seminar inevitably reflected the state of feminist thinking at the time. The Five-College area has always been a good place to be for those of us in women's studies, but we have never been completely isolated from the tensions and schisms which have rent other communities. Problems which we seemed to have escaped were at best ameliorated, at worst buried or disguised by the nature of the fairly homogeneous culture of a small New England town. In particular, I am thinking about the problem of "difference," the ways in which we were/ are unlike each other, as well as unlike the patriarchal academy. This problem has been articulated in the very rich theoretical writing which has been pouring out in the past several years; it has also exploded in pain and rage at the very conferences which are supposed to bring us together.

Race, class, and sexual identification are dangerous to take seriously in our society, and we were white, mainly middle class, and generally private people. Not that we were ignorant of the truth that our various "privileges" and "oppressions" affected our work, but we were not yet ready to say how, in the way that we wanted to, with accuracy and passion. I don't know that anyone yet is absolutely ready to say how, but feminist theory has advanced to the point where it is possible to begin, has in fact begun. Meanwhile the world around us looks more hostile, more threatened by the possibility of radical change, and more unwilling to give up its traditional privileges. We need to go back to that sense of working together in a committed intellectual community, although it has to be a community which more truly reflects the diversities among women. Our experience seems like a luxury perhaps, but we all need community to test us and encourage us, I think, because unless our thinking is rooted there, it runs the risk of becoming too vulnerable to attack from outside or too sterile to nourish the action which should be its fruit.

Notes

1. The following list includes our major reading for the seminar: Berenice A. Carroll, ed., *Liberating Women's History* (Urbana: University of Illinois Press, 1976); Nancy Chodorow, "Oedipal Asymmetries and Heterosexual Knots," *Social Problems* 23 (1976); Dorothy Dinnerstein, *The Mermaid and the Minotaur* (New York: Harper & Row, 1976); Howard Gadlin, "Scars and Emblems: Paradoxes of American Family Life," *Journal of Social History* 11 (1978); Clifford Geertz, "Ideology as a Cultural System," in *Ideology and Discontent*, ed. David Apter (London: Free Press of Glencoe, 1964); Charlotte Perkins Gilman, "The Yellow Wallpaper" (1892), rpt. in *The Oven Birds: American Women on Womanhood, 1820–1920*, ed. Gail Parker (Garden City, N.Y.: Anchor Books, 1972); Lucien Goldmann, *The Human Sciences and Philosophy* (1952), trans. Hayden V. White and Robert Anchor (London: Jonathan Cape, 1969); Jane Humphries, "The Working Class Family, Women's Liberation and Class Struggle: The Implications of Nineteenth Century British History," *Review of Radical Political Economics* (1977); George Lichtheim, "The Concept of Ideology," in *The Concept of Ideology and Other Essays*, ed. George Lichtheim (New York: Random House, 1967); Jean Baker Miller, *Towards A New Psychology of Women* (Boston: Beacon Press, 1976); George Pickering, *Creative Malady: Illness in the Lives and Minds of Charles Darwin, Florence Nightengale, Mary Baker Eddy, Sigmund Freud, Marcel Proust, and Elizabeth Barrett Browning* (New York: Dell, 1974); Janice Raymond, "Introduction," *The Transsexual Empire* (Boston: Beacon Press, 1979); Adrienne Rich, "Towards a Woman Centered University," in *Women and the Power to Change*, ed. Florence Howe (New York: McGraw Hill, 1975); Adrienne Rich, "Women's Studies: Revolution or Renaissance," rpt. in *Women's Studies* 3 (1976); Alice Rossi, "Biosocial Perspective on Parenting," *Daedelus* (1977); Susan Sontag, "Fascinating Fascism," *New York Review of Books,* Feb. 1975; Susan Sontag and Adrienne Rich, "Fascism and Feminism: An Exchange," *New York Review of Books,* Mar. 1975; Jean Strouse, *Women and Analysis* (New York: Dell, 1974); Virginia Woolf, *Three Guineas* (New York: Harcourt Brace, 1938).

2. Goldmann, *The Human Sciences and Philosophy,* p. 106.

Institutional Racism and Sexism: Refusing the Legacy in Education

Bobbie M. Anthony-Perez

> Blacks live under the same exploitative system, with its built-in moral hierarchy and fixed places, which has held women at the bottom. In spite of profound differences in their experiences (particularly the differing monolithic oppression), economically and psychologically black and white women have often encountered the same problems, met the same resistance, and joined each other historically in the same struggles.
>
> Barbara Joseph[1]

Introduction

Since the latter part of the 1960s, complaints of racism and sexism aimed at educational systems in the United States have increased. Voices of feminist and Black scholars have reverberated within and without academe. Many men and some women have expressed resentment and confusion about the clamor and have ignored or disputed the complaints concerning racism and sexism in formal education.

Educational discrimination against women and Blacks in the United States has been similar in many respects, and the histories of Blacks and white women in educational institutions illustrate connections important to our examination of the racist/sexist tradition we share. These historical connections are important to our efforts to make changes, but common experiences have often been largely ignored by white male historians and social scientists. Heidi Hartmann notes the "need to develop a better understanding of racism . . . and the consequent differences in the experiences of Black and white women. Such an understanding is essential if we are to transform society as we desire."[2] Gloria Joseph points out that "in defining patriarchy, Black males must be separated out from white males."[3] Unfortunately, neither women nor Black men have been blameless in the development of racist/sexist problems encountered by women. Both have been accused of erecting barriers to effective coalitions.

Black men

> . . . men, until the advent of the Women's Movement, had a certain feeling toward women entering into traditional male areas of endeavor. . . . Many Black men, justifiably or nonjustifiably, have the feeling that Black women who are intelligent and have ability are too dominant, too assertive. I mean, it's a combination of sociological and psychological factors. Men are men.
>
> Shirley Chisholm[4]

Shirley Chisholm, a former school teacher and the first Black woman elected to the United States Congress, recounts facing many more obstacles because of being female than because of being Black. Chisholm, who recalls not staying with her severely injured husband once "because I was the only woman and the only Black sitting on the Rules Committee, and there was legislation moving in the Rules Committee at that time that would have affected women and affected the Black people in this country," was contested in her initial campaign on grounds that James Farmer, the Black civil-rights activist, would satisfy "needs" of Blacks for "a strong male image," a "man's voice in Washington," and deliverance from "matriarchal dominance."[5] Chisholm's situation was akin to that of Dr. Ruth Love, a Black woman who became superintendent of the Chicago Public Schools in 1982; her selection was opposed by a Black man on the Chicago Board of Education because of his presumption that Black youth needed a Black man to be a role model in the superintendency.

I am reminded of the time several years ago when I, a Black woman, stood up to speak during the question-and-answer period of a faculty-administrator forum conducted by the Black man who was then president of the university where I work. I couldn't believe my ears when the president said agitatedly, "Dr. Anthony, let a *man* speak." The auditorium was full of men and women, but no one else had signaled a desire to speak at the time that I stood up. I looked around the auditorium and asked, "Does some man wish to speak?" There was absolute silence. Nothing remained for the president to say except, "Well what is it, Dr. Anthony?" in a most impatient voice. The president must have blurted out his gut feelings, for it seems incredible that he would otherwise have embarrassed himself so. Luckily for him, I "kept my cool," for I could have justifiably exploded and embarrassed him all the more. I also remember 1981 when faculty members of my department were being nominated for committee positions. A white man, upon being nominated for secretary of a committee, promptly remarked, "That's a woman's job." I, just as promptly, reprimanded him for his sexist remark. In recent years Black women have recounted many similar experiences. Although there may be many exceptions, and there may continue to be more, it would presently appear that, as Shirley Chisholm states at the head of this section, "Men are men."

Black and White Women

> There is a battlefield (race, class, and sexual identity) within each one of us, another battlefield where we wage these wars with our own feminist colleagues . . . , and a third battlefield where we defend ourselves from male onslaughts both on our work and on the laws that govern our lives as women in society.
>
> Jane Marcus[6]

Quoting Pat Armstrong's view that "White feminists must come to terms with the circumscribing nature of their whiteness,"[7] Gloria Joseph takes feminists to task because "to date feminists have not concretely demonstrated the potential or capacity to become involved in fighting racism on an equal footing with sexism."[8] Increasingly, Black feminists are focusing attention on the ways racism operates independently from and together with sexism to oppress Black women.[9] However, Joseph emphasizes that "Black feminists have a crucial role to play in the present movement. They must include themselves from their own organized base."[10]

I wish here to review work on the commonalities of women's experiences in order to indicate the ways that Black and white women have been separated from each other partly through the slavery and discrimination practices that have prevented them from having strong voices in the academy.

Racism and Sexism Defined

Eleanor Schetlin, urging sensitivity to problems of racism and sexism within educational institutions, underscores definitional similarities between the two "isms": "Racism . . . is . . . a belief that race is the primary determinant of human traits and capacities and that racial differences produce an inherent superiority of a particular race. Sexism . . . is the belief that sex differences produce the inherent superiority of a particular sex."[11] Sexism has also been defined as "a specific case of the generic process of racism," with both sexism and racism "subsumed under the heading of prejudice."[12]

Stokely Carmichael and Charles V. Hamilton distinguish between two forms of racism: Individual racism "consists of overt acts by individuals . . . ; it can frequently be observed in the process of commission." Institutional racism "is less overt, far more subtle, less identifiable in terms of specific individuals committing the acts. . . . [It] originates in the operation of established and respected forces in society."[13] Both individual and institutional racism have been defined as action resulting in negative outcomes for members of certain groups, whether they be "racial, cultural, sexual, or ideological."[14] Thus, institutional sexism is perceived by some to be a specific instance of institutional racism.

Racism, and similarly sexism, "is built into organizations' ways of proceeding, eases the burden of personal guilt, and so is readily perpetuated."[15] The implication is that individuals aware of racism and sexism are able to assume a stance of "I don't like it, but there's nothing that I can do about it. That's the way the system works." Like it or not, individuals within institutions are strongly influenced to follow institutional policies, racist, sexist or not, noncompliance being grounds for harassment and, perhaps, severance.

It is in this context that I will present some remarkable parallels between racism and sexism in education throughout the history of the United States and recommend courses of action for scholars wishing to combat racism and sexism.

The Case of Education

. . . Women's Studies, diverse as its components are, has at its best shared a vision of a world free from sexism and racism. Freedom from sexism by necessity must include a commitment to freedom from racism; national chauvinism; class and ethnic bias; anti-Semitism as directed against both Arabs and Jews; ageism; heterosexual bias—from all the ideologies and institutions that have consciously or unconsciously oppressed and exploited some for the advantage of others.

National Women's Studies
Association Constitution[16]

The pervasiveness of racism and sexism in the United States' educational systems has continued over time despite certain gains made by women, Blacks and other "minorities." Discrimination has been prevalent in administration, admissions, programming, counseling, testing, textbooks, hiring, promotion, tenure, and compensation. Stephanie Shields[17] as well as Alexander Thomas and Samuel Sillen[18] describe how professional white men have contributed heavily to the discrimination by hypothesizing and reporting false evidence that women and Blacks are innately inferior to white men. Examples of how racism and sexism have thrived together historically in academe are provided by William McDougall, former Harvard professor and "Father of Social Psychology," and G. Stanley Hall, founder of the American Psychological Association and the "Father of Child Study." McDougall attributed childlike qualities and a "maternal" instinct to women and a "submissive" instinct to Blacks.[19] Hall declared that complete growth among members of the African, Chinese, and Indian races was comparable to that of white adolescents, and that all educational and social institutions for girls should prepare them for their "special" roles in domestic arts.[20]

Focus on Sexism

As Black and white feminists combine forces in the struggle against male supremacy and white supremacy, they must be willing to communicate and follow a format consisting of dialogue (with the purpose of mutual education), practice, more dialogue, and more practice—moving slowly but inexorably towards advanced levels of understanding and respect for one another's differences.

Gloria Joseph[21]

Throughout the history of the United States, Black and white women have been denied access to equal educational opportunities and have had to contend with discrimination in training and employment. Both psychological barriers and institutional factors such as admission practices, types of curricula and services adopted, and faculty and staff attitudes impede women's progress,[22] foster divisiveness among women and men, and distort what is recorded as scholarship.

Postsecondary admissions. Though a small minority of women were formally educated before the Civil War,[23] admissions have always favored males. The 1980 enrollment estimates by the United States Department of Education's National Center for Education Statistics (NCES) show that the number of women entering full-time higher education was 207,000 less than the number of their male counterparts. Two years earlier, though there were 2.5 million more women than men in the 18–34 age group, almost one-half million more men than women in the group were enrolled in college.[24] Enrollment rates have been increasing for women over the past few years;[25] however, more women than men drop out of college, for reasons that are explored in this volume.

Programs and Counseling. Sexism in educational programming has been as damaging as that in admissions. Females are still counseled into certain traditional areas, and sex-role socialization, even within schools and at early ages, helps to account for the concentrations.[26] Department of Health, Education and Welfare statistics for 1976 show that 66 percent of the girls in vocational education programs were studying low-paid office and "homemaking" skills. Enrollment of high school girls has been low in mathematics, which is required for many of the creative and well-paying technical and business fields in which women are underrepresented.[27] Current research provides no evidence that girls have intrinsically less interest in mathematical problem-solving than do boys.[28] The preponderance of male mathematics teachers, especially in advanced courses, might serve to signal mathematics as a male domain. Further, researchers in 1979 reported that test content in many educational programs is biased in the direction of males, and that performance on test items is affected by agreement between sex of the examinee and sex of persons referred to in the items.[29]

The pervasiveness of sexism in higher education is evidenced by the plight of women in law, medicine, psychology, dentistry, engineering, and physical education. In the latter area, sexism has been apparent in the funding of women's programs, admission to classes, team sport participation, employment, and equality of pay.[30] For the academic year ending 1979, women were 30.4 percent of the total enrollment in law; the corresponding figure for medicine was 23.2 percent; for dentistry,

14 percent; and for engineering, 10.6 percent.[31] In psychology, the social science that attempts to describe and explain behavior, sex discrimination is widespread in education, therapy, professional opportunities, training, and research.[32] Additionally, at the end of the 1980–81 year, 44.5 percent of doctorates in education went to women, but only 12.3 percent of doctorates in the physical sciences (including mathematics and computer sciences) went to women and only 30.3 percent of doctorates were awarded to women across all fields.[33]

Textbooks. Sylvia Lee Tibbetts, reviewing studies of sexism in books for children to determine whether publishers had eliminated bias in texts, concluded that their efforts have not gone far enough. "Books are either sexist or not," she argues; there is no such thing as "a little bit sexist," and readers should not be satisfied with materials that appear to be "less sexist" than before.[34]

Faculty role models in higher education. The American Association of University Professors reported that the number of women faculty actually decreased in 1975–76.[35] A preliminary NCES report showed that academic tenure had been granted to more than 68 percent of the men on college faculties in 1979–80 but to only 48 percent of the women, and that women held only about one-fourth of the full-time faculty positions during that period. Jack Magarrell summarizes the situation using NCES data for 1978–79: "Although the hiring of female faculty members increased in the past academic year, the total number of women on college and university faculties, like their salaries and tenure rates, remained substantially lower than those of their male colleagues."

This was to the detriment of women students, since male professors, who have their "standards," have traditionally assumed that women are not serious about their future as professionals and do not follow the "rules."[36] While a male literature teacher may lecture for years without mentioning women writers, a female student or teacher who focuses on women writers is often accused of not understanding or valuing the "standard." (And if she mentions homophobia, anti-Semitism, and racism, her work displeases the makers and keepers of standards all the more.) In a collection of essays detailing experiences of women who have faced criticism of their academic presence and work, Marcia Lieberman writes, "Ask, ask for whom the standards are raised; are they raised for you?"[37] The prevalent male attitudes toward women and their scholarship may account for a finding that female Ph.D.'s who had female advisors during graduate school were significantly more productive academically four years after graduation than were women who had male advisors.[38]

Pay. A Boston newspaper ad soliciting employees for government schools to be opened January 1, 1886, read, "The salary of male teachers is principals $60 a month, assistants $45; female principals $30, assistants $20."[39] In 1975, reports from college campuses indicated that salary differentials point to the operation of systematic practices which keep the salary of a woman faculty member below what she would be getting were she a man with similar characteristics.[40] Apparently, the situation is worsening: in 1975–76 the salaries of male professors averaged $3000 more than female professors, a larger gap than a year earlier.[41] The 1979–80 NCES data show the gap was more than $4000 for full-time faculty holding nine-month contracts and well over $7000 for those holding twelve-month contracts.[42] Salaries for women in 1979–80 averaged 18 percent and 26 percent less, for nine- and twelve-month contracts, respectively, than those of their male colleagues. Salary differentials existed at all levels and at all types of institutions. Men tended to receive higher salary increases than women.[43] The decline in 1974–75 of the percentage of women at the ranks of professor and associate professor[44] undoubtedly accounts, in part, for salary differentials.

Administration. Sexism in top positions is prevalent at all educational levels and is getting worse. The National Institute of Education reported that in 1975, 63 percent of elementary and secondary teachers were women, yet women were principals in less than 2 percent of the high schools and in only 18 percent of the primary schools. Out of 16,000 school districts in the country, only 75 were administered by women. These figures represent a serious setback for women. In 1928, only eight years after women won the right to vote, 55 percent of primary school principals were women.[45] In addition, a 1973 study at the junior college level revealed that only 3 percent of listed junior college presidents were female and that 71 percent of these were Catholic sisters heading women's colleges.[46]

Sex differentials in administrative positions are not based on ability. Reviewers of a twenty-year span of studies comparing various behavioral aspects of men and women principals and of a sixteen-year span of attitudinal studies found prejudice shown by most male teachers, school superintendents, and school board members against women serving as principals. The reviewers also concluded that the studies showed that women teachers were discouraged from seeking administrative appointments.[47]

Women who become administrators face problems stemming from exclusionary practices of male colleagues, including lack of information required for making important decisions. They are thought of as women administrators, rather than women in administration, a situation similar to that of minorities.[48] After such treatment, it is no wonder that women in student personnel administration and in other aspects of student personnel work were found to be more sensitive than their male counterparts to sexism in hiring top administrators, sexism within their profession, the need for Black faculty and administrators as role models, and the importance of the Women's Movement for higher education.[49]

Focus on Racism

> Unfortunately, our society has done such an excellent job of institutionalizing racism that . . . when situations occur that call for coalition, solidarity, or alliance, racism serves as a wedge which prevents groups from the strategic, systematic, and protracted cooperation which is needed for the attainment of common goals.
>
> Gloria Joseph[50]

Racism, like sexism, has operated throughout the educational arena. Poor educational facilities for Blacks in the United States were early sanctioned by law. Legal codes forbade the teaching of reading and writing to Black slaves, and these codes were strictly enforced.[51] During Reconstruction, the efforts of southern Blacks to acquire education typically met with violence. A Black woman recounted before an 1872 congressional investigating committee that "they would not let us have schools. . . . They said they would dare any . . . nigger to have a book in his house. We allowed last fall that we would have a schoolhouse in every district, and the colored men started them. But the Ku Klux said they would whip every man who sent a scholar there."[52] In 1954, the Supreme Court declared separate schools in the South to be in violation of the United States Constitution, but segregated schools, and often poorer schools for Blacks, exist despite the 1954 and subsequent decisions.

Postsecondary admissions. From earliest times to the present, despite gains in particular institutions, admission of Blacks to higher education has been low. Blacks are underrepresented in the technical sciences and severely so in graduate and professional institutions, while they are relatively overrepresented in education and the social sciences.[53] The entering class enrollment statistics for 1979–80 are telling: only 10.1 percent of the women and 8.2 percent of the men were Black.[54] Further, as Carol Gibson, education director for the Urban League in 1976, explained: "Many large schools attract black students, but when they get there they find only a handful of other blacks. They become racially isolated and this is directly related to the high rate of black college dropouts."[55]

Black colleges were created to fill an educational void resulting from discrimination; they are still filling the void created by declining admissions of Blacks to predominantly white colleges.[56] By 1899, Black graduates from Black colleges numbered 1,914 and from white colleges, 390. About one-tenth of these graduates were women.[57] Access for Blacks is still largely provided by schools established to provide separate education for Blacks.[58]

Programs. Educational programs designed to help Blacks often treat the culture of Blacks condescendingly, without consideration of the lifestyles, linguistic habits, and behaviors of Black people. The programs are founded on "cultural deprivation theories." There is still a view that Black history and experiences are not academically valid or significant.[59]

Toward the end of the 1960s, more and more minority group students were admitted to higher education, but because appropriate curricula and instructional procedures had not been developed for nontraditional students, high attrition rates resulted as did "deeper disillusionment" among these students.[60] Little progress was made in increasing enrollment of Blacks in fields traditionally foreign to them, even in the social sciences. In psychology, for example, the percentages of minorities and women did not change in the three-year period ending with 1972.[61]

The failure of education in Black communities cannot be charged to lack of interest among Blacks. Even before Emancipation, some Blacks slaves taught one another to read.[62] After the Civil War, despite their "two hundred and forty-five years of slave education and unrequited toil," there was an intense desire among Blacks for "useful knowledge"; T. T. Fortune wrote in 1903 that "if we have a vast volume of illiteracy, we have reduced it by forty percent since the war."[63] Blacks of all ages wanted to go to school. Day schools, night schools, and Sunday schools were always crowded; the facilities were not equal to the demand.

Funding. Racism in funding has influenced the amount and quality of education. Scholarships, salaries, and programs at all levels of education have been adversely affected.[64] Initially, the problem was perceived as being a Southern one. In the early twentieth century, Charles Chesnutt, an educated Black man, wrote: "In Georgia . . . where the law provides for a pro rata distribution of the public school fund between the races, and where the colored population is 48 percent of the total, the amount of the fund devoted to their schools is only 20 percent. In New Orleans, with an immense colored population, many of whom are persons of means and culture, all colored public schools above the fifth grade have been abolished."[65] About the same time, W. E. B. Du Bois wrote that the Black colleges were "almost a year behind the smaller New England colleges," that the college program was only 136 weeks in length, and that only three years of high school were required for college entry.[66] Du Bois relates that twenty years earlier, Negro public school teachers were better than most white public school teachers, but, because of encouragement for thorough preparation through scholarships and good salaries, there was a marked improvement of white teachers in the South. Statistics presented by Du Bois in 1903 show only 6.3 percent of Black college graduates became physicians. Today, because of medical school expense and admissions criteria, there is still a low ratio of Black doctors to the Black population; approximately one-fourth of all Black doctors are being trained at the predominantly Black medical schools, although more Blacks than before are enrolled at white medical schools.[67]

Black land-grant colleges are still discriminated against by state governments and the federal government in terms of funds granted, and, in general, Black colleges have a much lower salary scale than do white colleges. This is in line with a report that differences between salaries of Blacks and whites for jobs requiring the highest levels of education are greater than those for jobs requiring less education.[68]

Counseling. Counseling has been frequently cited as one reason for either low or faulty admissions of Blacks. In the word of an Urban League education director, high school guidance counselors are the "gatekeepers" to higher education for Blacks: "It's like when the white teacher questioned Malcolm X about wanting to be a lawyer and not a carpenter. . . . Some white counselors just don't see college as something for black students too."[69] Similarly, when Dr. Robert Williams, a Black professor of psychology at Washington University in St. Louis, was in high school, he was counseled to become a bricklayer.[70]

Counselors are accused of neglecting the psychosociological interactions of the Black client with his or her environment, counseling Blacks to adjust to an unjust mainstream environment, and using a model of intellectual, academic, and motivational deficit when clients are Black students.[71] One author who writes about white counselors' assumptions and advice notes that criticisms by Blacks of their treatment have struck a responsive chord among women.[72]

Testing. Many Black professionals look upon educational testing as a racist ally of white counseling. Generally, it is claimed, bias exists from the conception of the test to the utilization of the results; specifically, the major causes of test unfairness are test content, administration, use, and interpretation. Testing can result in harmful "ability" grouping and in erroneous labeling of students as mentally retarded.[73] Some tests merely measure white middle-class speech patterns, "whether you call it reading or mathematics."[74] Racism within trade unions has helped reduce the number of skilled Blacks,[75] as the unions have favored graduates from vocational schools requiring tests for entry.

Texts and Materials. Blacks have been virtually excluded from texts and curriculum guides in many public schools in the United States. When included, Blacks have been frequently stereotyped and presented inaccurately. Samuel Banks holds that "slanted textbooks and teaching have created a false sense of superiority in white children predicated solely on their color."[76] Some curriculum guides provide for separate, supplemental, elective materials about Blacks or "minority cultures" for interested students, but the accurate history of Blacks is still not incorporated into the total social studies curriculum.[77] In most textbooks, at both lower and higher educational levels, Black slaves in the United States have been depicted as happy and well treated, while Africa has been depicted as the home of backward, strange people.[78] Writing of post–Civil War times, professors at the University of California presented Blacks as having "no will to work" and the Ku Klux Klan as a group with responsible leaders which committed violence against Blacks as a reaction to violence against the Klan.[79] Morison and Commager of Harvard and Columbia, who didn't even bother to capitalize *negro*, as names of other groups at the time were capitalized, wrote in their 1942 text:

> As for Sambo, whose wrongs moved the abolitionists to wrath and tears, there is some reason to believe that he suffered less than any other class in the South from its "peculiar institution." . . . Although brought to America by force . . . the . . . negro soon became . . . devoted to his "white folks." Slave insurrections were . . . invariably betrayed by some faithful darkey. . . . Topsy and Tom Sawyer's nigger Jim were nearer to the average childlike, improvident, humorous, prevaricating, and superstitious negro than the unctuous Uncle Tom. [Slavery subjected] Booker T. Washington to the caprice of a white owner, his inferior in every respect *save pigment*. . . .
>
> If we overlook the original sin of the slave trade, there was much to be said for slavery as a transitional status between barbarism and civilization[80] (emphasis added).

Between those two quotations, the professors display an unbelievable amount of racism, including implications that Blacks are childish and on the order of animals. The racist attitude of these professors was still apparent in a 1977 edition of their book. Along with a new co-author, they write, "It is often forgotten that . . . victims of the system [slavery] who were shipped to North America were better off than those who remained in bondage in Africa [and,] in some respects, than many poor workers and peasants in Europe."[81]

Employment. Experiences I will cite in a section on institutional remediation point to the need for more Black professionals in education as well as for continued Black Studies, yet a finding of a 1975 national study was that there were small proportions of Blacks in white institutions, 10 percent of whom "were fully involved in ethnic areas." Only 28 percent were females, and there was a critical shortage of Black faculty in the natural sciences. Most of the Black faculty had been employed at the institutions from only one to three years. Almost 70 percent of the Black men (and, likewise, 70 percent of the women faculty) held the rank of instructor or assistant instructor. Fifteen percent of the men and 8 percent of the women were professors. Clearly, most Blacks were at the lowest paid ranks. Generally, Blacks with college degrees have earned less than whites with degrees.[82]

Administration. Blacks in administration have had to contend with myths just as have women administrators, although the myths for the two groups have not all been similar. Two sexist myths are that men perform better as principals and that teachers do not like to work for female principals.[83] Comparable myths for Black school administrators are that Blacks are less effective than whites with comparable training and that whites do not wish to work for Black administrators.[84]

Racism and Sexism in Review. The evidence is clear that both Black and white women as well as Black men have suffered oppression in the realm of education. In a following section, remedies for this oppression will be suggested. First, because they have encountered educational problems related to both their sex and their race, Black women will be discussed. At this point, it will simply be noted again that the oppression has occurred with respect to administrative appointments and functions, admissions, programming, counseling, testing, textbooks, hiring, promotion, tenure, and pay.

Black Females

> Black women of necessity have been more directly engaged in life-and-death struggles . . . combating racism and capitalistic exploitation of Black people, rather than chauvinism. And while male chauvinism is institutionalized, very few White women suffer the extreme exploitation that most Black women suffer day by day.
>
> Barbara Joseph[85]

Affirmative action and equal opportunity programs have been particularly limiting for Black women, as they are sometimes counted as women, and sometimes as Blacks, thus receiving only partial benefits of equity programs. For example, I deeply resented the fact that when a special equity fund was divided among women and "minorities" at my university, I received the $60 allocated to each "minority" person, but not the $30 allocated to each woman. This is typical of the well-known ploy whereby institutions count Black women as women on the one hand and as Blacks or minorities on the other when issuing statistics on institutional personnel. If I had been a Black man I would have received the same amount as I did as a Black woman.

Black female students have also been in a double bind. A college student remarked in an interview, "When people treated me differently in college because I was Black and female in things like counseling me on the choice of a major or making comments about my background or about Blacks, I wondered what was wrong with me."[86] White females have not generally been sensitized to the "double" discrimination against their Black counterparts. One white woman, wondering why special attention should be paid to attitudes about Black women, commented: "All of us women are isolated when a campus or major is predominantly male. Economics is a boys' club and women, regardless of color, are not part of the mainstream." She did admit upon questioning that she "has never thought about why" she did not socialize with the lone Black female out of the eight women included in the fifty or sixty senior economics majors at the predominantly male institution she attended.[87] It is because of circumstances similar to those cited in this section that Gloria Joseph says, "A specifically Black feminist approach is called for because the psychological dynamics that function among Black men and Black women in the context of existing economic conditions are qualitatively and culturally different from those of whites."[88]

Institutional Remediation

> Feminist sensitivity to social process is perhaps manifest most clearly in the ongoing, if not always successful, attempt in women's studies to fight against oppression on the basis of race, class, age, religion, and sexual preference as well as sex.
>
> Marilyn J. Boxer[89]

Many educational institutions have responded to charges of racism and sexism by establishing special offices for recruiting minorities and women as students and faculty. Under the rubric "Affirmative Action," institutions have devised various procedures seemingly designed to bring about equity. Affirmative action has been perceived as ineffective, but, also, by many white males, as a deterrent to the educational progress of white males.[90]

Black Studies

> . . . Black Studies remains a battle front for justice and equality.
>
> National Council for Black Studies[91]

As a result of protests against treatment of Blacks in educational institutions, brown-skinned people began to appear in material scheduled for use by Black school children.[92] At higher levels of education, many programs and departments of Afro-American or Black Studies have been established since 1966 at the urging of Black students.[93] The continuing need for Black Studies is illustrated by recent remarks of Black students on white campuses. One felt the constant need to prove herself to professors and peers because of stereotypes that Blacks are deficient and inferior. Another related: "It seems as if the whole class decided that I have nothing to contribute, nothing worth listening to. The professor may call on me and I may give an answer, but there is no comment, just silence. A few minutes later a white student will give my answer, rephrased, and be praised on his or her insight." A third student felt her experiences negated when factors pertinent to Blacks were omitted during a discussion of the extended family, a topic of high relevance to many Blacks. A fourth student recalled that when an assignment was turned in, "the instructor told me I couldn't have written it because it was too well done."[94]

Women's Studies

> Research and teaching would be not only *about* but *for* all women, guided by a vision of a world free not only from sexism, but also from racism, class-bias, ageism, heterosexual bias. . . .
>
> Marilyn J. Boxer and National
> Women's Studies Association[95]

The unprecedented rise of programs in the 1970s was prompted by women's awareness of how women and their knowledge have been treated in the past. According to Dana Hiller: "Women's Studies programs are in the university not only to change the curriculum but to generate research. Their initial *raison d'être* has been to give women students a sense of their own identity as well as past and present role models"[96] and to contribute to the restructuring of knowledge. The programs bring a new, vital perspective to traditional disciplines, challenging scholars to examine past assumptions, research designs, and data. Hiller states that by 1976, over 200 programs had been established in institutions of higher education in the United States and that over 5,000 women's studies courses had been offered. The number of programs had grown to more than 400 by 1982; however, relative to the number of institutions, the number of budgeted women's studies programs is still small.[97]

It is important that Women's Studies teachers consider the interests of special groups of women as well as the histories of these groups, not just in the United States but in other areas of the world as well. Such consideration is helpful to the fight for equality for all women. Eleanor Leacock notes, "There has never been a more pressing need for an international movement of women committed to pursuing the struggle for their liberation by uniting it with fights against oppression by class and by race."[98] Gloria Joseph points out that "when Third World women today struggle against their own oppression, they also struggle against oppression in general. They are more concerned with strategies for change than with theories about the origin of the basic division of dominance and submission."[99] When rape is discussed, developers or teachers of Women's Studies courses need also to consider the plight of Black women during and after slavery, for subsequent to the initiation of slavery, when Blacks from Africa were sold "in batches to merchants and other middlemen who bartered them for tobacco, rice, or indigo . . . both in the North and South, mulattoes soon became numerous."[100]

Recommendations

> It is imperative that women and minorities learn quickly to build a broad base of support through identifying the unity of self-interests among us. . . .
>
> Maryann Mahaffey[101]

Many recommendations have been made for reducing or eliminating institutional racism and sexism in the United States. Broadly speaking, they relate to consciousness and conscience being influenced by programs and protests, which are interrelated, of course. The academic scholar is favorably situated to become involved in following through on recommended actions, both as an individual and as a member of various groups, within the institution and within the community.

Those of us worried about mixing professional concerns with the social concerns of racism and sexism would be well advised to study the history of individual and group actions of females and Blacks in the United States and to find evidence of cooperation among women despite institutional pressures which work to separate them.

We would discover that some white women have suffered abuse to help Blacks. Included among them was Angelina Grimké, who spoke in homes, lecture rooms, and churches, and in 1836 published "Appeal to the Women of the South," on the subject of slavery.[102]

We could find that although few women's medical colleges existed at the time of the Civil War, those doors were opened early to Black women. We also find that many Blacks, including educators, addressed the issue of racism through speaking, writing, and attending conferences.[103] White women, especially white middle-class women, need to listen closely as Black women talk about the politics of skin color. However, it is also important to study the institutions and practices which have worked to separate women from each other, to study the ways that antiracist efforts have been associated with feminist efforts, and to study how those efforts can be strengthened.

Activities customarily expected of academicians and which usually are the bases of professional advancement permit the scholar wishing to address social problems to do so without impeding professional progress because of time limitations. The scholar desiring to combat racism and sexism could be guided in any of these activities—publishing, lecturing, attending conferences, participating in community events, developing programs or courses—merely by studying the productivity in the 1970s and early 1980s of females and Blacks in educational institutions.

The National Association for Women Deans, Administrators and Counselors, the National Women's Studies Association, the National Council for Black Studies, and the National Alliance of Black School Educators are examples of organizations that at least propose to eliminate racism and sexism in curricula and research so as to develop the potential of all humans. Audre Lorde, speaking at the 1981 NWSA meeting on racism, pointed out the relative ease with which white middle-class women can gather for discussions about racism and feminism but ignore the racism which keeps them from providing the kinds of support which would enable more than token Blacks to attend and participate. Yet, if she listens at the conferences, as well as works through literature provided by the organizations, the feminist scholar may learn of strategies for increasing the numbers of women and minorities in educational institutions: correcting inequities and alleviating the problem of few role models; receiving funds to develop programs designed to correct historical social wrongs inflicted on white women and Blacks; properly counseling women and minorities in relationship to personal, cultural, educational, and occupational matters; changing racist and sexist characteristics of the educational institution and the outer community; and developing appropriate coping mechanisms for life in male-dominated arenas.

The scholar whose special focus is either racism or sexism should, whenever possible, call attention to the similarities between the two.[104] The scholar should integrate concerns about racism and sexism into the curriculum, through illustrative material in all courses or through specific courses such as "Issues in Domination: Race and Sex," offered by the Department of Afro-American Studies at the University of California at Berkeley. The women in education who served as consultants or commissioners for the First National Women's Conference, held in 1977 at Houston, are examples of scholars who served both the larger community and the academic institution. The planks on educational and minority women and the Black Women's Plan of Action, all included in the report of the conference, are witness to the productivity of these scholars in the war against sexism and racism in education and related areas. The 1980 Richmond Conference, convened by Blacks and attended by many Black scholars, called for coalitions to eliminate racism and sexism through such actions as meeting only in states where the Equal Rights Amendment has been ratified and as supporting the Black Agenda drawn up by the conference.[105]

There are many other examples of scholars serving both the larger community and the academic institution. For example, Joyce Hughes, a Black law professor at Northwestern University who served as chairperson of the desegregation committee of the Chicago Board of Education, and the educators who vote for legislators with records favorable to civil rights in general and women's rights in particular are models of how scholars can successfully integrate institutional and societal responsibilities.

There *are* problems which must be analyzed and resolved in dealing with racism and sexism. First, the prime source of racism and sexism—white men—must be recognized. In the words of a Black woman speaking in 1979 of conditions in Alabama: "In the late seventies, the news in much of the South is Black involvement in politics. . . . Some signs of change dot the newspapers: a Black woman running for the Board of Education, and photos of Black babies, along with white children. But the pictures of power, the people running the state, are still all white men with hard eyes of the traditional South."[106]

The Black Women's Plan of Action, completed at the First National Women's Conference in 1977, included the following statement:

The white male power structure has been adept, historically, at shifting arenas of competition, limiting opportunities, and assuming the power of definition in an effort to misrepresent divisions of greatest import in fundamental social change, such as that between advantaged white males as a group and all other groups in the society, who by comparison are significantly disadvantaged. Moreover, as black women informed by our past we must eschew a view of the women's struggle which takes as its basic assumption opposition to men, as distinguished from organizing around the principle of opposition to the white male power structure's perpetuation of exploitation, subjugation, inequality, and limited opportunities based upon sex or race.[107]

The scholar must also be prepared to face the facts that not all women are receptive to the fight against sexism,[108] that not all Blacks are supportive of other Blacks or of strategies proposed for the liberation of Blacks,[109] that relationships between the sexes among Blacks have historically differed from those among whites,[110] and that white women generally have special relationships with the "common oppressor" just as do Black men, who share the oppressor's sex and are thus oppressed differently than are Black women. Yet, it is also important to know that Black women, like white women, have traditionally played the role of domestic in the home, and 83 percent of almost 6,700 Black women in a recent survey felt that "Black women encounter sexist attitudes and behavior as much from Black men as from White men."[111]

Educator Betty Johnson underscores the problem of Black women historically giving greater priority to racism than sexism, the opposite of the case for white women, and also notes that ethnic minorities have viewed the women's movement as "white middle-class."[112] However, the cooperation displayed by women of very diverse backgrounds at the Houston conference against sexism indicates that women can work out their differences to fight the battle against sexism and racism.

Results of a 1980 survey of almost 6,700 Black women suggested that they are probably very ready for joint combat against the twin allies of racism and sexism. Regardless of socioeconomic position, almost 95 percent felt that "Black women were all subject to the oppressive effect of racism and sexism." The majority believed that "sex discrimination will persist long after race discrimination is eliminated" and were "dissatisfied with the current affirmative action laws." Two-thirds "felt that feminist issues have relevance for Black women."[113] The white scholar should, therefore, not rely on unwarranted perceptions about receptivity of Blacks and other minorities to waging joint combat on the institutional and societal cancers of racism and sexism.

Minorities and women need the help of each other in consciousness- and conscience-raising. The improvements in the conditions of both groups have resulted largely from protest in various forms. Economic distress in the society at large must not be permitted to divide the groups which are the most distressed: women and minority men. The scholar committed to the destruction of racism and sexism must be vigilant in institutional matters related to employment, promotion, course and textbook content, counseling, admissions, testing, and attitudes. The scholar must not be afraid to help defeat racism and sexism by joining in class action suits, by providing expertise where needed, and by forming coalitions with those having similar goals, including liberated "common oppressors," or white males, within and without the institution. To exemplify concern for social injustices as well as the essence of scholarship, the scholar needs to weave social concerns into day-to-day personal and professional activities and into special scholarly endeavors such as publishing and participating in activities of professional associations.

As detailed above, educational racism and sexism have been widely prevalent throughout the history of the United States. Battles for education have been fought and won in certain areas, but the war continues. Continue it must because opponents of educational equity are fighting to roll back the discrimination calendar two decades or more even though educational parity has not been achieved for women, Blacks, and other minorities. There is common knowledge of present attempts to weaken affirmative action mandates and programs for the underrepresented. The battle (or war) is joined. Fighting either racism or sexism could become frustrating and exhausting. Fighting both could be even more so, but working together and with others, the underrepresented can surely win.

Notes

1. Barbara Joseph, "Ain't I A Woman," in *Women's Issues—And Social Work Practice,* ed. Elaine Norman and Arlene Mancuso (Itasca, Ill: Peacock Publishers, 1980), pp. 94–95.

2. Heidi Hartmann, "Summary and Response: Continuing the Discussion," in *Women and Revolution: A Discussion of the Unhappy Marriage of Marxism and Feminism,* ed. Lydia Sargent (Boston: South End Press, 1981), p. 372.

3. Gloria Joseph, "The Incompatible Ménage à Trois: Marxism, Feminism and Racism," in *Women and Revolution,* p. 101.

4. Shirley Chisholm, cited by Les Payne, "Mrs. Chisholm Calls It Quits," *Essence* 13, no. 4 (Aug. 1982): 132.

5. Ibid., pp. 72, 128. For related readings on Black male-Black female relationships, see Gloria Hull, Patricia Bell Scott, and Barbara Smith, eds., *But Some of Us Are Brave* (Old Westbury, N.Y.: The Feminist Press, 1982); *Twentieth Century Third World Women Writers, Black American and African: A Selective Bibliography* (Office of the Women's Studies Librarian-at-Large, the University of Wisconsin System); many issues of *Essence* magazine.

6. Jane Marcus, "Storming the Toolshed," *Signs* 7, no. 3 (Spring 1982): 623.

7. Pat Armstrong, SUNY Conference paper, 1972, cited by Joseph, "Incompatible Ménage," p. 102.

8. Joseph, "Incompatible Ménage," p. 105.

9. See, for example, Cherríe Moraga and Gloria Anzaldúa, eds., *This Bridge Called My Back: Writings by Radical Women of Color* (Watertown, Mass.: Persephone Press, 1981), which contains a bibliography, "Third World Women in the United States—By and About Us," as well as powerful, angry essays about racism, misogyny, elitism, and homophobia; Hull, Scott, and Smith, eds., *But Some of Us Are Brave;* Angela Y. Davis, *Women, Race, and Class* (New York: Random House, 1981).

10. Joseph, "Incompatible Ménage," p. 105.

11. Eleanor M. Schetlin, "Ethnic Minority Feminism: A Majority Member's View," *Journal of the National Association of Women Deans, Administrators, and Counselors* (NAWDAC) 41, no. 2 (Winter 1978): 48.

12. William E. Sedlacek, Glenwood C. Brooks, Jr., Kathleen C. Christensen, Michelle Harway, and Mary Strader Merritt, "Racism and Sexism: A Comparison and Contrast," *Journal of NAWDAC* 39, no. 3 (Spring 1976): 121, 126.

13. Stokely Carmichael and Charles V. Hamilton, *Black Power* (New York, Vintage Books, 1967), p. 4.

14. Sedlacek, et al., *"Racism and Sexism,"* p. 125.

15. Dorothy Newman and Associates, cited in Alan Pifer, *Black Progress: Achievement, Failure, and an Uncertain Future.* (New York: Carnegie Corporation, 1978), p. 12.

16. Cited by Marilyn J. Boxer, "For and About Women: The Theory and Practice of Women's Studies in the United States," *Signs* 7, no. 3 (Spring 1982): 677.

17. Stephanie A. Shields, "Functionalism, Darwinism, and the Psychology of Women," *American Psychologist* 30, no. 8 (Aug. 1975): 739–54.

18. Alexander Thomas and Samuel Sillen, *Racism and Psychiatry* (New York: Brunner/Mazel, 1972). See also Stephen Jay Gould, *The Mismeasure of Man* (New York: W. W. Norton, 1981), and Alan Chase, *The Legacy of Malthus: The Social Cost of Scientific Racism* (Urbana: University of Illinois Press, 1980).

19. William McDougall, *An Introduction to Social Psychology* (London: Methuen, 1913). For more recent versions of male and white supremacy on the part of social scientists, see Ruth H. Bleir, "Brain, Body, and Behavior," in *Psychology of Women*, ed. Juanita H. Williams (New York: W. W. Norton, 1979), pp. 87–98; *Black Psychology*, ed. Reginald L. Jones (New York: Harper and Row, 1972 and 1980); Myra Leifer, "Pregnancy," *Signs* 5, no. 4 (Summer 1980): 755.

20. G. Stanley Hall, "The Negro in Africa and America," *Pedagogical Seminary* 12 (1905): 350–68; G. Stanley Hall, *Adolescence* (New York: Appleton, 1904); G. Stanley Hall, *Youth, Its Education, Regimen, and Hygiene* (New York: Appleton, 1918).

21. Joseph, "Incompatible Ménage," p. 106.

22. Betty Blaska, "Women in Academe—The Need for Support Groups," *Journal of NAWDAC* 39, no. 4 (Summer 1976): 174.

23. Gerda Lerner, *Black Women in White America* (New York: Vintage Books, 1973).

24. Jack Magarrell, "Fall Enrollment Sets Record Despite Fewer 18-Year-Olds," *Chronicle of Higher Education* 21 (Nov. 10, 1980): 3–4.

25. Ronald A. Walk, ed., *Higher Education Deskbook, 1980–81* (Washington, D.C.: Editorial Projects in Education, Inc., 1980), p. 158; Magarrell, "Fall Enrollment," p. 4.

26. Blaska, "Women in Academe."

27. *The Spirit of Houston: The First National Women's Conference* (Washington, D.C.: National Commission on the Observance of International Women's Year, 1978), p. 35; Genevieve M. Knight, "Equity in Mathematics Education: A Set of Conferences," *Mathematics Teacher* 77, no. 3 (Mar. 1984): 235; Wayne W. Welch, Ronald E. Anderson, and Linda J. Harris, "The Effects of Schooling on Mathematics Achievement," *American Educational Research Journal* 19, no. 1 (Spring 1982): 151; *Higher Education and National Affairs* 32, no. 12 (Apr. 22, 1983): 5, and no. 35 (Dec. 16, 1983): 2; Subcommittee on Science, Research and Technology, *Symposium on Minorities and Women in Science and Technology* (Washington, D.C.: U.S. Government Printing Office, 1982); Bureau of the Census, U.S. Department of Commerce, *We, The American Women* (Washington, D.C.: U.S. Government Printing Office, 1984), p. 8.

28. Julia Sherman and Elizabeth Fennema, "The Study of Mathematics by High School Girls and Boys: Related Variables," *American Education Research Journal* 14, no. 2 (Spring 1977): 165. For findings on a gifted sample and related controversy, see Karl L. Alexander and Aaron M. Pallas, "Reply to Benbow and Stanley," *American Educational Research Journal* 20, no. 4 (Winter 1983): 475–77.

29. Ruth B. Ekstrom, Marlaine E. Lockheed, and Thomas F. Donlon, "Sex Differences and Sex Bias in Test Content," *Educational Horizons* 58, no. 1 (Fall 1979): 47–52. An advertisement of a *Handbook of Methods for Detecting Test Bias*, ed. Ronald A. Berk (Baltimore: John Hopkins University Press, 1982) states, "Charges that ability tests are biased against females and minorities are of increasing concern to professionals who administer and develop such tests or use their results to evaluate students or employees," *Educational Researcher* 11, no. 5 (May 1982): 25.

30. *Spirit of Houston.*

31. W. Vance Grant and Leo J. Eiden, eds., *Digest of Education Statistics* (Washington, D.C.: National Center for Education Statistics, 1981), p. 96. Of all first professional degrees conferred in given fields, respectively, for the 1980–81 academic year, women received 32.4 percent of law, 24.7 percent of medical, 14.4 percent of dental, and 3.6 percent of engineering. *Yearbook of Higher Education, 1983–84,* 15th ed. (Chicago: Marquis Professional Publications, Marquis Who's Who, Inc.), pp. 708, 716 (using preliminary data of the National Center for Educational Statistics, U.S. Department of Education).

32. Reesa M. Vaughter, "Psychology," in *Psychology of Women,* ed. Juanita H. Williams, p. 161.

33. Grant and Eiden, *Yearbook,* p. 708.

34. Sylvia-Lee Tibbetts, "Sex-Role Stereotyping in Children's Reading Material: Update," *Journal of NAWDAC* 42, no. 2 (Winter 1979): 7.

35. *Spirit of Houston,* p. 35.

36. Jack Magarrell, "More Women on Faculties; Pay Still Lags," *Chronicle of Higher Education* 21 (Sept. 29, 1980): 8; Rosemary Goad and Frances A. Plotsky, " 'Through the Maze': A Graduate Women's Workshop to Explore Professional and Personal Issues," *Journal of NAWDAC* 39, no. 3 (Spring 1976): 116.

37. Marcia Lieberman, "Ask, Ask for Whom the Standards Are Raised; Are They Raised for You?" in *Rocking the Boat: Academic Women and Academic Processes,* ed. Gloria DeSole and Leonore Hoffmann (New York: Modern Language Association of America, 1981), p. 7.

38. Elyse Goldstein, "Effect of Same-Sex and Cross-Sex Role Models on the Subsequent Academic Productivity of Scholars," *American Psychologist* 34, no. 5 (May 1979): 407–10.

39. Lerner, *Black Women,* p. 102.

40. Barbara R. Bergmann and Myles Maxfield, Jr., "How To Analyze the Fairness of Faculty Women's Salaries on Your Own Campus," *AAUP Bulletin* 61, no. 3 (Oct. 1975): 262.

41. *Spirit of Houston,* p. 35.

42. "Status of Female Faculty Members, 1979–80," *Chronicle of Higher Education* 21 (Sept. 29, 1980): 8.

43. Magarrell, "More Women on Faculties; Pay Still Lags," p. 8.

44. *Spirit of Houston,* p. 35.

45. Ibid.

46. Alice J. Thurston, "A Woman President?!—A Study of Two-Year College Presidents," *Journal of NAWDAC* 38, no. 3 (Spring 1975): 118–23.

47. Andrew Fishel and Janice Pottker, "Performance of Women Principals: A Review of Behavioral and Attitudinal Studies," *Journal of NAWDAC* 38, no. 3 (Spring 1975): 110–17.

48. Helen S. Garson, "Hurry Up Please It's Time," *Journal of NAWDAC* 38, no. 4 (Summer 1975): 168–72.

49. Marylee McEwen and Bruce Shertzer, "An Analysis of Differences in Professional Attitudes Beliefs between Male and Female Members of the College Student Personnel Profession," *Journal of NAWDAC* 38, no. 3 (Spring 1975): 136–43.

50. Joseph, "Incompatible Ménage," p. 92.

51. Patricia A. Butler, S. M. Khatib, Thomas O. Hilliard, Joseph Howard, Joseph Reid, Kenneth Wesson, Gwendolyn Wade, and Oscar Williams, "Education in Black Psychology: A Position Paper," in *Sourcebook on the Teaching of Black Psychology* vol. 1, ed. Reginald L. Jones (Washington, D.C.: Association of Black Psychologists, 1978), pp. 1–29.

52. Lerner, *Black Women,* p. 113.

53. Samuel L. Banks, "Blacks in a Multiethnic Social Studies Curriculum: A Critical Assessment," *Journal of Negro Education* 44, no. 1 (Winter 1975): 87; Gail E. Thomas, "Race and Sex Group Equity in Higher Education Institutional and Major Field Enrollment Statuses," *American Educational Research Journal* 17, no. 2 (Summer 1980): 171.

54. Walk, *Higher Education Deskbook,* p. 172.

55. Carol Gibson, in an interview with Frank Emerson, "How to Pick a College," *Black Enterprise* 6, no. 7 (Feb. 1976): 21. In 1982, 79 percent of Blacks ages 25–34 had completed high school; 13 percent had completed four or more years of college. William C. Matney and Dwight L. Johnson, "America's Black Population: 1970 to 1982, A Statistical View," *Crisis* 90, no. 10 (Dec. 1983): 15. About 70 percent of Blacks at white colleges never graduate. Tony Brown, "Black College Day in Historical Perspective," *Tony Brown's Journal* (Oct./Dec. 1983), p. 6.

56. Beverly Jensen, "Financial Aid," *Black Enterprise* 5, no. 8 (Mar. 1975): 63. Blacks averaged about 5 percent of the enrollment in predominantly white higher education institutions in 1978. Alex Poinsett, "Education and the New Generation," *Ebony* 33, no. 10 (Aug. 1978): 72.

57. W. E. B. Du Bois, "The Talented Tenth," in *The Negro Problem* (New York: James Pott, 1903), pp. 33–75. Of the 1,062,000 Blacks aged 18–21 enrolled in post-secondary institutions in October 1977, 60 percent were in two-year colleges, vocational schools, or technical schools. Of the other 40 percent, half (more than 200,000) were in predominantly Black colleges or universities. Poinsett, *Education,* p. 72. In 1981, Blacks constituted about 11 percent of the college population as compared to 7 percent in 1970. There were

more Black females than males. Matney and Johnson, *America's Black Population*, p. 14. In 1983, Black colleges produced more than 50 percent of the Black graduates though only 20 percent of Black students in college attended them. Brown, "Black College Day," p. 6.

58. Thomas and Sillen, *Racism and Psychiatry*. Schools for females are also filling a void. High school females from coeducational elementary schools were found to show more "fear of success" than their counterparts from female elementary schools, and women achievers have usually been products of women's, rather than coeducational, colleges. For example, see Grace K. Baruch and Rosalind C. Barnett, "Implications and Applications of Recent Research on Feminine Development," in Williams, citing R. Winchel et al., "Impact of Coeducation on 'Fear of Success': Imagery Expressed by Male and Female High School Students," *Journal of Educational Psychology* 66 (1974): 726, and M. E. Tidball, "Perspective on Academic Women and Affirmative Action," *Educational Record* 54 (1973): 130–35. Although 80 percent of Blacks attend white colleges today, less than 50 percent of them graduate. The historical Black colleges granted undergraduate degrees to 80 percent of all Blacks with advanced degrees from white universities and have 800,000 living alumni. Of all Black college graduates, 80 percent finished at these Black colleges. These graduates constitute a majority of Black lawyers, judges, physicians, Ph.D.s, military officers, and executives. Brown, "Black College Day," p. 6.

59. Butler, et al., "Education," p. 16; Banks, "Blacks," p. 82.

60. Lewis B. Mayhew, "American Higher Education Now and in the Future," *Annals of the American Academy of Political and Social Science* 404 (Nov. 1972): 48.

61. Janet M. Cuca, "Graduate Psychology Enrollment Still Up—But Not As Much," *APA Monitor* 5, no. 5 (May 1974): 10.

62. Samuel Eliot Morison and Henry Steele Commager, *The Growth of the American Republic*, vol. 2 (New York: Oxford University Press, 1942): 20.

63. T. Thomas Fortune, "The Negro's Place in American Life at the Present Day," in *The Negro Problem*, pp. 232, 233. Most studies from 1955 to 1975 of student educational and occupational aspirations indicate that aspirations of Black students and their parents equal or exceed those of white students of similar socioeconomic status. Edgar C. Epps, "The Impact of School Desegregation on Aspirations, Self-Concepts and Other Aspects of Personality," Jones, ed., *Black Psychology* (1980), p. 231. In 1982, more Blacks were attending and completing high school than ever before. Barbara J. Shade, "Afro-American Cognitive Style: A Variable in School Success?" *Review of Educational Research* 52, no. 2 (Summer 1982): 219. There was an increase in school attendance of approximately one-half million Blacks aged 3–34 between 1970 and 1981. Matney and Johnson, *America's Black Population*, p. 14.

64. The focus here is on college training, but see also Hymon T. Johnson, "Educational Planning in the Black Community: Basic Considerations," *Journal of Negro Education*, 44 (Summer 1975): 338.

65. Charles W. Chesnutt, "The Disfranchisement of the Negro," *The Negro Problem,* p. 90

66. DuBois, "Talented Tenth," p. 49.

67. In 1980–81, Black Americans accounted for 5.7 percent of the 65,189 students enrolled in U.S. medical schools, though 6.6 percent of the first-year class; in 1981–82, these figures were 5.8 percent and 5.8 percent, respectively. Slightly less than one-fourth of these students were enrolled at Howard, Meharry, and Morehouse, the predominantly Black medical schools. *Medical School Admission Requirements* 1982–83 and 1984–85 (Washington, D.C.: Association of American Medical Colleges). See also Richard Watkins, "On Becoming a Black Doctor," *Black Enterprise* 5, no. 7 (Feb. 1975): 20–21, and Rod Toneye's personal narrative of "Institutionalized Racism in the Medical Profession," *Science for the People* (Nov./Dec. 1982), pp. 21–24.

68. John R. Hill, "Presidential Perception: Administrative Problems and Needs of Public Black Colleges," *The Journal of Negro Education,* 44, no. 1 (Winter 1975): 59; Phyllis Zatlin Boring, "Antibias Regulation of Universities: A Biased View?" *AAUP Bulletin,* 61, no. 3 (Oct. 1975): 254; J. Gwartney, "Changes in the Non-White/White Income Ratio," *American Economic Review,* 60 (Dec. 1970): 872, cited in D. Stanley Eitzen, *Social Structure and Social Problems* (Boston: Allyn and Bacon, 1974), p. 218.

69. Gibson, "How to Pick a College," pp. 20–21.

70. Robert L. Williams, "The Silent Mugging of the Black Community," *Psychology Today* 8 (May 1974): 34.

71. R. Jones, ed., *Black Psychology;* in the 1972 edition of *Black Psychology,* see Martin H. Jones and Martin C. Jones, "The Neglected Client," p. 196; Edward J. Barnes, "Counseling and the Black Student: The Need for a New View," pp. 213–24; William A. Hayes and William N. Banks, "The Nigger Box or a Redefinition of the Counselor's Role," p. 225.

72. William M. Banks, "The Social Context and Empirical Foundations of Research on Black Clients," in *Black Psychology,* ed. R. Jones (1980), pp. 285, 287.

73. LaMar P. Miller, "Testing Black Students: Implications for Assessing Inner-City Schools," *Journal of Negro Education* 44, no. 3 (Summer 1975): 410–12.

74. Frank Brown, "Assessment and Evaluation of Urban Schools," *Journal of Negro Education* 44, no. 3 (Summer 1975): 382.

75. Fortune, "The Negro's Place," in *The Negro Problem,* p. 230.

76. Banks, "Blacks in a Multiethnic Social Studies Curriculum: A Critical Assessment," pp. 84, 86.

77. Ibid., pp. 84–85.

78. See Butler et al., *Education,* p. 17; Banks, "Blacks in a Multiethnic Social Studies Curriculum: A Critical Assessment," p. 86; John D. Hicks and George E. Mowry, *A Short History of American Democracy,* 2nd ed. (Boston: Houghton Mifflin Company, 1956), p. 269.

79. Hicks and Mowry, *A Short History,* pp. 381, 400, 401.

80. Morison and Commager, *Growth,* vol. 1: 537, 539.

81. Samuel Eliot Morison, Henry Steele Commager and William E. Leuchtenburg, *A Concise History of the American Republic: An Abbreviated and Newly Revised Edition of the Growth of the American Republic* (New York: Oxford University Press, 1977), p. 202.

82. Dennis P. Andrulis, Ira Iscoe, Melvin P. Sikes, and Thomas Friedman, "Black Professionals in Predominantly White Institutions of Higher Education—An Examination of Some Demographic and Mobility Characteristics," *Journal of Negro Education* 44, no. 1 (Winter 1975): 6–11; C. Sumner Stone, "The Psychology of Whiteness vs. the Politics of Blackness," *Educational Researcher* (Jan. 1972), cited by Frank Brown, *Assessment.*

83. Fishel and Pottker, *Performance,* p. 110.

84. Charles W. Townsel, "The Urban School Administrator—A Black Perspective," *Journal of Negro Education* 44, no. 3 (Summer 1975): 428. Townsel identifies problems specific to Blacks in administration just as the *Journal of NAWDAC* identifies problems specific to women in administration.

85. Joseph, "Ain't I a Woman."

86. Julianne Malveaux, "Black Women on White Campuses," *Essence* 10, no. 4 (Aug. 1979): 78–79.

87. Ibid., p. 78.

88. Joseph, "Incompatible Ménage," p. 93.

89. Boxer, "For and about Women," p. 677.

90. Ketayun H. Gould, "Goals and Timetables vs. Quotas: Nondiscrimination or Reverse Discrimination?" *Journal of NAWDAC* 40, no. 1 (Fall 1976): 3–6; M. Louise McBee, "A New Day," *Journal of NAWDAC* 38, no. 4 (Summer 1975): 187; see also Robert L. Williams and Horace Mitchell, "The Testing Game," in *Black Psychology,* ed. R. Jones (1980), p. 487.

91. National Council for Black Studies, conference brochure.

92. Banks, "Blacks in a Multiethnic Social Studies Curriculum: A Critical Assessment," p. 84.

93. Harry Edwards, *Black Students* (New York: Free Press, 1970), p. 61. See also for example, R. Jones, ed., *Sourcebook on the Teaching of Black Psychology.*

94. Malveaux, "Black Women on White Campuses," pp. 102, 106, 109.

95. Boxer, "For and about Women," pp. 661–62.

96. Dana V. Hiller, "Women's Studies Emerging," *Journal of NAWDAC* 41, no. 1 (Fall 1977): 3.

97. Ibid.; *Spirit of Houston,* p. 37.

98. Eleanor Leacock, "History, Development, and the Division of Labor by Sex: Implications for Organization," *Signs* 7, no. 2 (Winter 1981): 491.

99. Joseph, "Incompatible Ménage," p. 98.

100. Allan Nevins and Henry Steele Commager, *A Short History of the United States,* 6th ed. (New York: Alfred A. Knopf, 1976), p. 46.

101. Maryann Mahaffey, "Foreword," in *Women's Issues and Social Work Practice,* ed. Elaine Norman and Arlene Mancuso (Itasca, Ill.: Peacock Publications, 1980) p. xiii.

102. Oliver Johnson, *William Lloyd Garrison and His Times* (Boston: Houghton, Mifflin, 1881), p. 259.

103. Lerner, *Black Women,* p. 77; see Booker T. Washington, W. E. B. DuBois, C. W. Chesnutt, W. H. Smith, H. T. Kealing, P. L. Dunbar, and T. Thomas Fortune, in *The Negro Problem.*

104. See illustrations of this type of scholarship in Garson, "Hurry Up," p. 168; Joseph L. White, William D. Parham, and Thomas A. Parham, "Black Psychology: The Afro-American Tradition as a Unifying Force for Traditional Psychology," in *Black Psychology,* ed. R. Jones (1980), pp. 57–58.

105. Staff of the Joint Center for Political Studies, *National Black Agenda for the '80s, Richard Conference Recommendations* (Washington, D.C.: Joint Center for Political Studies, 1980).

106. Pamela Douglas, "The 80s," *Essence* 10, no. 7 (Nov. 1979): 115.

107. *Spirit of Houston,* p. 274.

108. Janet Dreyfus Gray, "Married Professional Women: How They Feel About the Women's Movement," *Journal of NAWDAC* 43, no. 1 (Fall 1979): 29.

109. William H. Grier and Price M. Cobbs, *Black Rage* (New York: Bantam Books, 1969), p. 88; "How's Life," *Essence* 11, no. 1 (May 1980): 175.

110. *Spirit of Houston,* p. 273.

111. "How's Life," p. 170.

112. Betty Johnson, "Ethnic Minority Feminism: A Minority Member's View," *Journal of NAWDAC* 41, no. 2 (Winter 1978).

113. "How's Life."

Women in the Palace of Dahomey: A Case Study in West African Political Systems

Edna G. Bay

During the past dozen years, students of women in Africa have been preoccupied for the most part with questions of women's participation in national economic development and their status in contemporary society. Concentrating in the main on women in rural areas, scholars, most of them female, have produced macro and micro studies that trace women's loss of economic potential under colonial and independent government policies.[1] The delineation of this negative impact of development on women has been followed by a search for remedies by academics as well as development professionals. Together, these experts have prescribed a wealth of practical economic recommendations for the betterment of the lot of contemporary rural women in Africa. Their suggestions include small animal husbandry, tie-dying and soap-making, and home canning; the development of marketing or production cooperatives; the extension of government agricultural services and credits to women; and the creation of nonformal education networks directed at women's activities.

This recent literature on women in Africa, generated by committed scholars and supported by a sympathetic and predominantly female segment of the development community, has succeeded in integrating a significant women's perspective into the approaches of the Western-oriented and male-dominated development establishment. Clearly, feminist thinking has done great service in turning the attention of researchers involved in the Third World to questions of women's status and in focusing scholars' interests on applied research. Moreover, many of the developmental efforts proposed to improve women's livelihood have achieved laudable success. Yet this women's perspective suffers from disturbing limitations, possibly because it is tied so directly to short-term policy considerations. To the extent that this literature on African women is meant ultimately to provide the basis for policies that would improve African women's economic standing and status generally, it evidences major shortcomings.

First, this recent prescriptive literature on African women seldom confronts realities of power in contemporary male-dominated political systems. Applied researchers, in order to assure the general acceptability of their recommendations, take care that their projects rarely if ever question the status quo. Their hesitation is perhaps well founded, for male development professionals in particular express concern that, for the sake of what they perceive as "cultural considerations" or "traditional values," women-centered programs be designed so that they may never be construed as threatening to the power structure. The resulting projects are designed to create "pin money" for rural women and they effectively institutionalize women's economic marginality. In short, unless they press their concerns further than rural subsistence-level economics, development experts with feminist sympathies will be destined to help African women become, at best, more comfortable second-class citizens.

Second, recent development-oriented literature often assumes implicitly that African culture and the history of women in a given area of Africa are irrelevant to the contemporary needs of African women. Too often, recommendations are not based upon an understanding of women's usual obligations and privileges towards their families and their communities within the context of a given ethnic background; rather, academics and development professionals, including some who are African, seek adaptations of Western ideas and Western technology alone. Clearly, the past is irretrievable, even under the questionable romantic assumption that it represented a better way of life. Nevertheless, African women do have a heritage of political and economic participation in family and community that can and should form the basis for the building of programs for their betterment.

Finally, much recent literature on African women ignores the ideological implications of the study of the past. The histories of women in Africa are an unacknowledged heritage to contemporary women. A thread of continuity leads backward and forward, between past and present, linking the African past with the complexities of the contemporary amalgam of interethnic traditional systems and Western society. For African women, and for women throughout the world, an understanding of the past and its relation to the present may provide insights into society and self.

An analysis of these historical connections through a reconstruction of the political and economic activities of the women in the precolonial government of the kingdom of Dahomey, West Africa, reveals how African women participated in the formation and execution of national policies prior to the imposition of western modes.[2] Women's exercise of rights and prerogatives was an expected and indeed necessary element for the proper functioning of the state. Though the women here described constituted an elite portion of a ruling establishment, their roots permeated Dahomean society and thus their accomplishments appropriately stand as an element of the heritage of contemporary women. Although it is not possible to trace the lines of continuity from nineteenth-century women to their contemporary descendants, the cultural heritage of Dahomean women and particularly the sociopolitical structures and values extant in the precolonial period are a continuing element in the new social order.

Though my own field research experience was limited to Dahomey, many of the methodological problems I encountered are common to researchers of women elsewhere in Africa. Some such difficulties will be familiar to scholars dealing with women in a Western context; others are related to the problems of collecting and interpreting a historical tradition preserved orally; and yet others arise from the need to understand a culture inherently different from one's own. Historians of women in Africa are faced with the unpleasant reality that there are often limited possibilities to what we can ultimately know of women's precolonial past. Moreover, with a relative paucity of standard kinds of historical evidence, a researcher needs to employ an interdisciplinary approach and, at the very least, be able to apply evidence from the perspectives of linguistics, anthropology, political science, economics, and various literary traditions to the historical questions at hand.

The kingdom of Dahomey was located within the territory of what is today the People's Republic of Bénin.[3] It was created early in the seventeenth century and was ruled by a single dynasty for over 250 years until its conquest by the French in 1892. Authority in the kingdom was centralized in a monarchy whose capital was the inland city of Abomey, some sixty miles from the West African coast. There the king lived in a palace, or group of palaces, surrounded by thousands of female retainers or *ahosi,* a word that translates as dependents or wives of the king.

The *ahosi* performed a tremendous range of services in the name of the king. A good portion of them formed the king's standing army of women, elite soldiers considered by far the best fighting forces in the kingdom. Others are known to have had important political positions, holding ministerial office, acting as advisors to the king, and controlling the royal treasury. Some were priests and others judges in the palace. Virtually all worked both for the king and for themselves, at jobs that ranged from the menial to the highly responsible. In brief, the palace institution functioned as a small state within a state that, though separate from the kingdom as a whole, nevertheless could affect and be affected by the outside.

Unravelling the evidence to reconstruct this palace organization and the specific roles of women within it presents methodological difficulties that of themselves are worth consideration. There are written and oral sources of historical data about Dahomey and its palace women. Dozens of accounts of Dahomey were written by male European travelers—slave traders, abolitionists, government agents, and missionaries—who visited the kingdom beginning in the seventeenth century and continuing up to and through the conquest. The travelers generally recorded the dealings of men with other men. They spoke to and through male interpreters. Questions about women were answered by men, and women appear on the pages of their accounts only when their observable behavior did not conform to the Eurocentric stereotypes of the writers. Thus we read published accounts and archival records replete with descriptions of the fierce appearance of muscular "Amazon" soldiers, of the business acumen of market women, or of the exotic attire of hundreds of court ladies.

Recent African and non-African authors, trained in Western historiographical methods, have tended to give slight attention to the importance of women in the kingdom. In part, their omissions may be linked to the nature of the written historical evidence; historians tend to concentrate on the questions most richly supported by documentary evidence. Moreover, most recent historians have tended to define history as an accounting of the activities of men, a definition that corresponds to the attitudes of contemporary interpreters of the oral traditions of the kingdom.

The Dahomeans themselves preserve history in the form of oral narratives, maintained and recalled in several ways. Possibly most common are oral recitations related to the accomplishments of the kings. Such narratives of individual kings' administrations are preserved by professional chroniclers, male and female. In addition, individual families and congregations of the various Dahomean gods are charged with the guarding of versions of their own history. In some cases, religious observances in honor of the ancestral dead involve the ceremonial impersonation of significant men and women from the past. The performance of historical songs, too, is an important vehicle of history; generally considered to be the special province of women, songs recall the powers and acts of individuals, and the war exploits of the Dahomeans.

Much of this material demands explanation and interpretation before it can be integrated into historical reconstruction. Oral narratives are peppered with allegorical stories, proverbs, "strong names," and other references to the rich oral literary tradition that allude only obliquely to major historical events. The appearance of a long-dead ancestor in dramatic representation thus does not explain *why* he or she is remembered. Although preservation of the text of oral narratives and personification of ancestors is often done by women, in my experience only men were willing to offer explanations and opinions on the texts or to discuss this raw data of history in an analytical mode. Typically, such informants argued that the activities of women were not legitimately the concern of history.

Finally, oral narrative, because it depends on living memory, quite literally dies away with the elders who best remember the past, and each succeeding generation reinterprets the past in light of its own changed realities. At the time of my research, no one was still alive who knew the Dahomean palace as an adult, though several of my best informants had been children in the 1890s. As people moved in age further from the precolonial period, they tended more and more to assume that the changes brought about by colonialism had always existed in Dahomey. For example, the impact of Western culture has had dramatic effects on the nature of marriage traditions and particularly on the transfer of bridewealth, those payments in goods and services made by the family of the groom to that of the bride. Today, most descendants of Dahomey claim that in the past all children born of a woman belonged to the family of her husband, even if that family had not paid bridewealth or performed appropriate brideservice; however, documentary evidence shows that as recently as fifty years ago, children born to a woman for whom bridewealth had not been paid normally became members of the woman's family.[4]

Perhaps most important of all the problems of historical reconstruction, though, are the wider issues of analysis and interpretation that I faced with my Dahomean material and that any researcher who crosses cultural and linguistic boundaries must confront. Beyond the basic need simply to understand what one observes and is told is a deeper question related to seeing the world through perspectives similar to those of the people one studies. Particularly in the case of non-Western cultures, the category system used by people to comprehend and order their experience may vary dramatically from our own.

Very often, theoretical frameworks developed for Western-oriented data or, even more basically, assumptions of motives in human behavior, need to be questioned in a crosscultural setting. For example, the structures of the Dahomean and of several other West African precolonial political systems exhibit a female/male dualism which appears to be related to a division of labor and function in the social order. This dualism, which I will discuss below, does not correspond to the Western notion of nature vs. culture, however common that particular construct has been in the analysis of perceptions of women in the West. Moreover, participation in the political system and the immediate goals of political behavior differ in important ways in the Dahomean context from commonly assumed models of political behavior in the West. As a final example, anthropologists in dealing with women have sometimes presented a theoretical dichotomy between domestic and public realms in society; however, such a model is directly related to observations of human behavior in Western cultures and may not be relevant to African political institutions.[5]

This brief summary of my own work on women in the palace of Dahomey will outline three distinctive characteristics of that political system: (1) the institution of the palace and, by extension, the models of political interaction in Dahomean society were based upon and reflected common kinship structures; (2) forms of recruitment to the palace service suggest that the palace served as a major integrative and centralizing force in the kingdom; and (3) the palace as a female institution paralleled and mirrored similar male institutions in Dahomean society.

The organizing principles that supported the palace organization and indeed the entire political system of the kingdom of Dahomey were those of kinship. The institution of the *ahosi* appears to have developed out of the structure of the common polygynous household. In short, the palace was the family unit writ large.

Production in Dahomey, as in most of West Africa, was predominantly agricultural and was based on labor-intensive methods. Obviously, in such a system, the larger the household unit of production, the greater the potential for generation of wealth. It is little wonder that high status and wealth in Dahomey were associated with persons maintaining large numbers of dependents under their authority. Expansion of a given household could perhaps best be achieved by the acquisition of additional women, for women not only were productive agricultural workers and domestic managers, but in addition were capable of *reproducing* the labor force. Polygyny was thus a logical structure underlying the processes of gaining wealth in an agricultural and patrilineal society. Marriage in such a setting, as a mechanism for the acquisition of women and the expansion of the lineage, became a crucial focal point of negotiation between families, and institutions such as bridewealth and brideservice reflected the high value placed on the services offered by women. In Dahomey as elsewhere along the West African coast, a person's ability to offer a young woman under his or her control to another as a wife was a sign of great favor, appreciated as a mark of generosity and largesse on the part of the giver.

Within a single household, family members adhered to a strict hierarchy of position based on age. An individual's material and spiritual security lay ultimately in the lineage of his or her birth. Even though female members might depart from it to live with the families of their husbands, women and men alike were expected to fulfill material and ceremonial obligations, maintaining a lifelong loyalty to the lineage. The lineage in turn would assure basic necessities to its members, guarantee each a spouse, assist its members where possible in gaining rank or wealth in the broader society, and perform the necessary services to assure safe passage into the realm of the dead. Quite literally, the route for the solution of virtually any problem began at home.

On the level of the Dahomean monarchy, the king, by definition, was expected to maintain a massive household befitting the most wealthy and powerful person in the realm. Large retinues of wives, children, and slaves were commonly associated with kings along the West African coast, and early travelers to Dahomey confirm the pattern there. A visitor in 1724, for example, claimed that the king had "at least" 2,000 wives,[6] while a later sojourner estimated the female palace population in 1772 at between 3,000 and 4,000.[7] In the mid-nineteenth century, some 5,000 *ahosi* were estimated to live in the palace,[8] and its population reached a high of 8,000 just prior to the fall of the kingdom in 1892.[9]

Like wives in any common household, the king's *ahosi* were originally closely organized to accomplish the many tasks surrounding the support of their husband. They engaged in farming, oversaw the storage of foodstuffs, maintained the household buildings, and performed daily cooking and childcare tasks. At appropriate seasons, they prepared offerings and food for ceremonies. Moreover, each woman, as a right of marriage, continued productive economic activity for her own benefit, most typically in craft work or the processing and marketing of agricultural products. As the pressure of administrative needs increased, women began to assume wider roles in the developing internal bureaucracy. Over time, as the state expanded, the numbers of women increased and their duties were enlarged to encompass decisions and responsibilities with important implications for the nation as a whole. Where virtually no distinctions were drawn between the king's household as such and the machinery of state, a wife and minister became synonymous.

Visitors frequently argued that the kings trusted their women more than their male advisors. In truth, the women's comparative trustworthiness was assured by several factors. Culturally, married women were expected to obey and faithfully serve their husband's family, even though they maintained links with the lineage of their birth. A commoner's wife could divorce her husband or leave his house, but the palace women remained in the king's service for life. With no alternatives, women might just as well perform well for the king. Moreover, a reward system within the palace offered women strong incentives to work hard to win the monarch's favor and to use palace resources to their own and their lineage's advancement. Finally, as a physically separate institution that literally and figuratively surrounded the king and controlled access to his person, the palace appears to have been infused with an esprit, a sense of power, a feeling of participation at the center of control for the entire nation.

Thus the institutional structure of marriage provided the king and the kingdom with what was effectively both a household support system for the head of a wealthy lineage and the framework of a state bureaucracy. Women were drawn into the palace service from all levels of society; whatever their position in the palace and their physical relationship to the king, they were, in a strictly legal sense, wives to the monarch. In turn, like any common family head, the king presented women from the palace, some of whom were his own daughters, to representatives of other families, thus binding the royal lineage to others in ties of alliance and mutual obligation. As spokesperson for a nation, the king's presentation of palace women to visiting dignitaries representing foreign governments was at the same time the carrying out of foreign policy through the structure of kin relations. The Dahomeans carried the idiom of kinship a step further, for the monarchs tied their male aids to themselves through the form of marriage. A male minister, though he might maintain a household of his own, was bound to his husband, the king, through a set of mutual expectations and obligations that were based on the principles of common marriage ties. Like women in the palace, the most important male officers of the kingdom were called *ahosi,* wives of the king.

Women were recruited into the palace organization of Dahomey through a variety of means. At least by the nineteenth century and probably earlier, recruitment practices ensured the maintenance of what was effectively a cross-section, geographically and ethnically, of Dahomean life. Politically, this wide representation of total population had important implications for the integration of the kingdom and for the king's ability to maintain control over his subjects.

As early as the 1720s, agents of the king reportedly sought *ahosi* from among the citizenry of Dahomey.[10] By the nineteenth century, a court official, the *Kpakpa,* was responsible for recruitment. Every young girl in the kingdom was to be brought before the king's representatives, who visited each village in Dahomey at three-year intervals.

Girls judged suitable for the palace service were taken; their families notified the ancestors of this marriage to the king and token gifts were offered in the name of the monarch. Thus the king's marital control over the *ahosi* was legalized.[11]

According to informants, a lineage that wanted to "get ahead," and which had a nice daughter, one who was "fat and beautiful," would offer her to the king.[12] The offering of a daughter to the king established lines of authority and obligation, offering potential wealth to the lineage if the girl performed well in service or, in the case of wealthier families, symbolically linking a powerful lineage to the royal line.

Sources cite a third form of recruitment from among Dahomeans: women sent to the palace for various forms of misbehavior. Stealing, adultery, and general intransigence were said to result in enrollment in the palace.[13] In addition, a woman might be sent there as part of punishment meted out to an entire household whose head was found guilty of crimes against the state.[14]

The probable source of the greatest number of palace inhabitants, however, lay outside the confines of the Dahomean kingdom. Large numbers of women were brought to the palace as captives of war. Male and female prisoners captured by soldiers directly in the employ of the king were "bought" by the monarch, who rewarded his warriors with gifts of cowrie shells and cloth.[15] The king then sold some into the slave trade, used some in royal sacrifices, or assigned others to slave plantations. Women were usually integrated into the palace service. Girls of very young age could be brought up to be soldiers, while older women would be assigned a variety of roles.[16]

Ahosi were drawn, then, from among Dahomeans as well as from neighboring areas. Because they were recruited from all levels of society, palace women formed a powerful centralizing force within the kingdom. Most lineages could point to at least one daughter within the palace structure. Depending upon the rank and position she might achieve, the lineage could reap the advantages of gifts of slaves, land, women, and sinecures. More importantly, the lineage or family heads could enjoy a direct communications link with the very center of power in the kingdom, the palace at Abomey.

Female captives who became *ahosi* were additionally a vital channel of crosscultural influence. Religious practices can often be traced to women integrated into Dahomean society through the palace organization. A prime example is Hwanjile, a captive who became queen mother to one of the Dahomean kings, and who introduced three central gods to the Dahomean religious pantheon. Cultural institutions from the neighboring Yoruba peoples seem to have been established in large part through the impact of the presence of large numbers of Yoruba-speaking women who had been presented by the king as wives to leading Dahomean families. For example, one contemporary family credits its conversion to Islam to the influence of a Muslim Yoruba-speaking wife. Dahomeans further credit the introduction of an important sacred society to honor the dead to women captives. Many of Dahomey's greatest diviners, too, were descendants of female war captives and Dahomean fathers who learned their skill through relatives in their mothers' families.[17]

Once inside the palace, women and girls were placed in a complex system that reflected the social strata of Dahomean society as a whole. Initially, they were ranked according to socioeconomic position of their own lineages.[18] Foreign women, those captured in war or purchased as slaves, tended to occupy lower ranks, the youngest among them generally destined for training as soldiers. Over time, women might move to higher ranks. As in any polygynous Dahomean household, seniority gave earlier arrivals precedence over newcomers. In addition, a woman rose in rank through demonstrated outstanding service to the king. Military prowess in particular led to advancement and material reward.[19]

Related to the hierarchic ranking of women in the palace system was the organizational principle of doubling. As a microcosm of Dahomean society as a whole, the palace effectively doubled the social structure of the kingdom. But doubling in Dahomean life was more than a coincidental parallel in the organization of the king's household. Complementary duality was a central conceptual approach that permeated every level of human life in Dahomey. Examples abound of a constant pattern of pairing: male and female, right and left, military and ceremonial, royal and common, living and dead. The world itself was believed to be the creation of a twin deity, Mawu (female) and Lisa (male). The social and political structures of living beings were reflected in those of the realm of the dead. All human institutions, whether religious, political, military, or economic in nature, were characterized by a careful attention to doubling. For example, the internal affairs of every lineage and of the congregations of all deities in Dahomey were the responsibility of a male-female pair. Informants explain that doubling was necessary so that the female head could supervise women's work and the male, men's. But doubling was more complex than the male-female division of labor in Dahomean society. An individual, an office, or an institution, was often doubled not just by a single entity, but by a series of complementary others. The king, for example, was complemented by the queen mother, whose office will be discussed below; by a spirit being called his *tohossu,* said to be a deformed sibling destroyed at birth; by a distinguished ancestor believed to provide him a name and soul; and by a ceremonial figure representing himself as a prince.

Every office within the kingdom was held jointly by two persons, an official (usually male) outside the king's household, and a woman within the palace. The top policy-making body consisted of a cabinet of major officials, which in itself was divided into two groups, to the left and right of the monarch respectively. The cabinet included a prime minister, second minister, minister of war, minister of justice, treasurer, and so on. Male and female pairs were associated with each office, and were said to perform complementary duties. Witnesses at court agreed that both had to be present whenever matters pertaining to their charge were discussed. Public debates over national policy and affairs of state always included the active participation of both sets of officers.

The highest ranking position in the palace hierarchy of women, that of the queen mother, was a complement to the office of the reigning king. In keeping with the principle of doubling, the palace interior was divided into two major sections, controlled respectively by king and queen mother. The queen mother's court included male and female dignitaries; she received tribute from Dahomean subjects and showed favor to individuals, as did her reignmate.

In contrast to the royal origins of the monarch, the queen mother was always born of a common family, and in some cases may have been a slave. Though sources are contradictory, the weight of evidence suggests that the woman named queen mother was seldom if ever the natural mother of the king.[20] Rather, she was more likely a high-ranking wife of the reigning monarch's predecessor, who had worked in tandem with the would-be king to gain control of the throne. In a setting where a king might father well over 100 sons, ambitious princes who sought the highest office could well benefit from the assistance of well-placed and powerful women within the palace. Such alliances, which challenged and often overthrew the legal heir apparent, could result in the winning of great wealth and influence for the woman named queen mother. Moreover, the queen mother's material goods and title were inherited in perpetuity by female descendants in her lineage.

In the palace of precolonial Dahomey, in short, we have a situation where women exercised political rights and power and where they performed with intelligence and skill in a wide variety of endeavors. Women at the higher levels of the palace directly influenced decisions of national importance and amassed considerable economic power that they were able to bequeath to descendants in the families of their birth. As a cross section of Dahomean society, the palace inhabitants effectively represented their lineages at the centers of power and served as a communications link between the capitol and every portion of the nation. The foreign-born women in the palace, as transmitters of ideas, artistic traditions, social institutions, and religious beliefs, immeasurably enriched an essentially eclectic Dahomean society. But the political and economic importance of women in the ruling center of Dahomey was based not simply on an aberration at the level of the monarchy. Even though all Dahomean women were subject to a cultural ideology of male superiority, women acted under a tacit recognition of the right and need for women's presence and participation in affairs of family as well as affairs of state.

Outsiders to the palace expressed conflicting reactions to the *ahosi.* Some feared the women's powers. Others courted their favor because of the palace women's ability to influence and implement national policy. Many envied the riches that the women were able to bestow on their own patrilineages. The contradictory views of outsiders were reflected by the women themselves. The most highly honored and richest women in the kingdom dwelt in the palace, yet there is little evidence that any woman ever sought to join the *ahosi.* Moreover, there is no evidence that a feminist consciousness in the Western sense existed among the palace women. On the contrary, the record suggests that the Dahomean *ahosi* accepted the prevailing cultural denigration of their sex. For example, the women soldiers, universally recognized as the best warriors in the land, boasted:

> We march'd against Attahpahms as against men,
> We came and found them women.[21]

We were women, we are now men;
(King) Gezo has borne us again,
We are his wives, his daughters, his soldiers, his sandals.
War is our pastime—it clothes, it feeds, it is all to us.[22]

To the extent that we can speculate on the prevailing cultural values of the day, we may assume that the palace women sought solidarity, not with other women, but with members of their patrilineages. Achievement was valued in Dahomean society for it enhanced an individual's status within his or her lineage, assuring a respected place in this world and in the hereafter.

With the 1892 defeat of the Dahomean army, whose female troops fiercely resisted the superior technology of the French expeditionary force, the palace structure as it had existed under the kings was disbanded permanently. During the course of the early twentieth century, the differential standards of colonial rule—separate Western style schools for girls and boys, limits on the occupational level and type of training available to women, and the exclusion of women from political events involving traditional authorities—gradually ensured that women were seldom active in the public arena of Western-oriented politics. Yet the basic values that supported the development of the institution of the palace continued into the twentieth century. The lineage remained a central building block of a working political system, particularly on the local level, as well as the institution through which individuals sought material and physical well-being. Obligations of women and men to the lineages of their birth and to those of their spouses remained. So, too, did the rights of family members of both sexes and the expectation that women in particular would be active participants in decisions. In sum, although the political institution that allowed women direct and visible access to power on a national level was destroyed, the cultural values that undergirded its development continued into the modern era. In that sense, the foundation provided by the past can and should support the future of women.

Current scholarship on African women, particularly if it is directed toward public policy formation, should take cognizance of women's cultural and political heritage. Too often, studies that begin with a superficially Westernized, urban, here-and-now viewpoint have led to policies and projects designed to institutionalize African women's economic marginality. History tells us that such marginality is not inevitable and suggests that very different patterns have existed in the past.

Feminist scholars, both African and Western, have a responsibility to acknowledge the importance of African women's cultural heritage and to ensure that applications of their research appropriately reflect African women's prerogatives and status.

Notes

1. See, for example, Esther Boserup, *Woman's Role in Economic Development* (New York: St. Martin's Press, 1970); Irene Tinker, "The Adverse Impact of Development on Women," in *Woman and World Development,* ed. I. Tinker and Michele Bo Bramsen (Washington: Overseas Development Council, 1976), pp. 22–34; Achola Pala, *African Women in Rural Development: Research Trends and Priorities,* OLC Paper No. 12 (Washington: Overseas Liaison Committee, American Council on Education, 1976); Société Africaine d'Études et de Développement, *Social and Economic Development in Upper Volta: Woman's Perspective,* USAID (April 1978).

2. The field and archival research upon which this article is based was carried out under the auspices of the Foreign Area Fellowship Program. I would like to express my gratitude for that organization's generous support.

3. I will use the term "Dahomean" to refer both to persons who were citizens of the precolonial state and to contemporary descendants of the kingdom. The latter are today, of course, nationals of the People's Republic of Benin.

4. A. Le Hérissé, *L'Ancien royaume du Dahomey; Moeurs, réligion, histoire* (Paris: Larose, 1911), pp. 209–11; Melville J. Herskovits, *Dahomey, An Ancient West African Kingdom* 1 (New York: J. J. Augustin, 1938): 301; Rene Aho, "Le mariage chez les Fons," unpublished manuscript in possession of the author.

5. See, for example, Michelle Zimbalist Rosaldo, "Woman, Culture, and Society: a Theoretical Overview," in *Woman, Culture, and Society,* ed. M. Z. Rosaldo and Louise Lamphere (Stanford: Stanford University Press, 1974), pp. 17–42.

6. F. E. Forbes, *Dahomey and the Dahomans,* Vol. 1 (1851; reprinted London: Cass, 1966), p. 190.

7. Archibald Dalzel, *The History of Dahomey* (1793; reprinted London: Cass, 1967), p. 129.

8. Forbes, *Dahomey,* 1:14.

9. Le Hérissé, *L'Ancien royaume,* p. 26.

10. William Smith, *A New Voyage to Guinea* (1744; reprinted, London: Cass, 1967), p. 201.

11. Le Hérissé, *L'Ancien royaume,* p. 78; Paul Hazoume, *Doguicimi* (Paris: Larose, 1938), p. 131; Antoine Mattei, *Bas-Niger, Bénoué, Dahomey* (Grenoble: Impr. E. Vallier, 1890), p. 179.

12. Interviews: Abomey, July 11, 1972; Sept. 7, 1972.

13. Alfred Burdon Ellis, *The Ewe-speaking Peoples of the Slave Coast of West Africa* (London: Chapman and Hall, 1890), p. 183; Richard Francis Burton, "The Present State of Dahomey," *Transactions of the Ethnological Society of London* 3 (1865): 406.

14. Maximilian Quenum, *Au pays des Fons; Us et coutoumes du Dahomey* (Paris: Larose, 1938), p. 21.

15. Richard Francis Burton, *A Mission to Gelele, King of Dahome* (1864; rept. London: Routledge and Kegan Paul, 1966), p. 317; Forbes, *Dahomey*, 2:90.

16. Le Hérissé, *L'Ancien royaume*, p. 53.

17. Interviews: Sept. 7, 10, 1972; May 20, 1972.

18. J. Alfred Skertchly, *Dahomey as It Is* (London: Chapman and Hall, 1874), pp. 454–55.

19. Edna Bay, *"The Royal Women of Abomey"* (Ph.D. dissertation, Boston University, 1977).

20. See discussion of the office of queen mother in Bay, "Royal Women," p. 227–50.

21. Forbes, *Dahomey*, 2:108.

22. Ibid., p. 27.

4

The Medal of Excellence at Mississippi University for Women bears the engravings of four women who played significant roles in the university's history, including its founding mothers. The institution's mission has been to provide both a liberal arts education and vocational training to Mississippi's daughters, "a resource dearer than gold." Photo courtesy of the MUW Office of Public Information.

Section 4. On Methodologies

A number of important methodological issues turn upon the scholar's beliefs about the overarching categories of male dominance. For example, Marxist-feminist scholars ask about the structure of female-male relations within capitalism; they want to understand the origins, methods of perpetuation, and effects of the domination of women by men within a larger class stratification. Others argue that crossculturally, patriarchy precedes and is analytically independent of capitalism, and is institutionalized in the nuclear family. For some feminist scholars, the concept of patriarchy is general and transhistorical, but for others it is restricted to specific historical conditions. However conceptualized, patriarchy is an important, if problematic, concept for feminist scholars who are developing methodologies to deal with their concerns. Only research which acknowledges patriarchy can provide a genuine focus on women.

As a mode of perception, patriarchy is linked to what Marilyn Frye calls "the arrogant eye," a mode of perception, she suggests, in which traditional Western science and philosophy are grounded. The universe is—has to be—seen as ultimately intelligible to the arrogant perceiver, and woman as structured, organized, and formed to fit his needs and interests. From this starting point, Frye explores the consequences of this vision for women and feminist scholars, and posits a contrary mode of perception available to us only if and when we learn truly and generously to know ourselves and other women as independent beings.

Gail Paradise Kelly addresses what we might call "the androcentric eye." Only by dealing with the specifics of male dominance over women, she argues, can researchers perform accurate research. In the past, many researchers concerned with educational policy have asked questions such as, "Does educating women make for a better family?"

257

If this is the question, the answers will be measured only in terms of *family,* the effect of education on marriage age, marriage choice, number of children, and nutrition of children, and not in terms of *women.* "Women are not, and cannot be," she writes, "the center of research that begins with the question of how education affects institutions that women do not control and which, in most cases, oppress women." As her work indicates, feminist research increasingly does not accept, uncritically, the dichotomy between the public and the private spheres previously assumed by what has been termed "malestream" research.

Because of the methods, questions, and answers of most traditional historical research, historians, too, have perpetuated this dichotomy and assumed that only the public sphere is of much interest. This gives us what feminist historians have called a one-sex history. In contrast, they believe that feminist research must transform our view of the past, must infuse it with female life, must explore what has been outside the structure of accepted historical reality, and bring "the outside in." Thus Carroll Smith-Rosenberg and other feminist historians emphasize women's private histories. Hilda Smith argues, however, that this focus may present women's lives too much in a vacuum, unrealistically detached from the structural and attitudinal controls of a patriarchy hostile to their interests. Like Gail Kelly, she argues that "an understanding of the force of partriarchy should be the basis for all of women's history," although she goes on to say that it should not necessarily "be a continual part of the narrative itself." Each of these writers details how concern with the conditions of patriarchy affects the methodology of research, requiring new questions, such as the effect of women's oppression on female friendship, and reliance on new sources of data, including such local historical records as wills, marriage registers, physicians' records, and county histories.

Challenging our continuing dependence upon "research methodology," Dale Spender suggests we examine the assumptions and practices on which our own research is really based. Inscribing our personal and political commitments into our scholarship, we nevertheless draw back from using such fearful words. Though we may wish to believe that feminism draws strength from its openness to multiple realities, our academic training has not really prepared us to practice such multiplicity. Thus we may be quick to denounce patriarchal scholarship as propaganda that renders women valueless or invisible, yet we unconsciously substitute some equally doctrinaire feminist vision of "excellence," "objectivity," or "methodology." If we recognize propaganda as something we as well as others engage in, we can lift the taboo and become empowered to more openly and fruitfully explore and use the revolutionary scholarly processes and standards the propagation of feminism may entail.

Arrogance and Love

Marilyn Frye

Western philosophy and science have for the most part been built on the presumption of the intelligibility of the universe. This is the doctrine that everything in the universe and the universe itself can, at least in principle, be understood and comprehended by human intelligence, reason, and understanding.[1]

Western philosophy and science have for the most part been committed to the Simplicity Theory of Truth: the simplest theory that accounts for the data is the true theory. Theories are simplest which postulate the fewest entities, require the fewest hypotheses, and generate predictions by the fewest calculations.

The connection seems clear: only if the truth is simple can the universe be intelligible.

But why believe either of these principles?

The Bible says that all of nature (including woman) exists for man. Man is invited to subdue the earth and have dominion over every living thing on it, all of which is said to exist for man "for meat."[2] Woman is created to be his helper. This captures in myth Western civilization's primary answer to the philosophical question of man's place in nature: everything that is, is resource for man's exploitation.

If someone believes that the world is made for him to have dominion over and he is made to exploit it, he must believe that he and the world are so made that he *can*, at least in principle, achieve and maintain dominion over everything. But you can't put things to use if you don't know how they work. So he must believe that he can, at least in principle, understand everything. If the world exists for man, it must be usably intelligible, which means it must be simple enough for him to understand. A usable universe is an intelligible universe is a simple universe.

With this sort of world view, a person who identifies with "Man" sees with an arrogant eye which organizes everything seen with reference to himself and his own interests. This arrogant perceiver is a teleologist, a believer that everything exists and happens for some purpose, and he tends to animate things, imagining attitudes toward himself as the animating motives. Everything is either "for me" or "against me." This is the kind of vision that interprets the rock he trips on as hostile, the bolt he cannot loosen as stubborn, the woman who made meatloaf when he wanted spaghetti as "bad" (although he didn't say what he wanted). The arrogant perceiver does not countenance the possibility that the Other is independent, indifferent. The feminist separatist can only be a man-hater. Nature is called Mother.

The arrogant eye falsifies, but it also coerces. How one sees another determines how one expects the other to behave, and how one expects another to behave is a large factor in determining how the other does behave. Experiments show this is so: even rats learn faster in experiments done by people who have been told the rats were bred for higher intelligence; children whose teachers think they have high IQs show dramatic increases in their IQs.[3] Women experience this kind of coerciveness when men perversely impose sexual meanings on our every movement. Women scholars know the palpable pressure of a male colleague's reduction of our objection to an occasion for our instruction.

The arrogant perceiver's expectation creates in the space about him a sort of vacuum mold into which the other is sucked and held. But the other is not sucked into his structure always, nor always without resistance. In the absence of his manipulation the other *is* not organized primarily with reference to his interests. To the extent that she is not shaped to his will, does not fit the conformation he imposes, there is friction, anomaly, or incoherence in his world. To the extent that he notices this he can experience it in no other way than as something wrong with her. His perception is arrogating; his senses tell him that the world and everything in it (with the occasional exception of other men) is in the nature of things there *for* him, that she is by her constitution and *telos* his complement. He believes his senses. If woman does not complement him in perception, procedure, and judgment, there can only be something wrong with her. She is defective: unnatural, flawed, broken, abnormal, damaged, or sick. In the context, and in the eyes, of the academic, such a woman can only be stupid, illiterate, badly trained, crazy or, at the least, not a bonafide member of his discipline. The arrogant perceiver's norms of virtue and health are set up according to the degree of congruence of the object of perception with the seer's interests. And this is exactly wrong.

Though anyone might wish, for any of many reasons, to contribute to another's pursuit of her or his interests, the health and integrity of an organism is a matter of its being organized largely toward its own interests and welfare. The arrogant perceiver knows this in his own case, but he *arrogates* everything to himself and thus perceives as healthy or "right" everything that relates to him as his own substance does when he is healthy. But what's sauce for the gander is sauce for the goose. *She* is healthy and "working right" when *her* substance is organized primarily on principles which align it to *her* interests and welfare. Cooperation is essential, of course, but it will not do that I arrange everything so that you get enough exercise: for me to be healthy, *I* must get enough exercise. My being adequately exercised is logically independent of your being so.

The arrogant perceiver's perception of the other's normalcy or defectiveness, adequacy or incompetence, manipulates the other's perception and judgment at the root by mislabeling the unwholesome as healthy, and what is wrong as right, the interested as disinterested, the agreeable (to him) as true. One judges and chooses within a framework of values, notions as to what "good" and "true" pertain to. The simplest coercion (such as pulling a gun on a bank teller) leaves that framework alone and manipulates only the situation. The commercial advertiser may misrepresent particular items or options as good or good for you, but what we have here is the misdefining of "good" and "true." If one has the cultural and institutional power to make the misdefinition stick, one can turn the other wholly around the systematic congruence with one's self, with one's interest, by this simple trick. This is the sort of thing that makes the "reversals" Mary Daly talks about in *Gyn/Ecology* so evil and so dangerous.[4] If one does not get the concepts *right* and *wrong, healthy* and *unhealthy, true* and *untrue* right, and in particular if one gets them wrong in the specific way determined by the arrogant eye, one *cannot* take care of oneself and one *cannot* learn. This is the most fundamental kind of harm. It is, in effect, *mayhem:* a maiming which impairs a person's ability to defend herself. Mayhem is very close kin both morally and logically to murder.

One who would be publicly recognized as a tyrant or slaveholder, working with overt force, constructs a situation in which the victim's pursuit of survival, health, or understanding always requires, as a matter of practical fact in that situation, actions and interpretation which serve him. In the world constructed by the arrogant eye, this same connection is established not by terror but by definition.[5]

The Loving Eye

The attachment of the well-broken slave to the master has been confused with love. Under the name of Love, a willing and unconditional servitude has been promoted as something ecstatic, noble, fulfilling, and even redemptive. All praise is sung for the devoted wife who loves the husband and children she is willing to live for, and of the brave man who loves the god he is willing to kill for, the country he is willing to die for.

We can be taken in by this equation of servitude with love because we make two mistakes at once: we think of both servitude and love, that they are selfless or unselfish. We tend to think of them as attachments in which the person is not engaged becuase of self-interest and does not pursue self-interest. The wife who married for money did not marry for love, we think; the mercenary soldier is despised by the loyal patriot. And the slave, we think, is selfless because she *can* do nothing but serve the interests of another. But this is wrong. Neither is the slave selfless, nor is the lover. The slave is in a situation of utter dependence and peril where she cannot fail to interpret the other always with an eye to what will keep her from being killed or abandoned. Her eye is not arrogating, but it is the furthest thing from disinterested. One who loves is not selfless either.

If the loving eye is in any sense disinterested, it is not that the seer has lost herself, has no interests, or ignores or denies her interests; any of these would seriously incapacitate her as a perceiver. What is the case is that her interest does not blend the seer and the seen, whether empirically by terror or *a priori* by conceptual links forged by the arrogant eye. One who sees with a loving eye is separate from the other whom she sees. There are boundaries between them; she and the other are two; their interests are not identical; they are not blended in vital parasitic or symbiotic relations, nor does she believe they are or try to pretend they are.

The loving eye is a contrary of the arrogant eye.

The loving eye knows the independence of the other. It is the eye of a seer who knows that nature is indifferent. It is the eye of one who knows that to know the seen, one must consult something other than one's own will and interests and fears and imagination. One must look at the thing. One must look and listen and check and question.

The loving eye is one that pays a certain sort of attention. This attention can require a discipline, but *not* a self-denial. The discipline is one of self-knowledge, knowledge of the scope and boundary of the self. In particular it is a matter of being able to tell one's own interests from those of others, and of knowing where one's self leaves off and another begins. Perhaps in another world this would be easy and not a matter of discipline, but here we are brought up among metaphysical cannibals and their robots. Some of us are taught we can have everything, some are taught we can have nothing. Either way we will acquire a great wanting.

The wanting doesn't care about truth. It simplifies, where the truth is complex; it invents when it should be investigating; it expects when it should be waiting to find out; it would turn everything to its satisfaction, and what it finally thinks it cannot thus manuever, it hates. But the necessary discipline is not a denial of the wanting. On the contrary, it is a discipline of knowing and owning the wanting, identifying it, claiming it, knowing its scope, and through all this, knowing its distance from the truth.

The Beloved

We who would love women, and well, who would change ourselves and change the world so that it is possible to love women well, we need to imagine what the possibilities for women might be if we lived lives free of the material and perceptual forces which subordinate women to men. The point is not to imagine a female human animal unaffected by the other humans around it, uninfluenced by its own and others' perceptions of others' interests, unaffected by culture. The point is only to imagine women not enslaved; to imagine these intelligent, willful, and female bodies not subordinated in service to males, individually or via institutions (or to anybody, in any way); not pressed into a shape that suits an arrogant eye.

The forces which we want to imagine ourselves free of are a guide to what we might be when free of them. They mark the shape they mold us to, but they also suggest by implication the shapes we might have been without that molding. One can guess something of the magnitude and direction of the tendencies the thing would exhibit when free by attending to the magnitudes and directions of the forces required to confine and shape it. For instance, much pressure is applied at the point of our verbal behavior, enforcing silence or limiting our speech.[6] One can reason that without that force we might show ourselves to be loquacious and perhaps prone to oratory, not to mention prone to saying things unpleasant to male ears. The threat of rape is a force of great magnitude which is, among other things, applied against our movement about the cities, towns, and countryside. The implication is that without it a great many women might prove to be very prone to nomadic lives of exploration and adventure; why else should so much force be required to keep us at home?

But to speak most generally: the forces of men's material and perceptual violence mold Woman to dependence upon Man, in every meaning of "dependence": contingent upon; conditional upon; necessitated by; defined in terms of; incomplete or unreal without; requiring the support or assistance of; being a subordinate part of; being an appurtenance to.

Dependence is forced upon us. It is not rash to speculate that without this force much, most, or all of what most or all of us are and do would not be contingent upon, conditional upon, necessitated by, or subordinate to any man or what belongs to or pertains to a man, men, or masculinity. What we are and how we are, or what we would be and how we would be if not molded by the arrogating eye, is, *not molded to man, not dependent.*

I do not speak here of a specious absolute independence that would mean never responding to another's need and never needing another's response. I conceive here simply of a being whose needs and responses are not *bound* by concepts or by terror in a dependence upon those of another. The loving eye makes the correct assumption: the object of the seeing is *another* being whose existence and character are logically independent of the seer and who may be practically or empirically independent in any particular respect at any particular time.

It is not an easy thing to grasp the meaning or the truth of this "independence," nor is a clear or secure belief in it at all common, even among those who identify themselves as feminists. The inability to think it is one of the things that locks men in their eternal infantilism; it is one of the things that makes women endlessly susceptible to deep uncertainty in our political and epistemological claims and to nearly fatal indecisiveness in our actions.

When we try to think ourselves independent, to think ourselves women not mediated by men or Man, what we attempt is both prodigious and terrifying, since by our own wills we would be led to that fringe of the world where language and meaning let go their hold on our lives. So, understandably, we suffer failures of imagination and failures of courage.

We have to a great extent learned the arrogant boychild's vocabulary, and to identify with him and see with his eye; we have learned to think of agency and power very much as he does. What we may do when we try to imagine ourselves independent is just slip ourselves slyly into his shoes and imagine *ourselves* the center of the universe, the darlings of Mother Nature and the cherished sisters of all other women.

Much of the radical feminist art and theory which has nurtured my imagination has been characterized by occasional streaks of this kind of romanticism. Some of it is much influenced by such ideas of a "built in" perfect harmony among women and between women and Nature. Something of this sort is part of the romantic element in Mary Daly's *Gyn/Ecology;* it is in Susan Griffin's *Woman and Nature;* it is very prevalent (I do not say universal) in the literature and art of women's spirituality.[7] *The Wanderground,* a fantasy novel which has been very successful in feminist circles, develops such a romanticism quite explicitly.[8] This tendency of thought is markedly absent from two other feminist fantasy novels, *Walk To The End of The World* and *Motherlines,*[9] and these have been for that very reason disliked and criticized by some feminists for not presenting a feminist vision. The same failure of imagination which has seduced some radical feminist thinking into a rose-colored vision of ourselves and Nature has much more fundamentally shaped the "civil rights" wing of feminist thought. The woman who wants "equality" in many cases simply wants to be in there *too,* as one of the men for whom men's God made everything "for meat."

It has been suggested to me that we fail in these efforts of imagination partly because we insist on reinventing the wheel. We might give womankind some credit: we might suppose that not all women lead and have led male-mediated lives, and that the lives of the more independent women could provide material for the stimulation and correction of our imaginations. Women of exceptional gifts and creative achievements there are, and women whose lives do not follow the beaten path. But also, when one looks closely at the lives of the women presented by history or in one's own experience as exceptional, one often sees both some not-so-exceptional causal factors like the patronage of exceptional men (for which one must assume the women pay in some coin or other), and signs of peculiar fears and strange lapses of imagination.

Why did so powerful and individual a woman as Gertrude Stein speak only in code and hardly at all in public of her passionate relationship with Alice B. Toklas? Why did brilliant suffragists, white women, fail politically under the pressure of racism? Why did Simone Weil hate Jews and why did she think suffering would make her good? Why did Simone de Beauvoir adhere to the misogynist Jean-Paul Sartre? I know gifted lesbian feminist scholars who identify themselves as lesbian separatists who are passionately devoted to the project of making "the boys" in their fields recognize their work, talent, and intelligence; this makes no sense. And I have heard other feminist scholars whose accomplishments and spirit show them capable of material and intellectual independence talking about their husbands in ways that make it inexplicable that they remain married to these men. Feminist writing, especially autobiographical writing, is full of examples of the most disappointing of all the exceptional women to whom we would turn, to whom we have turned—the mothers, grandmothers, aunts, sisters, and cousins who have in our own real lives been our examples of strength, power, independence, and solidarity with other women, and of whom we say, almost grieving, "She really was/is a feminist lesbian, though she would rather die than be called by that name."

The answers to the puzzles all these women present are of course very complex and individual, but I think there is at least one common thread: there is in the fabric of our lives, not always visible but always affecting its texture and strength, a mortal dread of being outside the field of vision of the arrogant eye. That eye gives all things meaning by connecting all things to each other by way of their references to one point—the Man. We fear that if we are not in that web of meaning there will be no meaning: our work will be meaningless, our lives of no value, our accomplishments empty, our identities illusory. The reason for this dread, I suggest, is that for most of us, including the exceptional, a woman existing outside the field of vision of man's arrogant eye is really inconceivable.

This is a terrible disability. If we have no intuition of ourselves as independent, unmediated beings in the world, then we cannot conceive ourselves surviving our liberation; for what our liberation will do is dissolve the structures and dismantle the mechanisms by which Woman is mediated by Man. If we cannot imagine ourselves surviving this, we certainly will not make it happen.

There probably is really no distinction, in the end, between imagination and courage. We can't imagine what we can't face, and we can't face what we can't imagine. To break out of the structures of the arrogant eye, we have to dare to rely on ourselves to make meaning and we have to imagine ourselves beings capable of that: capable of weaving the web of meaning which will hold us in some kind of intelligibility. We do manage this, to some extent; but we also wobble and threaten to fall, like a beginner on a bicycle who does not get up enough momentum, partly for lack of nerve.

We have correctly intuited that the making of meaning is social and requires a certain community of perception. We also are individually timid and want "support." So it is only against a background of an imagined community of ultimate harmony and perfect agreement that we dare to think it possible to make meaning. This brings us into an arrogance of our own, for we make it a prerequisite for our construction of meaning that other women be what we need them to be to constitute the harmonious community of agreement we require. Some women refuse to participate at all in this meaning construction "because feminists are divided and can't agree among themselves." Some who do participate threaten to return to the father's fold or to write others out of the movement if unanimity cannot be achieved. In other words, we threaten to fail in imagination and courage like all the other exceptional and ordinary women, if our sisters do not or will not harmonize and agree with us.

Meaning is indeed something that arises among two or more individuals and requires some degree of agreement in perception and values. (It also tends to generate the required community and the necessary degree of agreement.) The community required for meaning, however, is precisely *not* a homogeneous herd, for without difference there is no meaning. Meaning is a system of connections and distinctions among different and distinguishable things. The hypothetical homogeneous community which we imagine we need *could* not be the community in which we can make ourselves intelligible, immediately, to and for ourselves.

The liberated woman cannot be presumed to "suit" us and such presumption will simply keep us from actually imagining her *free,* for in our own effort of imagination we impose upon her. If we feed our vision on images filtered through what we suppose to be our necessities, we will be disappointed and resentful and will end up doing violence.

We need to know women as independent, subjectively in our own beings, and in our appreciations of others.

If we are to know it in ourselves, I think we may have to be under the gaze of a loving eye, the eye which presupposes our independence and permits us to experience directly in our bones the contingent character of her relations to all others and to Nature.

If we are to know women's independence in the being of others, I think we may have to cast a loving eye toward them . . . and wait, and see.

The science of the Loving Eye would favor the Complexity Theory of Truth, would presuppose the Endless Interestingness of the Universe. The Lover would expect the Beloved to be what she is, which is not always agreeable.

Notes

1. This essay is adapted from Marilyn Frye, "In and Out of Harm's Way: Arrogance and Love," in *The Politics of Reality: Essays in Feminist Theory,* ed. Marilyn Frye (Trumansburg, N.Y.: Crossing Press, 1983). In that context, this discussion is part of a larger discussion of coercion, exploitation, and enslavement—of how the will, body, and intelligence of one person can be disintegrated and reorganized to the service of another's interests.

2. Genesis, 1:29.

3. See Naomi Weisstein, "Psychology Constructs The Female," in *Woman in Sexist Society: Studies in Power and Powerlessness,* ed. Vivan Gornick and Barbara K. Moran (New York: Basic Books, 1971), pp. 133–46, esp. pp. 138–39.

4. Mary Daly, *Gyn/Ecology: The Metaethics of Radical Feminism* (Boston: Beacon Press, 1978), p. 2, 30, passim.

5. The implicit comparison of the situations of women to that of enslavement should not be understood, as it usually would be by American readers, as

a reference to the enslavement of Black people by whites in pre–Civil War United States. I think here in terms of the enslavement of girls and women for sexual service, as described and documented in Kathleen Barry, *Female Sexual Slavery* (Englewood Cliffs, N.Y.: Prentice-Hall, 1979).

6. See Dale Spender, *Man-Made Language* (London: Routledge & Kegan Paul, 1980), pp. 43–50.

7. See, for example, the magazine *Womanspirit*.

8. See Catherine Madsen's review of Sally M. Gearhart's *Wanderground: The Stories of the Hill Women* (Watertown, Mass.: Persephone Press, 1979) in *Conditions* 7 (1981): 138.

9. Suzy McKee Charnas, *Walk to the End of the World* (1978) and *Motherlines* (1980), both brought out by Berkeley Publishing Co., New York.

Female Bonds and the Family: Recent Directions in Women's History

Hilda L. Smith

Research in women's history over the last decade, particularly the period 1975–1980, has evolved along lines both fruitful and potentially treacherous. Historians have written much more about women, have created vast new amounts of information about their daily lives, and have argued forcefully that a study of the past is incomplete without a knowledge of what happened within individual families and between individual women. Women's historians, however, have been less successful at using what they know about women's lives to re-evaluate historical writing generally. To an extent, they have chosen to do research and inform their readers about the facts of women's traditional roles, and to devote relatively less attention to women's participation in the public sphere or to their interactions with men outside of the domestic circle. This focus on the personal and individual lives of women has intensified in recent years.

This judgment is based on a quantitative study of articles on women's history appearing in ten major journals during the period 1975 to 1980, an analysis of historical dissertations focusing on women during the same period (collected from *Dissertation Abstracts* and the listing of dissertations in progress compiled by the American Historical Association), and a reading of the recent monographic literature on the history of European and American women. Articles and dissertations normally reflect the most current interests in a field, and here they demonstrate an even greater focus on women's private lives than do the books which, appearing in this period after the normal publication lag, represent the proportionately larger amount of research done on women's public activities, educational advancements, and feminist efforts during the late 1960s and early 1970s.

The articles published in the ten journals surveyed over a ten-year period make clear the growing interest in the family, sex roles, and sexuality, and waning interest in politics, reform, and the history of feminism.[1] During the period 1975 to 1980, in particular, there were only four articles dealing with education, seven on feminism and politics combined under one heading, and six others on reform. Many more of the articles examined women's private lives. There were twenty-nine alone on marriage and the family, and another eight on the issue of fertility, in addition to four complete issues devoted to that subject. There were thirteen articles on issues relating to women's sexuality, twelve others on sex roles, and four on the topic of the home. Of the 194 dissertations done on women's history and listed in *Dissertation Abstracts* for the period 1975 to 1980, only 20 were on feminism or the women's movement. The largest category, as might be expected, was biography, but these were often more private than public biographies, such as "Harriet Robinson and her Family" and "Abigail Adams, Domesticity and the American Revolution." The other major topic was women's work, and here it was consistently integrated with their role in the family. Out of 44 dissertations on women's work, only 8 discussed professional women.

Although these figures demonstrate a significant concentration of interest on familial, kinship, and friendship ties in women's lives, they may somewhat understate the degree of this interest. If one notes the journals which are most influential (i.e., whose articles are most often cited in notes by historians of women generally), they would probably be *Signs, Feminist Studies, The Journal of Social History,* and to a somewhat lesser degree, *The Journal of Family History* and *The Journal of Interdisciplinary History.* These journals have displayed an even more pronounced focus on women's private lives, publishing both entire issues and numerous separate articles on topics such as motherhood, kinship, and women's informal networks.[2]

Before discussing the significance of this concentration on women's private lives, we should consider a number of problems which emerged during the decade of the 1970s when the new field of women's history was in the process of defining itself.

Over the last decade, individual scholars have debated the relationships between the history of women and national histories and between
women's history and individual topical approaches such as economic,
demographic, and social history. These debates reflect the disagreement, among those concentrating on women, on what is meant by
women's history.[3]

Historians dealing with women do not necessarily raise questions
from an understanding of women's particular status within society.
Some simply add the feminine pronoun to their writing; where originally the abstract historical actor had consistently been *man* or *he*, now
the actor becomes *person* and *he or she*. This alteration is often made
without rewriting substantive historical development to take into account women's roles in the past. This change is particularly evident in
recent textbooks.[4] Similarly, authors of both textbooks and monographs when discussing a predefined area of research—say union leadership—may simply include a few women's names along with men's,
without attempting to rethink the whole process of leadership selection
based on an understanding of women's role in unionization. Moreover,
historians often intermingle women's history with family history or the
history of sexuality in such a way that the degree to which they are
focusing on women is unclear.[5]

It is crucial for us to distinguish between women's history as a
definable research field, and historical works that merely include some
mention of women. I would like to postulate two basic criteria for this
distinction. First, we must consider women as a group holding a unique
status within any given culture, existing across cultural and national
boundaries. This is not to say that all women have lived similar lives
despite varying historical settings, but rather that women in a given
setting have a common status and perform specified activities, solely
because of their sex. Just as class, religion, and geographical origin
create ties among those of like identity, so sex is a definable category of
shared experience. Second, we must ask questions relevant to women's
group experience, rather than, for example, about the development
of the family per se or about fertility in relation only to population
growth.[6]

In working from these two premises, we must seek methodological
principles that will rid us, as much as possible, of our biases against
assigning importance to women's roles in the past and enable us to pose
questions based on an understanding of women's group identity. We

must first confront our tendency to think of women in relational terms, as embodiments of feminine roles, or helpmates in all spheres of life, and thus secondary to the central action of the past. Second, we should not use traditional historical categories and simply fit women into them. If we study the marriage patterns of aristocratic women in order to shed new light on the gentry question in seventeenth-century English historiography we may be very far afield from the actual lives of those women.

To move beyond traditional historical categorization, historians of women have borrowed much from the social sciences concerning women's crosscultural behavior. Anthropologists, in particular, have been of special importance to women's historians in identifying cultural patterns in women's lives which historians could then test in particular historical settings. Borrowing from the social sciences, however, has also been problematical. Historians have sometimes accepted too readily social scientific views about women's shared characteristics which, at least implicitly, assume inherent sexual differences and encourage the view that women's nature exists outside of the social and economic conditions which define their brothers' existence.[7]

Further, we should be cautious about using prescriptive literature, or the descriptions of male contemporaries as our only or primary sources in re-creating women's past. In gaining access to women's past the researcher should be aware that often it is the single fact that one was a woman that is most crucial in discovering information about her. If the historian is interested in a seventeenth-century woman writer, for instance, more can be discovered by pursuing guides to early women's periodicals, listings of notable seventeenth-century women or almost any secondary work focusing on women, rather than from searching through general collections of seventeenth-century writings or secondary treatments of seventeenth century thought or intellectuals. Thus, for the researcher, a woman's sex often provides the most important clue to finding materials about her; such a search, however, is predicated upon acknowledging a group identity.

These considerations lead also to a greater use of local or comparative studies in research on women's history. National activities or identities have seldom been the crucial geographical unit in understanding the lives of women. Seldom have historians defined a nation's character by the characteristics of its female inhabitants, except perhaps through the manner in which they influence the present behavior of their husbands and the future behavior or their sons. When we speak of "an Englishman" or "an American" it is not a female image which comes to mind.

In turning to local or regional studies, we can deal with a unit sufficiently small to consider women's presence in a thorough manner. In this setting, the omnipresence of women in real life is an important guide in directing our search for historical materials. Rather than isolating one aspect of women's past, we understand women's history more clearly by studying a broad range of the surviving documents of small geographical and familial units. Wills, marriage registers, county histories, company or governmental records, physicians' books, and family papers all contain generally untapped information. The more unfocused our search among these documents, so long as it is a manageable unit, the more successful it may be. Women participated in virtually every segment of a community's life, and we distort that participation when we concentrate only, for instance, on family documents. Obviously, there is a limit to what one researcher can do, but we must remember that if we only view materials on women as wives and mothers, we will never know where they fit into the public structure of their community. On the other hand, the research can be just as limited by concentrating, for example, only on the woman worker. What is necessary, then, is to develop research questions, categories, and methods that illuminate the full range of women's lives, private and public, sexual and occupational, in kin groups and reform groups, across cultural boundaries and in the local community.

We have seen in the opening section that the emphasis in the field of women's history during the period 1975–80 has been heavily on the private realm, the interior of women's lives: their friendships, their homes, their families, and their sense of self. This emphasis on the daily life of "average" women grew out of conflicts with the kind of women's history done in the earlier heyday of the field, 1890–1930. Current historians of women wanted to develop something they called "the new women's history" which was to be more sound than the earlier scholarship on women, written mostly by members of the women's movement rather than by trained historians. Current women's history worked to differentiate itself from the previous studies of great women which Gerda Lerner termed "compensatory history" and Natalie Zemon Davis labeled works on "women worthies." To transcend the earlier hagiographic treatments of female leaders, more recent women's historians have allied themselves with the values and techniques of social historians. Thus the influence of social history, plus the desire not to be confused with what was considered the less-scholarly women's history of the early twentieth century, led historians of women to concentrate on studying women in the aggregate, women workers, and women's family role, in particular their economic and sexual functions within the home.[8]

This attention to women's private lives has now acquired important ideological and methodological components, and has led to a number of theories about how to do women's history, and about what is important about women's past or fundamental to our understanding of historical sex roles.[9] On the surface these theories sometimes appear in conflict, but while there is important disagreement among historians pursuing one theory or another, their analyses of women's past have produced similar results. These similarities appear not only in the kinds of women's experiences studied, but also in the analysis of such experiences.

Their essential likeness grows from the ways they have justified and elaborated on the central importance of women's private lives to our understanding of their position within a given society. One of the earliest and most influential of these studies was Daniel Scott Smith's discussion of American women's enhanced role in domestic decision-making during the 1800s. Terming women's greater authority there "domestic feminism," he argues that, in contrast to Gerda Lerner's view of women's declining status during the mid-1800s, women were coming to operate more as equals within the nineteenth-century family. His evidence for this is primarily demographic, and he uses it to demonstrate "that the wife significantly controlled family planning in the nineteenth century." A woman's increasingly definitive role in setting the terms for sexual intercourse and determining the numbers of children she would bear is linked to declining marital fertility, the increasing incidence of a female being the last child conceived, and the loss of paternal control over mate selection. He assumes that women more than men would desire female children, thus a final pregnancy resulting in a girl would indicate the woman's control over conception; that women had a greater interest in limiting family size than men, thus declining fertility would suggest growing female power; finally, that women gained more than men from a loss of paternal interference in their selection of a mate. He concludes by arguing that this was as much a feminist phenomenon as the women's rights movement, and of a more significant variety because it centrally affected the lives of all married women.[10]

There is, indeed, much useful material in Smith's article. It is helpful in focusing on women's choices in regard to demographic change, something generally avoided by demographers. It makes an important contribution in questioning the idealized notion of preindustrial families, in which in fact women often lived in close quarters with their husbands and children under an uncompromising patriarchal structure. The author, however, implies that to really understand women's lives we must look primarily at their role within the family, and this limited perspective poses certain difficulties. What women were doing in the family is viewed in a kind of void, isolated from the general social and political changes of the period. Economic shifts, growing urbanization, and removal of production from the home are linked to what the author terms " 'male' considerations." A peculiar distinction is made as to the way in which men and women came separately to a decision to limit family size. Smith says that the wife's "demand for a smaller family" may have been successful because it conformed so clearly to "the rational calculations of her husband" who was most influenced by economic factors. The work done and the income produced by large numbers of married women who took in boarders, who sewed or wrote novels at home apparently did not lead them to make "rational calculations" based on economic considerations.[11]

Another dubious feature of this article is the author's use of the term "feminism" to refer to any alleged enhancement in female power or position. The term is divorced from any ideological content; for instance, the woman who bears a third child so that she may have a daughter may be labeled a feminist in his analysis whether or not she perceives this as a "feminist" act. This removes feminism from the realm of thought and analysis to undirected action alone; thus, anything a woman does to enhance her position can be termed "feminist," whether or not she or society links it to the status of women generally. One wonders whether a poor seamstress's choice to give up her occupation to pursue the better-paying profession of prostitution would also be considered a feminist move.

Carroll Smith-Rosenberg, on a number of significant points, disagrees with Smith's domestic feminism, but she, as well, believes it is through women's personal lives that we can best understand their past. Smith-Rosenberg's important methodological essay "The New Woman and the New History" decries an overemphasis on women's public experience; her highly influential "The Female World of Love and Ritual: Relations between Women in Nineteenth-Century America" offers a case study of women's personal lives with the suggestion that these are central.[12] Like Smith, she argues that histories of the suffrage and feminist movements have little to tell us about the mass of women's lives. As Smith-Rosenberg states, "The most significant and intriguing historical questions relate to the events, the causal patterns, the psychodynamics of private places: the household, the family, the bed, the nursery, and kinship systems." She believes strongly that women's history has been interwoven too closely with the older, inapplicable categories of political history, and that we must now focus on what she terms "the non-political," namely "schools, factories, churches and religious revivals, hospitals, prisons, brothels." Not merely does she believe that we can understand the lives of most women and neglect the public sphere, she also contends we can know America's public past without studying women: "Women's suffrage has proved of little importance either to American politics or to American women; the transcendental movement would have existed without Margaret Fuller; the political events of the Progressive movement without Jane Addams."

Smith-Rosenberg makes a strong case for discussing women's personal and emotional growth, and for writing a history which truly reflects the realities of women's lives—not their lives as filtered through a study of political structures—but there are problems with this approach. Ellen DuBois has argued, for example, that an overemphasis on women's culture alone obscures the history of nineteenth-century American women. "From the point at which the woman's rights movement began to develop, it is impossible to understand the history of women's culture without setting it in dialectical relationship to feminism."[13] I would also argue that Smith-Rosenberg underestimates the importance of women leaders in directing or influencing public events. We simply cannot understand the failures and successes of Progressive politics without being aware of the efforts of Jane Addams and other women reformers during that period. Further, Smith-Rosenberg minimizes the significance of the denial of suffrage to one-half the population which, by enforcing division between public and private spheres and between men and women, could not have failed to affect negatively all aspects of women's lives.

Smith-Rosenberg, while downplaying women's public activities, assesses too generously the methods and materials of social history and demography for the study of women's history. She terms demographic records the "first truly detailed information concerning the life patterns of the working-class woman" available to the historian; however, these materials are often of little use in studying the woman's life outside the bounds of family formation and the birth and death of her children. Women are included in analyses of population shifts almost totally as passive beings; there is much detail about them in the descriptive portion of works of historical demography, much less or none at all in the portion devoted to discussions of causality. Demographic shifts are normally explained in economic, agricultural, or medical terms. Since men are seen as economic beings, alterations in their work patterns can and do influence the size of the family they choose to father. Alterations in women's lives, whether in terms of work, legal status or levels of literacy, are seldom used as explanations for general demographic change in a comparable way.[14]

Carroll Smith-Rosenberg does note that demographic data omit the emotional aspects of women's lives and give too little attention to family values. She does not, however, point out that demographers, in the information they collect and the analyses they make, show as much bias toward a male-centered definition of historical significance and assumed sex-role division as have political historians. Simply to shift the focus from the state to the family does not guarantee that the scholar will produce a scholarly analysis grounded in a women-centered understanding of women's past.

Smith-Rosenberg's essay on women's relationships during the nineteenth century effectively shifted attention from the relationship of the married couple—which had been so crucial to Daniel Scott Smith's analysis—to women's personal companionship. It was a woman-centered history in which "men made but a shadowy appearance." One may see Smith-Rosenberg's work on these relationships as the ultimate reaction to women being studied only as they interacted with men or as their lives touched institutions or areas defined as important by male historians.[15]

Although her account is useful and interesting, it does not provide the basis for a balanced history of women's past. As Smith-Rosenberg points out, women did not form close ties simply from reasons of personal inclination or choice; rather, the structural barriers between the sexes existing during the 1800s and the cultural values which sustained them often left women with little option to establish similar ties with men. As she notes, "American society was characterized in large part by rigid gender-role differentiation within the family and within society as a whole, leading to the emotional segregation of women and men." Further, these "supportive networks" were symbolically linked to and reinforced by women's passage through their traditional sexual functions: engagements, marriage, childbirth, etc. While she acknowledges these points, she does not incorporate them into her analysis, leading to a distorted, or at least incomplete evaluation of women's experience in nineteenth-century society.[16] To concentrate on these emotional ties among women, and especially to discuss only their favorable aspects and isolate them from the restrictions on women's public activities, runs some risk of giving legitimacy to society's acceptance of separate male and female spheres.

While Carroll Smith-Rosenberg's work concentrates on women's friendships both within and outside of the family, the work of Louise Tilly and Joan Scott aims to place women's work squarely within the family. An analysis of women's work would, presumably, take women's history outside the confines of the family to deal with these workers as independent economic units, yet Tilly and Scott have argued that to understand women's work one must understand the ways in which it functioned more to meet the needs of the family than of women as individuals. The particular subject of their interest is the European working class and peasant family of pre- and postindustrial society, particularly in the nineteenth century. They view the working-class family as a supportive, interdependent unit in which proceeds from the work of all members are pooled to take care of the needs of the family as a whole. They contend that preindustrial "family members worked in the economic interest of the family." Their language to describe this family interdependency is uniformly egalitarian; for example, they use the term "members" frequently. But, on the contrary, a contemporary whom they quote to support their arguments wrote: "The family and the enterprise coincide: the head of the family is at the same time the

head of the enterprise. Indeed, he is the one because he is the other. . . .
he lives his professional and his family life as an indivisible entity." This
contemporary language suggests a more patriarchal and less egalitarian
structure than Tilly and Scott have described.[17]

Scott and Tilly have disagreed convincingly with the work of Edward Shorter and his followers in the field of family history, such as
Carl Degler. They have also argued that women's interests and identity
are lost in a modernization framework that stresses greater sexual freedom as developing simultaneously with advancing industrialization and
individual autonomy. An illegitimate birth, for example, was obviously
experienced differently by the two sexes. The Scott and Tilly critiques
make clear their realization that women's interests are often being ignored or distorted by family historians.[18] Unfortunately, they do not
face this dilemma squarely in their own work. Their model of an interdependent, working-class European family plays down the normal
conflicts between husband and wife in a patriarchal family structure
and obscures women's needs. One could argue that in the preindustrial
family, the wife was doubly oppressed by the closeness of the family
unit. Not merely did her husband function as her political and legal
head, but he also functioned as her employer. Hard work does not
necessarily bring power or authority, and often in those regions of the
world where women must labor most strenuously, they have the least
say in the operation of politics, either within the home or the state.[19]

Smith, Smith-Rosenberg, and Scott and Tilly obviously had as their
purpose not to obscure women's past but rather to bring it more fully
into the center of the historical spotlight. While in many ways they
succeeded, by avoiding the issue of women's oppression, and thereby
failing to recognize or acknowledge the patriarchal structure which
controlled women's lives, they often appear to write women's history as
if these phenomena did not exist. One purpose of contemporary
women's historians has been to construct a more positive women's
history which does not continually see women only as victims. Yet one
can avoid mere reiteration of examples of women's oppression and still
write history informed by an understanding of how patriarchal control
functions as a significant element in women's lives. An understanding of
the force of patriarchy should be the basis for all women's history; it
should not necessarily be a continual part of the narrative itself.

The effort to present a more positive account of women's past has been connected with a growing interest in the work of Mary R. Beard. Berenice Carroll, Gerda Lerner, and Ann Lane, among others, have argued strongly for the importance of Beard's vision, especially as presented in *Woman as Force in History*. Beard argued that women have accomplished many great things in the past, and that their history was distorted both by historians and by nineteenth-century feminists who stressed the legal and economic restraints on women's lives.[20]

Lerner's interest in Beard is reflected in her 1977 book, *The Majority Finds Its Past,* and her earlier source book, *The Female Experience.* In *The Female Experience,* she correctly argues in favor of changing traditional historical categories and periods to bring them more in line with women's actual past. She decries traditionally male-biased history, and suggests that "to rectify this and to light up areas of historical darkness we must, for a time, focus on a *woman-centered* inquiry, considering the possibility of the existence of a female culture *within* the general culture shared by men and women."[21]

While Lerner sees this as merely a transitory stage in the ultimate transformation of American history generally, a number of structural limitations inherent in her arguments and selection of documents encourage a continued focus on women's separate identity. To move from traditional periodization, she suggests a life-cycle division as an alternative method of organizing the materials of women's past. Thus the first unit of her collection is termed "The Female Life Cycle," and women's past is divided according to "Childhood; Marriage, Motherhood, and the Single State"; "Just a Housewife"; and "Old Age, Sickness, and Death." These divisions constitute only one section of her collection, the second unit being entitled "Women in Male-Defined Society," but this organization suggests that by fulfilling traditional sexual functions and roles, women are outside "male-defined society." Women may have a greater freedom in their daily activities within the home simply because men are less apt to be about to command them, but the definitions and structures which direct and confine them there in the first place are the most fundamental norms of a "male-defined society." Looking at women's lives through their changing life-cycles may provide us with new insights as to how women's lives alter as they grow older, and how they share certain experiences only at a particular point in their lives. Yet if men's lives are not analyzed through their life cycles, and women's life cycles are seen as more crucial to understanding their history than men's, this approach may ultimately obstruct Lerner's goal of integrating both male and female experience into a non-sexist account of America's past.[22]

In assessing the advances made in the field of women's history over the past decade, we are obliged to ask ourselves some hard questions. We must question whether we are setting up norms for doing women's history that may direct it only to a study of the personal and private, to what is "woman-centered" in the most limited meaning of that term. We must also ask: to what degree has the success and popularity of such work rested on the fact that these traditional aspects of women's past are relatively non-threatening to male academics? To what extent does the rather inordinate interest of male scholars in the history of women's sexuality serve to provide them with titillating reading material and reinforce phallocentric views of women's nature?[23]

Estelle Freedman and Blanche Cook have argued strongly for the importance of treating women's separate institutions and lesbian experience historically.[24] Cook terms historians' omission of lesbian experience from the past "the historical denial of lesbianism" and links that omission with women's limited sexual options today and the oppressive control of the patriarchy. Freedman explicitly links relationships among women and separate female institutions to women's public effectiveness. She recognizes the potential for conservatism in a separate female sphere, stating that "the women's culture of the past—personal networks, rituals, and relationships—did not automatically constitute a political strategy." However, the female institutions developing out of the nineteenth-century women's movement escaped this conservatism. "As its participants entered a public female world, they adopted the moral radical stance of feminists such as Stanton and Anthony."

Although Freedman confronts more directly than Smith-Rosenberg the non-feminist potential of a separate women's sphere, she does not acknowledge sufficiently the conservatism of many of those connected with women's separate organizations during the late nineteenth and early twentieth centuries. Both Frances Willard and Jane Addams spoke of the necessity of preserving the family, the former linking up women's public involvement with issues of domestic purity while the latter supported protective legislation and worked diligently to enable women to fulfill their domestic roles more efficiently. Whether they initiated such efforts for strategic purposes rather than because of heartfelt convictions is more difficult to ascertain, but certainly it would be difficult to connect these aspects of their programs to the goals of radical feminism.

Studying relationships among women, the special difficulties and opportunities that women's sexual and domestic duties impose upon them, or the way in which women's status during different periods is determined by their place within the life cycle are essential to understanding women's past. But they are certainly not all of that past, and their study should not push aside, either consciously or unconsciously, a broader analysis of women's lives generally.

Finally, it may be that the most fundamental reason that historians of women have directed their attention to the private and personal in women's past has been a too uncritical attachment to the notion of women's autonomy over their own lives. But the search for women's autonomy must not lead us to close our eyes to the forces which have circumscribed and confined women's autonomy to a single realm. There is danger that current scholarship will encourage us to study women's lives in a vacuum, too separate from structural and attitudinal controls that are both pervasive and continual.

Notes

1. The journals included in this survey were *Signs, Feminist Studies, Journal of Social History, Journal of Family History, American Historical Review, Journal of American History, Past and Present, Journal of Modern History, Journal of Interdisciplinary History,* and *French Historical Studies.*

2. For special issues devoted to questions of female sexuality and the importance of the family see *Signs* 1, no. 4 (Summer 1976), *Feminist Studies* 4, no. 2 (June 1978) issue on motherhood, and two *Signs* issues focusing on "Women—Sex and Sexuality" (5, no. 4 [Summer 1980]; 6, no. 1 [Autumn 1980]). For issues devoted to the topic of fertility see the *Journal of Interdisciplinary History* (Spring 1976) and the *Journal of Social History* (Spring 1975; Fall 1978).

3. Renate Bridenthal and Claudia Koonz, "Introduction," *Becoming Visible: Women in European History* (Boston: Houghton-Mifflin Co., 1977), pp. 1–10; Natalie Zemon Davis, " 'Women's History' in Transition: The European Case," *Feminist Studies* 3 (Spring-Summer 1976): 83–103; Joan Kelly-Gadol, "The Social Relation of the Sexes: Methodological Implications of Women's History," *Signs* 1, no. 4 (Summer 1976): 809–23; Berenice A. Carroll, ed., "Introduction," *Liberating Women's History: Theoretical and Critical Essays* (Urbana: University of Illinois Press, 1976), pp. ix–xl. In the same volume, see Gerda Lerner, "Placing Women in History: A 1975 Perspective,"

pp. 357–67, and Hilda Smith, "Feminism and the Methodology of Women's History," pp. 368–84.

4. John M. Blum, et al., *The National Experience: A History of the United States* (New York: Harcourt, Brace Jovanovich, 1968 and 1973). From the second edition published in 1968 to the third released in 1973, *The National Experience* altered a sentence in its preface from "men make history" to "men and women make history" but altered little else in its coverage. The volume did, coincidentally, add Professor Willie Lee Rose to its list of authors with that edition. Such alterations are common with American textbooks, and they are imposed more by the editorial demands of presses than by any altered views on the part of authors. The most recent edition (1981) includes significantly more pages on women, but the coverage is still slight. For instance, the efforts of the Women's Trade Union League, the settlement house residents, and the suffrage activities of both NAWSA and the Woman's Party are discussed in one and one-half pages, while the Progressive movement is given a total of twenty-seven pages. Women are covered even more inadequately in Richard N. Current and Gerald J. Goodwin, *A History of the United States* (New York: Alfred A. Knopf, 1980). Thirty-one out of 904 pages are devoted to women, and the treatment is distorted; Susan B. Anthony and Elizabeth Cady Stanton are ignored in the authors' discussion of the nineteenth-century women's rights movement and introduced only in the chapter on Progressivism during a discussion of the suffrage victory (page 558).

5. Edward Shorter, "Illegitimacy, Sexual Revolution, and Social Change in Modern Europe," *Journal of Interdisciplinary History* 2 (Autumn 1971): 237–72. Here Shorter ignores that illegitimacy poses a quite different set of options and opportunities for men and women, and that women do not experience so readily the personal freedom and sense of mastery that he connects with the growing illegitimacy levels of the nineteenth century. See also Lawrence Stone, "The Rise of the Nuclear Family in Early Modern England," in *The Family in History,* ed. Charles E. Rosenberg (Philadelphia: University of Pennsylvania Press, 1975), pp. 13–57, and Edward Shorter, *The Making of the Modern Family* (New York: Basic Books, 1975). These works tell us a great deal of women's role within the family but rely heavily on prescriptive materials and do not sufficiently question women's absorption into familial roles.

6. For example, see Kathleen M. Davies, "'The Sacred Condition of Equality'—How Original Were Puritan Doctrines of Marriage," *Social History* 5 (May 1977): 563–80. This article is a quite thorough catalogue of Puritan writings about marriage but tells us little about the women in those marriages. Similarly, demographers seldom analyze women's role in the fertility level of a particular people. Changes in the numbers of children born are generally attributed either to external economic forces (defined as the male occupational sphere) or to famines or other uncontrollable natural phenomena.

7. Michelle Z. Rosaldo and Louise Lamphere, "Introduction," in *Woman, Culture and Society,* ed. Rosaldo and Lamphere (Stanford: Stanford University Press, 1974), pp. 1–15; Rosaldo, "Theoretical Overview," in the same volume, pp. 17–42. For a discussion of some of Rosaldo's later reserva-

tions about the universality of the theoretical overview she propounded in *Woman, Culture and Society* especially over the general application of "sexuality asymmetry," see her "The Use and Abuse of Anthropology: Reflections on Feminism and Cross Cultural Understandings," *Signs* 5, no. 3 (Spring 1980): 389–417.

8. Gerda Lerner's critique of earlier women's history, "New Approaches to the Study of Women in American History," appeared originally in the *Journal of Social History* 3, no. 1 (Fall 1969): 53–62. Her subsequent, more "woman-centered," approach to women's past is demonstrated in her collection of essays, *The Majority Finds Its Past: Placing Women in History* (New York: Oxford University Press, 1969). Natalie Zemon Davis, surveying research on the history of European women before the surge of interest in the topic during the last decade, employed the term "women worthies" to describe earlier works which had focused on great women. See her " 'Women's History' in Transition: The European Case," *Feminist Studies* 3 (Spring/Summer 1976): 83–103.

9. The goal is to work outward from women's personal experiences to their public activities, rather than to describe those activities in detail or reevaluate their impact on American society. See Nancy Cott, *Bonds of Womanhood* (New Haven: Yale University Press, 1978); Carroll Smith-Rosenberg, "Beauty, the Beast, and the Militant Woman: A Case Study in Sex Roles and Social Stress in Jacksonian American," *American Quarterly* 23 (1971): 562–84; Blanche Cook, "Female Support Networks and Political Activism: Lillian Wald, Crystal Eastman, Emma Goldman," *Chrysalis* 3 (1977): 43–61.

10. Daniel Scott Smith, "Family Limitation, Sexual Control, and Domestic Feminism in Victorian America," *Clio's Consciousness Raised*, ed. Mary S. Hartman and Lois Banner (New York: Octagon Books, 1976), pp. 119–36. See especially pages 123–29 for his discussion of women's growing importance in nineteenth-century couples' decision-making, especially in the area of family limitation.

11. Smith, "Family Limitation," p. 127.

12. Carroll Smith-Rosenberg, "The New Woman and the New History," *Feminist Studies* 3, no. 1/2 (Fall 1975): 185–98. In this essay and in her response to Ellen DuBois's questioning of the political implications of her approach (*Feminist Studies* 6, no. 1 [Spring 1980]), Smith-Rosenberg most thoroughly defends the importance of women's private lives to our understanding of their past. Carroll Smith-Rosenberg, "The Female World of Love and Ritual: Relations Between Women in Nineteenth-Century America," *Signs* 1 (Autumn 1975): 1–29.

13. Ellen DuBois, Carroll Smith-Rosenberg, and others, in "Politics and Culture in Women's History: A Symposium," *Feminist Studies* 6, no. 1 (Spring 1980): 28–64, debate the relative importance and political implications of studying women's past by focusing on their public activities or on a separate women's culture in the context of nineteenth-century America. Terming DuBois's view "a revisionist women's history," Smith-Rosenberg criticizes it for

ignoring "the experiences of the average woman," for relying on "an analytic framework which insists on the causal centrality of the political and ignores the economic, demographic, and institutional factors" of women's lives and for positing a nonexistent dialectic between feminism and women's culture (p. 55). Smith-Rosenberg, other than denying the dialectic propounded by DuBois, does not speak directly to the political implications raised in the earlier essay; rather, she speaks against elitist history, against focusing on the experiences of white middle-class women, and against studying only leaders.

14. Olwen Hufton's work on the length of female servitude, and the time required to accumulate a dowry, could provide a useful guide to explaining the late age at marriage of couples in early modern Europe, but the circumstances of women's work are rarely discussed in demographic explanations for late marital ages. See "Women and the Family Economy in Eighteenth Century France," *French Historical Studies* (Spring 1975), pp. 1–23. Demographers often assume a norm for female behavior and develop hypotheses about marriage, production of children, etc. based on that norm; yet Peter Uhlenberg, by simply asking not when but whether women married, found that only one-fifth to slightly over one-fourth of nineteenth-century Massachusetts women followed a "typical" life-cycle ("A Study of Cohort Life Cycles: Cohorts of Native Born Massachusetts Women, 1830–1920," *Population Studies* 23, pt. 3 [November 1969]: 407–20). Finally, demographers, when referring to such matters as pre-bridal pregnancies or the timing of sexual revolutions, reflect the sexual double standard. Although women are seldom seen in control of demographic phenomena, they are designated as responsible for sexual change. See, for instance, Daniel Scott Smith and Michael S. Hindus, "Premarital Pregnancy in America 1640–1971: An Overview and Interpretation," *Journal of Interdisciplinary History* 5, no. 4 (Spring 1975): 537–70. The authors note a changing "reality of allowing young men the political autonomy commensurate with their social and economic status," but ignore the involvement of women in the second Great Awakening, as well as women's participation in nineteenth-century reform movements. Yet when establishing sexual behavior, women are given much more credit, and they are called "the apparent source of the intergenerational transmission of premarital pregnancy in the eighteenth century" (p. 551). Demographers tend to see women in either one of two ways: as sources of increased population or as determinants of sexual mores. Seldom are they discussed as workers or as public figures, as are men. Such emphases encourage women's historians, when employing demographic research, to over-stress the sexual and private aspects of women's experiences.

15. Smith-Rosenberg, "The Female World," esp. pp. 1–3.

16. Smith-Rosenberg, "The Female World," p. 9. Smith-Rosenberg does not sufficiently relate her discussion of rigid sex role divisions to her glorification of women's relationships; for instance, see p. 14: "They valued each other. Women, who had little status or power in the larger world of male concerns, possessed status and power in the lives and worlds of other women." One wonders whether such relationships could survive women's equal involvement in men's activities?

17. Louise A. Tilly and Joan W. Scott, *Women, Work, and Family* (New York: Holt, Rinehart and Winston, 1978), p. 21.

18. Louise A. Tilly, Joan W. Scott, and Miriam Cohen, "Women's Work and European Fertility Patterns," *Journal of Interdisciplinary History* 6 (1976): 447–76. The authors contend that Edward Shorter did not study women's history thoroughly and based his explanations for the rise of European illegitimacy rates among working class women during the nineteenth century on preconceived, and often ill-founded, views about industrialization's naturally leading to greater female emancipation. It is their opinion that by studying women's lives more closely he would have discovered that "no change in attitude . . . increased the numbers of children," but that "old attitudes and customary behavior interacted with greatly changed circumstances . . . and led to increased illegitimate fertility."

Joan W. Scott, in a review of Carl Degler's *At Odds: Woman and the Family in America From the Revolution to the Present* (New York: Oxford University Press, 1980), notes his greater attention to women's importance than that shown by earlier historians of the modern family. Yet his work, which she terms "an attack on historians and feminists who trace the roots of women's current discontent to the nineteenth-century ideology of domesticity," paints an overly-rosy and inaccurate picture of women's growing autonomy during the 1800s. He fails to acknowledge the "conflict between domesticity and women's autonomy" and thus links positively the greater emphasis on a separate female sphere and women's quest for individuality ("The Making of the Modern Family," *Washington Post Book World*, June 29, 1980).

19. The work of Tilly and Scott, among others, has encouraged much recent research into women's work and its interaction with their family responsibilities. Two such works are Leslie W. Tentler, *Wage Earning Women: Industrial Work and Family Life in the United States, 1900–1930* (New York: Oxford University Press, 1979) and Winifred D. W. Bolin, "The Economics of Middle-Income Family Life: Working Women during the Great Depression," *Journal of American History* 65 (June 1978): 60–74. Both of these studies minimize the conflict between women's personal interests and those of the family. Tentler is too critical of the work setting—where women often found the greatest opportunities for socializing—and too uncritical of the allegedly autonomous setting of the home, to which women often retreated after a brief working career. There is slight attention given to the husband-wife relationship and little recognition that the husband might exercise a control over his wife's aspirations and working conditions similar to that previously wielded by her employer. Bolin also relies on data and interpretations which do not allow for conflicting interests for husbands and wives within marriage. Studies of women's work in Greek and Turkish villages raise questions about the status women gain from the importance of their labor to the survival of their family. See Fatma M. Cosar, "Women in Turkish Society," and Mary-Jo Delvecchio Good, "A Comparative Perspective on Women in Provincial Iran and Turkey," in *Women in the Muslim World,* ed. Lois Beck and Nikki Keddie (Cambridge, Mass.: Harvard University Press, 1978), pp. 124–40, 482–500, on the impor-

tant economic role played by large numbers of Turkish women which contrasts strongly with their weak familial, religious, and legal status. For a discussion of the work of Greek women and their familial subordination see Ionna Lambri, *Social Change in a Greek Country Town: The Impact of Factory Work on the Position of Women* (Athens: Center of Planning and Economic Research, 1965). Ester Boserup's classic study, *Women's Role in Economic Development* (London: Allen and Unwin, 1970), demonstrates that the status of women declines with modernization but makes it quite clear that women's hard work, especially in polygamous families in North Africa, does not guarantee them power within the family. To demonstrate women's greater importance within the family when their labor is essential for its survival, one must demonstrate not simply the fact of the labor, but also women's personal gain from their economic contributions.

20. Berenice A. Carroll, "Mary Beard's *Woman as Force in History:* A Critique," in *Liberating Women's History: Theoretical and Critical Essays,* ed. Berenice A. Carroll (Urbana: University of Illinois Press, 1976), pp. 26–41; Gerda Lerner has written about Mary Beard in a number of places beginning with her 1969 article "New Approaches to the Study of Women" and more recently in "The Challenge of Women's History," in her *The Majority Finds Its Past* (New York: Oxford University Press, 1979), 168–80. For the most thorough analysis of Mary R. Beard's life and work, plus a collection of essays written throughout her career, see *Mary Ritter Beard: A Sourcebook,* ed. Ann J. Lane (New York: Schocken Books, 1977).

21. Gerda Lerner, *The Female Experience: An American Documentary* (Indianapolis: The Bobbs-Merrill Co., 1977); Lerner, *The Majority Finds Its Past,* p. 178.

22. Lerner, *The Female Experience,* "Contents," pp. v–vii. Work on the aging process in men and life-cycle analyses of their historical experience have focused on very different phenomena than such research on women, e.g., men's growing "individuation," their experiences at school, their adolescence, their varying types of employment, their status as heads of independent households, and finally their decline into old age. This work is quite sex-stereotyped without always explicitly noting that it is accurate only for men's experience; it implies, often explicitly, that only men have the potential to reach independent adulthood. Again, presented in a descriptive fashion, often ignoring the ideological implications of these sex differences both for the past and the present, such work legitimizes the permanent division of male and female experience. For examples of these studies see the essays in "Part Three: The Stages of Life," *The American Family in Social-Historical Perspective,* ed. Michael Gordon, 2nd ed. (New York: St. Martin's Press, 1978).

23. Some of the more important work by male historians on the history of sexuality includes Edward Shorter's two articles "Illegitimacy, Sexual Revolution and Social Change in Modern Europe," *Journal of Interdisciplinary History* 2 (1971): 261–69 and "Female Emancipation, Birth Control and Fertility in European History," *American Historical Review* 78 (1973): 605–40; Carl N. Degler, "What Ought To Be and What Was: Women's Sexuality in the

Nineteenth Century," *American Historical Review* 79 (December 1974): 1479–90. The chapter on sexuality in Lawrence Stone's *The Family, Sex and Marriage in England, 1500–1800* (New York: Harper and Row, 1977), pp. 546–612, uses examples only from male sexual experience but analyzes the material as though it were about both sexes. Finally, a number of demographic studies document various sexual revolutions, including Daniel Scott Smith's "The Dating of the American Sexual Revolution: Evidence and Interpretation," *The American Family in Social Historical Perspective*, 2nd ed. (New York: St. Martin, pp. 426–38); Smith and Hindus, "Premarital Pregnancy in America"; John R. Gilis, "Servants, Sexual Relations, and the Risks of Illegitimacy in London, 1801–1900," *Feminist Studies* 5, no. 1 (Spring 1979): 142–73.

24. Estelle Freedman, "Separatism as Strategy: Female Institution Building and American Feminism, 1870–1930," *Feminist Studies* 5, no. 3 (Fall 1979); Blanche Cook, "Female Support Networks and Political Activism."

Failures of Androcentric Studies of Women's Education in the Third World

Gail Paradise Kelly

Before 1970, scholars virtually ignored the study of women's education in the Third World nations of Africa, Asia, Latin America, and the Middle East. They did so despite the vast proliferation of research on these countries throughout the 1960s which sought to trace the relation between school expansion; economic, social, and political development; and social justice and welfare. The absence of scholarship on women is even more shocking in view of the dramatic growth, since the 1950s, of female enrollments at all educational levels in most of the Third World nations.

Beginning in the early 1970s, research on the education of women in the Third World first challenged the assumption that the determinants, patterns, and outcomes of female education could be studied in the same manner as men's. More recently, this scholarship has raised new questions about the effect of education on women's lives and society, and has led to new methodologies for studying women's education.

Acknowledgment of Gender Roles, but not Gender Systems

The reason research on women's education was neglected until the 1970s is obvious. Most scholars believed it was not worth studying because women's roles were presumed immutable, confined to the domestic sphere, notably the family, which admitted but one type of organization and sex role division of labor. The few sketchy studies of women's schooling available indicated that women had lesser access to education, dropped out of school more frequently than men, achieved less well than men, and did not appear to enter the workforce in the modern sector of the economy in as great a proportion as men in jobs commensurate with their training.[1]

Studies of actual school achievement were almost nonexistent. It was presumed that the pattern of female versus male scholastic achievement identified in Western capitalist societies—notably the United States, Great Britain, Germany, and Sweden—held also in the Third World.[2] The few studies actually carried out seemed to bolster such assumptions with the notable exception of the largely ignored studies of Chile. Few scholars asked whether variations both within and among Third World nations existed; instead, they focused on establishing differences between males and females and assumed the differential outcomes of education were not likely to be modified.

In short, most researchers did not even consider the existence of patriarchy. They studied complex issues surrounding access to education, educational processes, and educational outcomes the same way for women as for men, and refused to recognize the gender-linked social relationships through which women are defined.

Studies conducted in this fashion, in current as well as past research, have a host of policy ramifications, given the present political activities in Third World countries. In the 1960s, most governments in these areas had allocated considerable sums of money to expanding educational opportunity. In countries like Kenya and Nigeria, up to 25 percent of the national budget was earmarked for schooling.[3] In other Third World nations, the percent was smaller, but still very large. Most government officials considered education an investment in economic development and assumed that schooling increased individual productivity, made industrialization possible by training a skilled labor force, and encouraged economic entrepreneurship.[4] By the late 1960s, the literature was dominated by correlational studies indicating that in countries with the greatest diffusion of formal education, the GNP per capita was highest, and that schooled individuals earned higher wages than those who were unschooled.[5] Despite the confusion between correlation and causation in this research literature, it became the basis for unprecedented government education expenditures and school expansion in Asia, Africa, and Latin America.

By the mid 1970s, it became clear that education had not produced the desired results. In most countries, educational expansion seemed totally unrelated to economic development, and in some countries it became associated with economic stagnation.[6] Government officials in Tunisia, for example, actually cut back educational expenditures and considered abandoning plans for universal primary education.[7] In the process, women's education was seen as an unnecessary "frill," even a "bad risk," given the scarcity in resources and the differences in male/ female educational outcomes research had documented.

Thus the research of the past, shaky though it was, has provided government officials a rationale for denying women an education, thereby often creating greater gender inequalities in income and power.[8] In many Third World nations, women traditionally have been employed in subsistence agriculture, petty trade, and handicrafts. Mechanization of agriculture, the spread of industrial production, and new marketing mechanisms have displaced women's work and/or changed its nature.[9] Since education has become the only avenue to employment in the new economic structures, women are often barred from employment or confined to unskilled, low-paying work, often at wages below subsistence. This fosters their increased economic dependence on men and has undermined their power and authority within domestic as well as public life. In short, the old patriarchical tradition of Western capitalist economies is being transferred to many Third World countries, aided and abetted by educational research which acknowledges different work experiences of women and men but not hierarchical gender systems.

Problems with Traditional Research

Traditional research begins with the proposition that women's lives naturally center on domestic, private life to the exclusion of public (social, political, and economic) life. Much of this scholarship perceives, implicitly or explicitly, public life as secondary, or "unnatural," for women, for example, as a product of poverty or broken marriage. It limits itself to determination of whether education affects or improves "domestic" life.[10] The research nexus therefore becomes that of marriage, fertility or reproductive patterns, children's nutrition and health, and children's achievement in the schools.

While research on these issues acknowledges the differing experiences of women and men, it does so in ways quite different from scholarship generated by feminists. Women are not at the center of such research; rather, the family as traditionally defined is. The research is not necessarily concerned with whether education improves women's lives nor how or whether education gives women greater control over their lives; rather, it asks questions about the impact of women's formal education on the family. These studies have found at best a tenuous relationship between the number of years of education on the one hand and, on the other, marriage choice, marriage age, number of children, children's nutrition and health, and children's subsequent educational attainment and achievement. While it is the case that the more education a woman receives the older she is likely to be when she marries, it is also the case that the marriage age for all women is rising, and it is not clear that increased schooling is responsible for this trend. Once class is taken into account, educated women do not always have fewer children who are better nourished or better achievers in school. There are, of course, enormous variations among and within Third World nations and, because of them and the limitations of the research questions, this research has been unable to draw conclusions about the overall impact of women's formal education on the family.

The Recognition of Patriarchy or Pitfalls of Scholarship

Studies of women's education which either ignore or uncritically accept patriarchy and presuppose a strict dichotomized domestic/public division for women and men make unwarranted assumptions about women and about schools. Both kinds of scholarship basically ignore the realities of most women's lives, for women are neither totally confined to the domestic sphere, nor totally free of it when they enter public life. Marriage, reproduction, and child rearing are but some, although important, aspects of women's lives; their primacy in women's experiences varies widely by culture, social class, and economic organization in the Third World. Women's participation in public life is profoundly affected by marriage, child bearing, and child rearing in ways different from men's.[11] Because of this, one cannot assume, as do many of the researchers on women's education, the bifurcation of public and private spheres. Any research which rests on one to the exclusion of the other cannot help but be inconclusive and inaccurate, for it denies women's reality. Second, the acceptance, by white researchers in particular, of a bifurcation between public and private of necessity places the heterosexual family or the society at the center of research, which is tantamount to posing patriarchical institutions and their maintenance as a central research focus. (See Marsha Houston Stanback's essay in this volume.) Women are not, and cannot be, the center of research that begins with the fundamental question of how education affects institutions that women do not control and which, in most instances, oppress women.

This is one of the pitfalls of research on women's education in the Third World that rises from either denial or unquestioning acceptance of patriarchy. The research also presumes that schools are neutral institutions divorced from gender systems. Nowhere does the research acknowledge that schools, through their locations, curriculum, and structure, may in fact produce the kinds of asymmetrical outcomes that have been described in the research. Perhaps women do not go to schools because schools are not available to them; perhaps they do not achieve well in schools because the schools to which they have access are of lower quality than those which males attend; perhaps they do not achieve well in school because they are taught not to achieve through years of in-school socialization. In short, the research has tended to treat the school as a neutral institution that makes no distinction between males and females. Differences in outcomes, consequently, can only be seen as "natural."[12] The assumption of neutrality has been made with little knowledge of the types of education given to women versus men and the processes associated with them. Research has considered only the number of years in school, not the quality and content of the education. As long as the school is presumed "neutral," one need not study what goes on in school and how that affects the outcomes of education. The acceptance of the school as a Skinnerian "black box" may account for inconclusive results regarding the effects of educating women.

Recent research, influenced greatly by feminism, has begun to place women at the center of research and has sought to determine how education changes women's lives rather than how education affects "society" or "the family." Recognition of patriarchy and its consequences is the key to such scholarship: the new research assumes women's roles are socially rather than biologically derived. It inquires whether social institutions like schools contribute to maintaining sex-gender systems and how schools might be changed to counter them.

Women at the Center of Research

Putting women at the center of research on schooling, combined with understanding sex-gender systems, has shown more fully why the pattern of women's educational attainment and achievement exists and how it might be changed. Research that does this is new. What follows will highlight the major differences between it and previous approaches.

For example, traditional scholarship never adequately explained why women go to school, or fail to go. Some scholars argued that social or cultural constraints accounted for lack of female education. More specifically, it has been posited, for example, that *purdah* (seclusion of women), practiced in Islamic nations and embedded in those cultures, explained why women's education rates were so low. But variation in women's educational enrollments is greater among nations that practice *purdah* than between those that do and those that do not, and women's enrollments in school have grown markedly in these countries since 1965.[13] Women have greater participation rates at all levels of education in Kuwait, Iran, and Tunisia, than they do in much of non-Islamic Asia and Africa. In fact, *purdah* in some cases has meant greater, rather than lesser, educational opportunities for women despite the fact that such participation does not necessarily imply equality for women in the society. Second, there is great variation among women within any given Islamic nation. To some extent, this variation can be explained by class: daughters of the middle class attend school more often than daughters of urban and rural poor. This is not always the case, for girls more often go to school, regardless of parents' occupations, when schools are available to them, culture and class not withstanding. In short, recent scholarship has demonstrated that a general "cultural constraint" explanation tells us very little; rather, it has shown that the way in which policy planners make schools available to women is more crucial. Third, if general culture constraints are not taken as major explanatory factors, one can also see how the quality of education, also a function of government choice, affects female enrollments. When high-quality schools are opened to women, women attend; they do not choose to go to third-rate schools. Also, clearly established is the fact that women's educational participation is dependent on the *type* of education offered to them. Schools which prepare women for prescribed familial roles tend not to be attended for they are redundant.[14] Finally, recent scholarship has found that, if education is related to a tangible reward structure, even if sex-segregated and in the context of *purdah,* women will attend school in increasing numbers.[15]

Recent scholarship also shows that the level of economic development, or industrialization, does not predict levels of female school enrollments, as some past scholarship has suggested. In Chile, for example, women are more equitably represented at all levels of the school system than they are in the U.S., Japan, or Canada, where per capita income and the contribution of manufacturing to the GNP is higher.[16]

In fact, in Chile, the quality of women's education is better than men's. The more highly educated a woman is in Chile, the more likely it is that she can enter high-paying professional and technical occupations. This is not to say that discrimination does not exist in the labor force; rather, because of discrimination, women need more schooling than men to enter those sectors of the labor force where qualification becomes more critical than prejudice. Women, given these circumstances, stay in school longer than men in order to reap the same economic rewards.

While for feminists it comes as no great surprise that social institutions such as schools support hierarchical gender systems, for scholars of education in the Third World it came as a revelation. Studies have begun to show that not only is the education offered to women in most parts of the Third World qualitatively inferior to that offered men, but that schools impart different social messages to their male and female students. Two studies of school textbooks, one carried out in Brazil, the other in India, have shown women portrayed as subservient to men, confined to domestic chores, and unable to benefit from education.[17] The Indian study found that these images are not always based on Indian traditions, and over time have become stronger in the texts, despite avowed government policies to correct sex inequality in education. Why this is the case is open to conjecture, but the trend, found also in Brazil and the United States, suggests some school materials used in the Third World are reproducing in those countries some of the patriarchical relations of Western capitalist societies. This linkage needs to be explored in greater depth, given the extensive aid programs in textbook development between industrialized and Third World nations.

Not only has current research documented that schools impart different messages to females than to males through the formal curriculum, it has begun to show that the "hidden" curriculum operates similarly. Such work was pioneered by Vandra Masemann in her study of a Ghanaian secondary school.[18] Western-style schools reproduced in their staffing patterns the authority structures and social organization found in the West. Biraimah's study of a Togolese secondary school, conducted in 1979, found similar results; however, Biraimah went one step further. In extensive interviews with students, she found that girls resisted the roles proffered by the schools. While aware of the schools' messages, they did not internalize them. Rather, the more educated they became, the more they dismissed the schools' teachings.[19] We do not yet know the significance of such resistance, but its existence raises major issues about whether schools, despite their structural and curricular attributes, can be used by women to better their own lives, regardless of the imposition of new sex-gender systems. Biraimah's work has allowed scholars to see women not as passive victims, but rather as active agents who attempt to shape their own destinies.

While such studies direct our attention to the study of schooling—especially what is taught in school—and the ways in which girls re-negotiate knowledge transmitted in the institution, they also contribute to our understanding of the ways in which we might view the impact of education on women. Traditionally, scholarship has shown that women's education has not led in the same way as men's to participation and status in public life. This is undeniable, but instead of concluding that because of this women are "bad risks" as far as education is concerned, feminist scholars have begun to ask whether women use schooling to mediate the impact of domestic life on public life and vice-versa. Feminist scholarship has not accepted the bifurcation between the two presumed by previous scholarship. The research question becomes, instead, how does education change the impact of marriage, reproduction, and child-rearing on women's roles in society. Does education allow women to obtain greater power and authority in both spheres? One study, conducted in Upper Volta, showed that women would not participate in educational programs unless such programs were likely to have a tangible effect on their domestic burdens.[20] Literacy and numeracy skills were irrelevant; rather, women chose to attend only those classes that would introduce technologies that would free them from the tedium of household tasks. Otherwise, women had no time for education. The Upper Volta study begins with women's reality and shows not only how women's daily lives, given patriarchical family structures and unequal burdens, affect whether they or their daughters will attend school, but also that women chose to be educated, or remain uneducated, on the basis of their assessment of whether education helps them to ameliorate their domestic as well as public lives.

Traditionally the only distinctions researchers made among women were the same as were made among men: class, region, and ethnicity.[21] While these represent important distinctions, they presume that marriage, reproduction, and child bearing have the same impact on men as they do on women; feminist scholars have shown that this is not the case. Those who have studied women's participation in public life, notably in the workforce, know that marriage drives women from the workforce; child bearing and rearing have a similar effect unless productive employment is integrated into the household. This trend operates differently for different categories of women. Poverty tends to drive women into the workforce. Single women or female heads of households, regardless of class, are represented in greater numbers within the workforce than married women or married women with small children. Scholars, like Wainerman,[22] have begun to assess the impact of education, not in terms of whether it is the same for women as for men, but rather in terms of whether education changes the pattern of women's withdrawal from public life at times of marriage, child bearing, and child rearing. She has found, in her groundbreaking 1980 study, that women of all classes who are educated tend to sustain themselves in the workforce and resist the usual pattern of increased dependency on male income and the erosion of their status that has accompanied industrialization. Education, as she suggests, mediates the impact of domestic relations and restrictions on women's participation in public life. Her findings are very much in agreement with those of Biraimah and McSweeney and Freedman, for they highlight the fact that women use education to mediate the impact of patriarchy and its intensification due to economic trends. We still do not know, however, from any of these studies why and how education seems to have this effect. More research is needed that relates what schools teach and what girls learn in school to understand how women use the education they receive.

New Directions

Recent research suggests that women want to, and individual women are in some cases able to, use schooling to better their lives, but it has not been able to show whether education does so for all women and can be used in and of itself to improve women's position in society. Study after study has shown that despite the expansion of schooling for women, their position, relative to men, especially in the economy and workforce has not improved; rather, in many countries it has deteriorated.[23] Why this is the case is not easily explained without further research, and that research cannot limit itself to considering schools and their relation to society in a one-nation perspective.

Some scholars have argued that the deteriorating status of women, despite their increases in educational attainments, is directly traceable to the failure of individual nations to industrialize.[24] They claim that if industrialization were to occur, then women's status relative to men's would improve, especially given the gains in women's education. Such analyses assume, without evidential bases, that the status of women in relation to men in already industrialized nations of Western Europe and North America where education is universal for both males and females on the primary, and often on the secondary levels, is substantially better than that of women in the Third World. This is somewhat debatable. Because of this, others have argued that the deterioration of women's status within the workforce of the Third World nations is a necessary concomitant of capitalist development that education cannot mediate.[25]

It is impossible, given the present state of research, to arrive at a definitive explanation for the deterioration of women's status within the economies of most Third World nations as industrialization has progressed, or the role of women's education in this process. It is important, though, to point out some of the difficulties involved in making statements about the relationship between increases in the education of women and their status in the workforce. These difficulties have to do with how one analyzes changes in women's roles and with the geographic boundaries within which most analyses have been based.

Most of the research documenting the changes in women's participation in the economy consists of correlations of population characteristics that have been used to study men. A few studies, like Wainerman's, depart and consider the structure of the family and child rearing and how they influence women's participation in a nation's economy. Wainerman suggests, in a study confined to Paraguay and Argentina (both with capitalist economies and differing levels of industrialization), that education increases women's labor force participation and lessens their dependency on males. But Wainerman says nothing about women's *status*, relative to men's, within the economy. Clearly, scholarship needs to explore, through the use of women-centric measures, whether the mediating effect Wainerman found relates to changes in their status within the workforce.

We have little ability to assess, through correlational data, the impact of schooling, and this presents a second difficulty in the existing research on women's education and its relationship both to their participation in and status within the economy. Scholarship to date has related increases in the number of women within certain sectors of the economy and increases in the number of women educated, finding the two have little to do with one another. *It has not studied women who are educated* and traced their work and family lives. It could be that increases in the number of women entering the workforce, or failing to enter the workforce, reflect young single women who seek jobs at an earlier age than their contemporaries who are in school until age nineteen or twenty-five. Third World populations are young; what may seem a trend now may not reflect the impact or lack of impact of education; the research findings may reflect instead the inadequacy of correlational data to detect new trends. To assess the relation of women's education to changes in their status, we need to study the social and economic realities of the lives of *educated* women relative to educated men, something which scholarship has yet to do.

The research studies that we have on women's education and the workforce are, for the most part, one-nation studies. These studies, and a very limited range of them, have been used to argue that the phenomena observed are characteristic of all nations as they develop. However, we have no idea of the impact of women's education on the position of women in the workforce in revolutionary socialist societies, since no such research has been done. We can only guess that what we have observed in non-socialist Third World nations results from modernization or the spread of capitalism until we compare these findings with those from Third World countries like China, Cuba, and Tanzania.

Comparative research has not only neglected analysis of the impact of education on women's position in socialist and non-socialist Third World countries; it has also failed to assess whether changes in women's position noted in Third World countries exist in advanced industrial societies, which in most instances control Third World economies. Most of the research has presumed that the factors influencing the roles of women and the use women can make of education exist solely within the boundaries of a single nation-state. Most deny the impact of neo-colonialism and the international market. The extent to which the economies of Third World nations are controlled by capitalists from the industrialized nations of Western Europe and the United States has been ignored in the literature.[26] The importance of extending our analyses of the impact of education on women beyond national boundaries cannot be overstated, since it is entirely possible that the extent to which women can use educational institutions to gain control of their lives is dependent on the degree to which patriarchical institutions operating *outside* of the nation-state allow women to use institutions in this manner. In other words, the content of and opportunities for schooling for Third World women may be closely tied to education systems for women in the advanced capitalist societies which control the Third World. In this case, it is important to know whether the changes feminists are making in the educational systems in countries like the United States have any role in changing the schooling available to women in the Third World. Comparative studies can begin to deal with these questions.

Feminist Scholarship and the Study of Women

This review of research has raised more questions than it has answered about the education of women in the Third World. Throughout, I have emphasized the vast gains in knowledge, research perspectives, and methods developed over the past decade. Yet our knowledge is sparse because research in this area has only recently begun. The kind of questions researchers have addressed reflects the newness of the field. The questions that have been studied—and not studied—also reflect the differences between traditional and feminist research on the study of the education of women. Unless future research is conducted in full recognition of patriarchy as an institution that can and ought to be changed, and takes women's lives and realities as its starting point, the results may have little to do with emancipating women or bettering their lives. Research, as I have pointed out, can serve to oppress women. In the past it has been used to provide a rationale to deny them education on the grounds of supposed sex differences that make them "bad risks" in school.

Feminist scholarship, however, is distinguishable from other scholarship on women in that its methods, frameworks, concerns, and questions are directed to changing women's lives and freeing them from oppression. For feminist scholars of education in the Third World, our goal is to find ways in which schools can be made a force to better women's private and public lives. We cannot know the effects of changing the numbers of women going to school, the length of time they remain in school, or the results of curricular innovations, until we develop ways to assess those changes. The first step is to orient our study toward women's realities.

Notes

1. See, for example, Marie Eliou, "Scolarisation et promotion feminines en Afrique francophone (Cote d'Ivoire, Haute-Volta, Senegal)," *International Review of Education* 19, no. 1 (1973): 30–46; Jacqueline Chaubaud, *The Education and Advancement of Women* (Paris: UNESCO, 1970). Excellent review articles include Mary Jean Bowman and C. Arnold Anderson, "The Participation of Women in Education in the Third World," *Comparative Education Review* 24, no. 2, pt. 2 (Summer 1980): S13–31 ("S" indicates special issue here and subsequently); Jeremy D. Finn, Loretta Dulberg, and Janet Reis, "Sex Differences in Educational Attainment: A Cross National Perspective," *Harvard Educational Review* 49 (Nov. 1979): 477–503; Rati Ram, "Sex Differences in the Labor Market Outcomes of Education," *Comparative Education Review* 24, no. 2, pt. 2 (Summer 1980): S53–77; M. Kotwal, "Inequalities in the Distribution of Education Between Countries, Sexes, Generations, and Individuals," in *Education, Inequality and Life Chances* 1 (Paris: OECD, 1975): 31–109. The term *Third World,* used in many of these publications, is itself problematic and needs additional attention.

2. For a review of this research, see Jeremy D. Finn, "Sex Differences in Educational Outcomes: A Cross National Study," *Sex Roles* 6 (Feb. 1980): 9–26.

3. See Ernest Stabler, *Education since Uhuru* (Middleton, Conn.: Wesleyan University Press, 1969); David Abernethy, *The Political Dilemma of Popular Education: An African Case* (Stanford: Stanford University Press, 1969).

4. There is a vast literature on this subject. An excellent review article is Irvin Sobel, "The Human Capital Revolution in Economic Development," *Comparative Education Review* 22, no. 2 (June 1978): 278–308.

5. See, for example, William S. Bennett, Jr., "Educational Change and Economic Development," *Sociology of Education* 40 (Spring 1967): 101–14; David C. McClelland, "Does Education Accelerate Economic Growth," *Economic Development and Cultural Change* 14 (April 1966), 257–78; George Psacharopoulous and Keith Hinchliffe, *Returns to Education: An International Comparison* (San Francisco: Jossey-Bass, 1973).

6. See Sobel, "Human Capital"; Abernethy, *Political Dilemma;* Donald K. Adams, "Development Education," *Comparative Education Review* 21 (June/October 1977): 296–310.

7. Marie Thourson Jones, "Education of Girls in Tunisia: Policy Implications of the Drive for Universal Enrollment," *Comparative Education Review* 24, no. 2 pt. 2 (Summer 1980): S106–23.

8. Ester Boserup, *Women's Role in Economic Development* (New York: St. Martin's, 1969).

9. Ibid.; Norma S. Chinchilla, "Industrialization, Monopoly Capitalism and Women's Work in Guatemala," *Signs* 3, no. 1 (Autumn 1977): 38–56; Glaura Vasques de Miranda, "Women's Labor Force Participation in a Developing Society," ibid., pp. 261–74.

10. Two excellent reviews of such research are: S. H. Cochrane, *Education and Fertility: What Do We Know?* (Baltimore: Johns Hopkins University Press, 1979); Robert Levine, "Influences of Women's Schooling on Maternal Behavior in the Third World," *Comparative Education Review* 24, no. 2, pt. 2 (Summer 1980): S78–105.

11. See Guy Standing, "Education and Female Participation in the Labor Force," *International Labor Review* 114 (Nov./Dec. 1976): 281–97; Catalina H. Wainerman, "The Impact of Education on the Female Labor Force in Argentina and Paraguay," *Comparative Education Review* 24, no. 2, pt. 2 (Summer 1980): S180–95.

12. A good example of such research is Bowman and Anderson, "Participation of Women"; Boserup, *Women's Role.*

13. Audrey Smock, *Women's Education in Developing Countries* (New York: Praeger, 1981).

14. Bowman and Anderson, "Participation of Women"; see also, G. McSweeney and Marion Freedman, "Lack of Time as an Obstacle to Women's Education: The Case of Upper Volta," *Comparative Education Review* 24, no. 2, pt. 2 (Summer 1980): S124–39.

15. Ernesto Schiefelbein and Joseph Farrell, "Women, Schooling and Work in Chile: Evidence from a Longitudinal Study," *Comparative Education Review* 24, no. 2, pt. 2 (Summer 1980): S160–79; Bee-Lan-Chan Wang, "Sex and Ethnic Differences in Educational Investment in Malaysia: The Effect of Reward Structures," *Comparative Education Review* 24, no. 2, pt. 2 (Summer 1980): S140–59.

16. Schiefelbein and Farrell, "Women, Schooling and Work."

17. Narendra Nath Kalia, "Images of Men and Women in Indian Textbooks," *Comparative Education Review* 24, no. 2, pt. 2 (Summer 1980), S209–23; Patricia Greenleaf, "Sexism in School Texts in Brazil," unpublished paper, Indiana University, 1979.

18. Vandra Masemann, "The Education of Girls in a West African Boarding School" (unpublished Ph.D. dissertation, University of Toronto, 1975).

19. Karen Coffyn Biraimah, "The Impact of Western Schools on Girls' Expectations: A Togolese Case," *Comparative Education Review* 24, no. 2, pt. 2 (Summer 1980): S196–208.

20. McSweeney and Freedman, "Lack of Time."

21. See, for example, Remi Clignet, "Social Change and Sexual Differentiation in the Camerouns and Ivory Coast," *Signs* 3, no. 1 (Autumn 1977): 244–60; Bowman and Anderson, "Participation of Women."

22. Wainerman, "Impact of Education."

23. Chinchilla, "Industrialization, Monopoly Capitalism"; Martha Maldonado Van Zuiden, "Participation of Women in Education and the Peruvian Labor Force," (Ph.D. dissertation, State University of New York at Buffalo, 1980); Boserup, *Women's Role;* Judith Van Allen, "Modernization Means More Dependency," *The Center Magazine* (May/June 1974), pp. 60–67; Nadia Yousseff, *Women and Work in Developing Societies* (Berkeley: University of California, Institute of International Studies, 1974). See also, Isabelle Deblé, *The School Education of Girls* (Paris: UNESCO, 1981).

24. See, for example, Elsa Chaney and Marianne Schmink, "Women and Modernization: Access to Tools," in *Sex and Class in Latin America,* ed. J. Nash and Helen I. Safa (New York: Praeger, 1975), pp. 160–82; Yousseff, *Women and Work.*

25. See, for example, Chinchilla, "Industrialization, Monopoly Capitalism."

26. James D. Cockcroft, Andre Gunder Frank, and Dale L. Johnson, *Dependency and Underdevelopment* (New York: Anchor Books, 1972); Introduction, P. G. Altbach and Gail P. Kelly, eds., *Education and Colonialism* (New York: Longmans, 1978); Robert P. Arnove, "Comparative Education and World Systems Analysis," *Comparative Education Review* 24, no. 1 (February 1980): 48–62; Philip G. Altbach, "Servitude of the Mind? Education, Dependency and Neocolonialism," *Teachers' College Record* 72 (December 1977): 188–204. Only Chinchilla, "Industrialization, Monopoly Capitalism," attempts to make this connection for women in the case of Guatemala.

On Feminism and Propaganda

Dale Spender

Propaganda: Association, organized scheme, for propagation
of a doctrine or practice; doctrines, information, etc. thus
propagated; efforts, schemes, principles of propagation

Concise Oxford English Dictionary

"For centuries women have been living under a male dictatorship.
It is a dictatorship that controls the channels of communication and
which produces propaganda designed to enhance the image of the dic-
tators and to justify their rule." I wrote this statement for a popular
article and can readily substantiate it on academic grounds because it
sums up my research over the last few years: having become convinced
that one of the crucial sites for feminist action is the control of information, I have been concerned with identifying the fundamental agencies
of control and examining their operation.

Some surprising understandings have emerged. One is that propaganda is what other people do: we wisely assume that our own reference group, whatever it may be, deals with the facts, with truth, and
that it is the "other," an alternative or opposing reference group, that
uses propaganda. Few of us are prepared to explore openly our own
engagement in the production of propaganda; on the contrary, from the
British Broadcasting Commission to reputable scholars, we vehemently
deny our own use of it. Not even historians have made an issue of the
extent to which they employ it, despite an awareness that no battle has
ever led to a report of the same facts from opposing forces. No matter
whom one consults, God was on their side.

Producing propaganda is *not* a scurrilous activity which only the
villains of the "other side" resort to; on the contrary, all human beings

307

construct a partial view of the world, generally a self-interested and self-confirming view, so it is usual to expect that fellow human beings will accept its plausibility if not share its meanings. Few people want to appear "crazy"; most want their reality confirmed. My objection, then, is not to the way human beings make sense of the world but to the way in which one particular interest group can appropriate disproportionate power and control so that its partial and self-interested view is made the legitimated or orthodox view without discussion.

"Self-made-propaganda" seems to be a taboo topic; even the limited discussion which does take place on propaganda is in the context of what others do, and this can be both perplexing and problematic. Why is it taboo? What are the consequences of raising it as an issue and of declaring "these are my research findings: they are propaganda for they are part of an organized scheme for the propagation of a doctrine or practice"?

It would be relatively easy for me to adopt the conventional position and to assert that my research and my reports are in the realm of facts and truth, while alternative views are biased and false and serve political and/or patriarchal ends. Were I to do so, there would be no discussion and the reality in which only "others" use propaganda would continue unquestioned. But for many reasons I find it unacceptable to maintain that reality.

First of all, it is conventional to insist on one's own impartiality while pointing to the partiality of others, and conventions are always open to scrutiny and change. Second, I have to acknowledge that to many I am "other"; those who see my research as propaganda are just as prone to devalue it (generally by referring to it as "polemic") as I am to criticize theirs as partial and self-interested.

The problem could be solved if it were possible to refer to some overarching authority, an entity devoid of interest or partiality who could arbitrate. Such an authority could not be human, however, for in the process of becoming human one must take on a language, a culture, a system of reference which contains within it particular assumptions, values, and partialities which preclude the option of neutrality. This requires us minimally to acknowledge that there is more than one reference system and that every reference system from political parties to personal friendships seems to have within it not only the means of legitimating itself but of discounting alternatives.

This is where feminists have the advantage. In my own case my "formative years" occurred before the feminist renaissance with the result that I was properly reared in a patriarchal frame of reference and for many years was able to accept without undue difficulty the facts and truths of a male-dominated society. I believed the propaganda. I could (and still can) work within that frame of reference, operate it, make sense of it, start with its assumptions, and follow its line of reasoning to reach its truth. Then came the women's liberation movement and my reference group changed. I developed new assumptions and followed different lines of reasoning and was led to conclude very different truths. I swapped camps some of the time and began to see the battle from the other side—as well! This has left me in the position of having dual reference systems which, while they do not command my allegiance equally, nevertheless serve as a checking point for each other.

Many feminists have access to this double view of the world, yet a survey of feminist literature suggests that this is not a well-developed topic. Where the issue is raised it is sometimes seen as a problem and is couched in terms of women being unable to free themselves from the patriarchal frame of reference. There are allusions to being fettered, to sliding back, to making the old mistakes, but I can find no statements about the positive aspects of this dual vision. Yet surely this is a positive feature of feminism? For me, feminism has been mind-shattering, enlarging my horizons in ways impossible to imagine within the patriarchal frame of reference in which I was reared. It has been an explosion of my vision and values.

For me, it was not possible simply to exchange one reference system for another. There is no clear-cut division in my life where I threw over patriarchal values, joined the opposing forces, and from that day on embraced feminist ones. Of course I became a feminist—that is a clear and definite memory—but I still lived and had to operate in a patriarchal reality. It was not a case of being converted from one ideology to another, of declaring that now I had found the true faith; it was much more a case of viewing the world with double vision.

Feminism provided me with a set of alternative explanations, a means of checking patriarchal truths and finding them wanting. Feminism provided me with a way of getting outside the patriarchal frame of reference and that is a liberated place to be. But equally, the patriarchal frame of reference, on occasion, allows me to get outside the feminist mind-set and, in the interest of justice, that is sometimes a place where I want to be.

Over the years I have not always found this position a popular one. Heresy—"opinion contrary to the accepted doctrine" (OED)—is no less prevalent than propaganda and is intimately connected to it. Declaring that feminism has no greater monopoly on truth than does patriarchy does not always win friends and influence people, and it frequently provides "others" with fertile ground for criticism. In good conscience, however, there is no other position that I can adopt.

My years of research have led me to conclude that men control the channels of communication in our society. Through those channels have flowed their formulations of the way the world works. In these formulations men have started with themselves as the reference point and explained the world in relation to themselves. They have been the norm and all who are not in their image have been "other." Their view reflects but one side of humanity and their truths are but half-truths.

It would be possible to adopt a mirror-image feminism. It is possible—and necessary at times—to begin with the premise that women are the norm, that we are the positive reference point for knowledge. Within such a framework men can appear distinctly incapacitated. It is even possible to suggest that they organized privileged social arrangements for themselves because they felt so inadequate and wanted compensation for their inability to meet the standards of the positive female norm. I do not wish to discredit this thesis. It is at least as true as male claims for male superiority. It is just as valid to assert that patriarchy is compensatory as it is to assert that it is natural. From my perspective, though, it is just as misguided to accept either assertion as the whole truth, as more than a partial view. As long as partriarchy begins with the premise that the male is the positive norm, and feminism begins with the premise that the female is the positive norm, then the war of propaganda simply continues to be waged. Both sexes are simply starting with their own personal dimensions, promoting a positive image at the expense of the other.

Women have a better case for doing so at the present time. Extenuating circumstances are justification for the argument that it is now women's turn. For centuries men have been propagating a positive view of themselves, simultaneously portraying women in a negative light, even to the extent of distorting or removing evidence of women's achievement from the repositories of readily available knowledge.[1] Redress is definitely in order.

Real power differences between the sexes mean that men's propaganda gets a much wider airing and is able to recruit or sustain many more "followers." Men's enhanced view of themselves is the substance of education, the content of media, the basis for scholarship, and after so much positive promulgation about the male sex, for so long, merely in the interest of balance it is time for a change.[2]

But it is not just that this propaganda which inflates men and deflates women is as tiresome now as it was in 1925 when Dora Russell noted that "anybody who has anything abusive to say about women, whether ancient or modern, can command a vast public in the popular press and a ready agreement from the average publisher" while the reverse does not apply;[3] it is also that within the framework that a male-dominated society has set up, the means of discrediting anything other than the male dominant view have also been encoded. While men are dominant and take up most of the positive space—physically, verbally, semantically—then the absence or invisibility of women appears plausible and justifiable. While, for example, history is presented as the history of the male line, as Virginia Woolf put it, then the historical absence of women, the ostensible failure of women to contribute to our contemporary cultural formation, makes the present subordination of women seem reasonable. Yet it is not that women have not made as much history as men, as Matilda Joslyn Gage and Mary Ritter Beard have so dramatically demonstrated;[4] it is that the propaganda of a patriarchal state leads us to see the so-called sense of current social arrangements.

This schemata of propaganda is one which feminists have been initiated into, and it is understandable that it should influence our own way of working in the world. We have been inducted into a world view in which it is reasonable to set up one sex as "other," to advocate a conspiracy theory whereby the "other" is responsible for the evils of the world, is made the scapegoat for all ills, and is held to be humanly flawed. Having grown tired of this simplistic and sadistic classification scheme, women in a male-dominated society seek a change, and understandably seek it, at least at first, in terms that we know.

Yet as a theoretical position, mere reversal will not stand up to close examination. Nor can I as a feminist sustain it as a fundamental frame of reference, although I am not adverse to making use of it occasionally to provide a "learning experience" for males who do not ordinarily understand how it feels to be on the receiving end. I cannot with a clear conscience, however, live my life on the principles that patriarchy has taught me (even if the positions are reversed) and accept women as the norm, men as flawed and "other," lacking in some human capacity and solely responsible for the world's ills. As a feminist I want something better than the propaganda model that I inherited, partly because it was within the model that I learned that it is the dominant as well as the oppressed who are brutalized by the construction of dominance and oppression. It is no *vision* to replace patriarchal propaganda with feminist propaganda but simply another reworking of what is already familiar . . . and faulty.

It is because I think it necessary to break out of these sterile molds of making sense of the world that I want to draw attention to the propagandistic nature, to the partial, personal, and political characteristics of the way human beings—*all* human beings—operate in the world. It is because feminism now in many respects is simply doing what patriarchy has done that I want to acknowledge the peculiarities of our processes. But no established or conventional means exist for debating this issue; there is no recognized forum for discussion. If all that we know is propaganda, the personal and partial perspective of the observer, with the particular view of those in power imposed as the prevailing and complete view, then I think it is imperative that we should be passionately concerned with an analysis of the way we make sense of the world, with an examination of our own value system and an exploration of the limits of our own propaganda. If all frames of reference including our own are closed systems containing within themselves the means for their own legitimation and for the outlawing of the systems of others, then our minimal commitment should be to understanding frames of reference. We should at least try to go beyond the closed system we have inherited, and which we have emulated, rather than simply settle for the exchange of one system for another. There is nothing that suggests to me that it is inevitable that we be confined to the processes of reasoning which we currently use.

It is because my entry into feminism led me to query the criteria of credibility in patriarchy that I can no longer be comfortable with some of the conventions of the academic world. How can we, within feminist scholarship, where we have based so much of our case on the recognition that the personal is political, how can we continue to use terms like standards, excellence, objectivity, and proof without stating WHOSE standards, excellence, objectivity, and proof they constitute? It is not enough to change the faces of those in power; what is required is a transformation of power itself, and a starting point would be to acknowledge the mechanics of power.

This is no abstract issue for me, but rather part of my daily life. The power to decree what is good and what is not, to decide what will be published and become part of the reservoir of knowledge, is a significant power. It is the power of the gatekeeper. The bulk of my research has been devoted to understanding the role of gatekeeping although I have concerned myself primarily with the way that male gatekeepers have excluded women's voices from many branches of learning. I have become a "specialist" on the methods that the male gatekeeper uses to project positive images of himself and the techniques that he employs to discredit and exclude "others" whose experience, values, and truths do not support his own views or interests.

Yet I, too, act in a comparable way as a gatekeeper, and I do it with women as well as men. I, too, have a partial view of the world, a view constrained by my color, my class, my cultural milieu, and my country of origin. It is because I find no consolation in repeating the error of *his* ways that I am concerned that feminists find a way of recognizing and re-ordering our partiality.

My daily life includes editing an academic journal and other publications. I am required to make decisions about what is excellent, acceptable, needs revising, or should be rejected. I cannot adopt the customary mode of claiming that my own standards are fair, impartial, and above reproach while those of gatekeepers in general (and male gatekeepers in particular) are to be deplored. I am as much a victim of patriarchy and its frame of reference as is anyone else who tries to make such decisions. It would be absurd for me to try and argue that my standards, my notions of excellence, are better than those which have gone before, because I would know that these are the very same arguments that male gatekeepers, appointments boards, selection committees, and review bodies—sometimes with sincerity—have used to keep women out of the sphere of influence. It is the very same logic that has decreed that a woman's experience is not of the same order as a man's, that a woman's authority is not as justified as a man's, that a woman's creativity is not as developed and a woman's reasoning is not as reliable[5]—and I know that the case can be substantiated within the frame of reference in which it is raised.

What does it mean if everything I select conforms to my own value system? I have a personal, partial view of the world which contains within it the means of validating and the means of discounting views which are not my own. This has significant implications for the material which I judge to be good. Add to that the fact that those who contribute legitimation to the enterprise such as editorial boards, referees, and editors generally share my view. I respect their judgment.

What would it mean if I selected material which did not reflect my own values, which I did not think excellent or scholarly, or even useful? What would it mean if I worked with colleagues whose judgment I did not respect?

I do not expect an instant resolution to this dilemma, but I do think it time for debate. Out of my own dissatisfaction with prevailing practices I have tried a few experiments and kept extensive research notes, but so far whenever I have sought a forum in which I can be accountable for my gatekeeping actions, there is more than reluctance to take up the topic. Sometimes I have found substantiation for my thesis that every reality contains within it the means of discrediting what it cannot accommodate and it seems that some of these issues cannot be readily accommodated.

I have tried making public, provocative statements, for example that I select material which reinforces my world view, which I like, which makes me feel good . . . and which comes to my attention when I get out of the right side of the bed. The response has always been that such a process of selection is not *fair;* the fact that I am raising the issue precisely because I know it is not fair seems to be overlooked. Usually there is an insinuation that I am not competent, that I have not yet learned to recognize high standards and excellence. There have even been offers of assistance from those who are convinced that they would be able to recognize excellence and who have asserted that their value system and knowledge are far superior to my own. Needless to say, these were not the particular responses I was seeking. I even tried writing articles, documenting the way in which material is chosen for publication; I tried editing articles on the topic; and I have helped my sister in her research on a book about gatekeeping.[6] But still the response to this powerful and provocative issue is frequently negative.

I have published articles with which I do not agree and have earned new praise from some who have congratulated me on seeing, at last, the light of day, while others have watched me closely for further signs of deterioration, and I have edited collections in which there are articles which challenge to the core my own value system but which I have refrained from "editing." I have requested those who do not share my view to be guest editors of the journal for which I am responsible, and I have been greeted on occasion by suspicion.

So what is to be done? It is simply not possible to publish everything; some selection has to be made and some criteria invoked. Surely there is a saner form of decision-making than that which currently persists; surely there is a way of making explicit the power dimensions of such a process in a manner which allows for the operation of power?

I cannot accept that it is beyond us to make clear the standards by which judgments and methods are made; I do accept that nothing less than this is necessary for our feminist practices to be in agreement with our theories of the personal and political.

In the matter of gatekeeping, the personal is fundamentally political; on the matter of research topics, research methods, findings, reports, publications, and appointments, the personal is crucially political. Those who engage in these activities are participating in the propaganda of our society and cannot claim refuge with the justification that they are in possession of superior knowledge and that propaganda is something which is made by "others."

Notes

1. Dale Spender, *There's Always Been a Women's Movement This Century* (London: Pandora Press, 1983).

2. Lynne Spender, *Intruders on the Rights of Men: Women's Unpublished Heritage* (London: Pandora Press, 1983).

3. Dale Spender, *There's Always Been A Women's Movement*, p. 113.

4. Dale Spender, *Women of Ideas and What Men Have Done to Them: From Aphra Behn to Adrienne Rich* (London: Routledge and Kegan Paul, 1982).

5. Dale Spender, "The Gatekeepers: A Feminist Critique of Academic Publishing," in *Doing Feminist Research*, ed. Helen Roberts (London: Routledge and Kegan Paul, 1981), pp. 186–202; Dale Spender and Lynne Spender, eds., *Gatekeeping: The Denial, Dismissal and Distortion of Women, Women's Studies International Forum* 6, no. 5 (1983).

6. Spender, "Gatekeepers"; Spender and Spender, eds., *Gatekeeping;* Lynne Spender, *Intruders on the Rights of Men.*

5

In the Alma Mater mural by Edwin H. Blashfield painted in 1908 for the City College of New York (City University of New York), a male graduate, in the center, has just lit his torch at the altar of learning and is about to start on the voyage of life. At his side Alma Mater points upward at the seated figure of Wisdom who holds the earth in her hands. The ten seated female figures represent the great universities of the world; below them male figures represent the arts and the sciences. In the foreground are the people, "men of all classes," including students in academic robes and in football and baseball uniforms. Description from S. Willis Rudy, *The College of the City of New York: A History 1847–1947* (New York: The City College Press, 1949), p. 260. Photo courtesy of the CCNY Office of Public Relations.

Section 5. On the Body

We have talked about feminist scholarship within and across boundaries. Another kind of movement takes place when a scientist's perceptions begin to be shaped by feminist issues. Most feminist scholarship, certainly most theory, has taken place in the humanities and social sciences. We include in this section several writers trained in the sciences, writing here on the female body. While the findings themselves should be of interest, these three essays are also valuable examples of feminist scholarship. They embody different fields and thus different approaches to data; further, they warrant comparison in terms of the degree to which their authors have politicized their study of the body.

Carol Sue Carter, a behavioral endocrinologist, is concerned with the complex links between physiological events and behavior; her essay seeks to provide a context which will demystify, in part, the controversial literature on hormones. In her review, she faults much of this literature on scientific grounds, noting that experimenter bias and poor controls have characterized the study of hormones until quite recently. (It has also been characterized by its low priority as a research project.) On the other hand, although she believes that "women cannot assume that the doctor . . . always knows best," and acknowledges the risks associated with synthetic hormone treatments, her analysis remains within the "givens" of her field.

Maureen A. Flannery is sharply critical of the training most medical students receive in conducting breast and pelvic examinations; she argues that the language even in relatively progressive programs fosters a notion of women as passive recipients of health care. The training program she designed is based on a woman-centered model of women as active health care consumers, competent to act as responsible clients and as instructors of medical students. Her program was carried out in the context of a relatively young, community-based medical school. As she notes, the members of the women's health collective at Harvard Medical School, who pioneered pelvic examination training, discontinued their program on the grounds that its feminist orientation was too radically at odds with the rest of the medical education establishment.

While Carter and Flannery study the body within established institutions, Susan C. Wooley and Orland W. Wooley argue that obesity is a political problem before it is a medical, psychiatric, or behavioral problem, and that its treatment must consequently begin with political analysis. Reviewing the literature on obesity across many fields, they are pessimistic about the ability of the scientific and medical communities even to interpret the facts accurately. Their paper draws intriguing parallels between women and obese people as political constituencies, viewing both groups as marginal to the dominant power structure; similarly, they view the women's movement as one successful model for a movement toward "fat liberation." Their citation of feminist writers is an important departure from traditional scholarly writing in their field.

In shorthand terms, these three approaches demonstrate the ambiguities of the encompassing term "feminist scholarship": Carter practices scholarship on issues of feminist concern; Flannery describes a program which introduces certain aspects of feminist process into an otherwise nonfeminist educational environment; and the Wooleys, dealing with a subject area long ignored by feminists, conclude that a feminist analysis provides a more fruitful foundation for the study of obesity than the assumptions of traditional research.

Hormones: A Biobehavioral Perspective

C. Sue Carter

"Hormones" are often invoked as explanations or excuses for many of the actions of women, yet we are only beginning to understand the influence of hormones, and in particular the reproductive hormones, on human physiology and behavior. My own interest arises both from a desire to understand my own gender and from my academic research, which since 1969 has focused on the area known as behavioral endocrinology. In this field, literally thousands of carefully controlled animal studies have provided the basis for theories about how hormones affect physiology and behavior. For human subjects, though, we are largely dependent on observations of naturally occurring phenomena, for example, the rather loose correlations between the menstrual cycle, menopause, and physiological or behavioral changes. Clinical data provide another source of information—for example, reports of pathological events including endocrine abnormalities, and the effects of medically prescribed hormonal treatments. Experiences reported by women themselves provide yet another source of data, one that was neglected for too long, and which the women's movement has strengthened.

My perspective, then, is that of a biobehavioral scientist, also a woman, attempting to draw from and synthesize these varied findings and in turn illuminate our understanding of the link between hormones and behavior in some clinically relevant way. Behavioral endocrinology is a relatively recent field. Ideally, it requires the rare cooperation between behavioral scientists trained in physiology or endocrinology (itself rare), clinicians with access to appropriate patient populations, and informed human subjects. My own work, characteristically for the field, uses laboratory animals as subjects. Reliable human behavior studies are still rare, in part because until recently women's behavior was not generally considered interesting by the male scientists and physicians who have dominated the field in the United States. Behavioral work in other countries has focused on women but has tended to lack methodological sophistication. This is a problem, for in contrast to animal species, human behavior is almost never solely determined or regulated by hormonal events: complex interactions among experiential and physiological factors are the rule, and concepts like "cause and effect" are rarely strictly applicable.

This review summarizes contemporary investigations of reproductive hormones in the human female and tries to highlight some of the basic issues. I should make clear, however, that those of us in this field are only beginning to grasp the complexity of these issues: one can critique existing clinical practices, but scientific evidence permits us few certainties at present. The disputes within the medical community on such questions as the advisability of hormone treatments mirror disputes between scientists and within the community at large. Some sources suggest that hormone treatments should be avoided at virtually all costs, while other equally concerned investigators argue that at least some women receive benefits from such treatments that outweigh the risks. As a scientist, at the present moment, I must conclude that many critical medical questions remain unanswered. As a woman, I feel equally strongly that women must participate in the determination of their own health care and that no doctor, no matter how well intentioned, always "knows best." With this inconclusive preface, I will proceed to discuss the biochemical bases of hormone action, changes during the female life cycle, issues related to synthetic hormone treatments, and apparent links between hormones and behavior. I hope discussion of the conceptual and interpretive confusion that often accompanies empirical evidence will demystify some of the issues related to hormone actions and their risks and benefits, and that it will encourage women to participate actively in the medical research and decisions that affect their bodies.

Background

The biological "purpose" of the female mammalian reproductive system is to produce eggs, or ova, provide for fertilization by sperm, and subsequently protect the developing offspring until it is independently viable. Hormones, biochemical agents carried by the bloodstream, regulate and integrate a number of different reproductive functions.[1] In general, hormonal effects are rather broad-ranging and slow. Hormonal actions and hormone levels along a chain of biochemical events are regulated by feedback mechanisms to meet physiological or environmental challenges.

In medical practice, hormonal levels are commonly altered by providing exogenous—synthetic—hormones. Most of the synthetic hormonal agents which women take in oral form, like the birth-control pill, are designed to break down slowly in the digestive tract. To provide a more physiological or naturally occurring form of a hormone, it is usually necessary to inject the hormone as an oil-suspension or place it in a capsule under the skin. The latter methods have the disadvantage of being difficult to regulate if for any reason the hormonal treatment needs to be turned off.

Hormone levels can also be altered by removing the endocrine secretory organ. In females, for example, levels of a number of hormones decrease following removal or the ovaries. As I will explain, ovarian hormone levels also vary naturally as a function of puberty, the menstrual cycle, pregnancy, or menopause.

Female Endocrine Organs and Reproductive Hormones

The *ovary* produces eggs during ovulation as well as the hormones known as sex steroids. A general subcategory of steroid hormones includes the estrogens, of which estradiol, estrone, and estriol are three naturally occurring examples. In addition, progestagens are secreted by the ovaries. Females may also produce androgens, of which the hormones testosterone and androstenedione are examples. Although androgens are usually found in higher concentrations in males than in females, they may nonetheless have important functions in the female as well. In general, all of the natural reproductive hormones exist in both males and females, and it is the level and timing of their occurrence that differentiates the sexes.

Ovarian function is regulated by *pituitary* hormones including the *gonadotropins,* of which luteinizing hormone (LH) and follicle-stimulating hormone (FHS) are examples, and *prolactin.* The pituitary in turn is under the influence of brain hormones, produced in a region of the central nervous system (CNS) that is described as the hypothalamus. These CNS hormones are sometimes collectively called *hypothalamic releasing hormones* because their primary function is to determine the "release" of pituitary hormones into the blood stream. The most critical brain hormone involved in timing ovulation and other female reproductive processes is known as either gonadotropin releasing hormone (GnRH) or luteinizing hormone releasing hormone (LHRH). Since both LH and FSH release can be influenced by GnRH, that name will be used in this paper. Another CNS chemical known as *dopamine* regulates the pituitary release of prolactin, although in this case the role of dopamine seems to be primarily inhibitory: higher dopamine levels prevent prolactin release. Because the CNS has ready access to the outside world through the sense organs and to physiological changes inside the body, brain hormones can play a vital role in integrating environmental events with reproductive physiology.[2]

Hormonal Events during the Life Cycle

Sexual differentiation. Genetic or chromosomal sex is determined at the time of fertilization. The sex chromosomes carry information which determines the maintenance of appropriate gonadal tissue. During fetal development, tissue is present that can become either ovaries or testes; typically, only one type of gonad is retained and the other is lost. If testes are retained and functional, they may begin to secrete androgens as early as the second month of gestation. These androgens are essential to permit the development of a masculine genital anatomy, including the growth of a penis and development of a scrotum. In the absence of androgens, and probably even in cases in which the ovary is not active, a feminine body type, including a clitoris, vagina, and labia, develops.[3] We don't know the precise role of fetal hormones in human sexual development. In laboratory animals, we know that the presence of androgens during early development can shift reproductive anatomy, physiology, and behavior in a masculine direction. While we originally assumed that estrogens were irrelevant to sexual development, recent animal research suggests that at least some of the important CNS functions of androgens may be manifest after these so-called male hormones are converted into an estrogenic form. (This conversion is possible within many cells of the body including the brain.) Growing evidence suggests that estrogens may also play a role in normal development for both sexes.[4]

Menstruation. Adult, nonpregnant female primates experience roughly monthly cycles in hormone and egg production, which are most easily detected by the periodic loss of uterine wall tissue. The parts of the ovary housing each egg, called follicles, are primarily responsible for estrogen production. In the first part of the menstrual cycle, estrogen production rises. Ovulation then occurs and a follicle which has just ovulated takes on a different form and function, and is called the corpus luteum. The phase of the menstrual cycle immediately following ovulation is known as the luteal phase and is characterized by the secretion of high levels of progestagens, produced by the corpus luteum, and continued estrogen production. In the premenstrual phase of the cycle, both estrogen and progestagen levels decline and when these hormone levels become insufficient to sustain the tissue lining the wall of the uterus, menstrual bleeding occurs.

The precise timing of ovulation is believed to be tied to a surge of hormones and can be influenced by the synthetic estrogens and progestins of oral contraceptives and by such external and internal factors as stress and malnutrition.

Puberty. Functional hormonal effects during infancy and childhood are generally viewed as relatively weak, but during adolescence readily observable anatomical and behavioral changes accompany dramatic increases in steroid hormone production. The earliest change heralding female puberty is breast development, the onset of which precedes the first menstrual cycle (menarche) by about two years. We believe that the adrenal glands secrete hormones responsible for breast development and the subsequent onset of pubic and axillary hair growth.[5] Between ten and fourteen years of age, most females experience the menarche and at this time are exposed to the cyclic fluctuations of estrogens and progestins characteristic of menstrual cycles, although the earliest menstrual cycles may be irregular and in some cases without ovulation. Estrogens eventually serve to terminate growth, and increases in height in girls are rare after about seventeen years of age.

We don't know what determines the age of puberty, although body weight or more precisely the ratio of fat to lean tissue seems to be monitored in some way so that most women approach a normal adult body size by the time they become capable of reproducing. Some relationship between body size and the onset of menstruation is also suggested by observations that women who experience dramatic weight loss due to malnutrition, dieting, or disease, or who alter their body fat composition through intensive exercise, such as long-distance running, may become acyclic or anovulatory.

Pregnancy. Another remarkable period of hormonal change for women occurs during pregnancy. Some of the earliest hormonal events of pregnancy depend on secretions from membranes surrounding the fertilized egg. These tissues are involved in the implantation of the egg in the uterine wall and produce nonsteroidal hormones responsible for certain early signs of pregnancy. Ovarian activity is altered in early pregnancy and progesterone secretion does not show the expected premenstrual decline. (The name progesterone signifies the essential progestational activity of that hormone.) As pregnancy progresses, a placenta develops and this complex organ takes on many of the secretory functions of the ovary and pituitary gland. Most female reproductive hormones levels are elevated throughout pregnancy; menstrual cycles are suppressed. At birth, progesterone levels drop.

Prolactin is probably also essential during pregnancy, but its best known reproductive function is seen during lactation. Suckling, and probably other cues from an infant, as well, promotes prolactin production and release. Prolactin in turn facilitates milk let-down and nursing. Many women, although not all, do not ovulate while nursing, and this reproductive suppression may reflect the high levels of prolactin released during lactation. (There also is good evidence that excessive prolactin can be responsible for infertility in some non-lactating women, and drug treatments are now available that effectively reverse this form of infertility.)[6]

Menopause. At approximately 50 years of age, with a range of 35 to 60, women begin to experience the symptoms of the menopause or climacteric. The medical definition of the menopause is the "final menstrual period that occurs during the climacteric" and the climacteric refers to "that phase in the aging process of women marking the transition from the reproductive stage of life to the nonreproductive stage."[7]

At the time of menopause there is a complete depletion of eggs and follicles. The human female has about 600,000 primitive egg cells at birth.[8] Although only a few hundred of these eggs actually go through the process of ovulation, a large number of follicles also are necessary for estrogen secretion in each menstrual cycle. Thus, there is a gradual loss of follicles, and the eggs that they contain, from puberty through menopause.

Variability exists in the pattern of climacteric-related hormone changes. Some women apparently undergo an abrupt cessation of cycles, while others may have irregular cycles for months or years prior to their final menstrual period. In either case, there is an eventual cessation of progresterone production and a decline in estrogen levels, accompanied by elevations in the pituitary luteinizing (LH) and follicle stimulating hormones (FSH).[9] Some women maintain relatively high postmenopausal levels of estrogens, and these women are presumably less likely to experience many of the symptoms of menopause. Postmenopausal estrogens are believed to result from the biochemical conversion into an estrogen of androstenedione; one important site of this conversion is fatty tissue, and women who are overweight may experience fewer menopausal symptoms than thinner women.[10]

Estimates of the percentage of women who experience "distressful symptoms" during the climacteric vary from 25 to 90 percent.[11] The most reported symptoms of the menopause are "hot flashes or flushes."[12] These changes in body temperature may last for a few seconds to a few minutes and are characterized by sensations of warmth followed by redness of the upper body and subsequent perspiration and chilling.[13] Although flushes can be prevented by estrogen therapies, the immediate cause of hot flushes is not known; they tend to occur in synchrony with pulses of the pituitary hormone LH.[14] Fluctuations in LH itself cannot, however, be directly responsible for hot flushes because women without pituitary glands, and therefore without LH, still experience hot flushes. In our laboratory studies, we have found that direct injections of GnRH into a region of the rat brain involved in the control of temperature result in rapid increases in body and brain temperature. Menopausal women probably experience analogous surges in GnRH. An understanding of this mechanism should help us develop ways to control flushing. While many women are not bothered by flushing, for others it can be extremely disruptive and may indirectly contribute to a variety of other serious problems including insomnia, irritability, and perhaps even depression.[15]

Vaginal atrophy also follows menopause and is sometimes treated with estrogens. In this case the hormone may be applied locally as a cream to the vaginal tissue; however, estrogens applied in this manner do enter the general circulation and we cannot assume that their effects are limited to the vagina.

Many of the physical and emotional changes that some women

experience following menopause may be related to declines in ovarian hormone secretion.[16] For example, thinning of the skin and urinary bladder, bone decalcification and softening called osteoporosis, cardiovascular diseases, and a variety of other physical and behavioral changes have been attributed to the hormonal events of the climacteric. It is difficult, however, to document a *causal* relationship between hormone levels and these disorders, and the research literature in this area remains controversial.

Hormone Treatments and Replacement Therapies

Hormones have been administered during every phase of the female life cycle. The "therapeutic" and contraceptive applications of steroid hormones, heavily promoted in the 1950s and 1960s, were seen as medical advancements. At last it seemed that effective contraceptives were available, and, thanks to continued postmenopausal treatments with estrogens, it was suggested that women could remain "forever feminine."[17] Hazards and disadvantages of these treatments were either not recognized or were deliberately minimized.

This rosy view of hormone treatments has been challenged in the last decade.[18] It is now clear that even the most apparently beneficial treatments are not without elements of risk. In part because of the questions and concerns of feminists, the original atmosphere of optimism has been replaced by apprehension and caution on the part of both patients and their physicians.

Oral Contraceptives

The most popular methods of hormonal contraception involve daily "pills" containing a combination of synthetic estrogens and progestins. Pills are taken for twenty or twenty-one days followed by a seven-day withdrawal from the drug. Among these products are contraceptives with brand names such as Brevicon, Demulen, Enovid, Loestrin, Modicon, Norinyl, Norlestrin, Ortho-Novum, Ovcon, Ovral, Ovulen, and Zorane.[19] So-called mini-pills are also marketed which contain only a progestin. Three examples of the mini-pill are Micronor, Nor-Q.D., and Ovrette. These compounds may come in various dosages.

Pregnancy is most effectively prevented by the combination pills, and if the dosage schedule is followed, they are about 99 percent effective. Mini-pills are somewhat less effective. These hormonal contraceptives interfere with ovulation primarily through effects on the brain (hypothalamus) and pituitary gland.

Risks of oral contraceptives. The side effects and adverse effects reported for the oral contraceptives are numerous and vary in severity.[20] Among the more dangerous effects attributed to the pill are blood clots which may impair lung, heart, or brain function, increases in blood pressure, liver or gallbladder disease, or severe depression. Women taking oral contraceptives may also experience weight gains, nausea, breast enlargement (including tenderness and secretion), changes in the eyes requiring adjustment of contact lenses, impaired color vision, and increased susceptibility to vaginal infections and venereal disease. It is not uncommon for women to fail to experience menstrual bleeding either during the seven-day withdrawal period or when they stop oral contraceptives for longer periods of time. Some women may experience long-term disruptions in fertility after discontinuing oral contraceptives,[21] and even those women able to conceive immediately may be wise to avoid pregnancy for six months or more because of a suspected increase in fetal abnormalities reportedly seen in that period.[22] Various serious risks from oral contraceptives tend to increase with age and may be higher in smokers than nonsmokers.

It has been argued that the risks of pregnancy are greater than those associated with the use of oral contraceptives. This is statistically correct. However, the careful use of other methods of contraception, such as a diaphragm or condom plus spermicide, provides excellent pregnancy protection with almost no risks.[23] It is my opinion that virtually no woman capable of reading this article should be deliberately exposing herself to the potential hazards of the pill.

Postmenopausal Hormone Treatments

Contemporary estrogen replacement therapies tend to incorporate either conjugated estrogens or synthetic nonconjugated estrogens. The conjugated compounds may be derived from biological sources or can be manufactured synthetically. The best known example of a conjugated estrogen is estrone sulfate, isolated from pregnant mares' urine, and sold under the trade name of "Premarin." About 80 percent of women taking estrogens for menopausal symptoms received Premarin.[24] Ethinyl estradiol is a common example of a nonconjugated synthetic estrogen. (Ethinyl estradiol is also found in oral contraceptives.) Finally, nonsteriodal estrogenic compounds such as diethyl stilbesterol have also been used widely in estrogen replacement therapies.

Estrogen therapies for menopausal symptoms are most often administered as pills, given for a period of three weeks followed by a one-week nontreatment period. Continuous or less frequent treatments may also be prescribed. Estrogens are readily absorbed through the skin and mucose membranes such as the vagina; therefore, creams or suppositories, often used intravaginally, will also increase estrogen levels, both at the site of application and in other parts of the body through distribution in the blood stream.

Risks of estrogen treatments. Probably the most infamous estrogenic compound is the synthetic drug diethyl stilbestrol (DES). Beginning as early as the 1940s, DES was widely administered during early pregnancy in attempts to maintain gestation in women believed to be at risk for spontaneous miscarriage. These treatments were not effective but physicians nonetheless continued to use them. Finally, in the early 1970s[25] it became obvious that a very rare form of vaginal cancer was appearing in young women (the so-called DES daughters) exposed to this drug when their mothers were treated with DES in pregnancy. Unlike most other possible side effects, this particular disorder could be clearly related to DES treatment since it was virtually unknown in untreated women. Although most DES-exposed women have not developed cancer, they and DES-exposed males as well may be at risk for other serious problems including reproductive sterility.

DES has also been used for the treatment of postmenopausal symptoms, to suppress postpartum milk production in women who chose not to nurse, as a morning-after contraceptive given to prevent pregnancy in otherwise unprotected women, and for the treatment of some cases of breast and, in men, prostate cancer. Many of these applications of DES have been reduced or eliminated because of the apparent danger of this drug; however, DES continues to be of commercial importance because it is used as a method for fattening domestic cattle. DES treatment is supposed to stop well before animals go to market, but this apparently does not always happen and there is evidence that DES-contaminated beef may continue to reach the dinner table. The possible effects of long-term exposure to dietary DES are not known.

There are other problems. Estrogen treatments, particularly if given continuously and in the absence of progestins, may cause an excessive growth of the uterine wall, resulting in symptoms known medically as endometrial hyperplasia. The degree of severity of this condition is difficult to determine and even well-trained pathologists may differ in their interpretations of tissue samples taken from an over-stimulated uterus.

The *diagnosis* of endometrial cancer increases for women receiving estrogen treatments.[26] There have been claims that estrogens "cause" cancer. Alternatively, it has been suggested that pre-existing cancerous cells, along with normal uterine cells, may proliferate under estrogen treatment. It is possible that the estrogen-stimulated uterus is more likely to be diagnosed or possibly misdiagnosed as containing cancerous cells, because hyperstimulation of the uterus is typically used as a possible indication of cancer. Finally, women who receive estrogens may differ in many ways from women who do not seek medical treatment or who elect to refuse estrogen therapies. All of these factors complicate the interpretation of the relationship among hormonal factors and the diagnosis and/or occurrence of cancer.

Similar considerations exist in attempts to analyze correlations between estrogen therapies and various other health disorders. Nonetheless, there is some indication that the use of synthetic estrogens such as those in oral contraceptives is associated with an increased incidence of blood clots, which may in turn can cause malfunctions in the heart, lungs, brain, and other organs. The risks of these symptoms are less severe in women receiving biologically derived conjugated estrogens.

There is some evidence that breast cancer, hypertension, gallstones, and diabetes may be slightly more prevalent in long-term estrogen users; however, these relationships are even more controversial than those described for uterine cancer and blood clotting.[27]

Benefits of estrogen therapies. Given all of the possible risks associated with estrogen therapies, the obvious question arises regarding why any doctor would prescribe, or any woman would accept, such treatments. Relief from hot flushes and/or thinning of the vaginal wall are the most accepted medical reasons for recommending estrogen therapy. In most cases, estrogens eliminate hot flushes within two to three days. Less effective, but sometimes used for hot flushes, is a compound known as Bellergal. This drug combines a sedative (phenobarbital) with drugs intended to act on that part of the nervous system which regulates perspiration. Minor tranquilizers, such as Librium, Valium, or Miltowns, or antidepressants are also sometimes used in an attempt to reduce hot flushes or related menopausal symptoms; however, all of these drugs have their own risks and none is as effective as estrogens.[28]

Softening or decalcification of bones may lead to decreases in height, including the "dowager's hump," and increase in bone fragility, known as osteoporosis. Estimates suggest that as many as 25 percent of women over 60 may experience spinal deformities as a result of this condition.[29] Older women may also experience bone fractures and associated serious complications, including death. It has been argued by some physicians that the positive effects of estrogens in preventing or reversing these symptoms outweigh the possible cancer hazards associated with estrogen treatments.[30]

Osteoporosis becomes a particularly serious problem in premenopausally ovariectomized women. Researchers agree that this disorder is most likely to appear in women who are deprived of ovarian secretions relatively early.[31] The symptoms associated with osteoporosis can also be treated by increasing dietary calcium, vitamin D, and through exercise. The benefits of the latter treatments are accepted by most experts, while the practicality of estrogen therapies for the prevention of osteoporosis predictably remains a source of medical controversy. The potential benefits of progestins in the treatment of osteoporosis also needs further study.[32]

Estrogens plus progestins. To produce progestins in a form that can be taken orally, it is necessary to modify the naturally occurring progesterone molecule. Examples of these synthetic progestins include medroxyprogesterone, norethindrone, and megestrol. In the currently marketed oral contraceptives, estrogens and progestins are combined in a single pill. Oral contraceptive tablets are generally not considered suitable for the treatment of postmenopausal symptoms.[33]

A commonly recommended approach to the treatment of menopausal symptoms involves the use of a progestin on the final seven to ten days of a twenty-one to twenty-five day course of estrogen treatment. Both drugs are then discontinued to permit a menstrual-type of bleeding. There is growing evidence that this treatment procedure is safer than the use of estrogens alone,[34] and many physicians now feel that it is unethical to prescribe estrogen therapies in the absence of progestagen treatments.

Some women, and some physicians, may be resistant to the idea of reinstituting postmenopausal bleeding; however, Gambrell has reported that the incidence of uterine cancer in postmenopausal women receiving an estrogen-progestin-withdrawal treatment is lower than in *untreated* or estrogen-alone treated women.[35] This finding is of considerable importance and demands further investigation. At present there is not enough information on the long-term effects of progestins to determine whether there may be hazards or unacknowledged side effects for these hormones as well.

Androgens. Although there has been medical interest in the possible use of androgens since at least the 1940s, there is resistance to treating women with these compounds. Some physicians continue to advocate their use, claiming behavioral and physical benefits,[36] while others feel that masculinizing side effects such as facial hair growth and acne are so common as to make androgen treatments impractical.[37]

Behavioral Changes Associated with Hormonal Events

The Menstrual Cycle

It has long been claimed—or assumed—that women exhibit behavioral changes that correlate with the menstrual cycle.[38] The earliest systematic study of mood changes in the menstrual cycle was published in 1942.[39] Women patients, from a population in psychoanalysis, reported more positive emotional feelings in the first (follicular or estrogenic) half of the cycle. These women tended to be seen as more passive and less outgoing following ovulation (the luteal phase). During the premenstrual period, these investigators found the women they studied to be tense, anxious, and more hostile. Subsequent research on other groups of women has supported the assumption that similar patterns of feelings are *reported* even in unselected or normal populations; however, such self-report studies are often conducted by asking women to retrospectively describe their feelings for a period of up to one month. In addition, expectations may play a role in such responses. For example, in one recent study[40] women who were actually on their sixth to seventh premenstrual day were told that the investigator could accurately detect their next menstrual period. The women were randomly divided into two groups. Those deceived into believing that they would menstruate in a day or two reported more negative feelings than those led to assume that they would begin to menstruate in seven to ten days. Paige[41] also found indications of cultural conditioning in the report or experience of menstrual symptoms: women from more traditional or religious backgrounds reported more severe symptoms. Cultural factors can temper women's perceptions of their own feelings and research openly targeted at finding menstrual cyclicity in emotional behavior is typically successful, almost certainly in part due to preconceived notions on the part of the subjects regarding what should be reported. Feminist scholars are helping to highlight the political context of medical research.

Even in light of these problems, there remain clear indications that many women do in fact experience cyclic changes in mood. For example, when women were simply asked to "tell us about some experience you had," themes of anxiety, death, and mutilation were more likely to be expressed by women when they are studied in the premenstrual phase than when they were questioned at approximately the time of ovulation. Women receiving oral contraceptives, and thus having more stable hormone patterns, did not show this pattern of variation.[42]

Emotional cyclicity may be correlated with menstrual cyclicity; however, attempts to show corresponding changes in other aspects of female behavior have been generally unsuccessful. Objective measures of *performance* including tests of reaction time, intelligence, academic performance, and so forth do not typically vary with the menstrual cycle.[43]

Reproductive hormones and behavior. Physiological explanations of premenstrual depressions in psychological mood have tended to emphasize the steroid hormones. Specifically, it has been proposed that declines in estrogen and/or progesterone predispose some individuals to become susceptible to emotional disturbances such as irritability or even clinical depression.

One of the most vocal and controversial advocates of hormone treatment for premenstrual symptoms is the British physician Katharina Dalton.[44] She has developed an endocrinological explanation for psychological changes in the premenstrum based on the notion that women experiencing such symptoms have insufficient amounts of progesterone. Dalton reports success in treating various adverse symptoms associated with the menstrual cycle and other reproductive events including menopause and stresses the importance of using natural progesterone as an injection or implant rather than a synthetic progestin such as those found in oral contraceptives. Other investigators conducting similar studies have not reported the same findings.[45]

Some researchers have proposed a number of estrogen-deficiency theories to explain premenstrual mood changes.[46] For example, one group of investigators suggests that some women may be particularly resistant to estrogen's effects and recommends large doses of exogenous estrogens as a therapy for depression, especially in cases in which other treatments have been unsuccessful.[47] The doses of estrogens reported necessary to relieve psychological depression are much higher than those typically used for postmenopausal treatments. Although E. L. Klaiber and his associates reported no physical ill-effects from these treatments, their study was relatively short-term and involved small numbers of women.

Some women experience marked cyclic weight gains, due at least in part to water retention during the premenstrual period. Many women take diuretics in an attempt to reduce menstrual symptoms. However, diuretic-induced water loss generally is not successful in controlling premenstrual mood changes, and there is at present no convincing evidence that changes in tissue water-balance or the factors that control this system are directly responsible for premenstrual irritability or depression.[48]

A final (and most recent) hormonal candidate for involvement in premenstrual mood changes is the pituitary hormone, prolactin, and/or the hypothalamic system which regulates prolactin release. Drugs that inhibit prolactin release reportedly reduce premenstrual symptoms.[49] The reliability of this treatment should be investigated.

Cautions

Although one influential source of information for American physicians[50] concluded that estrogens were not effective in the treatment of "anxiety, depression, or other emotional symptoms," a recent survey of gynecologists indicates that many doctors have confidence in the behavioral effectiveness of estrogen therapy; about 95 percent of the seventy-five physicians surveyed reported that they believe that "the benefits of estrogen therapy to the menopausal woman far outweigh the risks."[51]

The presence of several contradictory reports and indications that biochemically inactive placebos can produce equivalent or nearly equivalent improvements suggests that the behavioral effects of standard estrogen therapies are probably partially situation-dependent and in part depend on the expectations of the patient.

Such contradictory evidence is of course not proof that estrogen may not have important behavioral effects under some physiological circumstances. For example, the suggestion by Klaiber et al.[52] that clinically depressed women may be resistant to the behavioral effects of estrogens is of interest and may provide insight into the behavior of at least some postmenopausal women. These studies do reveal the contradictions and difficulties involved in sorting through the medical research on hormone treatment. The research indicates that menstruation and menopause, historically neglected topics for physicians and other scholars, are now receiving serious attention, yet scientists and physicians have not, in general, felt a need to give explanations to the women who are the target of the investigations and advice. Passive involvement is not likely to be a healthy situation itself and may contribute to depression. Those studied *could* be treated as students, encouraged to attend sessions sponsored by health facilities where women could receive information including treatment options, and learn how to compile their own health charts, keep records, and perform some tests themselves. This would be a healthy addition and correction to the present situation in which women are treated more as passive problems than as participating individuals.

Notes

1. A hormone is classically defined as a chemical agent produced by a specialized tissue (endocrine gland) and released into the blood stream which carries the chemical to target organs or tissues in other parts of the body.

2. S. S. C. Yen, "Neuroendocrine Regulation of the Menstrual Cycle," in *Neuroendocrinology,* ed. D. T. Krieger and J. C. Hughes (Sunderland, Mass.: Sinauer Associates, 1980), pp. 259–72. For a more general collection, see *The Menstrual Cycle:* Vol. 1, *A Synthesis of Interdisciplinary Research,* ed., Alice J. Dan, Effie Graham, and Carol P. Beecher (New York: Springer, 1980), and Vol. 2, *Research and Implications for Women's Health,* ed. Pauline Komnenich, Maryellen McSweeney, Janice A. Noack, and Sister Nathalie Elder (New York: Springer, 1981).

3. John Money and Anke A. Ehrhardt, *Man and Woman, Boy and Girl* (Baltimore: Johns Hopkins Press, 1972).

4. C. D. Toran-Allerand, "Sex Steroids and the Development of the Newborn Mouse Hypothalamus and Preoptic Area In Vitro: Implications for Sexual Differentiation," *Brain Research* 106 (1976): 407–12.

5. M. M. Grumbach, "The Neuroendocrinology of Puberty," in *Neuroen-*

docrinology, ed. D. T. Krieger and J. C. Hughes (Sunderland, Mass.: Sinauer Associates, 1980), pp. 249–58.

6. R. W. Kirby, T. A. Kotchen, and E. D. Rees, "Hyperprolactinemia—A Review of Recent Clinical Advances," *Archives of Internal Medicine* 139 (1979): 1415–19.

7. Wulf H. Utian, *Menopause in Modern Perspective* (New York: Appleton-Century-Crofts, 1980), p. xi.

8. Theodore B. Krouse, "Menopause Pathology," in *The Menopause,* ed. Bernard A. Eskin (New York: Masson, 1980), pp. 1–46.

9. Yen, "Neuroendocrine Regulation."

10. Utian, *Menopause in Modern Perspective.*

11. Paula Weideger, *Menstruation and Menopause* (New York: Alfred Knopf, 1975); J. Studd, Schakravarti, and O. Oran, "The Climacteric," *Clinics in Obstetrics and Gynecology* 4 (1977): 3–29.

12. Bernice L. Neugarten and R. J. Kraines, "Menopausal Symptoms in Women of Various Ages," *Psychosomatic Medicine* 27 (1965): 266–73.

13. A. K. Rakoff, "Female Climacteric: Premenopause, Menopause, and Postmenopause," in *Gynecologic Endocrinology,* ed. J. J. Gold (New York: Harper and Row, 1975), pp. 356–76.

14. R. F. Casper, S. C. C. Yen, and M. M. Wilkes, "Menopausal Flushes: A Neuroendocrine Link with Pulsatile Luteinizing Hormone Secretion," *Science* 205 (1979): 823–25.

15. C. Lauritzen, "Oestrogens and Endometrial Cancer: A Point of View," *Clinics in Obstetrics and Gynecology* 4 (1977): 145–67. C. Lauritzen and P. A. van Keep, "Proven Beneficial Effects of Estrogen Substitution in the Postmenopause—A Review," *Frontiers of Hormone Research* 5 (1978): 1–25. See Rosetta Reitz, "What Doctors Won't Tell You about Menopause," in *Seizing Our Bodies,* ed. Claudia Dreifus (New York: Vintage, 1978).

16. Lauritzen and van Keep, "Proven Beneficial Effects"; Utian, *Menopause in Modern Perspective;* Eskin, ed., *The Menopause.*

17. Robert Wilson, *Forever Feminine* (New York: M. Evans, 1966).

18. Reviewed by Barbara Seaman and Gideon Seaman, *Woman and the Crisis in Sex Hormones* (New York: Rawson, 1977).

19. J. M. Long, *The Essential Guide to Prescription Drugs* (New York: Harper and Row, 1980), pp. 472–77.

20. Long, *Essential Guide;* Seaman and Seaman, *Women and the Crisis in Sex Hormones.*

21. Ibid.

22. Long, *Essential Guide.*

23. Seaman and Seaman, *Women and the Crisis in Sex Hormones.*

24. J. L. Marx, "Estrogen Drugs: Do They Increase the Risk of Cancer?" *Science* 191 (1976): 383–82.

25. A. L. Herbst, J. Ulfelder, and D. C. Poskanzer, "Adenocarcinoma of the Vagina: Association of Maternal Stilbestrol Therapy with Tumor Appearance in Young Women," *New England Journal of Medicine* 284 (1971): 878–81.

26. Utian, *Menopause in Modern Perspective.*

27. Ibid.

28. Ibid.

29. G. S. Gordon, "Postmenopausal Osteoporosis: Cause, Prevention, and Treatment," *Clinics in Obstetrics and Gynecology* 4 (1977): 169–78.

30. C. J. Dewhurst, "The Role of Estrogen in Preventative Medicine," in *The Menopause,* ed. R. J. Beard (Baltimore: University Park Press, 1976), pp. 219–45.

31. Utian, *Menopause in Modern Perspective.*

32. R. Lindsay, D. M. Aitken, E. B. MacDonald, J. B. Anderson, and A. C. Clarke, "Long-term Prevention of Postmenopausal Osteoporosis by Oestrogen," *Lancet: Journal of British and Foreign Medicine* 1 (1976): 1038–41.

33. Utian, *Menopause in Modern Perspective.*

34. Robert B. Greenblatt, Camran Nezhat, and Anthony Karpas, "The Menopausal Syndrome Hormone Replacement Therapy," in *The Menopause,* ed. Eskin, pp. 151–72. R. D. Gambrell, "The Prevention of Endometrial Cancer in Postmenopausal Women with Progestogens," *Maturitas* 1 (1978): 107–12.

35. Gambrell, "The Prevention of Endometrial Cancer."

36. Greenblatt et al., "The Menopausal Syndrome."

37. Utian, *Menopause in Modern Perspective.*

38. Weideger, *Menstruation and Menopause,* reviews these claims.

39. T. Benedek and B. Rubenstein, *The Sexual Cycle in Women* (Washington, D.C.: National Research Council, 1942).

40. Diane Ruble, "Premenstrual Symptoms: A Reinterpretation," *Science* 197 (1977): 291–92.

41. K. E. Paige, "Women Learn to Sing the Menstrual Blues," *Psychology Today* 7 (1973): 4–46.

42. J. M. Bardwick, "Psychological Correlates of the Menstrual Cycle and Oral Contraceptive Medication," in *Hormones, Behavior, and Psychopathology,* ed. E. J. Sachar (New York: Raven Press, 1976), pp. 95–103.

43. Mary Brown Parlee, "The Premenstrual Syndrome," *Psychological Bulletin* 80 (1973): 454–65. Barbara Sommer, "The Effect of Menstruation of Cognitive and Perceptual-Motor Behavior: A Review," *Psychosomatic Medicine* 35 (1973): 515–34.

44. Katharina Dalton, *The Premenstrual Syndrome and Progesterone Therapy* (Chicago: Year Book Medical Publications, 1977). See also the Federation of Feminist Women's Health Centers, *How to Stay Out of the Gynecologist's Office* (Los Angeles, 1981), pp. 37–38.

45. S. L. Smith, "Mood and the Menstrual Cycle," in *Topics in Psychoendocrinology,* ed. E. J. Sachar (New York: Grune and Stratton, 1975), pp. 19–58.

46. Reviewed by M. Steiner and B. J. Carroll, "The Psychobiology of Premenstrual Dysphoria: Review of Theories and Treatments," *Psychoneuroendocrinology* 2 (1977): 321–35.

47. E. L. Klaiber, M. Broverman, W. Vogel, and Y. Kobayashi, "The Use of Steroid Hormones in Depression," in *Psychotropic Actions of Hormones,* ed. T. M. Itil, G. Laudahn, and W. Herrmann (New York: Spectrum Publications, 1976).

48. Steiner and Carroll, "The Psychobiology of Premenstrual Dysphoria."

49. L. J. Benedek-Jaszmann and M. D. Hearn-Sturtevant, "Premenstrual Tension and Functional Infertility," *Lancet: Journal of British and Foreign Medicine* 1 (1976): 1095–98.

50. Anonymous, "Estrogens and the Menopausal Patient," *The Medical Letter* 15 (1973): 6–8.

51. J. A. Rust, I. I. Langley, E. C. Hill, and E. J. Lamb, "Estrogens: Do the Risks Outweigh the Benefits?," *American Journal of Obstetrics and Gynecology* 128 (1977): 431.

52. Klaiber et al., "The Use of Steroid Hormones in Depression."

Breast and Pelvic Examination:
A View from Both Ends of the Table

Maureen A. Flannery

During the past few years, new methods of instructing medical students in breast and pelvic examination have become popular in many medical schools.[1] The evolution of these pelvic teaching programs provides useful background for a consideration of the political implications of the involvement of lay feminists in medical education. My focus will be on the gynecological teaching programs described in the medical literature in contrast to those designed and run by community women.

The majority of "innovative" programs for teaching gynecologic examination differ from traditional methods by incorporating consenting women into the medical educational process, not as patients or subjects, but as participants and instructors. Apart from the content of the instruction, providing a "view from both ends of the table,"[2] this manner of teaching breast and pelvic examination introduces medical students to a model of doctor-patient relationships based on mutual participation and education.[3]

It is important to understand the radical nature of this approach: employing lay women to instruct medical students in the performance of breast and pelvic examinations potentially turns both teacher-student and doctor-patient relationships topsy-turvy.

A review of gynecologic teaching programs described in the medical literature, however, reveals little of a radical character. Somehow the potential of the approach—to demonstrate to future physicians the active and competent role of the woman consumer—is lost to medical educators, and, unfortunately, to medical students. An examination of the reports of these programs shows how this came about.

One striking feature of program descriptions is the variety of names given to the women who serve as instructor/models for medical students. In the majority of articles, the term used is negative: "nonphysicians," "untrained," or "trained nonmedical personnel." The language acknowledges the fact that the instructors are outside of the traditional medical education system, yet defines them solely by what they are *not* which invalidates their competency as lay women. Even when authors name the instructors as the consumers which they are, there is little acknowledgement of their qualification for that role. They are "simulated patients," "programmed patients," or "professional patients"—the latter conjuring up images of the worried-looking female filling up a waiting room with multiple images of herself in a widely-used drug advertisement. In one of the earliest programs, the woman involved in the teaching program was referred to as a "live mannequin," a term conveying perhaps the ultimate in passivity and incompetence.[4] The absence of a standard term for people who instruct medical students but who do not fit neatly into the rigidly hierarchical system of medical education may be due, at least in part, to the relative newness of the concept. However, the tone of the various terms reflects an uneasiness with the idea of incorporating anyone other than the properly "credentialed" into the education of physicians, an ambivalence which cannot help but be communicated to the medical students.

Since all these programs rely upon people not on the medical school faculty, it is important to examine how the schools went about finding participants. The "live mannequin" was sought out by "discreet inquiries among our hospital personnel" and was apparently a willing and indebted clinic patient at the hospital.[5] Another program required students to "bring their own" willing subjects for examination.[6] In a few instances, women's health groups sought out or were contacted by the medical schools.

Several authors evidence concern over the background of the women participants that is of questionable relevance to their roles as instructor/models. One author makes the point that although the women involved were "not prostitutes," they were all "single and sexually active."[7] Another study details the educational background of the "professional simulated patients," all of whom were either Ph.D. candidates in the behavioral sciences or registered nurses.[8] In their introduction to the students, these instructors list their credentials, apparently to enhance their credibility. Although their educational background certainly does not disqualify them from serving, it does not seem particularly relevant to sharing their experience as women having pelvic examinations. By emphasizing the "qualifications" of the instructors, this approach neglects one of the important messages of this instructional method: that *all* women regardless of social or educational background can become active participants in their own health care.

Once participants were gathered, the women generally did not play an active role in developing the objectives, structure, or content of the courses. The programs differ in the way in which women were prepared for their roles as practical instructors. After acknowledging that the members of the women's health group which provided instructors for his program were "concerned with the physician-patient relationship being based on mutual respect and free exchange of information," the doctor describes the training for these professional patients as an "indoctrination session," which hardly sounds like a reciprocal process.[9] Frazer and Miller, in contrast, emphasize that "practical instructors must be made aware of significant subjective aspects of being the recipients of optimal examinations."[10] Yet this was done by reviewing with the instructors the notes of a *male physician* who recorded his subjective impressions while undergoing an organ system physical examination. Although Frazer states that genital examinations were a particularly valuable part of his program, he does not describe the way in which practical instructors were prepared for teaching pelvic examination; one hopes that it was not by studying the observations of a male physician!

In all these cases, by not involving the women participants in decision-making about the program, the medical schools reject what they are supposedly trying to convey to their students with this approach to physical examination: that patients and consumers have many valuable things which they can effectively teach health care providers.

Many of the teaching programs, particularly ones in which women's health groups provide instruction, emphasize a "well-woman/activated-patient" approach to gynecological examination. This concern with health and patient education is unfamiliar in traditional medical education. Partly because of its strangeness, often the educational emphasis of the examination is subverted into a "useful technique" for encouraging relaxation. When this occurs, students do not learn that the major purpose of the encounter is to make the woman more competent and aware of her body; they see it simply as a way to make her easier for physicians to examine. The "well-woman" emphasis on normalcy is also an unfamiliar one for medical schools. Hale and Schiner describe the excitement engendered by the occasional presence of an "abnormal pelvis" among the "professional patients" in his group.[11] It is instructive both that he refers to the "pelvis" (ignoring the woman who inhabits it) and also that as an example of an "abnormal" pelvis, he cites early pregnancy.

Several articles more directly express the ambivalence which many medical schools feel toward these new and different programs. Some authors describe difficulty in obtaining acceptance for their program among the medical school faculty and staff.[12] In most schools, the practice teaching sessions are considered "extras"; the course is required but the sessions with women instructors are generally optional.[13] Even in schools with successful programs, commitment to integrate them fully into the curriculum is often lacking.

In light of these reservations and ambivalences, one wonders exactly why medical schools became so interested in this method of teaching gynecologic examinations. One reason, expressed in a number of the papers, is economic. Godkins cites reduction in physician faculty time as one of the major assets of the program.[14] In this case, volunteer women were sought out because the prostitutes who were once used for instruction were not satisfactory: they were too costly (at $25 an hour) as well as inarticulate and often physically abnormal. Holzman's program was cost-effective because the women were paid only $15 an hour, obviously much less than would be paid to physician faculty.[15] In addition to financial considerations, there is occasional acknowledgment of the exploitation inherent in traditional methods of teaching pelvic examinations using "volunteer" patients who did not have the opportunity to give informed consent and were often "unwilling victims of the system."[16] In general, however, sparing unwilling poor women from repetitive and inept exams by inexperienced students is considered a by-product of the new examination procedure rather than a major incentive for the change.

In contrast, concern for women "victims" of the medical education system was a major motivating force for women involved in several programs developed by lay feminists. The Rockford, Illinois, Pelvic Teaching Group came together to provide an alternative to the existing program in which medical students learned to perform examinations in the local health department on poor and young women who were often undergoing their first pelvic examination. The Rockford program differs from the programs discussed in the literature in a number of other ways. The lay "practical instructors" from the beginning demanded and were given independent faculty status. Recruitment of new members into the teaching group was by the group itself from the larger Rockford women's community, with a willingness to participate in program planning and implementation the only requirement for joining. The content and structure of the teaching sessions were developed by members of the group, drawing heavily upon their own experiences with gynecologic examinations. After the first year's orientation, conducted by women physicians and nurse-midwives, the Pelvic Teaching Group oriented new members itself with a series of self-help, consciousness-raising, and skill-sharing sessions.

At the beginning of its second year of teaching medical students, the Pelvic Teaching Group learned that the Women's Community Health Center in Boston, one of the earliest women's groups to participate in a pelvic teaching program,[17] had discontinued its program and "strongly discouraged other groups of women from participating in similar programs."[18] Members of this group charged that they were being "undervalued and underpaid"; they felt they were not recognized for their lay competency by an institution which was more interested in a "readily available supply of women's bodies" than in a real commitment to their teaching program.[19] They decided to direct their efforts towards self-help groups for lay women and urged other feminists to do likewise.

This action brought the Rockford women together to discuss the future of their program. Although in general given full responsibility and free rein in planning and implementation, they, too, had experienced some difficulties in dealing with the medical school. They had heard jocular remarks from the local physicians about the sort of "loose women" who would agree to participate in the group. One faculty physician (male) insisted that vertical insertion of the speculum was "more comfortable" than the suggested horizontal approach and was unwilling to accept the fact that a group of ten women had tried both ways and thought otherwise; indeed, students reported that he strongly criticized them for performing examinations in the way that the group had taught them. They also found that although they had instructed students to perform an examination in which a mirror demonstration was an integral part, the community health centers in which the students performed the majority of their pelvic examinations had no mirrors and support staffs that often discouraged them from using the educational approach. Following extensive discussions among themselves and with the administration of the school, the group decided to continue teaching while placing continued pressure on the medical school for a full commitment to the program.

At the same time, involving increasing numbers of women in the teaching program became important as members examined the ways in which their involvement increased their self-care abilities. From the experience of sharing knowledge and performing examinations on a number of women during the sessions, they gained a sense of the range of normalcy; this increased their competency in deciding when to seek medical attention. By learning the technique of breast and pelvic examination, they learned "what questions to ask" and therefore were able to be more effective and assertive in obtaining information from health professionals. And finally, by intimate involvement with medical education, they demystified the health care system and gained a new ability to assess quality of care.

For the Rockford women, living in a community in which a woman-controlled health center with an active self-help program was not a possibility for the near future, the continuation and expansion of the Pelvic Teaching Program provided a way to make some impact on women's health care in the community. The experience of the Boston group provided them with an increased political consciousness about the implications of their involvement with the medical education system.

Considered in the context of the gynecologic teaching programs described in the medical literature, the experiences of the Rockford and Boston teaching groups raise a number of important questions.

First, are these programs effecting any basic changes in medical education or health care? Although radical social change was hardly a goal of the internally-controlled programs discussed earlier in this chapter, the women in Rockford and Boston saw themselves as part of a movement. For the Women's Community Health Center group, this meant working toward "basic changes in the medical system as part of changing the overall structure of society: for instance, a breakdown of hierarchical relations among provider and consumer in which the provider has a monopoly over skills and information, women providing health care for women, and an end to 'for profit' medical services."[20]

Certainly the design of the programs, in which lay women teach future physicians an important and necessary skill, addresses the issue of hierarchy both in medical education and in health care; however, it is impossible to ignore the fact that the students with whom the lay women share their skills will go on to use them in a system in which male doctors treat women patients in for-profit settings. Indeed, as Bell points out, the very techniques developed to make pelvic examinations more comfortable and empowering for women can easily be subverted into techniques for efficiently "managing" patients, thus reinforcing the male-dominated, hierarchical, and money-conscious American health care system.[21]

The Rockford and Boston experiences raise another, related, concern: can lay activists retain control over their programs within medical schools, or is co-optation inevitable? In the first two protocols that the Boston women implemented at Harvard, control remained firmly in the hands of the medical educators; when they proposed a "third protocol" which confronted basic power relationships in its more explicitly feminist content and structure, medical schools found the program unacceptable. The Rockford program began as a cross between the internally developed programs and feminist-controlled programs like Harvard's, since the medical school considered a feminist resident physician the program's "director" despite her relatively minor role in the ongoing program. After three years of establishing itself within the medical school, however, the program functioned autonomously without the involvement of medical school faculty or physicians. The issues of control in this case became more subtle but no less critical: even though the Pelvic Teaching Group maintained control over the content and process of the teaching program, the women discovered that the medical school had enormous power to undermine its teaching in the remainder of the curriculum. Given the prestige and power relationships in medical education, one belittling remark by a male professor/ physician could easily negate the teaching efforts of a group of lay women. It is, ironically, more difficult for women involved in an "accepted" and ostensibly woman-controlled program to confront the attitudes within the medical school which diminish the impact of their instruction.

Given the minimal impact of these programs on medical education and the difficulties in maintaining a feminist program within an inherently sexist system, it is clear that the pelvic teaching programs represent an "interim reform" at best.[22] As feminists, we must then ask ourselves how much of our limited energy we should devote to the training of future physicians, inevitably detracting from the struggle for more radical changes in the health care system. By following the Women's Community Health Center group in abandoning attempts to work within the medical educational system and concentrating instead on providing health care for women by women, teaching only in self-help settings, we would be working more directly toward basic change. This approach, however, is presently not reaching the majority of women who have been conditioned into dependence on health professionals, particularly low-income, minority, and working-class women. Pelvic teaching programs *are* reaching these women directly by sparing them inept exams by inexperienced students, and indirectly by changing the attitudes of at least a few of the physicians upon whom they depend for their care.[23]

Hard questions, these. Their discussion is at the heart of feminist theory and strategy. Women who, like the Rockford group, decide to continue to work with medical schools need to concentrate on strategy. If existing programs have not effected any major changes in the system, are improvements or modifications of approach or program likely to do so? If so, what? If co-optation is likely but not inevitable, what are the most effective strategies for maintaining control over programs? How can we work to integrate feminist values into the entire medical curriculum?

On the other hand, groups like the Women's Community Health Center that choose to use their energy teaching women in self-help settings, abandoning attempts to work within the medical educational system, must dedicate themselves to the task of making self-help and woman-controlled health care a reality for the majority of women presently unreached by this approach.

Just as input from "the other end of the table" is essential if medical schools are to produce physicians capable of sensitive health-caring, challenge from women dedicated to health care by women for women is necessary for feminists working within medical education.

Notes

1. J. Magee, "Bridging the Communication Gap," *Female Patient* 1 (1976): 31–33.

2. J. Magee, "The Pelvic Examination: A View From the Other End of the Table," *Annals of Internal Medicine* (1975), pp. 563–64.

3. J. A. Billings and J. D. Stoeckle, "Pelvic Examination Instruction and the Doctor-Patient Relationship," *Journal of Medical Education* 52 (1977): 834–39.

4. These terms are used in the following papers, respectively: Billings and Stoeckle, "Pelvic Examination Instruction"; B. S. Schneidman, "An Approach to Obtaining Patients to Participate in Pelvic Examination Instruction," *Journal of Medical Education* 52 (1977): 70–71; N. B. Frazer and R. H. Miller, "Training Practical Instructors (Programmed Patients) to Teach Basic Physical Examination," *Journal of Medical Education* 52 (1977): 149–51; T. R. Godkins, D. Duffy, J. Greenwood, and W. D. Stanhope, "Utilization of Simulated Patients to Teach the 'Routine' Pelvic Examination," *Journal of Medical Education* 49 (1974): 1174–78; G. H. Johnson, et al., "Teaching Pelvic Examination to Second-Year Medical Students Using Programmed Patients," *American Journal of Obstetrics and Gynecology* 121 (1975): 714–17; R. W. Hale and W. Schiner, "Professional Patients: An Improved Method of Teaching Breast and Pelvic Examinations," *Journal of Reproductive Medicine* 19 (1977): 163–66; J. F. Perlmutter and E. A. Friedman, "Use of a Live Mannequin for Teaching Physical Diagnosis in Gynecology," *Journal of Reproductive Medicine* 12 (1974): 163–64. One wonders how much influence the attitude implied by calling the instructor a "mannequin" had on the structure of the program. It is interesting that this program required the women to undergo *sixteen* examinations per session. The authors note that "this number (16) of examinations per session has not proved to be especially difficult for the mannequin." The women in the Rockford program found three examinations per session the limit of tolerance.

5. Perlmutter and Friedman, "Use of a Live Mannequin."

6. Schneidman, "An Approach to Obtaining Patients."

7. Johnson, et al., "Teaching Pelvic Examination."

8. Gerald B. Holzman, Dianne Singleton, Thomas F. Holmes, and Jack L. Maatsch, "Initial Pelvic Examination Instruction: The Effectiveness of Three Contemporary Approaches," *American Journal of Obstetrics and Gynecology* 129 (1977): 124–29.

9. Hale and Schiner, "Professional Patients."

10. Frazer and Miller, "Training Practical Instructors."

11. Hale and Schiner, "Professional Patients."

12. Perlmutter and Friedman, "Use of a Live Mannequin."

13. Billings and Stoeckle, "Pelvic Examination Instruction"; Schneidman, "An Approach to Obtaining Patients."

14. Godkins, et al., "Utilization of Simulated Patients."

15. Holzman, et al., "Initial Pelvic Examination Instruction."

16. Perlmutter and Friedman, "Use of a Live Mannequin."

17. J. Norsigian, "Training the Docs," *Healthright* 1, no. 4 (1975): 6; Women's Community Health Center, Inc., "Experiences of a Pelvic Teaching Program," *Women and Health* 1 (1976): 19–20.

18. Women's Community Health Center, Inc., "Report on the Pelvic Teaching Program," *WCHC Annual Report* (1977), pp. 9–10.

19. For an excellent description and analysis of the development of the Women's Community Health Center program, see Susan Bell's article, "Political Gynecology: Gynecologic Imperialism and the Politics of Self-Help" in *Science for the People* 11 (1979): 8–14.

20. Susan Bell, "Political Gynecology," p. 9.

21. Ibid.

22. Ibid.

23. In my experience, the students most open to the feminist approach to gynecologic examination are precisely those most likely to practice in not-for-profit clinics which serve minority and working-class women.

Women and Weight Obsession: Redefining the Problem

Susan C. Wooley and Orland Wayne Wooley

Obesity is a major problem in this country and it is primarily a problem for women. After skin color, excess body fat is probably the most stigmatized physical feature, but, unlike color, weight is thought to be under voluntary control. Efforts to lose weight consume an enormous amount of energy, interest, time, and money of women in all social classes and of all ages. For many women, concern with weight leads to a virtual collapse of self-esteem and sense of effectiveness. This is a result not only of a failure to achieve slenderness but the interpretation placed on failing. Unfortunately, most women struggle to comprehend their experience armed with a mass of misinformation.

Experts in the field of obesity have failed to convey the simple truth in terms that make it understandable: there is *no known cause* of obesity and, with the exception of treatments more dangerous than obesity itself, *no known cure*. Overweight people do little if anything out of the ordinary to cause themselves to be fat, and once fat, only the most extraordinary behavior will enable them to become and remain thin.[1]

It is precisely because thinness is unattainable by more than a fortunate few in our society that it is so valued. Not surprisingly, attempts to sustain semi-starvation in the pursuit of increasingly stringent ideals of slenderness usually fail, creating new problems.[2] A few feminists and other writers, whose work will be noted here, have begun to articulate some of the important political implications of these facts.

We thank Sue R. Dyrenforth for her contribution to this work. An earlier version of this essay appeared in *Women's Studies International Quarterly* 2 (1979), 69–92.

Their thesis grows out of the documented failure of reducing diets to achieve their purpose, the stigmatization of overweight, and the selective pressure on women to achieve unrealistic cultural ideals.

A Closer Look at the Facts

Etiology and Treatment of Obesity

A 1959 review of obesity treatment outcomes concluded that approximately 4 percent of patients entering outpatient diet clinics were successful in losing as much as 40 pounds and keeping it off for 2 years.[3] A 1978 update covering 112 new reports suggests little improvement, with an average weight loss of 11 pounds and generally inadequate follow-up.[4] Efforts to improve the success rate have included the controversial and sometimes fatal intestinal bypass, gastric stapling, jaw-wiring, brain lesioning, and fasts, which in addition to having high failure rates are now known to carry significant risks.[5] Early reports of behavioral treatments suggested improved success rates, but these results have not been borne out.[6] The discrepancy may be partially attributable to the populations treated in early studies. When applied to samples containing older patients with more severe obesity, the great majority of patients still fail to achieve significant losses.[7] Behavior modification treatments are based on the myth of teaching "normal," in the sense of average, eating behavior. The "normalization" of intake patterns usually achieved in these programs may do much to alleviate distress over eating but does not necessarily lead to weight loss.

This is because obese people do not, on the average, eat any more than anyone else. John S. Garrow reviewed the findings of thirteen studies relating body weight to food intake measured by a variety of methods varying in precision and the extent to which they allow observation of habitual behavior unaffected by measurement techniques.[8] Of these, twelve show the intake of the obese to be the same or less than that of the lean subjects. Interestingly, the one measure which demonstrated greater intake by overweight subjects was considered by the authors to have been validated in its accuracy by this result, while an alternative method, showing no differences, was judged imprecise, indicating how widespread was the assumption of overeating by obese people at the time the study was conducted.[9] A number of additional studies have supported this conclusion, and despite continuing skepticism no effective rebuttal has been offered.[10]

It also has not been possible to isolate any distinctive features in the eating styles of the obese. In the rat, limiting access to food so that the daily ration is consumed in an hour or two causes greater fat storage than when the same amount of food is consumed in a pattern of small frequent meals.[11] Although there is some suggestion that infrequent meals are associated with obesity in humans,[12] the generality and meaning of the finding remain unclear. Recent surveys of eating patterns and styles have produced no evidence that, on the average, the obese differ from the lean in the timing, duration, speed of consumption, or composition of meals or snacks.[13] Important unknown variables may yet be discovered but, so long as they remain unknown, they are of no use to the overweight person, and the continuing failure to uncover such variables despite careful scrutiny decreases confidence that any relevent differences in eating behavior in fact exist. The point is not that all overweight people consume small amounts of food but that intake, as well as other characteristics of eating behavior, shows the same rather large distribution in overweight as in lean samples. For every overweight person who eats a given amount, there is a person who remains lean on the same diet. Obviously, it involves an inferential leap to suppose that the appetite of the former is less compelling or regulatory of behavior than that of the latter.

Conventional wisdom concludes on the basis of these findings that the obese must, therefore, be less physically active. One paper demonstrating equivalent food intake in obese and lean subjects concluded in telling language: "in obesity sloth may be more important than gluttony."[14] There are, in fact, some studies showing the obese to be less physically active as well as approximately an equal number finding no differences.[15] Data on activity levels require cautious interpretation, however. Because of the greater weight to be moved, the heavy person expends more energy carrying out the same movements, and appropriate corrections must be made to determine the calories expended. Measurement methods sufficiently unobtrusive not to affect normal activity levels tend to be inaccurate, while precise observation techniques usually influence natural behavior. Certain types of observation, for example the filming of obese adolescent girls engaged in sports, are likely to be unrepresentative because of the self-consciousness of the subjects.

If one person grows fat on a diet on which others stay lean, there is, of course, a difference in overall expenditure of calories. What is at issue is how much of that is attributable to behavioral differences over which the individual has actual or potential control. Garrow has argued that among people with primarily sedentary occupations, the contribution of intermittent periods of vigorous physical activity to the total daily energy expenditure is surprisingly small and unlikely to account for large deviations in weight. Our own clinical experience with activity diaries tends to support this conclusion, for periods of strenuous activity are frequently found to be followed by periods of compensatory rest, so that there is no net gain in caloric expenditure as a result of planned exercise, and sometimes there is a net loss. Reviewing all available data, Garrow concludes: "It is probably a fair summary to say that obese people (especially women) tend to do less muscular work than thin people, but the contribution of this effect to overall energy balance is quantitatively small. The range of individual variation in energy intake and expenditure is many times greater than the difference produced by different levels of muscular activity. Inactivity may contribute to obesity, therefore; but it cannot be a main cause."[16]

It should be noted that even data which support the hypothesis of inactivity among the obese bear primarily upon the contribution of activity level to perpetuation of obesity. No data exist to suggest that inactivity precedes obesity and is, therefore, etiologic in the development of obesity. Prospective studies of the kind required are unfortunately very difficult to do.

How is this possible? If the obese do not eat more, or exercise less, what, then, does account for obesity? There is no single, generally accepted answer, but the following findings are relevant:

1. The range of normal variation in metabolic rate is, in fact, rather large. Rose and Williams assembled matched pairs of people—identical in weight, age, sex, and activity level as measured by pedometers—one of whom habitually consumed twice as much as his or her control to maintain the same body size.[17] This metabolic difference can be divided into two components: basal metabolic rate, or calories expended in a fasting state at rest, and the additional calories expended in metabolic activity and performance of physical work. Differences in resting metabolic rate alone may account for variations in energy expenditure of as much as 400 or 500 calories daily, while total expenditure of sedentary subjects has been observed to vary by as much as 770 calories a day.[18] Note that these differences exclude the effects of

habitual activity since they are obtained under very restricted laboratory conditions, and, though larger than most people realize, are within
the range of normal variations and are not manifested as abnormalities
of thyroid metabolism or any other clinical indices of metabolic function.

2. There is a variable tendency to adapt to increases in caloric
intake by increasing caloric expenditure, not through exercise but
through production of excess heat (thermic effect). Studies of overfeeding of lean volunteers show that weight gain is rarely as high as predicted, and that in some lean individuals the ability to dispose of excess
calories is so pronounced that it is nearly impossible to make them fat,
even when they are fed several thousand excess calories a day for long
periods of time. Ethan Sims and his colleagues, who have conducted
extensive studies of experimental obesity, comment in one paper that
graduate students do not make suitable subjects, since for naturally lean
individuals becoming obese was a full-time job.[19] Two comparative
studies of the thermic effect shown by obese and lean human subjects
found that the obese were less wasteful of calories, while a third found
no difference.[20]

Studies of genetically obese animal strains have also shown that
excess fat may be acquired in the absence of overeating, the imbalance
occurring through low energy expenditure. Interestingly, the difference
appears not as a low basal metabolic rate in the obese animals, but as an
inability to show normal increases in metabolic rate in response to
overfeeding or challenges such as cold exposure or infusion of norad-
renalin. Indeed, the deficit is so pronounced that despite their insulating
layers of fat, the obese animals die at temperatures at which lean animals can survive. Total energy expenditure is "normalized" (and weight
gain halted) only when body mass is increased sufficiently to achieve a
supernormal basal metabolic rate. In discussing these findings, James
and Trayhurn speculate that in primitive societies with long histories of
food shortages, there has been a natural selection for individuals with
efficient metabolisms, as indicated by high rates of obesity when food
becomes abundant.[21] In Western cultures, availability of food has permitted the survival of both efficient and inefficient genotypes, resulting
in considerable variability in body weight on similar intakes.

3. There is also a tendency to reduce caloric expenditure when
food is limited. This is reflected in decreases in resting metabolic rate of
15–40 per cent, decreases in spontaneous activity, and decreases in the

energy cost of a *given task,* i.e., walking on a treadmill.[22] Thus, the complaint of the obese that they stop losing weight on fixed diets is frequently true, although others do not believe them and, what is worse, they frequently do not believe themselves. More than one woman has wondered if she had become a sleepwalker and ate in fugue states.

Again, the ability to conserve calories in the face of shortages—a once highly adaptive response—shows great individual variability. Comparative data suggest that obese patients with low initial metabolic rates show the greatest decrease during food restriction.[23] In the classic studies of semi-starvation of normal volunteers conducted during World War II by Ancel Keys and his associates, subjects were reduced to 80 percent of initial bodyweight on an average of 1800 calories/day, a level well above that at which many fat people can reduce.[24] The two fascinating volumes which came out of this study chronicle the obsessive preoccupation with food and loss of interest in other activities which developed during semi-starvation and the voracious eating which occurred during the refeeding period with some men eating as many as 11,000 calories/day but complaining that they still felt hungry. This remains the best description of the reducing diet and its aftermath. The fact that a person has more fat makes it no easier to lose, and perhaps harder.[25]

4. It seems possible that dieting—the major treatment of obesity—may also be a major *cause* of obesity. Although some people gain very large amounts of weight in short periods of time (usually during overwhelming stress, illness, or pregnancy), for most, obesity is a gradually progressive condition in which weight losses and gains are alternated.[26] We would like to suggest the possibility that, in at least some individuals, overreaction to mild obesity—to a body weight which is within the normal distribution typical of all physical traits—may predispose those individuals to further weight gain.

As noted earlier, dieting reduces metabolic rate and caloric expenditure during activity, and some of these functions may not recover immediately. P. C. Boyle and his colleagues reported that rats subjected to food restriction later gained 29.6 grams on an amount of food which produced a gain of only 1.6 grams in control animals.[27] In other words, there was nearly an eighteen-fold increase in metabolic efficiency following weight loss. The participants in the study conducted by Ancel Keys and his associates, when allowed to return to their original weights after semi-starvation, were found to have in-

creased adipose stores by an average of 40 percent.[28] It seems possible
that nature might have equipped us with adaptive mechanisms to conserve calories when food shortages occur, but not before, without the
means for the complete reversal of this adaptation.

In addition to altering metabolic responses to food, starvation alters psychological responses. The experience of dieting and being hungry gives food a heightened importance, creating an increasingly
obsessive preoccupation with eating. Starvation is alternated with periods of loss of control, so that there is a progressive dissociation between biologic hunger and eating. It is perhaps for this reason that
chronic dieters lose the ability to sense calories (i.e., relative states of
repletion/depletion) that is found in normal subjects.[29]

All these facts help to explain the near inevitability of weight gain
after diets. An implication of this line of reasoning is that greater social
acceptance of natural variability in body weight might go a long way
toward preventing more severe obesity, as well as preventing the suffering and loss of productivity stemming from weight obsession.

Health Risks in Obesity

An objection which is usually raised to this argument is that obesity is inherently unhealthy and that it is for this reason, rather than
escape of social disapproval, that people should strive for thinness. It is
highly doubtful that any health risks are associated with mild obesity;
moreover, there is increasing question about the validity of long-
accepted attribution of certain diseases and risk factors to obesity. In a
1975 review published in the *New England Journal of Medicine,*
George V. Mann became one of the first to challenge the relationship
between obesity and (1) high blood pressure: "There is little to support
the widespread dogma of health education programs that regard obesity as a cause of high blood pressure and treatment of obesity as a useful
way of managing high blood pressure"; (2) heart disease: "The contribution of obesity to coronary heart disease is either small or nonexistent. It cannot be expected that treating obesity is either a logical or a
promising approach to the management of coronary heart disease";
and (3) cholesterol levels: "A recent report from the Cooperative study
of Renovascular Hypertension found . . . no correlation of [cholesterol]
with either obesity or high blood pressure."[30]

In truth, if health criteria were used to define obesity, the problem
would be nearly defined out of existence. Moderately obese people are,

if anything, more healthy than thin people. According to data obtained in the Framingham study,[31] the middle 60 percent of women live longer than the thinnest and fattest 20 percent, but within the 80-pound range there is no relationship at all between degree of fatness and mortality. Mortality rates among women in the heaviest and lightest 20 percent are equivalently elevated, but both live longer than men in the most favorable category. Still, almost all victims of the diet/obesity industry are women.

Ancel Keys concludes on the basis of a review of the thirteen prospective studies which now replace the old data collected by insurance companies that "the idea has been greatly oversold that the risk of dying prematurely or of having a heart attack is directly related to . . . relative body weight."[32] Reuben Andres of the National Institute on Aging goes even further: "Not only does advice on the subject of obesity need to be reappraised but . . . research into possible *benefits* of moderate obesity would be worthwhile."[33] In a study specifically of women, H. Noppa and associates found an inverse relationship between mortality and obesity. In other words, *the thinner a woman is, the greater her chances of an early death.*[34]

Even if correlations are found between weight and certain diseases, this is not, of course, evidence of a causal connection. Both may be due to an unknown third factor. Some factor associated with overweight, such as genetic differences in metabolism or the effect of frequent weight loss and gain, may be the actual cause of disease. It has been argued that weight vacillations may indeed have injurious effects on health. Finally, the status of the overweight as a stigmatized minority may generate stresses which are in part responsible for development of disease. Study of a community with a high incidence of overweight but in which obesity was socially acceptable found levels of heart disease and diabetes below the average for slender Americans.[35]

The point is not that severe obesity is without any risk, but the advice to lose weight through dieting as a remedy for illness is certainly pointless if it cannot, in fact, be carried out. Treatments which reliably produce weight loss, such as gastric and intestinal bypass, entail significant risk themselves, and there is no evidence that their use increases longevity; in fact, the reverse may well be true. Slimming efforts undertaken to improve health must, in summary, be critically evaluated. The belief that universal efforts to achieve "ideal weight" will actually result in improved health must be regarded as an oversimplification of a very complex and poorly understood set of relationships.

Attitudes toward Obesity

What can be done? What good is the right to be fat if it is merely the right to be a social outcast? Perhaps we are too pessimistic about the potential for change, considering the impact of other recent social movements. Several elements of these deserve mention in the hope that they can be put to use in changing social attitudes toward obesity. First, there must be public protest when the media or other professional groups are intentionally or unintentionally insulting. An example of a relatively subtle insult is an ad by a pharmaceutical company depicting a young doctor shaking his finger at an older overweight woman who sits with an expression of shame. Its appearance in a journal for physicians specializing in the treatment of obesity suggests that it is an appeal to the anger and frustration physicians feel on attempting to apply treatments which do not work, seemingly because patients fail to comply. The same journal featured an ad in which a female patient protested, "But doctor, I eat like a bird," while the physician conjured up an image of a vulture. This ad was so popular that it has been featured as a comic opening in many a professional talk.

Broader cultural attitudes are reflected in newspaper, magazine, and television coverage. Here is an example of an insult so outrageous it hardly deserves mention, except that it was printed in *Time* magazine: after a cover story on Boston Symphony conductor Sarah Caldwell, this letter to the editor appeared: "I am proud to see women take their place in music. However, one cannot regard Sarah Caldwell as anything but a big blob of blubber." Why did *Time* print this hate-mail? Imagine reading: "I am proud to see the disadvantaged taking their place in music. However, one cannot regard X as anything but a lazy nigger."

Social acceptance of minorities requires exposure. Blacks were first seen on television commercials in the sixties. Their increased visibility, since then, has reflected and fostered some cultural change. In an analysis of the appearances of overweight characters in the thirty most popular American television shows, it was found that overweight females— but not males—were highly underrepresented, especially overweight white females (only 1 in 131 continuing characters, and 2 in single appearances).[36]

Obesity as a Feminist Issue

Numerous studies document the hatred of obese children by other children and by adults.[37] The impact this hatred has on the individual child is probably irreversible. It is not only the obese child who suffers from this hatred; anti-fat attitudes learned in childhood no doubt become the basis for self-hatred among those who become overweight at later ages and a source of anxiety and self-doubt for anyone fearful of becoming overweight. But we would argue, further, that (1) fat is a woman's problem; (2) fat is an ethical, political problem more than a medical, psychiatric, or behavioral problem; (3) society must develop different attitudes toward and treatments of obesity. Studies of attitudes toward endomorphic children reveal that children of both sexes, and of all body builds, adopt the prevailing negative stereotypes associated with endomorphy. However, at later ages, beginning with adolescence, females are more affected than males by this prejudicial climate.[38]

Fat is a Woman's Problem

Kurtz had eighty-nine male and eighty female white, middle-class college students rate themselves (using the semantic differential)[39] on thirty "body concepts" (including profile; size of bust/chest, hips, waist; body build; weight). He concluded: "The hypothesis was confirmed that college women have a more clearly differentiated body concept than men. This finding suggests a greater awareness and concern over bodily appearance may be more acceptable in the female than in the male."[40] He also found that the females rated their bodies higher on the "evaluative" dimension of the semantic differential than the men, but saw their bodies as less "potent" and less "active." He speculates that "greater body differentiation and high evaluation in the female is related to her lack of actual social or political power in American society."[41]

Clifford reports that 194 adolescent females, eleven–nineteen years of age, were more dissatisfied with, or more critical of their bodies, than were 146 male adolescents of the same age range. These subjects rated forty-five "body-satisfaction" items; the females rated weight, looks, legs, waist, and hips lowest, while the five features least liked by the males were weight, waist, teeth, running, and posture. "Females may be more critical of their bodies because of the relatively greater amount of emphasis placed on buying clothing, personal adornment, and standards of beauty and appearance for women."[42]

Sidney M. Jourard and P. R. Secord present evidence that there is a shared "ideal female figure" and that, among sixty female college students, satisfaction with one's own height, weight, bust, waist, and hips was a function of how closely matched perceived and ideal dimensions were. As a group, these women perceived themselves as too tall, as weighing too much, as too big in the waist and hips, but not big enough in the bust. The researchers report:

> The size specifications of the ideal female figure in our culture seem to be rather restrictive, i.e., they are difficult to attain. In general, the ideal could be paraphrased: "It is good to be smaller than you are in all dimensions except bust." None of the women in our sample had physical dimensions that were identical with all of their ideal self-ratings, and none of the women rated positively all of their body parts. . . . Since "ideal" proportions appear to be difficult for many women fully to attain in our culture . . . the ideal . . . is indirectly responsible for much anxiety and insecurity among members of that sex. . . . [The] ideal . . . produces self-hate, guilt, and insecurity when it is not fulfilled [and this accounts] for the apparently widespread efforts among women in American society to mold and sculpture their bodies toward the ideal, by corsetry, dieting, exercise, and camouflage.[43]

Helen I. Douty and her colleagues report that 59 percent of female college students rated themselves low on "satisfaction with figure," even though "few of these Ss would attract negative attention because they were obviously different from societal expectations."[44] If these women, who as a group were within the "desirable weight" limits used by medical and behavioral investigators and therapists to define obesity, are dissatisfied with the way they look and are presumably adversely affected by this dissatisfaction, then it is a safe bet that women whose weight is higher than these limits are even more dissatisfied and adversely affected.

Sally B. Beck and her associates report that 115 college women rated silhouettes of female figures with large buttocks, large breasts, and a "proportionately 'large' overall" female figure as less preferred than silhouettes of figures with small buttocks, "moderately small" breasts, and a "proportionately 'moderate' overall (standard)" female figure.[45] On the basis of these results and of personality test scores, the authors speculate: "Women who select smaller female breasts and buttocks are, in general, less traditionally feminine individuals who desire to achieve in many ways and to pursue academic goals. . . . The women of this study may associate the more ample female body with a culturally stereotyped picture of the woman as 'wife and mother,' while the smaller (thinner) female body is associated with greater personal career freedom." These results show that college females prefer smallness in women. A study by Katherine A. Halmi and her colleagues showed that ten- to eighteen-year-old females (from Iowa City schools) consistently overestimated the width of their own face, chest, waist, hips, and "the greatest depth from front to back of the body below the waist."[46] These studies together suggest that, in general, young females see smallness as an ideal, but perceive themselves as falling short of that ideal.

Fat is a woman's more than a man's problem because less deviation from "ideal" is allowed women. A study by L. F. Monello and Jean Mayer reveals the psychological/emotional price paid by women whose body builds are not within acceptable limits.[47] Responses to projective tests of 100 obese girls, thirteen to seventeen years of age, attending a weight reduction camp were compared to those of 75 nonobese girls (same age range) attending a "typical summer camp next door." Highly statistically significant differences between the two groups were found. The obese girls scored higher on items measuring "passivity," "withdrawal," "blocking responses," "family conflict," and "concern about weight status." These authors note the close similarity of this pattern of characteristics with that shown by ethnic and racial minorities: "When obese subjects demonstrate attitudes similar to those resulting from ethnic and racial prejudice, it is not farfetched to say that obese persons in the United States may form a minority group suffering from prejudice and discrimination." They compare the obese girls' "obsessive concern" with weight to chronic feelings of helplessness, anxiety, and impending doom experienced by victims of racial discrimination and anti-Semitism.

One of our adult patients made the following entries in her journal:

How did I ever arrive at this severe state of self-hatred? Little by little over the years, I had been prodded, badgered, passed judgement on by so many people who had been important in my environment. Mother, sister, brother, husband, children, in-laws, distant relatives, and friends. Soon it seemed everyone had to be thinking the same thing. Until my self-esteem eroded to a point almost beyond tolerating (15 November). The more I hated myself the better a job I thought I was doing. The hate snowballed until I was so encumbered by lack of self-esteem that I entered a state of inertia (16 November). A mountain of fat, great volumes of larded flab, covered with over-stretched and sagging skin. Buried deep within is a bit of joy slowly drowning in the emollient folds. Hope too is suffering the death-agony, going down for the third time in the enormous body of fat. There is only one cure for the indignities. . . . Marking time, counting calories, recording activities, avoiding people, hiding misery, extravagantly wasting my life (29 December).

Two additional studies show that the price paid by women having a "deviant" body build can be more than just psychological/emotional. P. B. Goldblatt and colleagues report data collected from 1,660 adult residents of "Midtown Manhattan" which demonstrate that compared to thin women, overweight women are much less likely to achieve a higher socioeconomic status than their parents, and much more likely to be downwardly socially mobile. No such relationship was found among the men studied. They also report that, although the percentage of *men* who were "thin" was about the same for all three social classes (i.e., 10 percent, 9 percent, and 12 percent for low, middle, and high socioeconomic status), the percentage of *women* who were "thin" was directly proportional to the social class level (9 percent, 19 percent, and 37 percent for low, middle, and high socioeconomic status, respectively). The authors state: "In the Midtown [Manhattan] society we do not have to look far to see the image of the slim, attractive female as portrayed throughout the popular culture. . . . A selection process may operate so that in any status-conferring situation, such as a promotion at work or marriage to a higher status male, thinner women may be preferentially selected over their competitors."[48]

H. Canning and Jean Mayer found that among the 1964 graduating classes in the high schools of a large middle-class suburban community, the percentage of overweight females was 23.3 percent, whereas the percentage for overweight female college freshman in "one of the Seven Sister colleges" was 11.2. Moreover, while 51.9 per cent of the nonobese high school women went to college the year after graduation, only 31.6 per cent of the obese girls did. The obese and nonobese women did not differ on objective measures of intellectual ability and achievement or on the percentage who applied for college admission. The corresponding figures for men were: 18 percent of the high school seniors and 13 percent of the college freshmen at an unspecified Ivy League school were obese; 53.3 percent of the nonobese and 49.9 of the obese high school students went to college, a difference not statistically significant.

Canning and Mayer state: "If obese adolescents have difficulty in attending college, a substantial proportion may experience a drop in social class, or fail to advance beyond present levels. Education, occupation, and income are social-class variables that are strongly interrelated. A vicious circle, therefore, may begin as a result of college-admission discrimination, preventing the obese from rising in the social-class system."[49]

The articles discussed so far have been primarily empirical, and conclusions have been more or less constrained by the findings. There are a number of papers which, although they do not include new data, reach similar conclusions and take stronger stands on the issues raised by this knowledge.

W. J. Cahnman, in a paper entitled "The Stigma of Obesity," concludes on the basis of the last two studies discussed above that "obesity, especially as far as girls are concerned, is not so much a mark of low [socioeconomic status] as a condemnation to it."[50] Margaret Mackenzie states: "As a cultural disease, obesity is not limited to those who weigh more than the ideal. Especially among women there are those who believe they are obese [even] when they weigh less than the insurance norms. Usually, their idea of the normal for themselves comes from their notion of what their husbands or lovers expect of them."[51]

Fat as a Political Rather than a Medical Problem

Recognition that relative fatness may be normal for women casts the problem into a new form: understanding and modifying the social forces which serve to distort women's natural form. Critics take different positions concerning which social forces are most responsible, and thus what remedies should be advocated.

Anne Scott Beller writes, "Female fleshiness is a fact of biological life and one that has every appearance of having been programmed into the species long ago by nature. . . . In the context of the new feminism, therefore, it may be well to remember that, for whatever reasons, the present model is one that has by and large been imposed on women by women: men's pinup magazines have usually dealt in somewhat more biometrically realistic images and ideals."[52]

Robin Morgan writes in *Ms.* Magazine: "And what about confronting the very space our bodies inhabit; who defines it? In this patriarchal world, space-taking by a woman is seen as unattractive and attraction is the one bargaining power she is allowed." Men have assigned to women "the realm of the physical. The result [is] that women feel at once mired in and alienated from [their] bodies. . . ."[53]

Marlene Boskind-Lodahl, in "Cinderella's Stepsisters: A Feminist Perspective on Anorexia Nervosa and Bulimia," deals with "bulimarexia," a syndrome of binge-eating followed by purging and/or starving common among college women. She believes that bulimarexics accept the "stereotype of femininity—that of the accommodating, passive dependent woman."[54] Elsewhere, Boskind-Lodahl and Joyce Sirlin write: "We came to understand that the bulimarexic's problem is that she identifies too strongly with what she perceives as the proper female role. She doesn't reject her femininity; she becomes a caricature of it."[55]

Aldebaran, in *The Journal of Radical Therapy*, writes: "Most people who worry about their weight are women, and fat is a woman's problem. The current standards of beauty are set so thin that there is hardly any woman who does not consider herself 'overweight.' And women are brought up to regard [their] bodies as objects to be sacrificed for beauty. There is no doubt that a chief reason why the truth about fat and eating is ignored by doctors and psychotherapists is because fat is seen as a 'trivial' woman's issue. Mass starvation of women is the modern American culture's equivalent of footbinding, lipstretching, and other forms of woman-mutilation."[56]

Susie Orbach takes a position which is *politically* compatible with those of Boskind-Lodahl and Sirlin and Aldebaran, i.e., fat is part of the greater problem of sexual inequality, but, implicitly assuming that they are "compulsive eaters," she hypothesizes that fat women overeat *because of,* or *in response to,* the conditions of sexual oppression: "Fat is a social disease, and fat is a feminist issue. Fat is not about lack of self-control or lack of will power. . . . It is a response to the inequality of the sexes. . . . For many women, compulsive eating and being fat have become one way to avoid being marketed or seen as the ideal woman."[57]

Cahnman states, "A moral problem is posed, if those who are not in fact responsible for their condition, nevertheless are held responsible for it." He speaks of a "moralistic diagnosis" which includes the "unspoken assumption that what is needed first and foremost in the treatment of the immature obese person is the repression of ravenous appetites; the corresponding materialistic therapy consists in a strict dietary regimen, with or without the assistance of drugs."[58]

Aldebaran asserts: "It is incredible that no one has protested how psychological assumptions about fat people contradict material evidence. Most fat people do *not* eat more than most slim people. Most fat people do *not* want to be fat."[59] Elsewhere, Aldebaran argues that there is no way to know at this time whether fat is inherently healthy or unhealthy because virtually all studies quoted to suggest that fat is unhealthy were carried out on fat people who were severely persecuted for their weight, and were in most cases chronic dieters."[60]

Boskind-Lodahl and Sirlin concluded that they weren't dealing with a strictly psychiatric problem but with a problem of female socialization and its reinforcement by the media's steady bombardment of ideal female images.[61]

Calls for New Attitudes and Treatments

Deborah Berson and an author calling herself Cathy Fatwoman in the *Radical Therapist* seek to change the attitudes of thin women who want to "help" fat women: "Perhaps thin women are not aware quite how humiliating and powerless a position it is to be defended from persecution, supported and encouraged in a diet by a thin friend who someplace in her caring soul still knows she's better and luckier than you."[62]

Boskind-Lodahl and Sirlin used group therapy, "a social cure for a social neurosis":

> Female therapists were essential. They served as models for the younger women struggling to define new selves, and they shared their own struggles with problems of self-worth, body image, and acceptability to men. . . . We wanted the therapy to illustrate the limited ways in which our culture teaches women to see and use their bodies. . . . Since their low opinion of themselves seemed crucial, we encouraged the women to become more assertive . . . [and] to develop their own interests and activities independent of men in their lives. The therapists pointed out how women give men the power to demolish their

self respect by assuming that men define their worth in the first
place.

. . . [Eventually] the discussion drifted away from anger
and fear toward the joyous discoveries that it is possible to live
without desperately needing a man and that it is possible to
like men.[63]

Robin Morgan recommends that women (1) "confront those medical practitioners, drug manufacturers, and chemical corporations who
sell us our own disfigurements and deaths"; and (2) "continue saying
the unmentionable—cry rape and cry pornography . . . proclaim the
existence of fat, vaginal fungus, dandruff, and other unspeakables great
and small. Discover new ones and keep harping away at the old ones,
because their unmentionability grows back, reinforced daily by our
every waking moment.[64]

New Approaches to Treatment

These are the guidelines, based on our analysis of social and medical factors, we propose for those offering treatment to overweight
women. We believe women should accept no less.

1. Physicians and health care professionals should not impose
their values on patients by criticizing their weight or insisting on un-
wanted treatment.

2. Patients should be advised of health risks associated with obesity. However, the facts should be gathered to allow the most accurate
appraisal of the risk *to that individual,* rather than to obese people in
general. As we have noted, the true risks are not well known. This is all
the more reason not to insist on treatment carrying hazards for uncertain benefit.

3. When treatment is contemplated, the patient should be given
whatever information is available on the short and long term success
rate of that treatment. When not available, published success rates of
similar programs should be provided. Rational decisions require accurate information.

4. Patients should be helped to make autonomous decisions. To do
this, therapists must indicate that they will support patients' choices.

5. Patients who choose to remain heavy should be offered help in

adjusting to the consequences of this decision. The therapist who cannot provide such help should make an appropriate referral.

6. Patients who fail to lose weight should be offered help. Failing patients deserve concern and interest as much as successful ones, and ideally as much planning should go into the care of patients who do not lose weight as into the design of the weight loss program. At a minimum, exit interviews should be designed to assess the impact of failure and help clarify options. At best, treatments should be made available to help patients (a) maintain their weight and work on other problem areas in preparation for a renewed effort at weight loss, or (b) learn to live with themselves as they are.

7. Therapists should help to relieve undue pressures on the overweight to conform to social norms. This may require recommending therapy for families in which the patient's obesity represents an unresolved problem, helping the patient become more assertive with others, and helping her or him to combat discriminatory actions by schools, universities, employers, and manufacturers. Failure to illuminate the issues of sexism inherent in weight obsession is a failure of the therapist to address the central issue in many women's lives and an evasion of the real therapeutic task.

Notes

1. Susan C. Wooley and Orland W. Wooley, "Theroretical, Practical, and Social Issues in Behavioral Treatments of Obesity," *Journal of Applied Behavior Analysis* 12 (1979): 3–25.

2. Susan C. Wooley and Orland W. Wooley, "Eating Disorders: Obesity and Anorexia," in *Women and Psychotherapy: An Assessment of Research and Practice,* ed. Annette M. Brodsky and Rachel T. Hare-Mustin (New York: Guliford Press, 1980), pp. 135–58.

3. Albert J. Stunkard and M. McLaren-Hume, "The Results of Treatment for Obesity," *Archives of Internal Medicine* 103 (1959): 79–85. Throughout this paper the words used to describe heavier vs. slimmer persons are those used by the original researchers. For example, endomorphic is used by some investigators as a synonym for fat, chubby, or a "roundness and plumpness" of physique; "mesomorphic" and "ectomorphic" are used as synonyms for "average" and "thin" respectively. These three terms are descriptive and correspond only in a rough, general way to Sheldon's somatotypes (William Herbert Sheldon, *The Varieties of Human Physique* [New York: Harper, 1940]). Other

terms such as obese, overweight, chubby, and fat will be used to designate the relatively heavier groups examined in the studies being described and reflect the researcher's own descriptions of them.

4. Rena R. Wing and R. W. Jeffrey, "Comparison of Methodology and Results of Out-Patient Treatments of Obesity" (abstract), *International Journal of Obesity* 12 (1978): 495.

5. A. C. MacCuish, J. F. Munro, and L. J. P. Duncan, "Follow-up Study of Refractory Obesity Treated by Fasting," *British Medical Journal* 1 (1968): 91–92; J. A. Innes, I. W. Campbell, A. L. Needle, and J. F. Munro, "Long-term Followup of Therapeutic Starvation," *British Medical Journal* 2 (1973): 356–59; Rafael A. Lantigua, John M. Amataruda, Theodore L. Biddle, Gilbert H. Forbes, and Dean H. Lockwood, "Cardiac Arrhythmias Associated with a Liquid Protein Diet for the Treatment of Obesity," *New England Journal of Medicine* 303 (1980): 735–38.

6. Rena R. Wing and R. W. Jeffrey, "Comparison of Methodology."

7. Hal S. Currey, Robert J. Malcomb, Elizabeth Riddle, and Margaret Schachte, "Behavioral Treatment of Obesity: Limitations and Results with the Chronically Obese," *Journal of the American Medical Association* 237 (1977): 2829–31. A recent paper by Stanley Schacter, "Recidivism and Self-cure of Smoking and Obesity," *American Psychologist* 37 (1982): 436–44, reports a surprisingly high rate of well-maintained weight losses in an untreated sample of university personnel and residents of a resort town. The casual sampling procedure makes it difficult to interpret these findings, but, if true, they then could be taken to mean that those people who can lose weight do it without professional help. Perhaps these spontaneous cures include many of the simple overeaters who gain weight during transitory periods of stress or indulgence and who are able to return to a lower (possibly "natural") body weight without undue difficulty. If there is a physiological "set point" for weight, obviously people may at times exceed it, as well as fall below it. This finding does not alter the fact that the vast majority of people who seek help for weight loss and who are the targets of current research and treatment efforts belong to a refractory group with poor prospects for successful weight loss.

8. John S. Garrow, *Energy Balance and Obesity in Man* (New York: American Elsevier, 1974).

9. R. Beaudoin and Jean Mayer, "Food Intakes of Obese and Non-obese Women," *Journal of the American Dietetic Association* 19 (1953): 29–33.

10. T. Hanley, "The Etiology of Obesity," in *Obesity: Medical and Scientific Aspects,* ed. Ian M. Baird and Alan N. Howard (Edinburgh: E. & S. Livingstone, 1969).

11. H. Tepperman and J. Tepperman, "Adaptive Hyperlipogenis," *Federation Proceedings* 23 (1964): 73–75.

12. S. Hejda and P. Fabry, "Frequency of Food Intake and Relation to Some Parameters of the Nutritional Status," *Nutrition and Metabolism* 6 (1964): 216–28.

13. H. Kissileff, H. Jordan, and L. Levitz, "Eating Habits of Obese and

Normal Weight Humans" (classified abstract), *International Journal of Obesity* 1 (1978): 379; J. Mayer, Albert J. Stunkard, and M. Coll, "Eating in Public Places: There is No 'Obese Eating Style,' It's Where You Eat That Matters," paper presented at the Association for the Advancement of Behavior Therapy, Atlanta, 1977.

14. A. M. Thomson, W. Z. Billewicz, and R. Passmore, "The Relation Between Calorie Intake and Body-width in Man," *Lancet: Journal of British and Foreign Medicine* 1 (1961): 1027–28.

15. John S. Garrow, *Energy Balance.*

16. Ibid., p. 16.

17. Geoffrey Arthur Rose and R. T. Williams, "Metabolic Studies on Large and Small Eaters," *British Journal of Nutrition* 15 (1961): 1–9.

18. P. Warwick, R. Toft, and John Garrow, "Individual Differences in Energy Expenditure" (abstract), *International Journal of Obesity* 2 (1978): 396.

19. D. Miller, P. Mumford, and M. Stock, "Gluttony: Thermogenesis in Overeating Man," *American Journal of Clinical Nutrition* 20 (1967): 1223–29; D. Miller and P. Mumford, "Obesity: Physical Activity and Nutrition," *Proceedings of the Nutrition Society* 25 (1966): 100–107; Ethan Sims, R. Goldman, C. Gluck, E. Horton, P. Kelleher, and D. Rowe, "Experimental Obesity in Man," *Transactions of the Association of American Physicians* 81 (1968): 153–70; N. Ashworth, S. Creedy, J. Hunt, S. Mahon, and P. Newland, "Effect of Nightly Food Supplements on Food Intake in Man," *Lancet: Journal of British and Foreign Medicine* 2 (1962): 685–87; E. Sims et al., "Experimental Obesity."

20. M. L. Kaplan and G. A. Leveille, "Calorigenic Effect of a High Protein Meal in Obese and Non-obese Subjects" (abstract), *Federation Proceedings of the Federation of American Societies of Experimental Biology* 33 (1974): 701; P. Pittet, P. Chappuis, K. Acheson, F. de Techtermann, and E. Jequier, "Thermic Effect of Glucose in Obese Subjects Studied by Direct and Indirect Calorimetry," *British Journal of Nutrition* 35 (1976): 281–92; J. M. Strang and H. B. McLuggage, "The Specific Dynamic Action of Food in Abnormal States of Nutrition," *American Journal of Medical Sciences* 182 (1931): 49–81.

21. William P. T. James and P. Trayhurn, "An Integral View of the Metabolic and Genetic Basis of Obesity," *Lancet* 2 (1976): 770–73.

22. Michael Apfelbaum, J. Bostsarron, and D. Lacatis, "Effect of Caloric Restriction and Excessive Calorie Intake and Expenditure," *American Journal of Clinical Nutrition* 24 (1971): 1405–9; E. Drenick and H. Dennin, "Energy Expenditure in Fasting Obese Men," *Journal of Laboratory and Clinical Medicine* 81 (1973): 421–30; E. Burskirk, R. Thompson, L. Lutwak and G. Whedon, "Energy Balance of Obese Patients During Weight Reduction: Influence of Diet Restriction and Exercise," *Annals of the New York Academy of Science* 110 (1963): 918–46; George Bray, "Effect of Caloric Restriction on Energy Expenditure in Obese Patients," *Lancet* 2 (1969): 397–98; F. G. Benedict, W. R. Miles, and P. Roth, "Human Vitality and Efficiency under Pro-

longed Restricted Diet," *Carnegie Institute of Washington Publication* 280 (1919); Allan Howard, A. Grant, G. Challand, E. Wraight, and O. Edwards, "Thyroid Metabolism in Obese Subjects After a Very Low Calorie Diet" (classified abstract), *International Journal of Obesity* 2 (1978): 391–92; J. Brozek, A. Henschel, O. Mickelson, and H. Taylor, *The Biology of Human Starvation* (Minneapolis: University of Minnesota Press, 1950); R. H. Rixon and J. A. F. Stevenson, "Factors Influencing Survival of Rats in Fasting: Metabolic Rate and Body Weight Loss," *American Journal of Physiology* 188 (1957): 332–36.

23. M. Martineaud and J. Tremolière, "Mesures de la dépense calorique basale dans l'obesité," *Nutrition and Metabolism* 6 (1964): 77–85.

24. Ancel Keys et al., *Biology of Human Starvation.*

25. M. L. Glucksman, J. Hirsch, R. S. McCully, B. H. Barron, and J. L. Knittle, "The Response of Obese Patients to Weight Reduction—II: A Quantitative Evaluation of Behavior," *Psychosomatic Medicine* 30 (1968): 359–65.

26. A. A. Rimm, A. Hartz, and P. Barboriak, "Natural History of Obesity in 6967 Women between 50–59 Years of Age" (abstract), *International Journal of Obesity* 2 (1978): 489.

27. Peter C. Boyle, H. Storlien, and R. E. Keesey, "Increased Efficiency of Food Utilization Following Weight Loss," *Physiology and Behavior* 21 (1978): 261–64.

28. Ancel Keys et al., *The Biology of Human Starvation.*

29. Orland Wooley, Susan Wooley, and Barbara Williams, "Appetite Measure Made More Sensitive" (abstract), *International Journal of Obesity* 2 (1978): 495; Orland Wooley, Susan Wooley, and W. Woods, "Effect of Calories on Appetite for Palatable Food in Obese and Nonobese Humans," *Journal of Comparative and Physiological Psychology* 89 (1975): 619–25.

30. George V. Mann, "The Influence of Obesity on Health I and II," *New England Journal of Medicine* 291 (1974): 184–232, 227, 188.

31. Paul Sorlie, Tavia Gordon, and William B. Kannel, "Body Build and Mortality," *Journal of the American Medical Association* 243 (1980): 1828–31.

32. Ancel Keys, "Overweight, Obesity, Coronary Heart Disease, and Mortality," *Nutrition Reviews* 38 (1980): 297–307.

33. Reuben Andres, "Effect of Obesity on Total Mortality," *International Journal of Obesity* 4 (1980): 381–86.

34. H. Noppa, C. Bengtsson, H. Wedel, and L. Wilhelmsen, "Obesity in Relation to Morbidity and Mortality from Cardiovascular Disease," *American Journal of Epidemiology* 3 (1980): 682–92.

35. Clarke Stout, Jerry Morrow, Edward N. Brandt, and Stewart Wolf, "Unusually Low Incidence of Death from Myocardial Infarction in an Italian-American Community in Pennsylvania," *Journal of the American Medical Association* 188 (1964): 848–49.

36. Sue Dyrenforth, Dennis Freeman, Margaret Jaffe, and Susan Wooley,

"Differential Portrayal of Characters by Body Build Stereotypes on Prime Time Television," unpublished.

37. For a detailed review of these studies, see Orland W. Wooley, Susan C. Wooley, and Sue R. Dyrenforth, "Obesity and Women: A Neglected Feminist Topic," *Women's Studies International Quarterly* 2, no. 1 (1979): 81–92.

38. G. L. Maddox et al., "Overweight as Social Deviance," *Journal of Health and Social Behavior* 9 (1968): 287–98.

39. Charles Osgood, G. Suci, and P. Tannenbaum, *The Measurement of Meaning* (Urbana: University of Illinois Press, 1957).

40. R. M. Kurtz, "Sex Differences and Variations in Body Attitudes," *Journal of Consulting and Clinical Psychology* 33 (1969): 625–29.

41. Ibid., p. 628.

42. E. Clifford, "Body Satisfaction in Adolescence," *Perceptual and Motor Skills* 33 (1971): 119–25.

43. S. M. Jourard and P. R. Secord, "Body-cathexis and the Ideal Female Figure," *Journal of Abnormal and Social Psychology* 50 (1955): 243–46.

44. H. I. Douty, J. B. Moore, and D. Hartford, "Body Characteristics in Relation to Life Adjustment, Body-image and Attitudes of College Females," *Perceptual and Motor Skills* 39 (1974): 499–521.

45. S. B. Beck, C. J. Ward-Hull, P. M. McLear, "Variables Related to Women's Somatic Preferences of the Male and Female Body," *Journal of Personality and Social Psychology* 34 (1976): 1200–1210.

46. Katherine A. Halmi, Solomon C. Goldberg, and Sheila Cunningham, "Perceptual Distortion of Body Image in Adolescent Girls: Distortion of Body Image in Adolescence," *Psychological Medicine* 7 (1977): 253–57.

47. L. F. Monello and Jean Mayer, "Obese Adolescent Girls: An Unrecognized 'Minority' Group?" *American Journal of Clinical Nutrition* 13 (1963): 35–39.

48. Phillip B. Goldblatt, Mary E. Moore, and Albert J. Stunkard, "Social Factors in Obesity," *Journal of the American Medical Association* 192 (1965): 1039–44.

49. H. Canning and Jean Mayer, "Obesity—Its Possible Effect on College Acceptance," *New England Journal of Medicine* 275 (1966): 1172–74.

50. W. J. Cahnman, "The Stigma of Obesity," *Sociological Quarterly* 9 (1968): 283–99.

51. Margaret MacKenzie, "Self-control and Moral Responsibility, Competence, Rationality: Obesity as Failure in American Culture," paper presented at American Anthropological Association meeting, 1975.

52. Ann Scott Beller, *Fat and Thin: A Natural History of Obesity* (New York: Farrar, Straus & Giroux, 1977).

53. Robin Morgan, "The Politics of Body-image," *Ms.* 6 (Sept. 1977): 47–49.

54. Marlene Boskind-Lodahl, "Cinderella's Stepsisters: A Feminist Per-

spective on Anorexia Nervosa and Bulimia," *Signs: Journal of Women, Culture, and Society* 2 (1976): 341–56.

55. Marlene Boskind-Lodahl and Joyce Sirlin, "The Gorging-Purging Syndrome," *Psychology Today* 10 (Mar. 1977): 50–52, 82–85.

56. Aldebaran, "Fat Liberation—A Luxury? An Open Letter to Radical (and Other) Therapists." Quotations taken from an unpublished manuscript supplied by the author. This article subsequently appeared in *State and Mind* 5 (1977): 34.

57. Susie Orbach, *Fat Is a Feminist Issue: The Anti-Diet Guide to Permanent Weight Loss* (New York: Paddington Press, 1978).

58. W. J. Cahnman, "The Stigma of Obesity," pp. 286–87.

59. Aldebaran, "Uptight and Hungry, the Contradiction in Psychology of Fat," *RT: Journal of Radical Therapy* 5 (1975): 5–6.

60. Aldebaran, "Fat Liberation—A Luxury?"

61. Boskind-Lodahl and Sirlin, "The Gorging-Purging Syndrome."

62. Cathy Fatwoman and Deborah Berson, "The Fat Story of Eating as an Act of Revolution," *RT: Journal of Radical Therapy* 4 (1974): 16–17.

63. Boskind-Lodahl and Sirlin, "Gorging-Purging," pp. 50–52, 82–85.

64. Morgan, "The Politics of Body-image."

6

FRIENDS MEET
by
LARKIN HARRISON
COMMISSIONED IN HONOR OF
EUTICE COLLEGE CENTENNIAL

Section 6. On the Relationship between the Personal and the Professional

The authors in this section speak in more personal voices. They describe their own professional existence as feminists, exploring the intersections between professional and personal experience. On the one hand, they argue, with other feminist scholars, that personal and political values can influence and inform scholarship in important ways. At the same time, they note the ways in which socialization and professionalization act to undermine feminist values. These papers, then, identify a series of attitudes toward patriarchy and explore the relationship of the feminist scholar toward the patriarchal institution. Each of these writers has, within the framework of these texts at any rate, a talisman with which to ward off patriarchal oppression. For Pauline Bart, it is her commitment to the study of women. For Judith Hicks Stiehm, it is her position as a female in what has been a wholly male and wholly alien institution. For Marcela Lucero, it is her Chicana identity.

Pauline Bart does not care for the word "professional." She defines herself as a feminist and as a sociologist who uses the concepts and methods of her discipline to demystify the world for women. EVERYTHING IS DATA, reads a t-shirt she designed, BUT DATA ISN'T EVERYTHING. "We must create our own tradition," she writes, "and present our own data and judge the work by our own standards." In this essay, she traces her own career briefly, beginning with her early decision to study women (which predated the women's movement); her puzzled male colleagues could not understand how anyone so "hip" could want to study anything so "boring."

375

Judith Stiehm contrasts the "rigorous, androcentric training" most feminist scholars receive with the need to break with that training if we are to do good feminist scholarship. For Stiehm, feminism entails a commitment which is at once intellectual and moral. As feminists, we must continue to enter such alien environments as the military academies and carry out analyses of force, war, and the military establishment. Only in this way can we understand the consciousness peculiar to those who believe themselves our protectors, and thus come to understand how our own consciousness as protectees has unconsciously been shaped.

Marcela Lucero describes the Chicana feminist as "tricultural" in her knowledge of the Anglo, the Chicano, and the feminist cultures. The Chicana feminist scholar is additionally challenged in trying to study an activist, revolutionary population not easily accessible through traditional research resources. For Lucero, personal experience (her own and her students') became, necessarily, a critical resource for teaching and research. As additional resources are identified or created, the Chicana feminist scholar's challenge is to make them more widely accessible, to use them, without relinquishing the activist Chicana heritage.

All these papers bear upon that issue raised by Audre Lorde: can one use the master's tools to dismantle the master's house?[1] The papers in this section examine the fundamental processes of doing feminist scholarship and collectively suggest, perhaps, that the systematic effort to honor personal experience as a legitimate source of knowledge and integrate its realities into academic work offers us, in effect, new tools to build a new kind of house.

Note

1. "The Master's Tools Will Never Dismantle the Master's House," paper delivered at The Second Sex conference, New York, and reprinted in Cherríe Moraga and Gloria Anzaldúa, eds., *This Bridge Called My Back* (Boston: Persephone Press, 1981), pp. 98–101.

A Feminist in Military Academy Land; or, Men and Their Institutions as Curiosities

Judith Hicks Stiehm

Feminist scholarship remains a difficult achievement. To win a doctorate we must, almost inevitably, submit to rigorous, androcentric training. To do feminist work, which values women and takes them and their perspectives seriously, we must also, almost inevitably, break with or overcome the boundaries of our disciplines. Minimally, we turn to new subject matter. Methodological changes could involve the use of new variables (for example, age differential between spouses), or the use of antithetical or contrary thinking to increase intellectual self-consciousness. Reconceptualizations which lead to "scientific revolutions" are rare and, particularly in feminist thought, do not usually occur at the most competitive institutions. There men do the defining; further, since opportunity is so restricted, the standard for excellence has a tendency to narrow and to acquire an increasingly conventional cast. How, then, can feminists hope to acquire the kind of centeredness that takes them beyond their education? What circumstances make it possible to work as an *un*self-conscious feminist?

To some degree I had that unself-conscious feminist experience while researching the first year of women's integration into the U.S. military academies.[1] For personal reasons having to do with age, family composition and background, for intellectual reasons rooted in my work on nonviolent resistance, and for situational reasons related to the intensely masculine culture of the academies, I had the luxury (for a feminist) of feeling myself central and my male subjects marginal. I was able to perceive well-established, well-regarded American institutions not as "normal" but as curious.

During my work, the personnel associated with the academies were both cooperative and accessible yet sometimes they seemed as alien as if they came from Mars. I felt confident that my own detachment led to a fair analysis. At the same time, though, I assumed that most male social scientists would have seen and interpreted differently, for they have had training in the role of offering protection and have grown up understanding the obligation, as citizens, to serve their country. In contrast, I, like most women, have been taught to protect only children; moreover, few of us have been taught to be ready to risk or sacrifice ourselves in the nation's defense.

The fact is that the profession of arms has been reserved for men. Indeed, it is possible that some men elect it *because* women are excluded from it. However, because the draft ended in the early 1970s, and because the young women of the 1960s had failed *travailler pour l'armée* by producing numerous sons, the U.S. military made the decision to recruit an unprecedented percentage of women. It also assigned those women to an unprecedented number of "nontraditional" jobs. The public has mostly overlooked this, although women's entrance into the academies (a "revolutionary" event according to West Pointers) did attract attention. That event also gave scholars like myself a rare opportunity—that of studying a well-defined example, bounded in time and space, of mandated sex integration.

The academies' integration was legislated by Congress and the president in 1975 in the spirit of offering equal educational and employment opportunity. In opposing women's entrance, military personnel argued that the relevant question was not opportunity but whether or not women should serve in combat. They argued that the academies were schools for combat officers only, and also that this was a simple matter of economics: training which cost more than $400,000 should not be given to persons who could not be used wherever and however they were needed.

Actually the military was right. Combat was and is the root issue. It defines the profession of arms and is at the core of military mythology. Part of that mythology says women can and should be protected by men. This belief is shared widely by women and men. Indeed, it sometimes seems that one way men know they *are* men is by assuming protective duties. Feminists need to ask why men reserve this role for themselves. They need to examine the relationship between military service and political citizenship. They need to ask what it means to be offered and to accept protection. They need to think about how a protector differs from a predator and which of the two exercises the greater control over a protectee.

Few feminists and civilians have asked such questions. Most research on the military has been done by men who are civilians but who have also served or were liable for service in the military. Their attitude toward the military is often fatalistic. I believe my womanly exemption enabled me to see it as curious; I believe, too, that the military is an excellent subject for sex role research.

Men dramatize there the role they monopolize. They write the role of protector large. Feminists simply must come to understand how even the *possibility* of having to be a protector shapes men's thought and action. Only then can we understand how being a protectee *shapes* our thought and action.

Much of my early career was driven by individual, negative reactions. When I first began graduate study as a new mother, a woman lawyer sniffed, "Well, you don't have to finish." That guaranteed that I did. After having two more children and earning my Ph.D., I applied for an opening at the university in which I was already teaching. The response was that I would not be interviewed because "you are the kind of person who won't be visible." That moved me quickly into my professional association, where I helped found its women's caucus, and to a good deal of women's organizing. My intellectual work, though, continued to be done alone, without colleagues, without contacts, without discussion, without funding. When my first book was finished, it went quietly onto library shelves. Almost no one knew it was being written; no audience expected it; it went largely unread.

The military project was entirely different. It began with an idle conversation but at every step it was a positive and social enterprise. I filled an address book with the names of people whom I asked (always as an equal) for advice (not for help). My new self-confidence was partly the result of publishing a first book but it was also associated with becoming forty. That milestone was a time of great pleasure for me for it meant I had finally "grown up." I could no longer be patronized or indulged. I could stop fearing that I would mellow and have to retract my views. I began to keep a diary for the first time. Although hardly menopausal, I began to understand the centeredness of those older women who define the world from where they stand without hesitation or apology.

A second factor contributing to my woman-centeredness was my family. With myself and three lively daughters at every breakfast and dinner, my husband had to account for the male view as though it were "the other."

Third, as Director of the University of Southern California's Women's Studies Program (now the Study of Women and Men in Society, or SWMS), I had begun to participate in substantial discussions with other feminists, and to find all-woman groups the norm for serious discussion.

Finally, more and more I began to see "important" men not as authoritative but as foolish. I found it curious that the mere mention of women's entrance into the academies drove strong men to silly statements (General Hershey: "You might as well recruit people in wheelchairs"; General Westmoreland: "The academies are no place for freaks"; West Point Superintendent Berry: "If women come to West Point, I will resign!"). Why were the military's elite so distraught about having to do what other elements of the military (ROTC, OTS) had been doing for some time? It seemed clear to me that these men required examination. Thus, the troubled men of the military, not the eager women applicants, became my specimens, my objects of study.

My perception of curiousness was genuine. It was not a trick played on myself by myself in order to expand consciousness. It was not a method intended to distance myself from male-defined culture (although thinking of men as peculiar might be useful as a method). I really did think their behavior wondrous. I even found myself amused by, rather than angry about, their uproar. Hundreds of social scientists made inquiries about studying the integration transition; they, however, wished to study the new element—the women. I think I was the only one who wished to focus on the continuing element—the men.

I wanted to study the academies and their personnel for another reason. In my first book I had attempted to describe nonviolent philosophies as their practitioners would have.[2] I was not and am not a pacifist, but I must have been successful in my endeavor to speak for that position because at least one reviewer wrote that my book would have been more compelling if my (pacifist) bias had not been so thinly disguised. In any event, when I finished that work, it occurred to me that persons committed to the threat and use of force needed study too.

I had subsequently been searching for the right vehicle to investigate the thinking of those who chose "the profession of arms."

In general the military is a good subject for feminist research. Sexism is so obvious and unapologetic there, and manliness so important and obtrusive, that there is no need to argue about its existence. Moreover, it is so exclusively a male environment that most feminists haven't thought about it much. Because we have had so little to do with it, we have not internalized men's assumptions. Thus it is—forgive me—nearly virgin territory.

This is important. In graduate school we are taught about value-free research and most of us understand the limits of that view. When we are being intellectually rigorous, we try hard to identify values we hold which might affect our analysis. Only rarely do we approach a subject so foreign to us as to be as exempt from value considerations as John Stuart Mill claimed religion was for him. For me the military was such an environment. I found I had few assumptions about or standards for it. In fact, I was consumed with curiosity for almost the entire research period. Only when I began to yawn during interviews on my last visit did I realize that I had, indeed, gotten the data. By then I knew more details about the integration program than anyone, and because of the rapid rotation of the Academy's personnel, my account was almost sure to be news even to some of those who'd been important participants in the program.

Getting Started

At the American Political Science Association convention in the late summer of 1975, I struck up a conversation with the man in front of me in the hotel checkout line. He turned out to be an Air Force colonel and a friend of the best man in my wedding seventeen years before. He mentioned casually that women would enter the Air Force Academy (and the other military academies) in the class of 1980. I quizzed him about the people in charge, how to reach them, and whether any research was planned. At U.S.C.'s new-faculty reception several weeks later, I met the new director of the Marine Institute, an Annapolis graduate and recent Navy retiree. He sketched the organization of the Department of Defense for me and taught me to speak, or at least to understand, militarese. Thus began a nine-month effort to obtain permission and financing for a twelve-month research project which would document the integration of women into the U.S. Air Force Academy. That nine to twelve ratio is important: getting started took almost as much time and effort as doing the work. Stubborn persistence was an important part of what carried me through those nine preparatory months which (unlike pregnancy) required constant initiating behavior. Also important was the personal transition I had made from a defensive feminism (which was not just negative) to a positive feminism (which is not necessarily offensive).

Acquiring the access and money to do my case study involved energy and risk. My first set of inquiry letters went out October 3, 1975. (President Ford would sign the law providing for integration within the week.) More letters and a brief proposal went to the academies' information offices in December. Correspondence went to the Department of Defense, Office of Manpower and Reserve Affairs, in January 1976. Then follow-up phone calls began. In February I arranged to attend a Rand conference on military manpower, where I made contact with men and women wearing uniforms; to avoid blunders I memorized rank and insignia. Interestingly, at the Rand conference there were more papers on women than at a typical political science convention, more papers by women (who apparently were more eligible for Rand and government jobs than university jobs), and more research that attempted to present a woman's view if not a feminist view. For instance, one Navy paper showed that as men are promoted they like the Navy more and more; as women are promoted they like it less and less; the explanation given was not that the women were misfits, but that as they were promoted they became more and more isolated, and less and less sure that rank would bring them full opportunity.

In March the Air Force Academy asked if I could come there to discuss my proposal. I said, "Yes," canceling a class and investing my own money in the round-trip ticket. With this public and financial commitment I deliberately put myself in a position where success became imperative. The head of the academy's Behavioral Science Department met me for breakfast at the Sheraton Motel near the academy gate. I had on my first hosiery in eighteen months, wore a suit-dress, and had with me a borrowed winter coat.

Over the next two days I was introduced to key personnel throughout the academy's units. Most of the introductions were at the level of colonel or lieutenant colonel; the one woman officer who was working on women's integration was a captain. Something interesting developed. Although the officers' career choice was very different from mine, these officers were men I "knew." They were my age, they had children the age of my children, they were small-town, mid-America, white Protestants who referred to each other as "Christian" almost as casually as one refers to peers in an academic community as "bright." These were, in fact, the only kind of people I had known until I left home at twenty-one. Thinking back, I then remembered that at least three of my high school boyfriends, including the one whose track medal I had worn my senior year, were now professional officers. I knew their language; I knew how to be a "good sport." Moreover some of them knew my "best man" who had graduated from West Point, done his thesis on West Point cadet socialization, and was writing a book of his own—on change at the military academies. Ironically, the one unit that was difficult for me to tap was the academic unit. In fact, the officer with a degree in precisely my area—and his degree was from *my* university as well—was aloof, careful, and unhelpful. What does this mean? For one thing it may mean that men who are professionally most like us are the most threatened; that the men we may think we have the most in common with are those least likely to acknowledge it. On the other hand, officers in the military and physical education divisions found me "human" (though unusual) and seemed to be as interested in what I was doing and thinking as I was in them. Indeed, one pilot said, "I sure would like to meet your husband"—meaning, I suppose, that he'd like to see what kind of a man coped with me.

The officer in charge of my first visit was a small man whose Ph.D. was from Mississippi. This is the kind of man I would ordinarily expect to be threatened by me. He wasn't. Later I called someone long distance to ask, "Why isn't this man hostile toward me?" The answer was simple and instructive: "He's a colonel." I began to understand the meaning of rank. I was also surprised to find that many important military men are small in size. Even though I had once written an article on "invidious intimacy," pointing out that we artificially pair to emphasize the difference in size between men and women, somewhere I had absorbed the myth that military professionals are hulking physical specimens whose very presence intimidates.[3] I also learned that chivalry is still a large part of all male-female behavior in the military; wives of officers, for example, are still referred to as the officers' "ladies." Women are handled with delicacy, and a flat "no" is a rare response. More typically an event will not occur, a document will not arrive, or a call will go unanswered. A final clearance occurred during my March visit. Antonia Brico, the conductor, was addressing the cadets and the colonel's wife came to the talk ostensibly to hear her. However, it was arranged that she and I attend the lecture together. I managed the situation by discussing teen-age daughters and showed pictures of mine. I was cleared.

Following this initial visit, it was agreed that I would be invited to document the first year of women's integration through interviews and the reading of planning documents. In the interviews I would use a set of general questions as well as particular questions. I would be completely responsible for my own financing and publication arrangements. On the advice of other scholars who had worked with the military, I did not press for any particular arrangements or guarantees. No discussion about access or clearance occurred. (The plan was that I would visit the academy for blocks of one or two weeks over the first year of integration. In fact I was at the academy for close to three months. I made seven visits there, one to West Point and two to Annapolis.)

My proposal was picked from all the rest, I believe, because (1) the climate was right, (2) I was vouched for by someone somewhere, (3) I wanted to study the permission-givers, not the intruders, and (4) the permission-givers were committed to and certain they would do such an excellent job that they thought they could only profit by having an outside observer. It may have helped, too, to have been associated with a conservative university.

Doing research requires money as well as access. Until 1976 I had supported my own research which was done in libraries and on my own time. This project, though, required funds for travel, room and board, and released time. Just as I had gone social in trying to obtain access, I now began asking everyone I knew (including my department chair in a formal interview) for advice on getting support. The time was April. The women would arrive in two months!

My university's development officer wanted to help. He heard "women," though, and immediately gave me the names of a number of off-beat foundations; *they* heard "military" and said, "No, thanks." Break number one came six weeks later when a young woman program officer at Russell Sage whom I have never met gave me $3,000 left in her account at the end of the fiscal year. That was at the beginning of June. I left to do my first field work June 13, plunging into the work as though all problems were solved. In fact none of them were. Ultimately a Ford

Foundation program officer, Mariam Chamberlain, would support the project with discretionary funds. She acted with little in the way of a formal proposal from me but with my summer of hard work already completed.

Working in Military Academy Land

My first working visit occurred in June. When I called at 8 a.m., I found that my official sponsor (the chair of Behavioral Science) was out of town and would be gone for my entire visit. The captain he had asked to be my liaison had made no plans or arrangements and seemed to have few ideas as to what I should do. The formal structure was obviously not going to facilitate my work. Doctoral training in political theory also gave few clues as to what to do. Fortunately, I had recently seen Robert Redford and Dustin Hoffman in *All the President's Men*. The skills for acquiring information dramatically presented there turned out to be adequate. Although there was no "Deep Throat," there were women officers (of low rank) scattered throughout the Academy. There were also minority officers, and officers about to retire. Moreover, I was an object of some interest in that closed institution, and several wives had their husbands invite me to dinner. By playing lunch-hour squash I found I could chat with sweaty-togged senior officers, and by attending cadet athletic events I could meet more junior officers. The point is that there were naturally sympathetic networks, there were confident and curious people who came to me, and there were various times and places for asking impertinent questions. During my first stay I was in the Bachelor Officers' Quarters (BOQ); this meant I had a military roommate (a rotating one) and a chance to talk with a variety of official women visitors. This was advantageous. After my first visit, however, the BOQ was always "full." I think I was probably not authorized to stay there, but rather than indicate that I should not have stayed there at all it was handled in this way.

There was nothing unobtrusive about my presence. In that confined environment any civilian woman who was not a wife or a secretary was an anomaly. Because of my multiple visits, however, I became familiar, and because the administration had clearly signaled that the integration was to be a success, and even that it *was* a success, people were generally willing to talk about the process and to associate themselves with it.

Many civilians see the military as beyond supervision or scrutiny. Nevertheless, the military—at least at an installation like the academy—sees itself as operating in a goldfish bowl. Public relations are an important part of what happens at Colorado Springs, and having nearby Congresswoman Pat Schroeder on the Armed Services Committee and Air Force Major General Jeanne Holm at the White House as Ford's advisor on women and later as a member of DACOWITS (the Defense Advisory Committee on Women in the Services), and having news media regularly around, meant the academy's information office was sophisticated about observers generally, and experienced in responding to inquiries by and on behalf of women.

The Air Force Academy created an early-warning system for its first year of integration by having three women of moderately high stature and moderately feminist views in positions where they received information about the integration process and gave informal feedback. One was the first woman Distinguished Visiting Professor (DVP). A civilian sociologist, the DVP was hired to teach and to participate in a four-year research project following the women cadets from their entrance through their graduation. Her project and mine were noncompeting both as to subject and method. Also, she was a full-time academy employee who participated in academy social life and ceremony while I suffered and enjoyed the difficulties and benefits of being on my own.

The second was a lieutenant colonel who held a deanship and also acted as the base advisor on women. A savvy woman who had held a number of command positions, she assumed responsibility for managing the most ticklish problems associated with the women cadets, e.g., the cadet who became a mother at the academy's hospital. This brought relief to the men officers who would otherwise have had to deal with such novel events.

The third was myself. The three of us affected behavior simply by being there. We created self-consciousness in others; efforts to anticipate our responses affected (even though they did not control) policy choices. Sometimes our presence had a direct effect. In the matter of home hospitality for cadets, for instance, it seems clear that my questioning changed the behavior I was supposed to be observing. Once each summer doolies (entering cadets) were invited to dinner at the home of married staff and faculty. The idea was that cadets should see officers as normal, home-loving human beings "with wife, children, dog, and fireplace." Many of the women officers were not married, and believed that this practice (1) distorted reality and (2) meant that the doolies would not see women officers as "normal." This was told to me by one of the women officers. When I attempted to verify it the next day with the appropriate official, he indicated he would have to check on it. The following day he confirmed that the policy had been that only families entertained doolies, but that it had been changed for next year.

At the end of the first year all three of the women monitors left— the academics returned to their universities, and the colonel went to War College. At that time I asked an academy official how the academy planned to get the kind of feedback we had de facto provided. The answer seemed to be that the academy felt it had been so successful that such stimuli were no longer necessary. Integration had been "solved." In fact it hadn't. The following year would bring a marked attrition of women cadets in both the entering and second-year classes.

Notes on Being There

How did feminism affect my work? First, I took women seriously. I talked carefully not only to women officers, but to the secretaries and the librarians. As a feminist I knew military wives were important, too.

Second, I was slow to understand some of the things cadets told me. For instance "reverse discrimination" was a common theme in cadet discussion. This was true even though 90 percent of the slots were reserved for men! Only after numerous queries was I able to perceive that they empathized with the 157 men who were not there because the women *were* and believed that if admission had been gender-free and based on merit alone, women would not have done nearly so well. Since women doolies matched or surpassed men on SATs, gradepoint, and activities, this conviction had to have been based on physical performance. Since Air Force officers do not have tasks that require special physical strength, it became apparent that somehow this was a profound measure for them as men. I was also slow to understand how reluctant men are to respect the authority of women, how doubtful they are that other men will do so, and how bold a man must be to defend a woman as being equal. Indeed, the fact that women are better at something than men (such as flexibility) almost seemed to guarantee that it would not be considered an important criterion. I was even slower to grasp the intensity of the cadets' conviction that a double standard was practiced on behalf of racial minorities and their determination not to let "the same thing" happen with women. Finally, I failed to appreciate men's assumption that "runnin' 'em out" is an appropriate way of dealing with persons who are disliked.

Third, as a feminist who tends to think that at least women know about women, I nevertheless had to recognize that some of the gaffes during the integration process were the work of the young women whose job it was to prevent gaffes. For instance, incoming cadets are supposed to give themselves up to the service during basic training; in return, they are supposed to receive everything they require during that period. One such item was the brassiere. A slim woman officer okayed the ordering of lightweight stretch-to-fit bras. These were not adequate for large women doing heavy exercise, and soon after training began a supply officer found himself pushing a shopping cart at a downtown department store. The point is one feminists know but forget: *we* don't know about women in their varieties either. We may be more expert than men about women, but we are not experts just because we are women.

Fourth, while I knew that any successful integration program must work for many different kinds of women, not just for ideal women or superwomen, and that accordingly some would fail, some would change their minds, and some would excel and even "sell out," I nevertheless found myself quietly rooting for the women as a collective entity. It was not part of my job to judge and assess them. If it had been, I can only hope I would have been critical.

Fifth, feminists find it such a complex matter to define "feminism" themselves that perhaps I should not have been (although I was) surprised to find how little academy personnel knew about feminism or how hard put they were to recognize feminists in their midst. (The word "libber" was the operative description for an assertive, self-regarding champion of women's rights and responsibilities.) Since I believe that one can't conceal what one is or control what one is called, I pulled no punches. My hostess gifts during my first visit were copies of the *Life* magazine special issue on women. As I met people for the first time I was sometimes told, "You're not [as bad as] what I expected." (When I sprained my ankle and then fainted outside the commandant's office—then ended up on crutches—the academy must have been richly entertained at the sight of the temporarily crippled strong woman!) Still, there was little hesitation among academy personnel about expressing personal, "not to be attributed" reservations about women's attempts to play nontraditional roles.

As feminists, we should note some things about change. It is a process especially easy for administrators, who interact regularly with outsiders and pressure groups. On the other hand, alumni (and at the academy most faculty are also alumni) are especially reluctant to accept institutional change. If one lives in the past, after all, it is important that the present continue to resemble it. Also, the newest members of an organization may be the least flexible; they don't want what they are trying to join changed. At the academies the cadets were most recalcitrant about women's admission. Thus idyllic notions about "the next generation" may be foolish. It is, after all, older, confident men who can best afford to reason and to assimilate data and who may be most ready to relinquish part of their responsibilities. Young men cannot be expected to relish the doubling of competition which occurs when women enter a new field. In particular they may not want to compete with women during the period they are "becoming men"—that is, from eighteen to twenty-five—the time that people establish their work identity.

One last point should be made. As a political scientist I am by definition interested not only in power but in force, in "legitimate" violence. It is my contention that even if one is committed to the abolition of force, or at least to the equal distribution of potential for force, one must not be ignorant about the varieties of force and of legal, violent power existing and being used today. We must not let our distaste for force interfere with analysis. Naiveté is not innocence. Force exists, is real, and access to it will not be voluntarily shared. As one of my sympathetic male interviewees said several times, "Just don't think they're going to give any power to women. They won't. They won't."

Concurrent Research

Other researchers, including a number of women, studied the integration of the academies too. The sociologist Lois DeFleur, the Air Force Academy's distinguished visiting professor, worked at the academy during 1976–77 and with the academy through 1980. She worked with a team of faculty members and was funded by the Air Force. Her work focused on (1) male and female cadets' attitudes and beliefs about sex roles, (2) male and female cadets' interaction, and (3) women cadet's thinking and choices about their careers. Her research was done with the cooperation of the commandant of cadets, and official cadet records provided a data base for background variables. While the results of the research have been presented at professional meetings, DeFleur was not free to design the questionnaires as she alone saw fit, to sample the different groups she thought relevant, nor to control and use the data at her discretion. Her work required continual cooperation with a subject that was sensitive and that also held the purse strings.[4]

West Point has a well-established and well-regarded social science unit and also an office of institutional research. Even though (or because) the Army was unhappy about women's entrance, it decided to document thoroughly and carefully the effects women had on the institution and the effects the institution had on them. These reports, available through West Point's Office of Institutional Research, are collectively referred to as Project Athena.[5] Nora Kinzer, now an assistant to the Secretary of the Army, worked with the project and some of its findings are reported in her book *Stress and the American Woman*.[6]

The Navy was not interested in doing research on women's admission. The Navy tends not to reveal itself. No books have been written about that academy, there is no social science tradition there, and while one set of questionnaires testing the relationship between attitudes toward women and contact with women was completed during 1976–77, the Naval Personnel Research Lab investigators were not even allowed to visit Annapolis.[7] There a new anti-Zumwalt, anti-change spirit reigned and the chosen strategy was simply to treat women's integration as a non-event. (This was not necessarily a bad strategy. Further, Annapolis was the only academy to give a woman officer a command position during the first year of integration.)

Perhaps because it started late, the Coast Guard confined its research on women to the at-sea experience and seemed to derive pleasure from putting its women to sea successfully. By doing so, they showed up the Merchant Marine Academy which had been publicly embarrassed by its decision to expel the woman but not the man cadet who were found in bed together. The Coast Guard also seemed to enjoy showing the Navy that women could do well at sea since the Navy was (and is) determined not to do anything not legally required. The Coast Guard's consultant was a civilian sociologist, Constantina Safilios-Rothschild, who did participant-observation studies sketching the informal ways in which support (or lack of it) affected women's and men's learning and performance.[8]

All this research on women at the academies was presented at the Inter-University Seminar (IUS) and other professional meetings. The results were remarkably consistent and do not bode well for women's assuming the full range of military responsibilities. Specifically, men were opposed to women as cadets and strongly opposed to women's being in combat. Men and women also had very different perceptions about women's performance and effectiveness. Overall, the various attitude studies point to the conclusion that men find it hard to conceive of women as equals. Many see women's current military participation as aberrant, caused by the lack of a draft and by "women's lib" politics. Both these, they expect, will pass.

Conclusion

Feminists are committed to being intellectually and morally responsible. We are also committed to accepting a full share of social and political responsibility. This includes either participating in society's exercise of legitimate force or refusing to participate—but only for those logical and principled reasons which apply to men as well as to women. Thus, in my view, a feminist could be a pacifist but only so long as she or he believes this ethic to be appropriate for others, too, both women and men. To me what is wrong, what is indefensible, is to refuse to use force oneself but to accept, even to seek, protection by others. For too long women have called for peace while enjoying protection. They may have done so because they wished to avoid being either victims or executioners, but they have been guilty not guiltless, for they have permitted and even encouraged men to execute for them. As feminists, we must pursue the difficult task of assuming personal responsibility for critical analysis, moral choice, and political action.

If one excepts the pacifist literature, there is little thought recorded by women about force, war, and the military. Only recently have I and a few other feminists begun to do research on women and the military.[9] What is required now, though, are critiques which explore the broader range of issues, research which will not assume that war is inevitable and killing normal, research which uses political woman as the measure, rather than political man. Such scholarship, though, is likely to be so radical, so erosive of today's givens, that it may at first be treated as fantasy. Still, we have always known that truth is stranger than fiction.

Notes

1. Judith Stiehm, *Bring Me Men and Women: Mandated Change at the Air Force Academy* (Berkeley: University of California Press, 1981).

2. Judith Stiehm, *Nonviolent Power* (Lexington, Mass.: Heath, 1972).

3. Judith Stiehm, "Invidious Intimacy and Public Policy," *Social Policy* 6, no. 5 (Apr. 1976): 12–16.

4. See Lois B. DeFleur and David C. Gillman, "Sex Integration of the U.S. Air Force Academy: Changing Roles for Women," *Armed Forces and Society* 4 (Aug. 1978): 607–22.

5. The first volume in the project is Alan George Vitters and Nora Scott Kinzer's *Report of the Admissions of Women to the U.S. Military Academy (Project Athena)* (West Point, N.Y.: Dept. of Behavioral Sciences and Leadership, U.S. Military Academy, 1977).

6. Nora Scott Kinzer, *Stress and the American Woman* (New York: Doubleday, 1979).

7. Kathleen P. Durning, "Assimilation of Women Into the Naval Academy: An Attitude Survey," paper presented at the National Biennial Conference of the Inter-University Seminar on Armed Forces and Society, Chicago, Oct. 1977.

8. Constantina Safilios-Rothschild, Ronald A. Wells, and Marcelliuus Dijkens, "Women in a Male Domain: Attitudes and Reactions at the Coast Guard Academy," paper presented at the Inter-University Seminar on Armed Forces and Society, Chicago, Oct. 1977.

9. See "Women's and Men's Wars," special issue of *Women's Studies International Forum,* ed. Judith Stiehm, 5, nos. 3/4 (1982).

Resources for the Chicana Feminist Scholar

Marcela C. Lucero

As we approach the subject of feminist scholarship, each of us brings to the analysis our own background, conditioning, and area of specialization. My own involvement in Chicano Studies has run parallel to an interest in Women's Studies. These parallel interests and loyalties create tensions which are at the heart of Chicana feminist scholarship. While at some points Chicano and Women's Studies converge, they diverge at the ethnocultural level, for to speak another language implies another soul, another world view.

The Chicana, conditioned by two cultures, is fighting not only sexism but also racism, and in some cases marianism. Sexism is called "machismo" by the Chicana. The Chicana's outlook is not necessarily based on her bilingual capacity, but rather on the retention of those cultural values not easily grasped by Anglo liberals. The Chicana's research and writing may result in an esoteric effort comprehensible only to herself or to other Chicana scholars, yet, because some of the feminist values are the same ones Chicanos are emphasizing (more humanism, more personalism, etc.) Chicanas continue attempting to communicate as women.

The Chicana is neither an Anglo woman nor a Chicano man, yet she integrates simultaneously both viewpoints, while having empathy and sympathy with both conditions. Thus, she is hesitant to dissipate her time and energy solely on the feminist movement, which she may consider out of her class as an elitist movement that she is not comfortable with, and simultaneously may be disillusioned with the Chicano movement for not recognizing the importance of women's identity and

393

contributions. "Bicultural" may be a misnomer for the Chicana. She knows the Anglo, Chicano, and feminist cultures and may be considered a tri-cultural person in a triple-bind oppression. The three factors exist in the Chicana feminist scholar, that is, if she calls herself a "Chicana." Chicanas cannot yet control their own destiny, and they are not sure that their identity would be guaranteed with the women's movement.

It is understandable, then, that the Chicana has returned to the past to seek out women to serve as role models to motivate her not only to emulate those models but to want to write about the Chicana experience. Writing sometimes means research, and when it does, the Chicana feminist scholar is embarking on the most difficult academic challenge she will ever undertake.

Specific and Special Difficulties of the Chicana Feminist Scholar

Since there are few Chicana graduates of institutions of higher education, there is a scarcity of Chicana scholars who are undertaking systematic scholarship concerning Chicanas.[1] Those few who are researching Chicana contributions in every discipline must be prepared and willing to do research in unorthodox sources, for most traditional library resources do not list Chicanos in their subject classifications, much less Chicana women.

Chicano scholars have had great difficulty in researching history from a Chicano perspective since Anglo historians have omitted Chicano contributions to U.S. history or have presented the Mexicans and Chicanos pejoratively.[2]

Crucial to the Chicanos' situation is the fact that the land of their ancestors was conquered and brought partially within the U.S., and their language and history were eradicated or distorted. The older generation, however, has retained their language and history, even in the face of second-class citizenship and oppression or, perhaps, because of it. The proximity of and migrations from Mexico have also helped with this retention, or these parts of Chicano culture would have disappeared into the grave with this older generation.[3] The history does exist, but it must be retrieved from families or individuals who have preserved the oral tradition of history. In view of the systematic omissions by Anglo historians, we should hesitate to conclude that Chicanos, earlier called Mexican or Spanish Americans, were not writing and publishing before the 1960s. Moreover, Chicano historians have published, but their books are not readily available in public or even university libraries.

Problems

Thus, briefly and succinctly, the Chicana feminist scholar encounters many barriers to research which may take her into the barrio, into other states (for example, to the Chicano Studies libraries of California and Texas), and possibly even to Mexico. She must know how to read, write, and speak Spanish as well as English. She must have knowledge of the Chicano Studies libraries at various universities and must be able to gain access to them. Lastly, she must have the time, energy, and money to initiate and carry out the project.

If Women's Studies had a difficult time in assembling courses and teachers, the problem was compounded for the Chicana who wanted to offer a "La Chicana" course within the framework of Chicano or Women's Studies. Chicanas responded to this endeavor. The lack of curriculum material prompted many Chicana conferences whose position papers became the curriculum content for classroom use. Many of us are familiar with Enriqueta Vasquez's essay which appeared in *Sisterhood is Powerful,* but we might be reminded that this article emerged out of frustration with a Chicano conference where women stated that they did not wish to be liberated.[4]

Existing Publications and Resources

In 1971 the first national Chicana conference, sponsored by the YWCA, was held in Houston, Texas. That conference gave impetus to many Chicana publications, a few of which should be mentioned here. *Regeneración,* a journal published by Comisión Femenil of Los Angeles, California, covered many of the conference viewpoints.[5] Mirta Vidal's pamphlet, *Chicanas Speak Out,* gave an accurate account of the conference resolutions.[6] After that date, interest in Chicana issues began to be reflected in other publications.

Early in the 1960s, Dr. Sylvia Gonzales was writing poetry. She still is, but she has been writing more and more position papers about diverse subjects such as literary criticism and sociological treatises about the Chicana feminist, and has found her niche writing about the

Chicana intellectual, feminist scholar. In 1974, she published a book entitled *La Chicana piensa*.[7] She has followed that effort with many articles and poems and is probably the most prolific of Chicana writers.

Another Chicana, Dorinda Moreno of California, also published a book that same year entitled *La mujer en Pie de Lucha*.[8] This book was a compilation of newspaper articles concerning Third World women together with some creative work by Moreno and other Chicanas. Flo Saiz's *La Chicana* came from lecture notes and research for a course on the Chicana.[9] (The first such course was taught at the University of Colorado.)

Marta Cotera, author of *The Chicana Feminist*, has taken on the monumental task of researching the history of Chicanas in the United States.[10] Cotera, a librarian, has methodically kept notes from the many books she has come across in her work, and from this collection has written *Diosa y Hembra*.[11] Her research has taken her into the Chicano community (the barrio) and elsewhere to interview personally women still living who have contributed to the history of this country. Because she is an independent consultant and manages her own firm, she has the time to do this but not always the money. Cotera is still collecting anecdotes and biographies of the forerunners of the contemporary Chicana activist.

These three women financed their own publications and distributed them themselves or through Chicano press channels. These publications quickly sold out. It is still true today that Chicanas are publishing primarily through Chicano presses which then distribute the books.

Publishing activity began to flourish in 1973. Montal Educational Associates sponsored a project which brought together Chicana professionals from various disciplines to teach a course. Their bibliographies would then be published as a curriculum for future Chicana courses. The end result was *Estudios femeniles*,[12] published by the UCLA Extension Center, with Corrine Sanchez and Anna Nieto-Gomez as editors.

In 1976, and largely through the efforts of Dr. Sylvia Gonzales, Chicanas were invited to participate in the first Inter-American Women Writers Congress held in San Jose, California. It was there that Chicanas had an opportunity to meet and know many Latin American women writers, so well known in their own countries. It was also an opportunity for the editors of the Hispanic Women's Clearinghouse to learn and add names to their information base. The position papers presented at that conference were published by Pajarito Publications of New Mexico in a periodical called *La Cosecha*.[13]

Chicano publishing houses have been quite active publishing articles by and about the Chicana. Aztlan Publications at UCLA has published Rosaura Sanchez' *Essays on La Mujer* as well as a number of bibliographies.[14] The Chicana Research and Learning Center in Austin, Texas, published an annotated bibliography on Chicana writings.[15] Chicano newspapers such as Juan Rodriquez' *Carta Abierta* and Jose Armas' *Rayas* and *Caracol* all carry bibliographical references to Chicanas' works as well as personal interviews and book reviews.

The fact remains that today, when the Chicana's writings are marketable, there is still a scarcity of material by and about her. The prolific writers shift between writing political, socioeconomic, historical essays, and esthetic, creative literature, primarily poetry.

When I was asked to put together the literature section of *Estudios femeniles,* I encountered various problems.[16] Although I had a substantial background in literature (English, American, Spanish, and Latin American), I could not at first identify any appropriate women writers. True, there were Alfonsina Storni, Juana de Ibabouru, and Gabriela Mistral of Latin America (the latter was the twentieth-century Chilean poet who had won the Nobel prize in literature), but these women were not the role models that Chicanas were looking for. Chicanas were relating to women activists and revolutionaries. Alfonsina Storni wrote about the agonies of being a woman in a man's world, and eventually committed suicide. Gabriela Mistral had dedicated her life to writing after her fiance's suicide. She was a deeply religious woman, led an ascetic life, never married, and wrote about the children she would never have. I was left with male authors who had written about women. There were Federico Garcia Lorca's women, frustrated in unrequited love with remote possibilities of marrying, or if married had tragic wedding days, or could never bear any children.[17] These, too, left much to be desired—masterpieces, to be sure, but not the kind of literature that I wanted to bring into the classroom.

Thus I asked my women students to do some creative writing as a class assignment, and these works were read and analyzed in class. Many discovered their talents, and I saved and used some of this material for my classes on "La Chicana" which I taught at the University of Minnesota. The many handouts provided by the various teachers at the Montal seminar became the early content for this course.

In 1976 when editors Otero and Echevarria asked me to write about the Spanish surnamed women of Colorado for inclusion in the book *Hispanic Colorado,* again I was faced with a problem.[18] I was asked to write two articles: one about the Spanish surnamed woman of yesteryear, and one on the contemporary Chicana. The latter posed no problem for I had been born and raised in Colorado, but the research into past history became burdensome. I had few documents to rely on. The public library was not helpful. Fortunately, I had saved some pamphlets and articles from the 1940s and 1950s, and the rest had to come from memory and oral history tradition. My own grandmother had been born in Colorado in 1864 and lived until 1950, and I remembered her stories, as well as those of my mother, who was born in the first decade of this century and is still living. The oral tradition of history, plus the fact that I was born and raised in the oldest colonized area of Colorado, the San Luis Valley, helped to formulate the article on the lifestyle of yesteryear, although it was deficient in specific names and dates. I was aware that Olibama Tushar Lopez had done a history of the valley, and had focused on the customs, traditions, and folklore, but, again, material which dealt specifically with women and their issues was practically non-existent.[19]

My present research about the contemporary Chicana and her literature, which was also the topic of my Ph.D. thesis, encountered similar barriers. The only library I used is my personal one, my accumulated books, magazines and newspapers from my teaching in Chicano Studies. The poetry analyzed was compiled through personal interviews, telephone calls, correspondence, and travels. Since I put the material in a sociohistorical context, I dealt with Southwest Chicana writers primarily, so living in Minnesota made the gathering of materials difficult. Fortunately, there is a network of correspondence among Chicana writers and scholars.

Upon learning that the vacuum in written history exists, Chicana writers sometimes choose to create rather than to investigate. The writer, in her desire to catch up with other women writers, must produce in quantity, and the genres of poetry and essays lend themselves to that. Poetry is an art form economical in words and time; it is personal and gives a rapid catharsis of the emotions. The quest for identity brings about introspection, and this results in poetry as a means of communication with oneself and with the public. Moreover, poetry does not require the time of the longer forms of a drama or a novel. Perhaps that is why at this juncture the majority of Chicana writers prefer the essay or poetry in order to produce and to communicate.

It is necessary to have a historical consciousness to realize that all human efforts and products reflect a present which is itself a culmination of a certain past and which will in turn be a catalyst for future actions. Mircea Eliade, in *Cosmos and History: The Myth of the Eternal Return,* proposes that popular memory concerning historical facts endures about two hundred years before the facts get exaggerated and distorted into myth and legend. If that is the case, we must remember that 1848, the end of the Mexican-American War, is recent. In historical evolution, this means that the repercussions of that war are still reverberating; the wound is still healing. (The wound may be open and bleeding in Texas where the actual war took place.) The memory of that war, handed down through oral tradition and negative Anglo historians, is still fresh enough to remind Chicanos of the loss of their economic base (their land) and identity. The memory is sensitive to the conquered condition, sensitive because of the molding and perpetuation of the roles of superiority and inferiority vis à vis Anglos and Chicanos. WE ARE STILL LIVING IN THE POPULAR MEMORY OF THE HISTORICAL ANGLO-MEXICAN CONFLICTS OF 1848. That is why recording the histories of the older generations becomes so vital.

History is a continuum, and the contemporary Chicana is a sum total of all the historical actions that have preceded her. Even the Chicana who writes about herself and her emotions has a historical consciousness. She believes in art for people's sake, and not art for art's sake. The same could be said for feminist writers.

The Chicana belongs to all the oppressed groups of the United States, yet she seeks to communicate with all her oppressed counterparts. As Esther Ybarra-Kaw states, "Diversity within the Women's Movement need not mean disunity."[20]

Notes

1. It is usually at these institutions where methods of research are taught, and scholarship implies research. Only recently (the 1960s and 1970s) have Chicanos started attending the universities in any number. Chicanos, along with other Hispanics, and perhaps the Indians, have the lowest level of schooling in the United States. Another factor for the lack of Chicana scholars resides in the fact that scholarly activity implies leisure time and activity for the non-

university scholar. For faculty in the universities, research is a necessity, but here again, there are few Chicanos employed as faculty in the university systems.

2. One has only to consult Anglo historians on the Mexican-American War to learn that historians are not objective. One Chicano historian who analyzes the biases of Anglo historians is Rudolfo Acuña in his book *Occupied America* (San Francisco: Canfield Press, 1972).

3. The Colonials, or "Hispanos" as other Chicanos call them, are the Spanish surnamed Spanish people of northern New Mexico and southern Colorado. Up until the second World War, they had retained and preserved sixteenth-century traditions and dialect; Aurelio M. Espinosa's linguistic study of the 1930s suggests that this dialect will disappear with today's older generation. *Estudios sobre lel español de Nuevo Mejico* (Studies of New Mexican Spanish) (Buenos Aires: Instituto de Filologia, 1946).

4. Enriqueta Longauex y Vasquez, "The Mexican-American Woman," in *Sisterhood is Powerful*, ed. Robin Morgan (New York: Random House, 1970), pp. 379–84.

5. *Regeneración,* Los Angeles, Calif., Cómisión Feminil. Cómisión Feminil Mexicana Nacional was founded in November, 1972. It is located at 379 S. Lona Dr., Los Angeles, California, 90017. This Council has published *Regeneración* and *Encuentro femenil.*

6. Mirta Vidal, *Chicanas Speak Out* (New York: Pathfinder Press, 1971).

7. Sylvia A. Gonzales, *La Chicana piensa: The Social-Cultural Consciousness of a Mexican American Woman* (San Jose, Calif.: Mexican American Studies Dept., San Jose State University, 1974).

8. Dorinda Moreno, *La Mujer en Pie de Lucha* (San Francisco: Espina del Norte Publications, 1973). Moreno publishes *La razon Mestiza,* a Chicana newspaper, out of her office, Concilio Mujeres, 2588 Mission St., San Francisco, Calif. 94110. See also Moreno's publications (undated) *Colonization and the Mestiza: A Framework for Discrimination and the Chicana* and *Spanish-Speaking Women in the Media.*

9. Flor Saiz, *La Chicana: Preliminary Booklet* (Denver: n.p., 1973).

10. Marta Cotera, *The Chicana Feminist* (Austin, Tex.: Information Systems Development, 1977).

11. Marta Cotera, *Diosa y Hembra: History and Heritage of Chicanas in the United States* (Austin, Tex.: Information Systems Development, 1976).

12. Anna Nieto-Gomez, *New Directions in Education: Estudios femeniles de la Chicana* (Los Angeles: University Extension, University of California, 1974).

13. *La Cosecha* 3, no. 3 (1977).

14. Rosaura Sanchez, *Essays on La Mujer* (Los Angeles: Chicano Studies Center, University of California, 1977). The bibliographical publications from UCLA's Chicano Studies Center and Chicano Studies Library include R. Cabello-Argandoña, *The Chicana: A Comprehensive Bibliographic Study,* 3d ed. (UCLA CSC Bibliographic Research and Development Unit, 1976); Cristina Portillo, *Bibliography of Writings on La Mujer* (UCLA Chicano Studies

Library, 1976); *A Bibliography of References to Chicano/Raza Serials,* (UCLA CSL 1976); *A Comprehensive Listing of Chicano/Raza Serials* (UCLA CSL 1977); *A Listing of Dissertations Related to Chicanos* (UCLA CSL, 1977). Another helpful source is *HAPI: Hispanic American Periodical Index* (Los Angeles: UCLA Latin American Center Publications, 1975—).

15. Evey Chapa, *La Mujer Chicana: An Annotated Bibliography* (Austin: University of Texas Chicano Research and Learning Center, 1976). The Center is no longer in existence. Additional bibliographies include *Bibliography Relating Specifically to the Spanish-Speaking Woman* (San Francisco: Concilio de Mujeres, n.d., see n. 8); *Chicano Periodical Index: A Cumulated Index to Selected Periodicals, 1967–1978* and *1978–1981* (Boston: G. K. Hall, 1981 and 1983); Catherine Loeb, "La Chicana: A Bibliographic Survey," *Frontiers: A Journal of Women Studies* 5, no. 2 (Summer 1980): 59–74; *A Selected Bibliography of Works by Chicanas and Other Women Interested in Chicana Culture* (Monticello, Ill.: Vance Bibliographies, 1979); Arnulfo D. Trejo, *Bibliografía Chicana: A Guide to Information Sources* (Detroit: Gale Research, 1975); Francisco Garcia-Ayvens, *Quien sabe?: A Preliminary List of Chicano Reference Materials* (Los Angeles: Chicano Studies Research Center Publications, University of California, 1981); Barbara J. Robinson, *The Mexican American: A Critical Guide to Research Aids* (Greenwich, Conn.: JAI Press, 1980).

16. Nieto-Gomez, *New Directions.*

17. Lorca's trilogy of tragedies—*La Casa de Bernarda Alba, Bodas de Sangre,* and *Yerma*—is based on women's themes.

18. Marcela [Lucero] Trujillo, "The Spanish Surnamed Woman of Yesteryear," and "The Contemporary Chicana," in *Hispanic Colorado,* ed. Evelio Echevarria (Ft. Collins, Colo.: Centennial Press, 1976).

19. Olibama Tushar Lopez, "Pioneer Life in the San Luis Valley," *Colorado Magazine* 19, no. 5 (1942). More recent work includes Nan Elsasser, *Las Mujeres: Conversations From an Hispanic Community* (Old Westbury, N.Y.: Feminist Press, 1981); K. Lindborg, *Five Mexican-American Women in Transition: A Case Study of Migrants in the Midwest* (San Francisco: R & E Research Associates, 1977); M. B. Melville, *Twice a Minority: Mexican-American Women* (St. Louis: Mosby, 1980). Alfredo Mirande and Evangelina Enríquez, *La Chicana: The Mexican-American Woman* (Chicago: University of Chicago Press, 1980); and M. Mora, *Mexican Women in the United States: Struggles Past and Present* (Los Angeles, Chicano Research Center, University of California, 1980).

20. Esther Ybarra-Kaw, "Women: Taking Themselves Seriously," *The Minneapolis Tribune: Saturday Magazine,* Apr. 8, 1978.

Being a Feminist Academic:
What a Nice Feminist like Me Is Doing in a Place like This

Pauline B. Bart

When I was a little girl I wanted to be a cowgirl when I grew up. I listened to cowboy songs, had my parents buy me a skirt with leather fringes on it, and was an avid follower of Tom Mix and the Lone Ranger. Years later, as a sociologist, I learned that high-achieving women usually prefer male occupations in their early years—firefighter, police officer, doctor, and so forth. On the other hand, women who lead more traditional lives as adults played as children at being mothers and nurses. I recalled that neither category applied to me. When I became involved in women's studies, I realized that I had in fact followed the future that my early desire to be a cowgirl had presaged. I was engaged in a female variant of a male career.

I am a feminist sociologist, a scholar, not a "professional." I define myself in that manner, as both feminist and sociologist, because I attempt to use the tools of my discipline (such concepts as power, class, gender, ethnicity) as well as the methods of my discipline—notably interviewing—to demystify the world for women. The sociology of knowledge provides me with the analytic framework to make sense of what is happening to the world in general and to women in particular.

What I Study, Why I Study, and How I Study

I began by studying women as victims, the Portnoy's Mothers whose complaints landed them in mental hospitals.[1] Because the study

402

was completed in 1967, just before the women's movement started, people (i.e., men who had the power to hire) could not understand how anyone as "hip" as I was could study anything as uninteresting as women, much as Helena Lopata, studying housewives, was asked what that had to do with sociology. My study has important feminist implications because it is a cautionary tale telling what can happen to women who follow the traditional scripts. They are vulnerable to being left at middle age with existential depressions, feeling that their lives have been meaningless, and with no sense of self once they can no longer be full-time mothers and wives.

My next two major studies dealt with women who had transcended victimization: the members of an illegal feminist abortion collective, and women who had been attacked and avoided being raped. I will first talk about the former, called Jane or the Service. This group of laywomen, some of them Hyde Park housewives, learned to perform abortions, to assist at abortions, and to counsel women wanting abortions so that from 1969 to 1973 any woman at any stage of her pregnancy could get an abortion whether or not she had funds (the average fee was $50 to $75 but women who could not pay were not turned away). Eleven thousand abortions were performed from 1969 to 1973, no woman died, and the complication rate was roughly equal to that of New York when the state legalized abortion.[2] After Jane disbanded, following the Supreme Court decision to make abortion a matter between the woman and her physician, three of the women spoke to my seminar in women and health. They were spellbinding. I knew that this chapter in women's history had to be recorded, but at first these women did not want to become data. They considered it ironic for a group that was anti-professional and anti-academic to be interviewed by an academic. They also did not want to be portrayed as superwomen, since their ideology was that they were not different from other women. Since my women's movement credentials were suitable, however (I had "put energy" into feminist activities, my demeanor was not professional, and I did not have a grant—all sure proof of my not having been co-opted), they agreed to be interviewed and spread the word so that ultimately everyone contacted was interviewed. I wanted to learn from Jane how to make other feminist alternative institutions successful. (I did not know at this time that abortion rights would be so eroded that groups such as Jane might have to be reconstituted.) Indeed, because one of the papers I wrote about Jane had been widely circulated by the Boston

Women's Health Book Collective, a woman from New Zealand, where abortion had been made illegal, came to Chicago to learn from the women how to organize such a group in her area.[3]

My appointment is in a Department of Psychiatry in a medical school. I have been a lecturer at the University of California at Berkeley and a visiting professor at the University of California, Santa Barbara and Los Angeles, and at California State University, San Diego. But I have never had a regular appointment in a Department of Sociology. Because of this, in part, I have never been co-opted, and my outsider perspective has remained. If the Department of Sociology at Cal had had any sense, they would have given me an assistant professorship in an attempt to cool me out and dilute my feminist outsider politics (this pattern, called "find the chieftain" by anthropologists, characterized British imperialist ruling techniques). But I turned being at a medical school into an advantage: I decided to focus on issues of women and health because I was learning experientially what I had known intellectually: that doctors have enormous power, and that medical education and the pathways to it can result in a trained incapacity to deal with women as patients.

This lack of training was illustrated at my school for many years by the absence of a program for sensitizing emergency room staff, including the psychiatric resident who was routinely called in, to the proper treatment of women who had been sexually assaulted. Untrained physicians can compound the women's trauma, yet even though medical students requested such training as part of the required course in behavioral science and even though I offered to provide it, it was not included. Neither was there a program to detect battered women who came to the emergency room. In contrast, pediatric residents receive extensive training to detect battered children.

I am currently studying women who were attacked and avoided being raped. This research integrates the personal with the political—a fundamental principle of the women's movement—and both with the scholarly. It began in a very personal way with a telephone call at seven o'clock one morning in 1973 from a graduate student saying that she had been raped. I met her at the hospital and arranged for my roommate, a feminist therapist, to stay with her. Since she was enrolled in a seminar on women and health which met that afternoon, she met me outside the door just before the seminar and asked if it would be good for the class to hear about her experience. I said, "Yes," but added that the important issue was whether it would be good for *her*. She decided to share the story of her ordeal with the class and found that experience therapeutic.

Sometime after that I was asked to analyze the more than one thousand questionnaires which had been filled out by *Viva* readers who had been sexually assaulted;[4] in the process of writing up those data, I and other feminists were asked to attend a meeting to prepare a report to the state's attorney on how to improve services for raped women. We packed the meeting, which resulted in my chairing a subcommittee on hospital treatment of women who were raped, on which I included that graduate student, as well as other credentialed and non-credentialed movement women with concern and experience.[5]

I cared about the issue and knew the politics of rape analyses. I wished to challenge how research had traditionally been used to blame women—the women who were raped, the rapists' mothers, and the rapists' wives.[6] I knew where the blame for rape lay and it wasn't with the women.[7]

Now why did I decide to study women who avoided being raped? My first idea was to study a rape victim advocacy group in a hospital and examine the conflicts not only between the feminist advocates and the physicians but also among the advocates, the nurses, and the social workers who all were struggling over turf. I knew that there were respectable sociological theories that could account for this type of organizational behavior, but then I thought, "Why should I document the conflicts among women and feed into the patriarchal ideology that claims women cannot get along with each other"?[8] At that point I remembered that each time I spoke about rape, women would ask me what they should do when attacked. There was no data-based advice available, although police departments, feminists, and the notorious (in feminist circles) Frederick Storaska were giving women advice on how to behave under those circumstances.[9] In addition, I thought that study-ing rape avoidance and presenting women who had transcended vic-timization would have beneficial effects on the self-esteem of the women who read the research. I did not think this research could be used against women, although my current doubts have prompted me to take steps to prevent this. At any rate, after a long and painful process of revision and counter-revision, during which time I consistently slipped and referred to the proposal as my dissertation (because writing my dissertation was the last time I had felt so powerless about my work), I finally received a grant for what was at that point called "Avoiding Rape: A Study of Victims and Non-Victims."

I changed the language three times in labeling these women. I first called them "victims and non-victims" but after some time I realized that the term "non-victim" was inappropriate. It implied that all women could be described in terms of victimization. It further suggested that women who avoided being raped were *not* victims. In some sense they had transcended victimization, but, indeed, because someone had tried to assault them, they may have felt victimized. I decided to call them "avoiders." Then I learned that women who had been raped had participated in the Minneapolis Take Back the Night March wearing armbands which bore the term "Survivors." I also learned that a group at the Women's Building in Los Angeles called itself "Incest Survivors." In addition, a Chicago feminist who worked with women who had been raped told me she preferred the term "survivors" because it emphasized the positive aspects of the experience, i.e., the women's strengths in coping with the assult. Calling the woman a "survivor" rather than a "victim" might help her to internalize this more positive label and thus this change in terminology could function as a self-fulfilling prophecy. In light of this information I changed the terms to "survivors" and "avoiders." However, since that implies that the avoiders were not also survivors, in the last version the women are referred to as "raped women" and "avoiders." I may decide to make still further changes in my forthcoming book (e.g., "raped" and "not-raped" women).

To summarize, the idea for the research came from concerned women. I used my academic skills to conduct the research. The analysis and presentation of the research were influenced by feedback from women working on the problem in the "real world." In addition and reciprocally, some policy implications of the research were incorporated into the demands of the Take Back the Night Committee in Chicago, which met from June to September, 1980. The night of the Take Back the Night rally, I presented the strategies that seemed most clearly to differentiate women who had been raped from women who had avoided being raped. So the circle was closed: the idea came from women in the community and I presented the results to community women.

The Rape Papers

I can briefly summarize my findings as reported in a number of papers. In "Rape as a Paradigm of Sexism in Society," I note the endemic nature of violence against women which I found when interviewing raped women and rape avoiders and asking them about the prior violence in their lives.[10] Such violence takes various forms which I compare and contrast: rape by a known rapist, rape by a stranger, woman abuse, and incest. Individual and institutional responses to rape are discussed as manifestations of sexism, including the definition of rape, the ideology of the rapist as mentally ill, and the ideology of the imperative nature of male sexuality. The relevance of social class is addressed, since poor women cannot purchase the protection against street and other forms of stranger rape offered by taxis, private cars, and well-secured buildings. (It is not accidental that the rate of rape for black women is much higher than that for white women.)

As is by now well known, the institutional response to rape, that of the police, the courts, and the hospitals, frequently results in the woman feeling raped again. But it is not only these institutions that are guilty. The "helping professions" and criminology have also played a part in discrediting raped women, the former through an intrapsychic approach which frequently leads to blaming the victim and the latter through the use of the concept of "victim-precipitated rape" that also essentially blames the victim. This term refers to two differing definitions of the situation, with the male definition being legitimized. For example, a man and woman meet in a bar and have a drink together. The man thinks this behavior signals sexual availability while the woman thinks she is just being friendly. A man picks up a hitchiker and assumes that she is sexually available while she is simply looking for transportation. The institutional use of this term demonstrates a phallocentric approach to rape not only in the criminal justice system but also in allegedly scientific and objective criminology.

In my next paper, I examined the cases of thirteen women, each of whom, as adults, had been both raped and avoided being raped.[11] Such a study, analogous to identical-twin studies in that many background variables are held constant, made it possible to learn the impact of situational variables. The following factors were associated with rape avoidance: (1) attack by a stranger, (2) attack outside, (3) use of multiple strategies including screaming and physically struggling, and (4) the woman's primary concern with not being raped. The following factors were associated with being raped: (1) attack by a known assailant, particularly if they had had a current or prior sexual relationship with them, (2) attack inside, (3) use of only one strategy, usually talking (including pleading), and (4) the woman's primary concern with not being murdered or mutilated.

I then gave a case history of a woman who avoided being raped by two strangers in an alley and then was raped by her husband. She screamed and fought back in the alley, hitting one man in the head with a rock, kicking, and biting the other man's hand down to the bone. A police officer heard her screams, came by in a patrol car, and the assailants fled. Her husband insisted on having intercourse with her because she was his wife; she did not want to because he had told her he heard her scream and did not intervene. She reported: "He . . . tore my clothes off and me and him went round and round and he ended up doing it to me on the floor. You know he blacked my eye and everything. . . . he tore my clothes off me and slapped me and—I mean he did worse to me than the guy in the alley." He had, on this occasion, awakened her demanding sex because he said, "You're my wife and you belong to me." During their struggle he said, "Maybe you liked those guys the other night. Maybe you didn't tell me the truth, maybe." He knocked her down in the hall and there was nothing she could throw at him to defend herself, a strategy she had used successfully in the rape attempt. "I thought he would really hurt me that time. . . . I was really actually afraid of him that night."

She finally submitted to the rape "to get rid of him." She didn't have any plan to avoid the rape because "I always just thought your husband's not supposed to rape you . . . and if he does, what am I gonna do about it anyway? . . . What, are you gonna say 'My husband raped me'? People are gonna say you're crazy." When I asked her what she was doing and thinking during this time she said she was laughing hysterically because "first in my thought, you know, was . . . husbands can't really rape you, but I felt like he was raping me, you know what I mean." In response to her laughing hysterically, he became angrier and "he just got a weird look about 'im, like he could really kill ya. He grabbed me around the neck . . . cut my wind off." She continued telling how he had choked her several times when she was pregnant until she blacked out, and that made her angry because it could have hurt the baby. (The concern for the baby rather than herself is a response which logically flows from female socialization.)

When I submitted this paper for publication in a standard academic journal, albeit for a special issue on rape, the editors suggested that I substitute additional data for the case history, and I was asked how representative the case was. I was specifically asked how usual it was for a woman to be raped by her husband. I refused to remove the case study.

In "How to Say No to Storaska and Survive: Rape Avoidance Strategies," written with Patricia O'Brien, I took issue with Storaska, a popular speaker on rape avoidance whose book and film *How to Say No to a Rapist and Survive* are widely used by police departments and other institutions such as schools and hospitals.[12] He is notorious among feminist anti-rape activists and even among a few police departments for the following reasons:

1. His advice is not only undocumented (though he *claims* he has evidence that it is effective) but is wrong. For example, he suggests first cooperate with the rapist and then if the opportunity presents itself poke out his eyes. He says that women can't learn self-defense.

2. He demeans women by presenting them as cute little helpless creatures. It is precisely this traditional image of women that is related to the prevalence of rape in our society.

3. He makes huge fees from our bodies and our pain.

4. He claims certainty for his method.

In that article we used a convenience sample of 94 women 18 or over who had been attacked and avoided rape (n = 51) or who had been raped (n = 43) in the two years prior to the interview.[13] (This latter requirement was requested by the Center for the Prevention and Control of Rape Peer Review Committee so as to minimize distortion of past events.) Rather than use students, the traditional academic device when a non-random sample is difficult to obtain, I recruited women through public service announcements, ads and interviews in the media, flyers with tear-off sheets with a phone number to call (which I always carried and tacked up every place I could including, of course, women's bathrooms), and through networks of friends and acquaintances who publicized the study.

The interview had two major sections: situational and background. We asked the women to tell us what happened; we asked them additional questions about the assault *situation*. Then we asked them background questions about their childhood and adult socialization. When the data on childhood and adult socialization were analyzed, we found partial support for the feminist explanation of rape.

As put forward by Susan Griffin, Susan Brownmiller, and Diana Russell, among others, this analysis suggests that women are socialized to be rape victims rather than rape avoiders because women are taught that competent women, particularly women who can beat men at their own game, will lose their femininity and therefore their chance at love and marriage.[14] Thus, women so raised are set up to be rape victims. Indeed the women who avoided rape were less likely than were the raped women to give traditional responses on several dimensions. They were more likely to have said they wanted a career when they were asked what they thought their life would be like when they grew up and less likely than were the raped women to mention home and family. Their parents were less likely to have intervened when they fought physically with peers and siblings. They were more likely to be oldest daughters with major household responsibilities, a role that would reward competence and ability to deal with stress. They were more likely to know first aid and how to quell a broiler fire (but they were not more likely to know how to fix their cars). They were more likely to engage in regular physical exercise and to mention women in their personal lives as women whom they admired. They were more likely to know self-defense.

From the analysis of situational variables I found that avoiders were more likely to have used the following strategies: fleeing or trying to flee, physically struggling, and screaming. Women who were raped were more likely to plead, which one can assume reinforces the assailant's power trip. The most frequently used strategy, what we termed cognitive verbal, included talking, reasoning, flattering, conning. By itself it seldom worked and did not differentiate between the two groups. The women who avoided being raped would take advantage of environmental intervention. While sometimes this meant the police arrived, frequently the woman herself took advantage of the situation to escape, as when a siren caused the assailant to loosen his grip and the woman broke away and fled. Five women used no strategies (e.g., they were tied up, or they "froze"). All five were raped. So much for the advice that if you don't do anything he'll lose interest and leave, while

fighting will only excite him. The traditional advice on rape avoidance—to get him to see you as a human being, to use guile and wiles—
reinforces the traditional role of women just as traditional myths about
rape do.

Replicating the findings of the Queen's Bench Study, we found that
women who avoided being raped were more likely to use multiple
strategies.[15] The most common combination of strategies was screaming
and physical resistance. The modal number of strategies used was three
for avoiders vs. only one for raped women. (The mean number of
strategies was 2.53 for avoiders and 1.86 for raped women, a less
dramatic difference, however.) It appears that avoiders made a more
concerted effort to avoid rape using more active strategies, e.g., physical
resistance in contrast to pleading, than did women who were raped.
Why? Although we cannot answer the question of causality, we can
turn to some extremely provocative data on what each woman feared
most when attacked. Women who were most afraid of being murdered
or mutilated proved more likely to be raped, but women who were most
afraid of rape itself were more likely to be avoiders. Where fear of being
killed was the primary concern, the woman was more likely to comply:
often, such a woman would tell us that she hoped that by going along
with the rapist she would deter him from further and more horrible
violence. In the second pattern, the woman feared and/or was angered
by the idea of rape. Her mind filled with the determination not to be
raped and she tended not to perceive herself to be in imminent danger of
death or dismemberment. Under these circumstances, she seemed likely
to put up a more vigorous as well as successful defense. Statistically, 51
percent of the avoiders named fear of rape and/or determination not to
be raped as their main thought, while only seven percent of the raped
women reported this as their main concern. Conversely, 65 percent of
the raped women were primarily concerned with fear of death or mutilation in contrast to 37 percent of the avoiders.

These findings do not jibe with the pervasive folk wisdom that a
woman who puts up a fight merely contributes to the rapist's arousal
and sexual aggression without enhancing her advantage. Considering
that our sample included only five women who had been severely
beaten, the relatively high percentage of women who feared extreme
violence deserves further exploration. In my view these folk beliefs are
reinforced, and may indeed be caused, by media coverage of rape. This

coverage is such that one may infer not only that most rapes involve grisly violence, but also that once a woman is attacked, her chances of successfully avoiding being raped are very remote. Thus Linda Heath and her colleagues found that newspapers report (often sensationally) thirteen completed rapes for every one attempted rape.[16]

This thirteen to one ratio is very different from the findings of two major studies that explicitly collected data on the incidence of attempted vs. completed rapes. First, the Law Enforcement Assistance Administration (LEAA) "victimization" study that asked random samples of people about their experiences as crime victims found three attempts for one completed rape.[17] Second, even the Uniform Crime Reports, based only on crimes reported to the police, showed a ratio of three rapes per each reported attempt. Obviously, as many others have noted, *attempted* crimes are considerably underreported in these official statistics. In short, the newspaper differential reportage of completed and attempted rapes clearly distorts the underlying patterns. The reasons are not hard to fathom.

Journalist interns are told: "Look for sex and gore: bad news, good story; good news, bad story." It is clear that a woman breaking away from a rapist and fleeing is a "bad story" compared with a woman bloodily beaten, maimed, and raped. Heath and her colleagues suggest that since murders are more newsworthy than rapes, the possibility is exacerbated that "the media will present only accounts of rape which will grab the readers' interests."[18] By these criteria, the underreporting of both attempted rapes and rapes by men known to the women makes good journalistic sense—and heightens women's fears that an attempted rape is likely to be also an attempted mutilation and/or murder. A woman's perception that few women are able to avoid rape once attacked is similarly strengthened by such patterns of coverage. That *any* women avoid rape in the face of such propaganda testifies to their courage and ingenuity, and the LEAA estimate that women *do* manage to avoid rape by a ratio of three to one indicates the extent of such female determination.

The last paper, "There Ought to be a Law," was written with Kim Scheppele and addresses two questions:[19] What is the relationship between a woman's self-perception, the acts that occurred, and the legal definition of what occurred? Is the low rate of conviction for rape a result of women bringing capricious charges, which have no legal grounding? We found that almost all the women who said they were raped *were* either victims of rape or of deviate sexual assault under Illinois statutes. (One exception was a woman raped by her husband; this is not illegal under Illinois law.) Women's self-perceptions of having been raped or having avoided rape revealed that women defined rape to include penile-vaginal penetration, fellatio, and sodomy. Digital penetration, cunnilingus, fondling, and kissing were considered rape avoidance. Thus from the woman's perspective, rape is what is done *with* a penis, not what is done *to* a vagina. While cunnilingus is defined as deviate sexual assault (as are sodomy and fellatio), and classified as a felony, digital penetration is considered battery, which is only a misdemeanor. Because penetration digitally or with an object (also considered merely battery) is more serious than the usual events classified in that manner, we proposed a new law against a felony called sexual battery. (Illinois, like some other states, has since changed its sexual assault law to include non-penile penetration.)

Almost all the women who said they were raped met the legal definition of rape under Illinois law. Only two of the women whose self-definition was rape had no legal claim (no statutes were violated). Neither of these two cases was reported to the police. We concluded that the low rate of conviction for rapists reflects other factors which we believe are sexist in nature.

Feminism and Research Conceptualization, Methodology and Presentation

In structuring these studies and interpreting the findings, I made a number of feminist and political decisions:

1. I decided to use the *woman's* self-perception about having been raped or having avoided rape rather than the researcher's evaluation or the legal definition or some arbitrary guideline. I believe that women's constructions of reality have been systematically invalidated, particularly in issues of sexuality and in issues of violence. As a feminist researcher I did not want to continue in that patriarchal tradition. I consider the woman the best judge of what she experienced.

2. I decided to examine the background variables as well as the situational variables. I conceptualized the outcome (rape or rape avoid-

ance) to be a result of both background and situational variables. By including background variables I could test the feminist hypothesis that, in terms of their habits, their attitudes, their self-presentation, and their behavior, traditionally socialized females are set up to be rape victims rather than rape avoiders. "Appropriate" feminine conduct includes vulnerability and the belief that men are necessary and will protect women.

3. I decided to include newspaper treatment of sexual assault in the section on factors associated with rape and rape avoidance. Originally I thought that studying rape avoidance could have no untoward political effects; that is, the results could not be used against women. However, when one of the emergent findings was that women who were raped were primarily concerned with not being killed while women who avoided being raped were primarily concerned with not being raped, I could visualize headlines reading, "Raped women didn't care about being raped." Thus immediately after presenting the finding I included a section on why women are concerned with being murdered, and pointed out that the press coverage of rape and lack of coverage of rape avoidance would logically lead women to that conclusion. Therefore it would be more difficult to take the finding out of context than if I were to follow the more conventional paradigm and place the interpretation in a separate section from the findings.

4. I chose particular cases as examples. I most frequently use the case presented above of the woman who avoided being raped by two men in an alley yet was raped by her husband. I use it because the question of whether husbands can rape wives is the most controversial legal issue remaining in the struggle against rape. (Try to discuss it with a male and you will see.) In this case the husband's view of his wife as property, his sense of entitlement, and his physical brutality which forced her surrender are so clear that it would be very difficult even for a skeptic to call the behavior anything but rape. Another case I frequently use is that of a woman we call "the Queen of the Negotiators," who avoided rape even though she was attacked by an armed man while she was asleep, the most difficult situation for avoidance. That through her ingenuity and courage she was able to negotiate and fight her way out of the situation emphasizes the bravery and survival ability women have. Another woman stopped her rape by yanking her assailant's penis. When I read these cases to the audience at the Chicago Take Back the Night Rally, they cheered.

Inadequacies of the Standard Research Paradigm

The original interview schedule for the study was derived from standard criminological works on sexual assault. Thus we had questions which would enable us to gather detailed information on each member of a gang in gang rapes, which were infrequent in our study, but nothing in that literature prepared us for the general violence endemic to women's lives. The standard paradigm proved inadequate. Questions on incest, child molestation, and woman battering had to be added as well as a more detailed question on prior rapes and avoidances. Fortunately, since the research was exploratory and the interview unstructured, with complete freedom for the woman to talk about anything she wanted for as long as she wanted, we were quickly made aware of these lacunae and added the questions.

What proved even more interesting than the inadequacy of the standard model to get at the fabric of women's lives was the inevitable male reaction to my research presentations. As I spoke of the amount of violence in women's lives, I became increasingly careful to describe it as *endemic* and not a characteristic of the women in the sample "choosing victimization" or being "prone to victimization." (This is not to say that previous violence may not damage women's self-esteem and discourage their resisting further violence.) In each audience, at least one man (it never has been a woman) asked me if I were saying that these women were prone to victimization. Such experiences make it clear to me that in order to explore and present the female experience it is not enough simply to have female researchers. We must create our own tradition and present our own data and judge the work by our own standards.

Concluding Words

I designed a T-shirt which says "Everything is data." The next line says "But data isn't everything." It is true that the women whom I interviewed were data; it was, however, always very clear to me that first of all they were women. (Note that I refer to them as "women" and not as "subjects" in this paper.) Thus, when there was a conflict between my need to obtain information and their need to withhold it, I tried not to push.

I first faced this problem with the depressed middle-aged women I interviewed for my first study. They were not comfortable talking about sexuality. Their discomfort was demonstrated by their failure to respond to the sexuality card in a projective test made up of cards showing different stages and activities in a woman's life. So I did not insist they answer questions about sex. I also let the women infantalize me, or, as a member of the seminar on depression I attended at Yale suggested, I allowed them to treat me like the child they lost. Thus I answered their questions about my personal life, and when they learned I was divorced, I allowed them to give me advice on remarrying ("He should love the children") and force feed me, since some decided I was too thin and ignored my protests that I was on a diet.

I did not distance myself from them or from the women in the rape study. When one of the women cried I cried; she reminded me of my grandmother. This lack of distance caused psychic pain as I felt the sorrow of the depressed and sexually-assaulted women. Their stories entered my soul. After listening to and reading and analyzing the transcripts of the ninety-four women who were raped and nearly raped I am not the same person I was before. When issues of sexual assault come up and people trivialize them I respond with anger, though I don't know if this is because my threshold is too low or other people's is too high. Thus, when an administrator of a school where a woman had been raped said it wasn't rape because there was no sperm and besides she wasn't really hurt, I said publicly that he was either a fool or a liar or both. (Under Illinois law rape is defined by penetration, not ejaculation, and the person making the statement was a criminologist who should have known better.)

My method of data collection has proven effective in obtaining the information I want and is also therapeutic for the women interviewed, according to their evaluations. It is not usual in our society for people to be listened to carefully for as long as they want and to have the listener validate their world view.

As part of the women's movement, working in the women's community not only helps me choose topics to research but gives me useful feedback on my work. Women working in "the real world" are dealing with issues I am studying so we can have a mutually beneficial relationship which would not be possible were I simply to work in the academic community or, conversely, to leave the academic world for the "real world." It is unfortunate for both worlds that there is so little communication between them. In this paper I have tried to show how I integrate the two worlds so that we will not only have a sociology of women, we will also have a sociology by women and for women. That is what a nice feminist like me is doing in a place like this.

Notes

1. Pauline B. Bart, "Depression in Middle Aged Women: Some Sociocultural Factors" (UCLA 1967); University Microfilms, no. 68-7452, *Dissertation Abstracts*, 28, 4752-B, 1968.

2. For a fuller discussion, see Pauline B. Bart and Melinda Bart Schlesinger, "Collective Work and Self-Identity: The Effect of Working in a Feminist Illegal Abortion Collective," in *Workplace Democracy and Social Change*, ed. Frank Lindenfeld and Joyce Rothschild-Whitt (Boston: Porter Sargent, 1982); Pauline B. Bart, "Seizing the Means of Reproduction: A Feminist Illegal Abortion Collective, How and Why It Worked," in *Women's Health and Reproduction*, ed. Helen Roberts (London: Routledge and Kegan Paul, 1980), pp. 109–28.

3. Bart, "Seizing the Means."

4. Pauline B. Bart, "Rape Doesn't End With a Kiss," *Viva* 11 (June 1975): 39–41, 100–101.

5. Citizens Advisory Committee on Rape, *Report* (Advisory to Illinois State's Attorney Carey, 1975, unpublished).

6. Rochelle Semmel Albin, "Psychological Studies of Rape," *Signs* 3 (Winter 1977): 423–36.

7. J. Marolla and Diana Scully, "Rape and Psychiatric Vocabularies of Motive," in *Gender and Disordered Behavior: Sex Differences in Psychopathology*, ed. Edith S. Gomberg and Violet Franks (New York: Bruner/Mazel, 1979).

8. Pauline B. Bart and Anne Seiden, "Is Sisterhood Powerful?" *New Family/Old Family*, ed. Nona Malbin Glazer (New York: Van Nostrand, 1975).

9. Frederick Storaska, *How to Say No to a Rapist and Survive* (New York: Random House, 1975).

10. Pauline B. Bart, "Rape as a Paradigm of Sexism in Society," *Women's Studies International Quarterly* 2, no. 3 (1979): 347–57. The entire study is currently in press: Pauline B. Bart and Patricia O'Brien, *Stopping Rape: Successful Survival Strategies* (Elmsford, N.Y.: Pergamon Press, 1985).

11. Pauline B. Bart, "A Study of Women Who Were Both Raped and Avoided Rape," *Journal of Social Issues* 37 (1981): 123–37.

12. Pauline B. Bart and Patricia O'Brien, "How to Say No to Storaska and Survive: Rape Avoidance Strategies," paper presented at the annual meeting of the American Sociological Association, New York, 1980, and published as "Stopping Rape: Effective Avoidance Strategies," *Signs* 10 (1984): 83–101.

13. American Sociological Association, New York, 1980. A convenience

sample is a non-random sample obtained by any one of a number of methods, or by more than one method.

14. Susan Brownmiller, *Against Our Will: Men, Women, and Rape* (New York: Simon and Schuster, 1975); Diana E. H. Russell, *The Politics of Rape* (New York: Stein and Day, 1975); Susan Griffin, "Rape—the All American Crime," *Ramparts* (Sept. 1971), pp. 26–35.

15. Queen's Bench Foundation, *Rape Prevention and Resistance* (San Francisco, 1976).

16. Linda Heath, Margaret T. Gordon, Stephanie Riger, and Robert LeBailly, "What Newspapers Tell Us (and Don't Tell Us) About Rape," paper presented at the meeting of the American Psychological Association, New York, 1979.

17. Joan McDermott, *Rape Victimization in 26 American Cities* (Washington, D.C.: U.S. Department of Justice, Law Enforcement Assistance Administration, U.S. Government Printing Office, 1977).

18. Heath, et al., "What Newspapers Tell Us."

19. Pauline B. Bart and Kim Lane Scheppele, "There Ought to Be a Law: Women's Definitions and Legal Definitions of Sexual Assault," paper presented at the annual meeting of the American Sociological Association, New York, 1980, and published as "Through Women's Eyes: Defining Danger in the Wake of Sexual Assault," *Journal of Social Issues* 39, no. 2 (1983): 63–80.

7

Minerva, goddess of wisdom and the arts, stands in the hall at the top of the stairs in Rush Rhees Library, University of Rochester, across from her sister statue Industry. Designed for the River Campus by architect Philipp Merz, the two statues date from 1930. Photograph by Chris T. Quillen, courtesy of the University of Rochester Office of University Public Relations.

Section 7. On Resources

This section is concerned largely with the resources of the library, where certain principles have an impact on the storage and retrieval of materials for feminist scholarship. The issue of separatism versus integration, for example, bears directly on library research. When women and their concerns are given separate definition, it becomes easier to study them; in a room of one's own, one knows where to look. The categories used in the card catalog often constitute a problem for women; the ease with which one can carry out scholarship has to do with what has been named. Another issue is whether or not the user of resources is considered important: one effect of the women's movement is to give women as a user-constituency special importance, with identified research needs. In many cases, feminist librarians work closely with feminist scholars to search out sources for scholarly work. This sense of a shared enterprise is perhaps what the isolated scholar most lacks. One notion is that computer networks may help link feminist scholars, especially those otherwise isolated.

The resources needed for women's studies and feminist scholarship pose special problems of identification, classification, and retrieval. Dealing with some of these problms, Beth Stafford has published elsewhere an evaluation of bibliographies to identify and compare those most useful for general libraries and for researchers.[1] In this section, Cain, Hammell, and Pastine guide the scholar through the vast array of subjects and publications of the women's movement, pointing particularly to methods of searching in nontraditional and multidisciplinary sources; their overview suggests some principles that contribute to successful research efforts in women's studies.

Note

1. "Getting Started in Women's Studies: Some Basic Bibliographies," *Reference Services Review* 8, no. 3 (1980): 61–67.

Library Research in Women's Studies

Melissa McComb Cain, Kathryn A. Hammell, and
Maureen Pastine

In 1970 only a small number of women's studies courses were offered in American colleges and universities. Since then, this field of scholarship has rapidly grown to include over 4,000 courses and over 400 women's studies programs.[1] In addition, hundreds of faculty members in economics, history, literature, psychology, sociology, and other academic disciplines are revising their course curricula to offer a more comprehensive view of women's role in society and in particular fields of knowledge. Thus it is crucial for libraries to respond to the increased demand for research resources and services in feminist studies; both intensive collection development and active library instruction programs are needed to gather and make available materials on, by, and about women. This is not a simple task; past omissions in library reference resources, selection policies, and the organizing, classifying, and cataloging of library materials have created problems that must be resolved. But the matter of research in feminist studies is greater than library practices. Women's studies research raises some theoretical questions about knowledge—how, where, and by whom it is acquired, stored, legitimated, and shared. In describing library research in women's studies we hope to provide both theoretical and practical guidance for the feminist scholar.

Special Problems in Women's Studies Research

Because women's studies is a relatively new discipline, the number of reference books devoted to it exclusively is limited. Many are excellent, but some are hastily prepared publications with unfortunate omis-

423

sions, out-of-date information, and duplication of existing information. Thus the scholar must rely heavily on the reference sources available in other disciplines as well as those specifically designed for women's studies. The multidisciplinary nature of women's studies requires the librarian and the researcher to know and understand the organization and research possibilities as well as the limitations of an extensive range of reference materials. Because information exists in widely scattered sources, the librarian's role is vital. In summary, research in women's studies is a problematic and time-consuming endeavor and library users should ask for the guidance of a librarian.

A major difficulty in locating and acquiring women's studies resources is the lack of suitable guides to the literature. Several guides do exist but none is comprehensive. Recent bibliographical guides which promise to be of inestimable help are Jane Williamson's *New Feminist Scholarship: A Guide to Bibliographies* and Esther Stineman and Catherine Loeb's *Women's Studies: A Recommended Core Bibliography*. Williamson's book grew out of an independent study project that was begun in 1974 while she was a library science graduate student. At that time her publication *New Feminist Scholarship* included 73 bibliographies; by 1979 it included 391. Williamson demonstrates the maturity of feminist research and programs of study by offering an historical survey of bibliographies of bibliographies beginning in 1971 with the mimeographed, stapled sheets KNOW Press made available free of charge entitled the *List of Bibliographies on Women and Feminism*. She continues through the Winter 1977 issue of *Signs* in which Patricia Ballou published a comprehensive and acclaimed essay discussing sixty bibliographies and listing an additional sixty-two. Of the total 391 entries that Williamson presents, 215 are annotated. All entries are arranged by subject into thirty sections.[2]

Stineman and Loeb's intent differs from Williamson's in that they present, in considerable detail, a recommended core collection of book and journal titles that should be available in libraries responsible for supporting undergraduate women's studies curricula. All items listed in the twenty-six sections are deemed by the authors essential to the library collection, and both descriptive and evaluative annotations are included which compare and contrast similar works. *Women's Studies: A Recommended Core Bibliography,* based upon the University of Wisconsin's library holdings, should be a standard consulting tool for all academic and public librarians as well as others involved in the task of building and improving a women's studies library collection. The principal emphasis is on 1970s imprints and on in-print materials produced by commercial and university presses.

Another reason for the success or failure of a research effort is the library user's ability to access information in the card catalog, indexes, and abstracts by subject. Discriminatory subject headings are frequently found in indexing tools. To combat such problems, in 1974 the Council on Library Resources funded a project resulting in the compilation of the thesaurus *On Equal Terms*.[3] This thesaurus promotes change in antiquated and biased subject headings and allows for more effective identification of feminist study resources. Recommendations for future cataloging and indexing include the changing of such terms as WORKING WIVES to MARRIED WOMEN, EMPLOYMENT; MAMMIES to SLAVERY IN THE UNITED STATES—TREATMENT OF WOMEN HOUSEHOLD SLAVES; and SPINSTERS to SINGLE WOMEN. Such modification of subject headings is usually not retrospective so noting both "old" and "new" subject headings is suggested while conducting the literature search. In addition, standardized subject terminology (through the Library of Congress or Sears subject headings) is not always adopted by indexing and abstracting services; they frequently select their own subject terms to index articles in magazines, journals, newspapers, etc. This practice necessitates the compilation of lists of subject headings for each commercially produced index or abstract if a thorough search is to be undertaken. In a retrospective search, the scholar should be aware that more information on a woman may be found under her husband's name or family surname than under her own.

Another obstacle to women's studies research is that standard bibliographical sources for major American historical figures emphasize men rather than both women and men. For example, less than one-half of one percent of biographies in the *Dictionary of American Biography* are of women. The best scholarly biographical reference work focusing on women is the three-volume set *Notable American Women: 1607–1950* and the supplement *Notable American Women: The Modern Period*, extending coverage to women who died between 1951 and 1975. All pieces are insightful and well written by more than 700 historians, scientists, journalists, novelists, and literary critics.[4]

The Reference Collection (Including Bibliographies)

Reference collections include almanacs, collective biographies, dictionaries, directories, encyclopedias, guides, handbooks, statistical sources, yearbooks, and bibliographies. It is the responsibility of the reference librarian to introduce the researcher to appropriate volumes and relevant levels of information, suggest research strategy, and make the scholar aware of new reference tools that may be of use. Such works as the *Women's Rights Almanac,* the *Women's Organizations and Leaders Directory, Womanlist, Contributions of Black Women to America,* and *The Nature of Woman: An Encyclopedia Guide to the Literature* provide a starting point for serious study. In addition, reference works can be tremendous time-saving devices. For example, the compilation *Anthologies By and About Women: An Analytical Index* is an outstanding guide identifying and locating fugitive works of literature contained in collections of poetry, drama, essays and short stories, especially pieces by and about Black women and lesbians.[5]

Bibliographies provide the backbone for research and facilitate the scholar's awareness of the scope of writing and research in a specific subject area. Use of bibliographies is essential in the initial stages of research, and fortunately the last five years have seen a proliferation in the publishing of women's studies bibliographies. In addition to Stineman's, Loeb's, and Williamson's work already cited, two other publications, *Women: A Bibliography of Bibliographies* by Patricia Ballou and *Women's Studies: A Checklist of Bibliographies* by Maureen Ritchie, offer increased control and organization to the quickly multiplying area of feminist scholarship. Of special note are those sections in Ballou's bibliography covering ethnic and racial groups as well as geographic subjects. *Woman in America: A Guide to Information Sources* and *Guide to Social Science Resources in Women's Studies* are two helpful handbooks novice researchers should consult. Barbara Haber's paperback book *Women in America: A Guide to Books, 1963–1975, with an Appendix on Books Published 1976–1979* is a remarkable reference source which annotates and discusses 650 books relating to topics such as abortion, Black women, Native American women, health, rape, sexuality, and work. The publication begins with Betty Friedan's *The Feminine Mystique* and supplies the reader with a wealth of knowledge on the literature of American women.[6]

Even with this increase in published bibliographies, lesser coverage still remains in certain areas, such as of minority women; however, recent publications on ethnic women have begun to augment collections. *The Progress of Afro-American Women: A Selected Bibliography and Resource Guide, Black Lesbians: An Annotated Bibliography,* and *Resource Guide of American Indian-Alaska Native Women* exemplify this trend. Gail Schlachter's *Minorities and Women: A Guide to Reference Literature in the Social Sciences* is useful though a second edition is needed to bring it up to date.[7] G. K. Hall, Garland Publishing, Greenwood Press, ABC/CLIO, and Scarecrow Press have made commendable efforts to furnish bibliographies with access to both well-known and obscure works by and about women of color, women in antiquity, film, literature, music, politics, or theater. Such book-length publications are welcome, for in the past bibliographies were usually compiled by an individual and published in limited numbers on mimeo or offset presses, making them difficult, if not impossible, to obtain.

Finally, Andrea Hinding's two-volume *Women's History Sources: A Guide to Archives and Manuscript Collections in the United States*[8] is an excellent directory to approximately 18,000 obscure collections and repositories of primary source material. It represents the labor of 2,000 historians and librarians over seven years and emphasizes letters, diaries, personal papers, and manuscripts found in historical societies and libraries.

The best reference works published in a given year are identified in the May issue of the American Library Association's reviewing journal *Choice;* the list of "Outstanding Academic Books" names superior publications reviewed for the previous year. Each month, *Choice* lists new and significant books in a variety of academic disciplines. The *American Reference Books Annual* (ARBA), now in its thirteenth volume, is a comprehensive reviewing service for reference books and provides reviews of all reference books published in the United States during a single year. ARBA now devotes a section to women's studies.[9]

Special Collections

Major library research and special collections on women exist throughout the world. Researchers can find detailed information about content and location in *Biblioteca Femina: A Herstory of Book Collections Concerning Women; With Reference to Women: An Annotated Bibliography of Reference Materials on Women in the Northwestern*

University Library; and *BiblioFem: The Joint Library Catalogues of the Fawcett Library and the Equal Opportunities Commission Together with a Continuing Bibliography on Women.*[10]

The publisher G. K. Hall has made significant contributions to women's studies scholarship by making available catalogs of special collections such as the *Arthur and Elizabeth Schlesinger Library on the History of Women in America* from Radcliffe College's famous repository and *The Manuscript, Subject, and Author Catalogs of the Sophia Smith Collection* from the Women's History Archive at Smith College in Northampton, Massachusetts. Catalogs such as these are fundamental to research and should be consulted for citations to numerous titles which may be borrowed through interlibrary loan agreements. The catalogs are partly responsible for the phenomenal increase in the use of such great collections as the Schlesinger Library, where research visits have mushroomed from 247 in 1970 to more than 4,000 in 1980. (The library's acquisitions are growing to meet the demand—in 1968 the library had only 8,000 volumes but by 1980 20,000 volumes.)[11]

Other notable collections on women include the Fawcett Library (Britain's largest historical collection, with an emphasis on women's rights); the Special Collections Department at Northwestern University Library which houses over 800 cataloged periodicals focusing on women's issues and a substantial number of foreign language items; the Women's Collection at the University of North Carolina at Greensboro; the Galatea Collection on the History of Women in the Boston Public Library; the Cornell University Collection of Women's Rights Pamphlets; the Gerritsen Collection of Women's History at the University of Kansas; the Library of Congress; and the International Archief voor de Vrouwenbeweging in Amsterdam. A number of these special collections, or portions of the collections, are available in microformat to other libraries so the researcher should check to see if any of this material is on hand locally. Ritchie's bibliography (referred to earlier) lists thirty-two special library collections on women.

General Book Collections in Libraries

The circulating collection differs from the reference collection in being often less factual and more discursive in nature. An adequate lending collection in women's studies should include sufficient books in the following categories:[12]

Biographies of Women
(Including women as significant historical and cultural figures)

Economics and Women
(Including Consumerism, Domestic Employment, Employment Factors, and Women in the Labor Force)

Feminist Philosophy and Theory[13]

Psychology and Physiology of Women
(Including Assertion, Biocultural Conflicts and Behavior, Women and Sports, Fear of Success, Health and Hygiene, Lesbianism, Psychology of Sex Differences, and Self-Help and Therapy)

Sociology of Women
(Including Aging, Criminology, Demography, Family Life, Marriage or Alternatives to Marriage, and Role Theory)

Women and History
(Including Women in Society, Women's Movements—specifically, Suffragists and Women's Liberation, and Women's Rights)

Women and Politics
(Including Pressure Groups and Lobbying, Voting, Women and Political Parties, and Women as Politicians)

Women and the Law
(Including Abortion Laws, Equal Rights, Laws of Employment, Prostitution, and Sex Discrimination)

Women in Literature, Language, and the Arts
(Including Collections of Artistic and Literary Work by Women, Literary Criticism of Feminist Writing, Linguistic Studies and Sex Differences in Language, and Representation of Women in Literature, Music, and Art)

Women's studies book materials originate from both well-established mainstream publishing houses and informal small feminist presses. The mainstream publishers are responsible for the majority of books in most libraries' circulating collections. Currently the greatest percentage of books published are popular in scope and recreational in nature, with unprecedented numbers of works of fiction and poetry by women writers. Major scholarly works have been available through the university presses, but increasingly the mainstream publishing houses are introducing such works to the library market.

The reprint publishers' market is primarily an academic one and college and university libraries with serious collections in women's studies will provide Arno Press's respected series *American Women: Images and Realities, Women in America from Colonial Times to the 20th Century,* and *Homosexuality: Lesbians and Gay Men in Society, History, and Literature.*[14]

Publications in the field of women's studies are now so abundant (with many new titles published daily) that the librarian's dilemma is selecting titles which are individually suitable for a particular library's collection and clientele. Because of the tremendous demands required in keeping a collection current, retrospective collection development (severely needed in most libraries) usually suffers unless a staff member with expertise is assigned to work in this area; reprint, secondhand, and out-of-print catalogs must be promptly searched and frequently the library will have to advertise for individual titles.

In addition to the large, well-known publishers, the small feminist presses publish works that are true expressions of alternative perspectives. Often available only locally or regionally, these publications go largely unnoticed because of limited advertising, limited commercial indexing, and small press runs. Indexes designed to locate these items are the *International Directory of Little Magazines and Small Presses* and *Small Press Record of Books in Print.* Many women's journals receive, note, and review small press publications as does the *Small Press Review.*[15] Small press bibliographies should be considered as serious information sources and feminist publishers such as KNOW, Inc. (P.O. Box 86031, Pittsburgh, Pa. 15221) and The Feminist Press (Box 334, Old Westbury, N.Y. 11568) offer items of interest.[16] The value of these more restricted publications is inestimable when one realizes how conservative and incomplete works from better-known publishers have been.

Periodical Literature

Periodicals (journals, magazines, newspapers, indexes, and abstracts) are generally the best sources for gathering current information on women and can be used for retrospective study as well. Both the *Union List of Serials* and *New Serial Titles* are sources which give the historical development of journals and indicate in which U.S. libraries a particular title may be found.[17]

The number of feminist scholarship journals now available has increased dramatically over the last decade. The growth has been so staggering that in 1974 the Women's History Research Center at Berkeley was forced to admit the impossibility of creating and maintaining a comprehensive collection of women's journals. Because journals are costly, sporadic, and sometimes difficult to obtain and catalog, they are scattered throughout the major research libraries; use of interlibrary loan services is critical if the scholar is to have access to a wide range of articles. Feminist periodicals are of great importance for they present honest dialogue and alternative viewpoints without sensationalization. This is in contrast to popular trade journals, many of which have a history of inaccurate summaries and detrimental abridgement of feminist viewpoints.

By scope and content, feminist journals encompass such topics as cultural change, literature and the arts, health, political, legal, and financial status, and the educational discipline of women's studies. Periodicals that examine cultural change document trends in societal familial relationships, sex, and occupational roles, the growth of feminist consciousness, and so on. Scholarly journals include *Sex Roles: A Journal of Research* and *Signs: Journal of Women in Culture and Society;* *Signs's* strongly multidisciplinary emphasis makes it a major research source for feminist scholars in most fields. *Ms.,* a popular magazine, is a monthly forum where the larger community of women examine and share changes in their lives.[18]

Poetry, short stories, essays, and literary criticism are featured in the feminist literary magazines. *Motheroot Journal: A Women's Review of Small Presses* is an invaluable information and selection tool; *Room of One's Own: A Feminist Journal of Literature and Criticism* reviews women's writing; and *Women and Literature* includes criticism of women writers. Periodicals which encourage and record the lesbian voice include *The Ladder, Sinister Wisdom,* and *Conditions: A Magazine of Writing by Women, With an Emphasis on Writing by Lesbians.* Periodicals which express women's concerns within a regional context include *Bread and Roses* and *Feminary: A Feminist Journal for the South Emphasizing the Lesbian Vision.* Journals which explore women's contributions and participation in art, music, and film—often the first introduction for new women artists—are gaining prominence.

Camera Obscura: A Journal of Feminism and Film Theory and *Women's Art Journal* are two such titles. *Moving Out: Feminist Literary and Arts Journal* was one of the first feminist art magazines, starting publication in 1971.[19]

Women's periodicals which investigate health-related issues such as health care delivery for women, self-help, feminist therapy, and preventive medicine reflect growing interest and concern with the subject. The *Health-Pack Bulletin* and the *National Women's Health Network Newsletter* are important radical sources of health statistics.[20]

Periodicals that monitor women's political, legal, and financial status chronicle lobbying efforts, voting records, salary levels, legal status, legal rights, legislation, and levels of political participation. These publications appear frequently and often are prepared by government-related or independent political groups. The *Spokeswoman,*[21] a monthly Women's News Service publication, digests the latest in legislation and legal action affecting employment, abortion, health, and education.

Many professional organizations have sections or divisions which publish newsletters specifically designed to address occupational topics. These often include job lists for women, a partial answer to the traditional "old boy" referral system.

Journals that discuss the discipline of women's studies are the best sources of information on degree programs, curricula (including course design and syllabi), faculty, teaching departments, and surveys of research completed or in progress. *Connexions: An International Women's Quarterly, Frontiers: A Journal of Women's Studies, Resources for Feminist Research,* and *Women's Studies International Forum* are representative titles.[22]

Access to women's periodicals is often provided by specialized indexes because coverage in standardized tools is random and incomplete. The quarterly *Feminist Periodicals: A Current Listing of Contents,* published at the University of Wisconsin since 1981, reprints the tables of contents from over 30 major feminist journals with the bibliographic history of each title. *Current Contents,* published monthly, reproduces in a reduced format content pages from over 1,300 recent journals in arts and humanities, applied sciences, and social sciences. An author index and address directory enable the reader to write for reprints. The annual *Index Directory to Media Report to Women* conscientiously tries to identify feminist publications by publishing a directory to women's periodicals in each volume. *Women Studies Abstracts* regularly cites special periodical issues on women.[23]

Media Report to Women is also the best finding source for titles of feminist newspapers. One of the longest-lived examples is *Women's Press,* which began publication in 1970. The 1971–74 issues are part of the HERSTORY microfilm collection produced by the Women's History Library, Berkeley. *Women's Press,* published in Eugene, Oregon, carries extracts from feminist newspapers published in other cities. Most feminist newspaper coverage is of local news and events, but occasionally feminist interests and issues at the state and national level are examined. Characteristic of many small press publications, feminist community newspapers are frequently short-lived. Thus even in those few libraries subscribing to one or more of these newspapers, a researcher may find the library keeps only the current issues, or that the newspaper was published only a short time before it changed titles in its place of publication, skipped an issue due to financial constraints, or ceased publication. Libraries generally desire to acquire conventional, unbroken series of periodicals rather than risk feminist or other small press periodicals which may cease publication shortly after beginning. In addition, rapid inflation means periodicals must be carefully selected to stretch limited funding; the high theft rate of feminist journals, coupled with the cost of claiming missing issues or replacing mutilated ones, makes libraries wary of concentrated collection development in this area. Perhaps the best way to determine if a particular locale publishes a feminist newspaper is to contact the local book stores, particularly the women's book stores. Among the most significant of the women's newspapers is *Majority Report: The Women's Newspaper.* Begun in 1971 as a "feminist newspaper serving the women of New York," *Majority Report* later expanded its focus and audience until its demise in 1979. The women's movement was thoroughly studied at local, state, national, and even international levels. Current and historical items of interest were covered in all subject areas from politics to sciences to the arts. *Majority Report* was one of the few feminist newspapers indexed and consequently large academic and public libraries subscribed to it.[24]

A number of women's news periodicals could be considered both newspapers and news magazines. *Off Our Backs: A Women's News-Journal,*[25] just entering its second decade of publishing, is such an item. It is a high-quality, radical feminist tabloid that combines news of the women's movement with special features on women of various cultures, classes, and races; it also includes theoretical articles on topics such as women in the church, Third World women, and women and Marxism. It also prints fiction, poetry, and art.

In addition to the titles and types of newspapers discussed above, several noteworthy newsletters expressing women's concerns and legislation are published by major women's organizations. A popular newsletter is the *National NOW Times*,[26] published monthly by the National Organization for Women. Similar titles may be located through directories of women's organizations and sample copies may be obtained upon request or through membership.

All general information newspapers of local or national readership include articles relating to women's issues and cultural changes affecting women or women's role in society. Researchers should not overlook such newspapers as the *New York Times, Chicago Tribune, Wall Street Journal,* and *San Francisco Chronicle.* Most major city newspapers are indexed through such services as the *New York Times Index, Newspaper Index, News Bank,* and *Urban Affairs Library;* most local newspapers are not indexed, though limited subject and name access may be available in the files (or morgue) of the local newspaper office. Many libraries keep newspaper clippings files organized by subject and may offer useful information on local women's issues or prominent local women.

Computerized Indexing and Abstracting Services

Women's studies students and scholars should become familiar with the online computerized bibliographic and nonbibliographic data bases in their subject fields.[27] This relatively recent technology allows for speedy retrieval of information in an electronic format rather than by manual searching. Finding periodical literature relevant to women has been made easier by the number of abstracting and indexing services which have been put online, or in a computer system. Major college and university libraries have access to online search services through BRS (Bibliographic Retrieval Service), SDC (Systems Development Corporation), or DIALOG. Smaller college and university libraries and many public libraries may not have such access. Searching indexing services online allows for rapid retrieval of bibliographic citations and more comprehensive interdisciplinary searches. In addition to authoritative indexing terminology (most online data bases produce a subject thesaurus), many have what is called "free text searching"—searching key words in the title or abstract that may or may not be used as standard subject terms. Since 1973, *Sociological Abstracts* has included a section on feminist studies in each issue and it is now online. *Psychological Abstracts, Public Affairs Information Service, New York Times Information Bank, RIE* (Resources in Education), *Medlars, Dissertation Abstracts International, America: History and Life,* and various other indexing services have their data bases online. Most of these do not index material prior to 1970. Other problems with online searching include nonstandardized subject terms from data base to data base and cost. Despite these drawbacks, an online search may in the long run save the researcher countless hours of manual searching time and yield a larger number of useful citations. The joint thesaurus project of the Business and Technical Women's Foundation and the National Council for Research on Women is nearly complete, with publication (by Bowker) expected in 1985. The thesaurus, the first step in organizing a single national online computerized women's studies bibliographic data base, will contain about 4,000 terms that relate to issues of special concern to women.

Microform Reproduction

The recent focus on preservation of state and local historical society materials and the ongoing microform reproduction of major women's studies collections bring about more contact with and control of these rare materials. One of the best known and most highly regarded microfilm collections is *HERSTORY: Women's Newsletters, Journals, and Newspapers on Microfilm, 1956–1974,* a treasure of the contents of over 850 titles published by women's liberation, civic, religious, professional, and peace groups. Research Publications, Inc., is a distributor of the Women's History Research Center materials and has microfilmed Dr. H. Carleton Marlow's *Bibliography of American Women, Part 1.* This work covers the period up to 1904 and lists 40,000 titles. The bibliography includes information on women in medicine, science, history, anthropology, fine arts, humanities, law, theology, economics, and other disciplines. Research Publications has also produced a microfilmed work, *History of Women: A Comprehensive Microfilm Publication* which is a selection of material prior to 1920 culled from nine major women's studies library collections.[28]

Bell and Howell's *Cornell University Collection of Women's Rights Pamphlets on Microfiche, 1814–1892* and Microfilming Corporation of America's *National Woman's Party Papers, 1913–1974* on microfilm are necessary additions to a retrospective library research collection.[29] Many such microform and reprint collections are now available in public and academic libraries.

U.S. Government Publications

Local, state, federal, and United Nations government documents are a rich source of information for women's studies research. Numerous indexes exist to both federal and U.N. publications; best known is the *Monthly Catalog of U.S. Government Publications.*[30] For example, the U.S. Labor Department's Women's Bureau publications are listed in the *Monthly Catalog* and are of first importance for providing data on the development of womanpower resources, and the economic, legal, and civil status of women.

Significant examples of historical material published by the U.S. government may be found in the Congressional Information Services (CIS) *U.S. Serial Set Index* which began publication in 1789 with the fifteenth Congress. Items such as the Labor Bureau's extensive nineteen-volume *Report on Condition of Woman and Child Wage-earners 1910–1913* (also available on microfilm) and major addresses and reports on the consideration of women's suffrage in the 64th to 68th Congresses can be found in this index.[31]

Of special merit is the U.S. Government Printing Office's publication *Subject Bibliography Series*[32] (SB-111) which lists all in-print titles under the subject heading of Women. The current bibliography includes, for example, "Earnings Gap between Women and Men" (a twenty-two page study of tables and statistics); "Forcible Rape: An Analysis of Legal Issues"; and the "Legal Status of Homemakers." The entire bibliography or selected individual items can be obtained from the U.S. Government Office, Superintendent of Documents, Washington, D.C., 20402.

Resources in Women's Educational Equity (also available from the Superintendent of Documents) was an initial publication (begun in

1977) which cited and abstracted journal articles and government documents relating to the education of women. Sex differences and sex discrimination in education were the issues addressed. The U.S. Department of Health, Education, and Welfare's Office of Education was the publishing body. Finally, the publication *Journal of Reprints of Documents Affecting Women* reprinted precedent-setting documents including legislation, court decisions and opinions, and government and union rules.[33]

Historically, women have held a lower status than men in higher education, a fact that has influenced how women's interests and concerns are reflected in library cataloging and storage practices. Perhaps as women's enrollments in colleges and universities increase in the United States, traditional male biases against women and their scholarly contributions will decrease. In any case, women's current productivity is yielding a wide diversity of publications and rich body of resource material for continued scholarship.[34]

Notes

1. National Women's Studies Association, "Women's Studies Programs— 1980," *Women's Studies Newsletter* 8 (Winter 1980): 19–26, and "Graduate Programs in Women's Studies," *Women's Studies Newsletter,* 8 (Spring 1980): 24–26; Beth Stafford, compiler, "Women's Studies Programs," *Women's Studies Quarterly* 10, no. 3 (1982): 21–31.

2. Jane Williamson, *New Feminist Scholarship: A Guide to Bibliographies* (Old Westbury, N.Y.: The Feminist Press, 1979); Esther Stineman and Catherine Loeb, *Women's Studies: A Recommended Core Bibliography* (Littleton, Colo.: Libraries Unlimited, 1979); *List of Bibliographies on Women and Feminism* (Pittsburgh: KNOW, Inc., 1971), out of print; Patricia K. Ballou, "Review Essays: Bibliographies for Research on Women," *Signs* 3, no. 2 (Winter 1977): 436–50.

3. Joan K. Marshall, comp., *On Equal Terms: A Thesaurus for Nonsexist Indexing and Cataloging* (New York: Neal-Shuman Publishers, 1977).

4. *Famous American Women in the Dictionary of American Biography* (Available from the Reference Department, Charles Scribner's Sons, 597 Fifth Avenue, New York, N.Y. 10017); Edward T. James and Janet W. James, eds., *Notable American Women, 1607–1950: A Biographical Dictionary* (Cambridge, Mass.: Harvard University Press, 1971), 3 vols.; Barbara Sicherman and Carol Hurd Green, eds., *Notable American Women: The Modern Period: A Biographical Dictionary* (Cambridge, Mass.: Harvard University Press, 1980).

5. Nancy Gager, ed., *Women's Rights Almanac* (Bethesda, Md.: Elizabeth Cady Stanton Pub. Co., 1974); Myra E. Barrer, ed., *Women's Organizations and Leaders Directory* (Washington, D.C.: Today News Service, Inc., 1979); Marjorie P. K. Weiser and Jean S. Arbeiter, *Womanlist* (New York: Atheneum, 1981); Marianna W. Davis, ed., *Contributions of Black Women to America, 1776–1977* (Columbia, S.C.: Kenday Press, 1982); Mary Ann Warren, *The Nature of Woman: An Encyclopedia & Guide to the Literature* (Inverness, Calif.: Edgepress, 1980); Susan Cardinale, *Anthologies By and About Women: An Analytical Index* (Westport, Conn.: Greenwood Press, 1982).

6. Patricia K. Ballou, *Women: A Bibliography of Bibliographies* (Boston: G. K. Hall, 1980); Maureen Ritchie, comp., *Women's Studies: A Checklist of Bibliographies* (Lawrence, Mass.: Merrimack Book Service, 1980); Virginia R. Terris, ed., *Woman in America: A Guide to Information Sources,* American Studies Information Guide Series, vol. 7. (New York: Gale, 1980); Elizabeth H. Oakes and Kathleen E. Sheldon, *Guide to Social Science Resources in Women's Studies* (Santa Barbara, Calif.: American Bibliographical Center, CLIO Press, 1978); Barbara Haber, *Women in America: A Guide to Books, 1963–1975, with an Appendix on Books Published 1976–1979* (Urbana: University of Illinois Press, 1981).

7. Janet L. Sims, *The Progress of Afro-American Women: A Selected Bibliography and Resource Guide* (Westport, Conn.: Greenwood Press, 1980); J. R. Roberts, comp., *Black Lesbians: An Annotated Bibliography* (Tallahassee, Fla.: Naiad Press, 1981); Ohoyo Resource Center, *Resource Guide of American Indian-Alaska Native Women 1980* (Newton, Mass.: EDC, WEEA Publishing Center, 55 Chapel St., 02160, 1981); Gail A. Schlachter and Donna Belli, *Minorities and Women: A Guide to Reference Literature in the Social Sciences* (Los Angeles: Reference Service Press, 1977).

8. Andrea Hinding and Clarke A. Chambers, *Women's History Sources: A Guide to Archives and Manuscript Collections in the United States* (New York: Bowker, 1979), 2 vols.

9. *Choice,* 1964–, Association of College and Research Libraries (Middletown, Conn.: 100 Riverview Center, 06457); Bohdan S. Wynar, ed., *American Reference Books Annual,* 1970– (Littleton, Colo.: Libraries Unlimited).

10. Maryann Turner, *Biblioteca Femina: A Herstory of Book Collections Concerning Women* (Warrensbury, N.Y.: pub. by the author, 1978); Linda Seckelson-Simpson, *With Reference to Women: An Annotated Bibliography of Reference Materials on Women in the Northwestern University Library* (Evanston, Ill.: Northwestern University Library, 1975, addendum rev., May 1976); *Bibliofem: The Joint Library Catalogues of the Fawcett Library and the Equal Opportunities Commission Together With a Continuing Bibliography on Women* (London: Fawcett Library, City of London Polytechnic, 1978–), monthly, microfiche.

11. Radcliffe College, Arthur and Elizabeth Schlesinger Library, *Arthur and Elizabeth Schlesinger Library on the History of Women in America: The Manuscripts Inventories and the Catalogs of the Manuscripts, Books and Peri-*

odicals, 10 vols. (Boston: G. K. Hall, 1984); Smith College, Women's History Archive, *The Manuscript, Subject, and Author Catalogs of the Sophia Smith Collection* (Boston: G. K. Hall, 1975); Nan Robertson, "Special Libraries Are Putting Women's History Back in Circulation," *Chicago Tribune,* Jan. 18, 1981, sec. 12, p. 3.

12. Naomi B. Lynn, A. B. Matasar, and Marie Barovic Rosenberg, *Research Guide in Women's Studies* (Morristown, N.J.: General Learning Press, 1974), pp. 111–13.

13. Sherrill Cheda, "Feminist Philosophy and Theory: Resources," *Emergency Librarian* 4 (May/June 1977): 8–9.

14. Annette K. Baxter and Leon Stein, eds., *American Women: Images and Realities* (New York: Arno Press, 1972), 44 books-rpts; Leon Stein and Annette Baxter, eds., *Women in America from Colonial Times to the 20th Century* (New York: Arno Press, 1974), fifty-nine books-rpts; Jonathan Katz, ed., *Homosexuality: Lesbians and Gay Men in Society, History, and Literature* (New York: Arno Press, 1975), fifty-four books and two periodicals-rpts.

15. Len Fulton and Ellen Ferber, eds., *International Directory of Little Magazines and Small Presses,* 18th ed. (Paradise, Calif.: Dustbooks, 1982), annual; Len Fulton, ed., *Small Press Record of Books in Print,* 11th ed. (Paradise, Calif.: Dustbooks, 1982); Len Fulton, ed., *Small Press Review,* 1967– (Paradise, Calif.: Dustbooks), monthly.

16. Women's Center, Barnard College, *Women's Work and Women's Studies* (New York: Women's Center, Barnard College, 1971, 1972, and 1973/74), ceased publication. (Order 1971 and 1972 vols. from KNOW, Inc.; 1973/74 vol. may be obtained from the Feminist Press). This journal exemplifies the uncertain existence of small press publications, which often must rely on volunteer labor.

17. Edna Brown Titus, ed., *Union List of Serials in Libraries in the United States and Canada,* 3rd ed. (New York: The H. W. Wilson Co., 1965); U.S. Library of Congress, *New Serial Titles: A Union List of Serials Held by Libraries in the United States and Canada,* 1950– (Washington, D.C.: U.S. Library of Congress, Serial Record Division) supplements *Union List of Serials,* cumulated annually.

18. *Sex Roles: A Journal of Research,* 1975– (New York: Plenum Press, 227 W. 17th St., 10011); *Signs: Journal of Women in Culture and Society,* 1975–(Chicago: Univ. of Chicago Press, 5801 S. Ellis Ave., 60637); *Ms.,* 1972– (New York: Ms. Magazine Corp., 370 Lexington Ave., 10017).

19. *Motheroot Journal: A Women's Review of Small Presses,* 1979– (Pittsburgh: 214 Dewey St., 15218); *Room of One's Own: A Feminist Journal of Literature and Criticism,* 1975– (Vancouver, B.C., Canada: 1918 Waterloo Station, V6R 3G6); *Women and Literature,* 1975– (New Brunswick, N.J.: English Dept., Rutgers Univ., 08903); *The Ladder,* 1956– (Reno, Nev.: The Ladder Press, Washington Station, 89503; *Sinister Wisdom,* 1976– (Amherst, Mass.: P.O. Box 660, 01004); *Conditions: A Magazine of Writing By Women, With an Emphasis on Writing by Lesbians,* 1977– (Brooklyn: Box 56, Van

Brunt Station, 11215); *Bread and Roses,* 1977– (Madison, Wis.: P.O. Box 1230, 53703); *Feminary: A Feminist Journal for the South Emphasizing the Lesbian Vision,* 1970– (Chapel Hill, N.C.: P.O. Box 954, 27514); *Camera Obscura: A Journal of Feminism and Film Theory,* 1976– (Berkeley: P.O. Box 4517, 94704); *Women's Art Journal,* 1980– (Knoxville, Tenn.: 7008 Sherwood Dr., 37919); *Moving Out: Feminist Literary and Arts Journal,* 1971– (Detroit: Wayne State Univ., 169 Mackenzie Hall, 48202).

20. *Health-Pac Bulletin,* 1968– (New York: Health Policy Advisory Center, 17 Murray St., 10007); *National Women's Health Network News,* 1980– (Washington, D.C.: 224 7th St., S.E., 20003).

21. *Spokeswoman: An Independent Monthly Magazine for Women,* 1970– (Falls Church, Va.: Women's News Service, Box 2457, 22042).

22. *Connexions: An International Women's Quarterly,* 1981– (Oakland, Calif.: 4228 Telegraph Ave., 94609); *Frontiers: A Journal of Women's Studies,* 1975– (Boulder, Colo.: Women's Studies Program, University of Colorado, Hillside Court 104, 80309); *Resources for Feminist Research,* 1972– (formerly *Canadian Newsletter for Research on Women*) (Toronto, Canada: Dept. of Sociology, Ontario Institute for Studies in Education, 252 Bloor St. W., M5 1V6); *Women's Studies International Forum,* 1982– (formerly *Women's Studies International Quarterly,* 1978–82) (Oxford, Eng.: Pergamon Press, Headington Hill Hall, OX3 OBW).

23. *Feminist Periodicals: A Current Listing of Contents,* 1981– (Madison, Wis.: Women's Studies Librarian-at-Large, University of Wisconsin System, 112A Memorial Library, 728 State St., 53706); *Current Contents,* 1979– (Philadelphia: Institute for Scientific Information, 3501 Market St., Univ. City Service Center, 19104), covers Arts and Humanities, Agriculture, Biology and Environmental Science, Life Sciences, Clinical Practice, Engineering Technology and Applied Sciences, Physical, Chemical and Earth Sciences, and Social and Behavioral Sciences; *Index Directory to Media Report to Women,* 1972– (Washington, D.C.: Women's Institute for Freedom of the Press, 3306 Ross Pl., N.W., 20008), annual; *Women Studies Abstracts,* 1972– (Rush, N.Y.: Rush Publishing Co., Inc., Box 1, 14543).

24. *Media Report to Women,* 1972–(Washington, D.C.: Women's Institute for Freedom of the Press, 3306 Ross Pl., N.W., 20008); *Women's Press; A Women's News Journal,* 1970– (Eugene, Ore.: Women's Press Collective, Box 562, 97401); *HERSTORY: Women's Newsletters, Journals, and Newspapers on Microfilm,* 1956–1974 (Berkeley: Women's History Research Center, Inc., 2325 Oak St., 94708), ninety reels; *Majority Report: The Women's Newspaper,* 1971–79 (New York: Majority Report Co., 74 Grove St., Sheridan Sq., 10014).

25. *Off Our Backs; A Women's News-Journal,* 1970– (Washington, D.C.: Box 8843, 20003).

26. *National NOW Times* (newsletter), 1977– (formerly *Do It Now*) (Washington, D.C.: National Organization for Women, 425 13th St., N.W., Suite 1048, 20004).

27. One serviceable guide which offers an overview of online information data bases is Dorothy Williams's *Computer Readable Data Bases: A Directory and Data Sourcebook* (Washington, D.C., 1979; rpt. White Plains, N.Y.: Knowledge Industry Pub., Inc., 1982). A companion piece also by Williams, *Data Bases Online in 1981* (Washington, D.C.: American Society for Information Science, 1981), is recommended as well.

28. H. Carleton Marlow, *Bibliography of American Women: Part 1* (on microfilm) (Woodbridge, Conn.: Research Pub., Inc., 12 Lunar Drive, P.O. Box 3903, 06525, 1975); *History of Women: A Comprehensive Microfilm Publication* (Woodbridge, Conn.: Research Pub., Inc., 12 Lunar Dr., P.O. Box 3903, 06525, 1976).

29. *The Cornell University Collection of Women's Rights Pamphlets* (Wooster, Ohio: Bell and Howell, Micro Photo Division, Old Manfield Rd., 44691), containing 117 pamphlets published between 1814 and 1912, including reports from such organizations as the Men's League for Women's Suffrage and the Women's Rights Convention, 1859, microfiche; *National Woman's Party Papers, 1913–1974* (Sanford, N.C.: Microfilming Corp. of America, 1620 Hawkins Ave., 27330), microfilm.

30. *Monthly Catalog of U.S. Government Publications, 1901–* (Washington, D.C.: Supt. of Documents, U.S. G.P.O., 20402).

31. *U.S. Serial Set Index* (Bethesda, Md.: Congressional Information Service, P.O. Box 30056, 20814); *Report on Condition of Woman and Child-Wage Earners in the United States, 1910–1913* (LaCrosse, Wis.: Brookhaven Press, Division of Northern Micrographics, Box 1653, 2004 Kramer St., 54601), microfilm.

32. *Women: Subject Bibliography Series* (SB-111) (Washington, D.C.: Supt. of Documents, U.S. G.P.O., 20402).

33. WEECN, *Resources in Women's Educational Equity, 1977–80* (Washington, D.C.: Supt. of Documents, U.S. G.P.O., 20402); *Journal of Reprints of Documents Affecting Women, 1975–80* (Washington, D.C.: Today Publications and News Service, Inc., 621 National Press Bldg., 20045).

34. Eileen Mackesy, Karen Mateyak, and Diane Siegel, comps., *MLA Directory of Periodicals: A Guide to Journals and Serials in Languages and Literatures, 1978–79* ed. (New York: Modern Language Association of America, 1979); Andrea Chesman and Polly Joan, eds., *Directory of Women Writing* (Newfield, N.Y.: Women Writing Press, RD3, 14869, 1977); Polly Joan and Andrea Chesman, *Guide to Women's Publishing* (Paradise, Calif.: Dustbooks, 1978); Celeste West and Valerie Wheat, *Passionate Perils of Publishing*, vol. 4, no. 17 (Summer 1978) (San Francisco: Booklegger Press); *The Writer's Market, 1982* ed. (Cincinnati, Ohio: Writer's Digest Books, 1982), annual; *Literary Market Place: The Directory of American Book Publishing, 1982* ed. (New York: Bowker, 1982), annual; National Enquiry, *Scholarly Communication: The Report of the National Enquiry* (Baltimore, Md.: Johns Hopkins Univ. Press, 1979).

Witches' Tribunal, Halloween, 1984. Prior to the November presidential election, university and community women demonstrate at the Alma Mater statue against current economic and social policies. University of Illinois at Urbana-Champaign. Photograph courtesy of the News Bureau.

Contributors

PAULA A. TREICHLER grew up in Yellow Springs, Ohio, majored in philosophy at Antioch College, and earned a Ph.D. in psycholinguistics from the University of Rochester. Since 1972 she has been a teacher and administrator at the University of Illinois and served for several years as dean of students in the College of Medicine at Urbana-Champaign. She is currently a member of the faculty of the College of Medicine, the Institute of Communications Research, and the Unit for Criticism and Interpretive Theory; her research and teaching interests include medical communication and feminist theory. With Cheris Kramarae, she is co-editor of *Women and Language* and co-author of *A Feminist Dictionary: In Our Own Words* (London: Routledge and Kegan Paul/Pandora Press, 1985).

CHERIS KRAMARAE teaches courses on language and gender, language and power, and on the ethnography of speaking at the University of Illinois, where she is a faculty member in Speech Communication. Her writing on women and language includes many published articles and the book *Women and Men Speaking: Frameworks for Analysis,* published by Newbury House in 1981. She is co-editor (with Barrie Thorne and Nancy Henley) of *Language, Gender and Society* (Newbury House, 1983) and (with Paula Treichler) of *Women and Language;* until 1982, she was the U.S. editor of *Women's Studies International Quarterly* (now *Forum*).

BETH STAFFORD is Women's Studies/Women in International Development librarian and faculty member in Library Administration at the University of Illinois, Urbana. She has published articles on library research and materials in both women's studies journals and library journals. She has been Special Projects Editor for *Women's Studies*

443

444   *For Alma Mater*

Quarterly, and she is on the National Women's Studies Association
National Coordinating Council. During 1981–82 she was on a team of
four that received a Women in the Community grant sponsored by the
Schlesinger Library at Radcliffe College and funded by NEH for the
purpose of bringing together women's studies scholars and the community at large. Since 1982 she has been on the executive committee of
Black Women in the Middle West, an NEH-funded project designed to
collect and preserve documentation of Black women's lives and achievements, predominantly in Illinois and Indiana.

BOBBIE M. ANTHONY-PEREZ is a member of the faculty of the
Psychology Department at Chicago State University. She has five degrees, including an M.A. in mathematics education from the University
of Illinois at Urbana-Champaign and a Ph.D. in measurement, evaluation, and statistical analysis from the University of Chicago. She taught
extensively in the Chicago public school system at all educational levels,
especially as a certified mathematics teacher at the secondary level. She
served as psychologist for Head Start centers in the Chicago public
schools and has presented papers and organized symposia and work-
shops in the areas of education, psychology, mathematics, research,
evaluation, and social issues (race, sex, and minorities) at national and
international conferences in Europe, South America, Canada, and the
United States. She has published articles on classroom environmental
variables, spelling ability, evaluation of teachers, racism and sexism,
curriculum development, and racial factors in careers. She has received
many awards for her professional, civic, extracurricular, and religious
endeavors.

PAULINE BART, who describes herself as formerly a sloppy house-
keeper and permissive mother, received her Ph.D. in sociology from
UCLA in 1967. She is currently a faculty member in the Department of
Psychiatry in the College of Medicine, and in the Department of
Sociology, University of Illinois at Chicago. Although she has also
taught as a visiting faculty member at USC, UC Berkeley, San Diego
State University, UC Santa Barbara, and UCLA, she has never had a
regular position in a department of sociology. Therefore, she has never
been co-opted. She teaches seminars in sex roles and health issues, sex
roles and violence against women, and will be teaching seminars in
feminist theory and in motherhood. In addition to the articles men-

tioned in her essay in this book, she has written "Portnoy's Mother's Complaint," "A Funny Thing Happened on the Way to the Orifice: Women in Gynecology Textbooks," with Diana Scully, *The Student Sociologist's Handbook,* with Linda Frankel, and *Stopping Rape: Successful Survival Strategies,* with Patricia O'Brien (Pergamon Press, Athene Series).

EDNA BAY, an African historian who received her Ph.D. from Boston University, has done field and archival research on women in West Africa. While a faculty member in African studies at the University of Illinois, Urbana-Champaign, Dr. Bay served as first chair of the University's Women in Development Committee. Her publications include *Women in Africa: Studies in Social and Economic Change,* edited with N. J. Hafkin (Stanford, 1976), and *Women and Work in Africa* (Westview, 1982).

MELISSA McCOMB CAIN is English Librarian and faculty member in Library Administration at the University of Illinois at Urbana-Champaign where earlier she was assistant undergraduate librarian. She has written on the Motley Costume Design Team (British), a group of three women who designed in the 1930s. Currently she is doing research on British women costume designers in the 1930s and 1940s for a forthcoming book.

C. SUE CARTER, faculty member in Ecology, Ethology and Evolution, and Psychology at the University of Illinois, Urbana-Champaign, conducts laboratory research examining the hormonal bases of reproductive behavior and sex differences. These research programs have been funded by the National Science Foundation and National Institutes of Health.

ARLYN DIAMOND is a member of the English faculty at the University of Massachusetts. She received a Ph.D. from the University of California at Berkeley in 1970, where she also taught. She is co-editor of *American Voices, American Women,* published by Avon in 1973, and *The Authority of Experience: Essays in Feminist Criticism,* published by the University of Massachusetts in 1977. She is currently president of the faculty librarians' union at the University of Massachusetts and in between crises is working on a feminist analysis of courtly love in the medieval romance.

MAUREEN A. FLANNERY is a family physician practicing in rural southeastern Kentucky. During her three years at the Office for Family Practice in Rockford, Illinois, she was deeply involved in local women's health activities, including the Rockford Rape Counseling Center, the Resource Center on Women and Health Care, and the Pelvic Teaching Group (the Insiders). She has published articles on ethical issues in rural primary care and on health care in Appalachia. She served on the board and executive committee of the National Women's Health Network and currently chairs the Rural Health Committee.

MARILYN FRYE teaches philosophy and women's studies at Michigan State University. She is the author of *The Politics of Reality: Essays on Feminist Theory,* published by Crossing Press in 1983. She is currently working on the relationship between feminist theory and racism. During 1984–85 she was Visiting Scholar at the Center for the Study of Women in Society at the University of Oregon.

KATHRYN A. HAMMELL is head of the Acquisitions Department and a faculty member at the Library of the Health Sciences, University of Illinois at Chicago. For one year she was subject specialist in sociology and social work and worked in women's studies at the Education and Social Science Library on the Urbana campus of the University of Illinois. She was previously head of the Interlibrary Loan Department at the Library of the Health Sciences and also served as project coordinator for the Regional Online Union Catalog of the Greater Midwest Regional Medical Library Network.

GAIL PARADISE KELLY received her Ph.D. from the University of Wisconsin in 1975. As a member of the Department of Social Foundations of Education at SUNY/Buffalo, she teaches courses in Women and Education in Cross National Perspective, Education in Africa, Education in Asia, and Modernization and Education. In 1982 her book (written with Carolyn Elliott) *Women's Education in the Third World: Comparative Perspectives* was published by SUNY Press. She also has authored or coauthored numerous articles and book chapters on women and education from an international perspective. Her research interests include education and colonialism and African and Asian studies.

MARCELA C. LUCERO, formerly on the faculty of Chicano Studies at the University of Minnesota, was a faculty member and director of Chicano Studies at Adams State College in Alamosa, Colorado, until her death in 1984. She taught courses on La Chicana, the cultural heritage of the Chicano, and Chicano folk medicine. She published literary criticism and poetry, along with such articles as "The Terminology of Machismo." She was also interested in the methodology of feminist writers, Anglo-Chicanas, and the history of Chicanos and Chicanas.

SALLY McCONNELL-GINET is a faculty member and chair of the Department of Modern Languages and Linguistics at Cornell University. She has been actively involved in the Cornell Women's Studies program since 1973. She has published and given many talks in the general area of language and gender and co-edited *Women and Language in Literature and Society* (Praeger, 1980) with Ruth A. Borker, an anthropologist, and Nelly Furman, a literary scholar. Her research also includes semantic theory; she is currently completing *The Construction of Meaning,* a book on the "looseness" of linguistic meaning.

CAROL THOMAS NEELY, faculty member in English at Illinois State University, has published articles on Shakespeare's plays and sonnets. She co-edited with Carolyn R. S. Lenz and Gayle Greene *The Woman's Part: Feminist Criticism of Shakespeare* (University of Illinois Press, 1980) and is the author of *Broken Nuptials in Shakespeare's Plays* (Yale University Press, 1985). She has chaired or participated in numerous sessions on feminist criticism of Shakespeare at local, regional, and national meetings. She teaches Shakespeare, Renaissance poetry, Women in Literature, and composition.

CARY NELSON is Professor of English and Director of the Unit for Criticism and Interpretive Theory at the University of Illinois. He is author of *The Incarnate Word: Literature as Verbal Space* (University of Illinois Press, 1973) and *Our Last First Poets: Vision and History in Contemporary American Poetry* (University of Illinois Press, 1981), which includes an essay on Adrienne Rich. He is presently completing *Reading Criticism: The Literary Status of Critical Discourse.*

MAUREEN PASTINE, formerly undergraduate librarian and then reference librarian at the University of Illinois, Urbana-Champaign, has been active in women's issues for some time. She assisted with the compilation of *Women's Work and Women's Studies 1973–74,* published by The Women's Center at Barnard College in 1975, and has presented numerous papers on women's studies at professional meetings. She has also appeared on several panels on women's studies resources and women's issues such as one on women and power(lessness). Currently the library director at San Jose State University, she has extensive experience in reference work and is interested in library administration, children's literature, bibliographic instruction, small presses, and little magazines.

TEY DIANA REBOLLEDO is Director of Women's Studies and a member of the Department of Spanish at the University of New Mexico at Albuquerque. She has published articles on Chicana literature and poetry, and teaches courses on Latin American women writers, culture, civilization, and poetry, on Chicana writers, and on the new novel. Active in both academic and community activities, she is currently a member of the Modern Language Association's Commission on the Status of Women in the Profession and of the Nevada Women's Fund Board.

HILDA L. SMITH received her Ph.D. from the University of Chicago in 1975 and has been very active giving many presentations on women's history to a broad variety of groups during the past ten years. She was a founder and co-president of the Coordinating Committee on Women in the Historical Profession, starting in 1969. She has edited a national newsletter and chaired national meetings and was project director of the First International Conference on the History of Women in 1977. Now project director of the Council of Chief State School Officers in Washington, D.C., she has taught at the University of Maryland in College Park and at George Williams College in Illinois, and was acting executive director of the Maryland Committee for the Humanities. In 1982 the University of Illinois Press published her book, *Reason's Disciples: Seventeenth-Century English Feminists.* Her research interests include masculinity as a political concept in English thought.

DALE SPENDER is an active feminist who has written feminist books on language and has been the coordinating editor for *Women's Studies International Forum* since its inception. Her book *Women of Ideas and What Men Have Done to Them* was published in 1982 by Routledge and Kegan Paul in Boston. From Australia originally, she now lives in London. She has both taught courses and written on the subjects of the politics of knowledge and the intellectual aspects of sexism.

GAYATRI CHAKRAVORTY SPIVAK, who was born and educated in India, teaches English at Emory University. She is the author of a book on William Butler Yeats and the translator of Jacques Derrida's *Of Grammatology*, which includes a monograph-length introduction. She is well known for a series of essays on deconstruction and on its relation to issues raised by Marxism and feminism. She is currently at work on a study of the relationship between literary criticism and a critique of imperialism.

MARSHA HOUSTON STANBACK received her Ph.D. in interpersonal communication and rhetoric from the University of Massachusetts in 1983 and is currently head of the Communications Studies Program at Spelman College in Atlanta. She has published articles and presented conference papers on Black English, language and Black women, Afro-American communication, and communication and culture. She has taught courses on interpersonal communication, Afro-American literature, intercultural communication theory and research, and introduction to the mass media.

JUDITH HICKS STIEHM is Vice-Provost and a faculty member in Political Science at the University of Southern California, as well as former chair of the Program for the Study of Women and Men in Society. She teaches courses in political philosophy and on sex, power, and politics. She edited *The Frontiers of Knowledge* (University of Southern California Press, 1976), *Women and Men's Wars* (Pergamon, 1982), and *Women's Views of the Political World of Men* (Transnational, 1984) and authored *Nonviolent Power* (D.C. Heath, 1972) and *Bring Me Men and Women: Mandated Change at the U.S. Air Force Academy* (University of California Press, 1981). She was a founder of the Women's Caucus in Political Science.

ORLAND WAYNE WOOLEY is on the faculty of the Department of Psychiatry at the University of Cincinnati School of Medicine and is co-founder and co-director of the Eating Disorders Clinic. For years he has specialized in obesity research and in the treatment of obesity, eating disorders, and body image disturbance. He has been active in litigation and legislation involving discrimination against the obese.

SUSAN CLARK WOOLEY, faculty member at the University of Cincinnati, is clinical director of the Eating Disorders Clinic. Her major areas of research include psychosomatic disorders, eating disorders, and the cultural meanings of body size. Under her direction, the Clinic has been active in developing innovative, feminist treatments of obesity, bulimia, and body image disturbance.